RESOLUTION

DAVID RUTLAND is 11th Duke of Rutland and lives at Belvoir Castle, ancestral home of the Dukes of Rutland in north-eastern Leicestershire. His interest in history began when he was a child growing up in his family home, surrounded by ancestral portraits and possessions which he wished to learn more about. Since inheriting the dukedom in 1999, he has devoted himself to caring for the chattels in Belvoir Castle and, more recently, exploring the castle archives to produce this, his first book.

EMMA ELLIS completed a degree in politics and then 'ran away to sea' for a few years, undertaking numerous voyages including to Antarctica and Greenland. She became interested in the history of maritime exploration during the course of a circumnavigation of New Zealand. She subsequently undertook a Masters Degree in naval and merchant naval history at the Greenwich Maritime Centre, University of Greenwich. *Resolution* is her first book.

RESOLUTION

Two Brothers, a Nation in Crisis, a World at War

DAVID RUTLAND
and
EMMA ELLIS

Consultant: Richard Woodman

First published in 2017 by Head of Zeus Ltd

1 3 5 7 9 10 8 6 4 2

A CIP catalogue record for this book is available
from the British Library.

ISBN (HB) 9781784979911
(E) 9781784979904

Printed and bound by CPI Group (UK) Ltd,
Croydon, CR0 4YY

Head of Zeus Ltd
5-8 Hardwick Street
London
ECIR 4RG

www.headofzeus.com

In loving memory of
Imogen Skirving
1937–2016

Imogen Skirving, late owner of Langar Hall, gave us much encouragement and support towards completing this book. She will always be with us in spirit and much missed. She now lies at rest near the tomb of Admiral Richard Howe, whose family came from Langar.

'Since it is denied us to live long,
let us do something to shew we have lived.'

Lancelot 'Capability' Brown to
Charles, 4th Duke of Rutland,
1 October 1782

Contents

Foreword

BY THE 9TH EARL OF MANSFIELD AND MANSFIELD

As the lineal descendant of a man who knew the 4th Duke of Rutland well enough to dare to advise him on his errant behaviour, and who acted as guardian to his children following the Duke's untimely death, I was curious to discover more about the fortunes of the Manners family during the extraordinary eighteenth century. In *Resolution*, David Rutland and Emma Ellis have not only taught me a wealth of things I had not known before about this most fascinating and distinguished of families, they have also provided evidence to challenge the veracity of the celebrated opening lines of L. P. Hartley's *The Go-Between*: 'The past is a foreign country: they do things differently there.'

The Manners – and many of their contemporaries – lived lives shaped by a strong sense of duty. This can be seen in their family tradition of the dying paterfamilias instructing his sons to raise regiments and to accept public office for their country's benefit, rather than for their own. It was duty that inspired Charles Manners' acceptance of the expensive office of Lord Lieutenant of Ireland, as it did his fourteen-year-old brother Robert's decision to embark on a career in the Royal Navy.

The two brothers loved each other deeply throughout their tragically short lives, a fraternal bond that is manifest in their running away from Eton together and, perhaps most of all, in Charles's deep grief at the death of his younger sibling. It is fashionable to think of our forebears as being unemotional and somehow disconnected from one another, but the warmth of Charles's and Robert's relationship reveals this to be simply untrue.

And there are other abiding truths to be found in *Resolution*. While the two brothers enjoyed the good fortune to inherit wealth and an exalted social position, they put their nobility to beneficial use in their public roles. In Robert Manners' case, it is certain that had he lived his name would be as honoured in the annals of naval history as those of Cloudesley Shovell, Edward Boscawen, Earl St Vincent, Viscount Hood, the Cochranes, the Codringtons – and perhaps even Horatio Nelson himself.

Charles and Robert both upheld the great Manners tradition of service: the authors show them to be examples to us all.

Mansfield.

Preface

BY THE 11TH DUKE OF RUTLAND

Belvoir Castle, my home, stands high on the crest of a ridge overlooking the borders of three counties in the green and gently rolling rural East Midlands, about as far from the sea as anywhere in the country. Its ironstone fairy-tale turrets and towers, glowing golden in the evening sun, form a dramatic skyline above hillslope gardens that are abundant with roses and delphiniums in the summer months. Sweeping below it are grassy parkland, lakes and woodland with a magnificent canopy of English oaks, feathery, spreading cedars and the twisted trunks of ancient sweet-chestnuts. The site has been the seat of my ancestors for a thousand years; the castle's halls are lined with their portraits and its archives burst with their papers.

It was my father, the 10th Duke of Rutland, who first opened Belvoir to the public in 1952, and since that time the favourite story of our visitors has always been that of my family's eighteenth-century naval 'hero', Captain Lord Robert Manners. Children are especially fascinated by some unusual artefacts relating to his short life and gruesome death, placed by my father in a showcase near a portrait of him in naval uniform. When I was a child Lord Robert intrigued me too. Sir Joshua Reynolds' life-sized depiction portrayed a blue-and-gold-laced uniformed figure among endless paintings of red-coated army officers and silk-and-velvet-clad society hosts. Lord Robert's hand rests upon an anchor, and in the background are men-of-war under sail, set against a stormy sky. Every inch a man of action, Robert Manners had been a maverick who had joined the Royal Navy when he was expected to serve in the British army, and I was drawn to him because I too wanted to break from family tradition by joining the Royal Air Force.

My father showed me bound volumes of the letters Robert had sent home from the various ships in which he served, and one of my earliest memories is sitting on papa's knee and turning the pages with fascination, trying to decipher the eighteenth-century hand to see what adventures lay within. Robert's words scrawled across the pages, written perhaps as the ship was rolling in the waves, still sparkled in places from the sand thrown on them to dry the ink. The writing was more legible when the young man seemed happy, but was stained with ink blots when he was angry; there was a doodle or two when he was bored, and sometimes a hint of loneliness in between the lines.

My sense of connection with him was strong. From a young age, I longed to discover more about him – was he *really* a hero? Why had he joined the navy rather than the army, and why had a sort of reverential air about him descended to the present generation? How had cannon from a French warship captured by him come to be on the terrace at Belvoir Castle? I resolved to research his life and find out for myself what actually happened and who he really was. However, I did not get the chance until long after inheriting the castle, when my children approached maturity and I was able to find the time to do so.

After I began work in the spring of 2012, it quickly became clear that Robert's story would have to encompass his older brother Charles, the 4th Duke of Rutland, for their lives were inextricably linked. My starting point was my own archives, and going behind the heavy steel door each day made me think of C. S. Lewis's wardrobe as I entered a lost world, to dwell in the past and discover the lives of past generations through their letters and documents. And there was plenty of material there: the nature of the aristocracy and its zealous protection of land ownership via inheritance customs, with settlements, entail and trustees, meant that the relevant papers had been carefully guarded over the centuries.

I soon found myself utterly absorbed in a most engaging era of my family's history, as I and my co-author Emma Ellis explored the brothers' child- and adulthoods and their legacies, all of which brought a few surprises. Nevertheless, while some aspects of their stories emerged in great detail, others remained tantalizingly obscure. Together, we embarked on what evolved into a quest, discovering what, we became increasingly aware, was a powerful evocation of brotherly love and a family drama played out in the later eighteenth century, as the thirteen American colonies struggled to break free of Britain.

Robert, as we discovered, served at sea during the glorious era of the Georgian sailing navy, when wooden warships were extraordinarily sophisticated and complex in their build, manning and handling. He became a post-captain, commanding a major line-of-battle ship in the largest British fleet ever to operate so far from home waters up to that date. I was amazed to find that when he died, a monument to him was placed in Westminster Abbey, one of only a handful in that venerable place paid for by public subscription. He was considered at the time worthy of being secured 'from the oblivion which waits upon the many millions who in every century take their turns upon this stage of human life and depart undistinguished by the performance of any actions eminently great or good'. But the author of those words could not know then that Horatio Nelson would soon take such a prominent role upon the stage and would eclipse in the public eye many 'heroes' who had gone before him.

So it seems it was left to me to bring Robert back from neglect. Owing to the staggering amount of the Georgian navy's remarkable administrative records preserved in Britain's National Archives, Emma and I were able to look at the logbooks and musters of all the ships Robert served in, to find out on almost every day of his naval life where he was, who he was with, and even what the weather was like. Through these and my own archives we have been able to portray a rare, personalized insight of a very young officer at a time when warfare was still 'gentlemanly', when more sailors died from disease than actual fighting, and when a particular code of honour existed. It was also a time when many then unheard-of young officers, including Horatio Nelson himself, were learning their skills, to become famous a quarter of a century later – after the British embarrassment and loss of the American colonies could be quietly 'forgotten' amid the glare of resounding victories against France and Spain in the Revolutionary and Napoleonic wars.

This is not, though, a book set only upon the quarterdeck of a ship. Back at home, Robert's older brother Charles Manners – one of the country's great landowners and owner of Belvoir Castle – was a member of glittering, scandalous Georgian aristocratic society, where the lure of temptations contrasted vividly with the stern call of duty. But responsibilities came with that privilege, and Charles was expected to take part in the male-dominated political life of the nation during one of its most brilliant periods of Parliamentary debate, as argument raged over what, it transpired, were the birth pangs of the United States. The historical importance of America's revolutionary founding obscures the often overlooked fact that Britain was simultaneously fighting not only to preserve its 'First Empire' in America, but also involved in a global imperial war – against France, Spain, even the Dutch Republic – without any allies and with deep political divisions at home. This was the background to Charles's public life, and to the expectations of his public role. Bearing the title of the Duke of Rutland, he slid onto the historical page with less obscurity than Robert. And yet, his libertine tendencies left a rather one-sided view of him in the public eye. I am able, I hope, to set the record straight somewhat, for an unexpected twist occurred towards the end of his life.

The brothers were linked not just through their love for each other, but also because Charles was involved in the politics of the war in which his sibling was fighting. Between them, their lives offer parallel but utterly different insights into the same conflict. Threaded through their relationship was the thorny issue of the apparent 'unfairness' of primogeniture, where the hereditary title and the bulk of the family's property and wealth passed only to the oldest son while younger sons had to make their own way in the world. This undeniably conferred extraordinary privilege on Charles, yet it was not all it seems, for underlying was a more complex reality for the two brothers. In addition, both were trying to live up to the name of a celebrated father, Lieutenant General the Marquis of Granby, said to have been as famous in his day as Nelson was in his. It was a long shadow from which Charles and Robert struggled to emerge.

*

Using my own experience of aristocratic customs combined with Emma's knowledge of naval history, we have together attempted to portray the contrasting strands of Charles and Robert's lives in one story, under the watchful editorial eye of Captain Richard Woodman, a master of the art of evoking life in the Georgian navy. We have not attempted to present a comprehensive account of the period. While every author faces difficult choices about what to include and what to leave out, I rather concur with William Makepeace Thackeray, who wrote: 'It would require a greater philosopher and historian than I am to explain the causes of the famous Seven Years' War in which Europe was engaged; and, indeed, its origin has always appeared to me to be so complicated, and the books written about it so amazingly hard to understand, that I have seldom been much wiser at the end of a chapter than at the beginning, and so shall not trouble my reader with any personal disquisitions concerning the matter.' We have taken a similar view here, and only touched upon the causes of the American Revolutionary War, the details of the land campaigns, and eighteenth-century politics and naval administration where the context of the brothers' lives required it. (There are many well-written books elsewhere that provide much more detailed historical accounts.) But one of the things I enjoyed most while researching this book was discovering how intertwined my ancestors were in the events of this era, and even if they have not entered history as famous characters in the mould of Pitt the Younger or Cornwallis or Nelson, they are illustrative examples of young men – and women – 'of their time and class'. Through them, we can learn about eighteenth-century attitudes, mores and fashions among the men who governed and who served at the time of the American war, and see some of the roots of our modern society. I equally did not realize when I started this project how Charles and Robert sat at a pivotal moment of social change, when the seeds of the decline of families like mine were being sown. Perhaps, indeed, they even contributed to this evolution.

To set the scene in which the following story takes place, I would ask the reader to think of a drastically less crowded world, when Britain was populated by just 9 million people, and in which a further 2.5 million British subjects lived in the thirteen American colonies. One must imagine an England with endless green rolling hills and woodland broken only by provincial towns, villages and hamlets. The Industrial Revolution was beginning, and new experimental steam engines were just being developed to pump water out of mines or power early cotton mills; but there were as yet no vast chimneys belching smoke over row upon row of factory workers' dwellings. Neither were there any railways, and people relied on horses and horse-drawn vehicles. A glimpse of the future would have been visible in the growing network of canals that began to permeate the countryside: dug by gangs of industrious 'navvies', they linked the emerging centres that would soon be transformed into industrial powerhouses. But not quite yet. A large proportion of the population were tenant-farmers paying rent to the great landowners like Charles, and the most extensive sites of what we might regard as 'industry' were the naval yards of Portsmouth and Plymouth and those in London. The country was connected by a primitive network of roads and tracks, sometimes knee-deep in mud and beset with highwaymen, although better-bred horses, lighter carriages and the introduction of turnpikes – toll roads – were making travelling easier, safer and more comfortable. But still nothing moved very fast. It took two days to travel by road from London to Belvoir; today it takes three hours.

The reader should consider, too, that British society was hierarchical, without what we would regard as democracy, since a mere 14 per cent of adult males, and no women, were able to vote for Members of Parliament. Even so, this was more progressive than other European nations, and Britain's poorest sections of society were smaller too, as wealth trickled down more easily. The labouring classes in towns and cities were not entirely without a voice, particularly so in London, in which periodic eruptions from 'mobs' could – and sometimes did – influence government policy and even threaten sovereigns. Riots in the eighteenth century were commonplace, and with no police force yet in existence, soldiers were called on to suppress them. Popular unrest was feared, but not to the extent that it might sweep away the social order.

Ranked higher up were the 'middling sort', country squires and the like, and the growing urban middle class, men able to exert some political power by influencing elections. Above them were some 400 families, who between them owned a quarter of the land surface of Britain and dominated political power, including around 200 or so of the wealthiest landed gentry and 200 landed families with hereditary titles.

That elite held sway not only over Britain but also its empire – at this time a total of twenty-six colonies worldwide, primarily in North America, the West Indies and in the British East India Company's fiefdoms. Most of them provided a rich source of income and luxury goods, and were the object of competitive rivalry with other European imperialist nations. This was in a world whose true extent was still unknown, for while Australia had been revealed to Europeans, Antarctica had not. I found it interesting during my research to be reminded that convicts at this time were still being sent to the American colonies, rather than to Australia's Botany Bay. While explorers like Captain James Cook were setting off to find new lands, ostensibly 'discovering' them, the underlying aims were economic – to secure them before other nations could claim them to their financial advantage.

Africa's interior had yet to be colonized by Europeans, but thousands of slaves were being shipped annually across the Atlantic from African shores to the Caribbean 'sugar islands', to feed Europe's growing consumerism. The war for American 'liberty' in which Charles and Robert were caught up was complicated by national rivalries over the profits of slavery – rivalries that meant it effectively became a world war, as the French, Spanish and Dutch joined in. I find it remarkable to consider how a conflict on this gobal scale was managed in the days before radio, satellites, smartphones and email. People spent hours and hours writing letters, and yet the postal system was primitive, the first mail-coach not being introduced until 1784. Correspondence took weeks or months to travel to or from overseas, relying on ships sailing according to the vagaries of the weather and men on horseback.

So where did my family fit in this world? They were part of Britain's governing elite of 400 families, sharing a delicate balance of power with the king through their hereditary seats in the Houses of Lords and control of many of the seats in the Commons. They did not have the monopoly on political power, for many of the greatest statesmen were not drawn from their ranks, but certainly they had tremendous political significance and felt a responsibility for the way in which the country was run.

And what were these governing families like? What did their personal lives look like? Within this book is a microcosm of a class that formed the smallest, most exclusive, richest, most powerful and most land-based aristocracy of any in Europe. The impact of such privilege on individuals like Charles and Robert was not only political and financial, but emotional too, shaping personal attitudes and sense of self. They considered their hereditary rule as a right, and that it safeguarded the continuity of the state. My ancestors were a part of this belief system – priding themselves on honour and the good opinion of others through personal virtue and superior birth, for nobility carried with it certain expectations of correct behaviour in public and in private, and accomplishment was honoured as well as birth. Peers like Charles needed to play a substantial role in local communities in addition to wider national political or military duties, and managing the strenuous number of obligations meant a busy life travelling hundreds of miles all over England. Within this social group, my ancestors were among those who, since Magna Carta in 1215 and the 'Glorious Revolution' of 1688, sought to uphold Parliament against any slide back towards arbitrary rule by a monarch and his appointed ministers. My forebears were not democrats, but they joined others in paving the way for democracy through Parliamentary means.

Land was both the foundation and the symbol of a nobleman's power. This was reflected in grandiose lifestyles and country homes with fashionable décor, collections of paintings and magnificent sweeping parklands. Belvoir Castle stood prominent among these private palaces. The family name and title were important, but the ancestral home symbolized continuity, evoking strong emotional responses from each life-tenant whose existence linked the past and the future. Neatly summed up by the eighteenth-century politician and philosopher Edmund Burke, the lives of the nobles were 'a partnership... between those who are living, those who are dead, and those who are yet to be born'. In our own times, Sir David Cannadine, in *The Decline and Fall of the Aristocracy*, described how the aristocracy adorned the walls of their houses with ancestral portraits and planted trees for future generations, for 'more than any other class the noble families knew where they had come from, they knew where they were, and they hoped and believed they were going somewhere'.

But with this sense of self came the heavy weight of convention and expectation. Aristocratic men and women frequently endured unhappy marriages, which were considered little more than institutions for passing on life, name and property, in which the participants were bound by law, custom and convenience rather than ties of sentiment and affection. 'Marrying well' was paramount, and heiresses could bring financial aid to debt-ridden estates. What accompanied this pragmatism was an unromantic and unmoralistic attitude towards fidelity, shared by men particularly but also high-born women, other than in the matter of first ensuring there was a legitimate male heir in place. As for children, the practice of parents seeing little of them further reinforces a view of the eighteenth-century aristocracy as emotionally cold. In this respect, I leave the reader to make their own judgements from the narrative about my own ancestors. But I will add that the concept of marriage as purely dynastic was being altered by the emerging notion of romantic love, emotional fulfilment, companionship and celebration of family.

One privilege enjoyed by this class, which I found striking to consider, was their opportunity to indulge in intellectual speculation. Surrounded by servants to take care of their cooking, cleaning and so on, they had the time to study and to achieve a diverse range of accomplishments, priding themselves on erudite conversation and debate. This was particularly the case for aristocratic men, for, with some notable exceptions, this was still a century and more before society encouraged women to apply themselves to the world of ideas. But a young nobleman would be steeped in classical education, his behaviour and attitudes shaped by the lessons of Greek and Roman writers, before broadening his horizons through the vogue for the 'grand tour' around the Continent. Actual visits to Italy, especially Rome, increased the sophistication of the class, while the influence of the Enlightenment led to fertile debate upon the nature of the human condition and the new discoveries of science.

Many of the new ideas found practical application in the nascent Industrial Revolution. Its dimensions are beyond the scope of this book, but it may be helpful for the reader to understand that scientific notions and technical innovations would have been important and interesting to the likes of Charles and Robert, even if the brothers were conditioned by background to feel too superior to engage in 'trade' themselves. In addition to steam engines, there were the new agricultural machines, and while major industrial processes were in their infancy, the foundations of future industrial towns of the English North and Midlands were being laid. Many of the brothers' contemporaries were influential in the changes taking place. The polymathic Benjamin Franklin, for example, whose abstract ideas found expression in philosophy, politics and as a 'Founding Father' of the United States, was also involved in inventing the lightning conductor and refrigeration (and, incidentally, advocated love-matches versus marrying out of a 'thirst for riches'). Lord Sandwich, chastised and denigrated in Parliament for his stewardship of the navy, was a leading patron of the arts and of voyages of exploration. In Charles Manners himself, there is evidence of such engagement with the fast-changing world around him, for he was investing in canals and mines, in agricultural reform and improving roads; he was corresponding with friends about cotton mills, and he had some contact with Sir Richard Arkwright, whose mills in Derbyshire were located not far from Charles's property in that county, Haddon Hall.

At the same time – and partly in reaction to rationalism – this was also the start of the Romantic era, with its emphasis on aesthetic appreciation of the picturesque and the sublime, bringing new attitudes towards landscape, history and literature, suffused with a new sensibility of feeling. For those wealthy enough to do so, increased time was spent in leisurely activities, looking dreamily at landscapes, enjoying humour, celebrating family life and mutual delight in each other's company for its own sake.

Not everyone had the opportunities to satisfy their intellectual curiosity and aesthetic sensitivities. For the lower orders, life remained one of unrelenting toil in poor conditions, though the locations were changing, as the poor moved to the urban centres, away from the land. And at the very bottom of the pile in Britain's empire were the slaves. The practice of slavery was at last being attacked as a moral evil, at the same time as the rights of the individual were being advanced. Meanwhile, those with resources lapped up and savoured new experiences and indulgences, not all of them wholesome.

Charles and Robert may have been part of a social group who

believed their position at the apex of society was unassailable; but the
cracks were already beginning to show, and the reader will find some
of the reasons within this book. To a growing, ambitious and increasingly articulate middle-class, the families they represented appeared
corrupt, especially in the way they wielded influence through interest
and patronage. The renegade Englishman and revolutionary philosopher Thomas Paine, whose pamphlet *Common Sense* of 1776 inspired
the American rebels, had once been a customs officer in Grantham,
near Belvoir Castle. It is certain that, among others, he had the Manners family – my family – in his mind's eye when he talked of wresting
politics from the grasp of the aristocracy. By the end of the nineteenth
century, families like mine had been eclipsed as the economic elite,
undermined as the most glamorous social group, and superseded as
the governing class. A further century later, I was no longer able to
attend the House of Lords, after the reform of 1999 removed peers'
rights to hereditary seats. And so, my ancestors' story remains as a
portrait of aristocratic life more or less at its zenith, before an era of
unprecedented social change gathered full speed. It is a moment in
time on the journey to where we are now.

*

It was no easy task to piece together the lives of those who lived three
centuries ago and to understand their characters from their letters
when there is, of course, no one alive who knew them to ask. Further
challenges existed in that Robert's letters to Charles were undoubtedly
guarded, for they were often opened and read by censors; he could not
risk writing too much that, by being critical of either the government
or the Admiralty, would make him seem cowardly or traitorous. And
finding clues to emotions among dry account ledgers and settlement
documents is no easy task. Nevertheless, I should like here to pay a
tribute to my remarkable grandfather, the 9th Duke of Rutland, whose
extraordinary diligence between 1925 and his death in 1940 in sorting,
cataloguing, dating and binding manuscripts in the castle's archives
helped me on every single day of the research that went into this book.
Without him, my task would have been very much harder, and often it
seemed as if his hand were guiding me to find what I was after. I always

knew which documents he had looked at, for he carefully stamped each one with 'Belvoir Castle Manuscripts', using red ink. So I then did the same, but using green ink, so that future generations would know which ones I had looked at for this book.

In portraying the two brothers' characters, I saw elements of their personalities I recognized in myself; yet they were their own people, so I have tried to avoid endowing them with my own characteristics just because they were my ancestors. I have, I hope, also resisted the temptation of omitting anything that did not present them – or me – in a favourable light. It was helpful to have a co-author more objective than I, and we are also indebted to other historians who have provided further insights. Nevertheless, we recognize we may not always have been successful in our endeavours to be objective and, as they say, to understand a book you have to understand its author!

As for me, I never did join the Royal Air Force. A disability sustained at birth and inheritance of the dukedom in 1999 prevented me. Instead, I joined the Air Training Corps in 1974 aged fifteen and that was the start of what, at the time of writing, has been a forty-three-year involvement with an active organization that often changes for the better the lives of the young people who take part. I feel my continued support for the Air Training Corps is fitting, for the Marquis of Granby, who features in this book, was an early supporter of the Marine Society, which helped young people find a career at sea all those centuries ago.

Beyond that, I have spent my time engaged in all that is involved in protecting and preserving Belvoir for future generations, not just for my own family but as part of the nation's heritage. Whatever one's personal view of primogeniture, it has surely had the effect of safeguarding many historic buildings and large tracts of the rural English countryside from development. Although my estate is drastically reduced in size since the days of Charles and Robert, it is my hope that this book will help to increase the enjoyment and understanding of those who visit Belvoir Castle to see the art collection and various artefacts, and who walk through our beautiful woodlands and wander around our recently restored 'Capability' Brown-inspired landscape. I hope, too, that it will provide an illuminating portrait of a generation of my ancestors caught up in the world-changing turbulence of the war for America, and who largely made Belvoir what it is today.

Rutland

Duke of Rutland
Belvoir Castle
November 2016

Note to the reader

The prefix 'HMS' (His Majesty's Ship) was not in formal use at the time in which this book is set, and so we have not used it. Likewise, the marines did not become the Royal Marines until 1802.

Some confusion may be caused by courtesy titles – the 'Marquis of Granby' was the title given to the eldest son and heir of the Duke of Rutland, while waiting to inherit. If the Marquis of Granby also had a son and heir (i.e., three generations alive at once), this boy would have the courtesy title 'Lord Roos'. The family name was Manners. Ducal titles were, and are, not related to the county in which the person lived – so the Duke of Rutland did not live in Rutland and the Duke of Devonshire did not live in the county of Devon.

The office of prime minister emerged during the eighteenth century as a descriptive term, originally pejorative, for the minister chiefly concerned with advancing the government's agenda in Parliament. The term is used here, but formally the prime minister bore the title 'First Lord of the Treasury'.

In quotations, original spelling, punctuation and capitalization have been retained throughout. Square brackets have been used to indicate any deviation from the original or any added clarification. Most unreferenced quotations are from manuscripts at Belvoir Castle, which include, in addition to letters and account ledgers, some contemporary printed material such as Charles Manners' own copies of the *Parliamentary Register*. Quotes of speeches in Parliament have been taken from these and therefore have not been referenced. Any other unreferenced quotes concerning shipboard life have been taken from the ships' logbooks and musters in The National Archives, and are listed at the end of the book.

Finally, a note on money: determining modern monetary equivalents is notoriously difficult, because relative values of items change over time. As a rule of thumb, multiplying figures cited here by eighty should give an approximation of the amount today.

Maps

Great Britain and Northern Ireland

The Mediterranean

The Caribbean

North America

Great Britain and Ireland

N

IRELAND

ENGLAND

Etal Castle

Scarborough

Dublin

Liverpool

Grantham

Belvoir Castle

London

Greenwich

see inset

Isle of Wight

Plymouth

Falmouth

English Channel

Gosport

Portsmouth

Spithead

Isle of Wight

St Helens

Ushant

Brest

FRANCE

0   100 miles
0   150 km

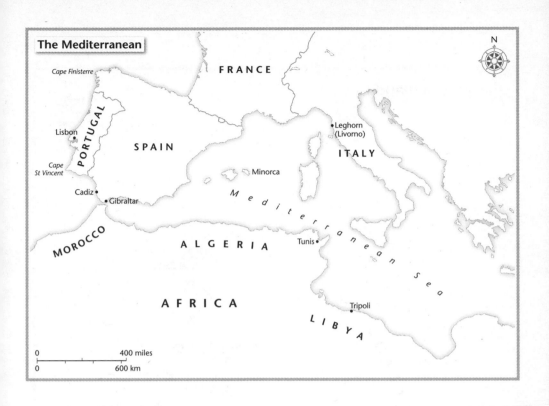

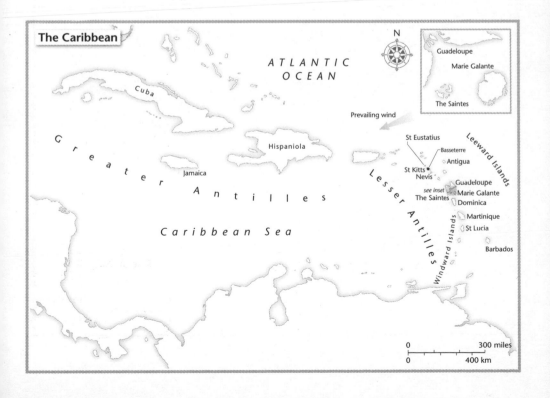

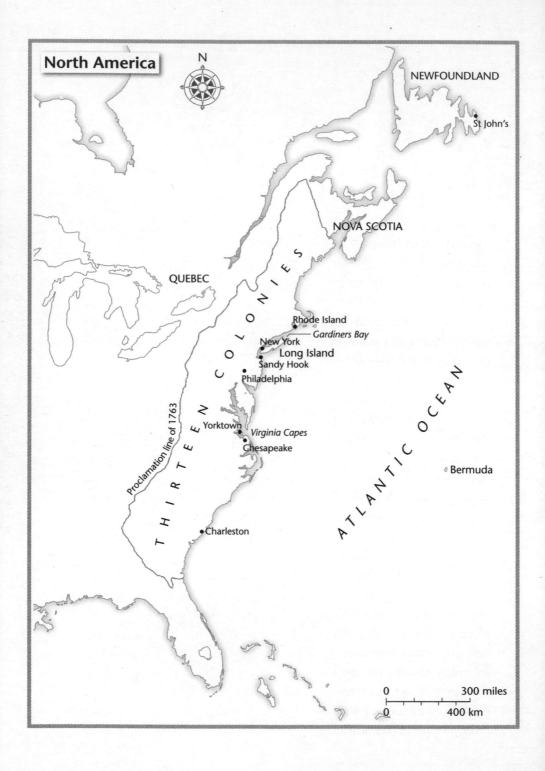

North America

N

NEWFOUNDLAND

St John's

NOVA SCOTIA

QUEBEC

Rhode Island

Gardiners Bay

New York

Long Island

Sandy Hook

Philadelphia

Yorktown

Virginia Capes

Chesapeake

Bermuda

Charleston

T H I R T E E N   C O L O N I E S

Proclamation line of 1763

A T L A N T I C   O C E A N

0   300 miles

0   400 km

Prologue

In the early hours of 26 October 1816, a horseman carrying a terrifying message was sent to find the Duke and Duchess of Rutland, who had gone to attend the races at Newmarket and were staying at their property of Cheveley Park. Rumours of smallpox in Cambridgeshire had caused them to leave their children behind, supposedly safe in their family home of Belvoir Castle. But the messenger brought shocking news: the castle was on fire.

John Henry Manners, 5th Duke of Rutland, bid farewell to his wife, called for a horse and set off at a breakneck pace to cover the 85 miles ahead of him. His anxiety increased when, still some distance away, he saw the inferno visible against the skyline, for the castle was built on the highest point of land for miles around. Galloping up the steep hill at ten o'clock that evening, he could see that the fire had already destroyed the newly built wing containing the Picture Gallery, and now the flames were engulfing the older part of the great house, where the children's rooms lay.

John Henry flung himself from his horse, gripped by fear. The children were at least safe. His friend Sir John Thoroton had rushed to their bedchambers and – finding the punctilious Nurse Griffith insisting the children put on their shoes and stockings – had carried them from the flames. John Henry now turned his attention to the possessions of seven centuries of ancestors. The castle's staff and tenants from the estate's nearby villages, alerted to the disaster, had risked their lives rushing to rescue what they could. In desperation, they lowered or threw out of windows furniture and paintings, and now the family's chattels lay scattered over the lawns. The cases of miniatures

1

from the Drawing Room had made it to safety, as John Henry discovered, and so had the contents of the Great Yellow Room. There, to his relief, were the *Seven Sacraments* painted by Nicolas Poussin – except he could only count six.

Outwardly he was calm. The fire was brought under control before the whole building was destroyed, and John Henry expressed his gratitude to his many helpers and privately thanked God that his children and the staff were safe. Inwardly, his heart was breaking, for his expensive attempt to rebuild his ancestral home and realize the vision of his father Charles, the 4th Duke of Rutland, was now a smoking ruin. Later, on enquiring as to how the fire started, John Henry was confused by varying accounts. Some said it had been ignited by an overset oil lamp in a workshop near the Guard Room. Others whispered 'arson'. Whatever the cause of the disaster, John Henry's ambitions now seemed to lie in charred ruins.

He had been only seventeen when, in 1795, he had started making plans for the reconstruction of Belvoir. The family lawyer, Joseph Hill, and the young duke's guardians, who included Prime Minister Pitt the Younger, had advised him not to do it after the whole estate had come perilously close to being lost, debts having blighted the family for years. But he had been a determined, headstrong young man who, when he did come of age and got married, sold land in outlying counties to raise sufficient money – just – for the ambitious plans.

Now, while the castle could always be rebuilt, gone forever were many irreplaceable possessions and artefacts. Contemplating the smouldering wreckage, John Henry recalled a previous, happier, occasion when the castle had glowed against the skyline. It was the time in late 1805 when every window held a candle burning inside a hollow turnip, when the entire family had walked to the bottom of the hill to admire the grand 'illumination' that was part of a national celebration for Admiral Lord Nelson's victory over the French and Spanish foe, off Cape Trafalgar. The triumph had been tinged with deep regret though, since Nelson had fallen in battle, mortally wounded by a musket ball in his spine, and some of the villagers had dressed their turnip lanterns with black crêpe to mark their hero's passing. John Henry's sense of history was moved by other, more personal, considerations. His uncle, Captain Lord Robert Manners, had been born in 1758, the same year as

Nelson. Coincidentally, it was also the same year in which orders were given to build the *Victory*, and Lord Robert would serve on this ship before it achieved lasting fame as Nelson's flagship. What struck John Henry at that moment of introspection was that, like Nelson, his uncle had fallen at a moment of victory and died of wounds acquired in the service of his country. But who now thought much about the Battle of the Saintes twenty-three years earlier, when Admiral Rodney defeated the French and restored confidence to a country reeling under the loss of its North American colonies? A friend, John Pitt, the 2nd Earl of Chatham, understood, telling John Henry that 'few feel as you do on the loss of Nelson'.

Now, a decade later, John Henry turned to the painful business of assessing the losses from the fire. Mercifully, the precious contents of the Evidence Room in the south wing had been spared as the wind had driven the fire elsewhere. The letters Uncle Robert had written at sea to John Henry's father, Charles, were safe, but the writing desk and its contents – letters from Charles and the family – were gone, lost in the inferno that had engulfed the two northern wings of the castle. One object saved was a tiny, detailed model of the ship Robert had commanded on that fatal day, when Rodney had engaged the French. The man-of-war had been named *Resolution*. At its bow was a miniature version of her figurehead, Shakespeare's Cleopatra clasping the asp, uttering: 'My resolution's placed…'

Resolution: a firm decision to do or not to do something, and a word much in use in Robert's time. To Benjamin Franklin, it was a desirable virtue: 'Resolve to perform what you ought; perform without fail what you resolve.' It was uncannily similar to the Manners family motto *Pour y Parvenir* – 'To attain one's object.'

1

'Isles of ice'

1772

'Isles of Ice'

The fourteen-year-old Lord Robert Manners stepped down from his carriage at Portsmouth Harbour, one sleeting April day in 1772, to catch his first heart-stirring sight of the 'wooden walls' of British sea power. He was familiar with fishing-boats at Scarborough and merchantmen lying in the Pool of London, but he had never before seen so many ships of war. Some were moored in the harbour, while others lay anchored in the waters of the Solent, at Spithead, just beyond the harbour's narrow entrance, their hulls and masts towering over the small craft that ferried men and stores out to them.

Known to his family as 'Bob', the youth was slender and handsome, with a fine aquiline nose and large dark eyes said to reflect the 'sensations which at the moment influenced his mind'. On that cold, wet April day, his eyes might well have revealed a mixture of excitement and trepidation, for in those great ships a young man could make his name and fortune – or die in the attempt.

The country was not at war, but the young Lord Robert was to join the 60-gun *Panther*, bound for Newfoundland, a posting that brought with it an element of danger. Britain had laid claim to the fishing rights upon the Grand Banks, off Newfoundland's coast, a decade earlier, at the conclusion of the Seven Years' War, and the *Panther*'s duty now was to protect the men from Devon, Cornwall and Dorset whose communities depended on their summer catches. Bringing the prospect of skirmishes with French and Spanish fishing-vessels, not to mention dense fog, loose icebergs and frequent gales, the Newfoundland station was said to be the most exciting of the peacetime options for a hopeful

young man. The *Panther* brought another advantage too, for she was
the Newfoundland governor's ship and would return to England for
the winter months. The milieu into which Robert was about to step
was utterly alien to him. It would completely change his life.

*

Robert should have joined the army. That was the expectation for a
boy whose grandfather was the 3rd Duke of Rutland, living at Belvoir
Castle in the English Midlands, and whose ancestors had a long tradition of military command. More particularly, Robert was a son of the
late Marquis of Granby, one of England's most celebrated generals.
But the circumstances of his young life had caused him to abandon a
path where, his military duties apart, he could spend time in leisurely
and sporting pursuits, dining on delicacies with titled, erudite guests,
attended by numerous servants. Instead, he had chosen to join the
navy as a midshipman – a trainee officer – and though just fourteen,
he was already considered almost too old to adapt to the arduous and
dangerous ways of a life at sea.

His new environment was certainly daunting. The *Panther* was
moored alongside an old hulk within the harbour and, stepping aboard
for the first time, Robert saw a confusion of ropes running from the
deck skywards; he would have to learn quickly the name and purpose of each one, along with the nautical slang that accompanied
the rigid daily routines by which his life henceforth would be governed. Around him was a new community of which he was, as yet, an
insignificant part: the *Panther*'s handful of officers, fifty marines and
four hundred or so other disparate crew – from drunkards to skilled
carpenters, from ageing and experienced seamen to 'landsmen' escaping unemployment, broken marriages or even the magistrates. One
young contemporary wrote of his naval induction with astonishment:
'I had anticipated a kind of elegant house with guns in the windows…
a species of Grosvenor Place floating about like Noah's ark… [but
found] the tars of England rolling about casks, without jackets, shoes
or stockings… the deck was dirty, slippery and wet; the smells abominable; the whole sight disgusting.'[1]

At least Robert was used to being away from home, having boarded
at Eton College from a young age, and some childhood contacts in

the service had helped prepare him for what to expect. But in taking leave of John Glover, the valet who accompanied him to Portsmouth, Robert felt the greatest wrench as his last tie with closest family was broken. In a moment of desolation, he was struck by the enormity of losing the companionship of his older brother Charles, left behind at his grandmother's house in London, and from whom he had barely been separated since birth.

Taking his sea-chest to his quarters on the orlop deck, Robert encountered the raw living conditions assigned to him and his three fellows – John Deeble, John Herring and Ralph Milbank: the 'cockpit', lying midway between the officers aft and the men forward, hence the designation 'midshipmen'. Situated well below the waterline, the cockpit's only light came from tallow dips, whose stench mingled with the miasma of bilge water, the wet and rotting timber and the ooze from casks of food,[2] rendering the air mephitic. Close by were quartered the marines, who acted as the ship's policemen should the seamen turn mutinous. As required by the service, Robert brought his own bedding, books, navigation instruments, and his midshipman's dirk and underclothes. As a well-provided-for boy, he may have had 'tarpaulins' (an oiled canvas coat) and a 'greygo', or early form of duffel coat, both of which would be necessary in the foul weather to be expected in the North Atlantic. He also had a uniform with white breeches and a knee-length blue coat with twelve buttons and turned-up white cuffs, which was intended to lend a measure of authority at a time when most seamen still wore 'slops'. From the very start of going to sea, Robert – eager to become an officer – was expected not only to learn all the tasks involved in sailing a ship, but also to lead men old enough to be his grandfather.

Several of his messmates had already been aboard for some time, and a neophyte, whatever his social rank, was soon made aware of his ignorance. Chivvied hither and thither, new boys were given no time to settle in, for the work of preparing the ship and stacking tier upon tier of barrels and sacks of stores for an ocean crossing of 2,000 nautical miles permitted no slacking. But for Robert, the excitement of going to sea meant more than the hardships. Finding a moment at the end of April 1772, he wrote cheerfully to his closest adult connection ashore, his maternal grandmother Charlotte Somerset. With relief, she relayed to his brother Charles that: 'I have had a letter from Bob who was well in health & spirits.' By the time the *Panther* emerged from the dry-dock on 2 May and took the tide out into the sheltered waters of the Solent, Robert would have grasped the essentials of his tough new existence. As the ship passed between the forts guarding the entrance to Portsmouth's harbour, he was perhaps reminded of his father, Lord Granby, who had repaired those forts in the 1760s while Master General of the Ordnance. Such a consideration was an uneasy legacy for a son determined upon taking such a different path to his forebears, emphasizing the enormity of his decision.

Before setting off on the ocean passage to Newfoundland, the *Panther* anchored at Spithead to make her final preparations. Here, vessels could take on additional powder, shot, food, stores and water while remaining in readiness to sail as soon as the wind and tide served. Lying offshore prevented the men from deserting, which was a constant worry for the officers when the distractions of women and taverns were within sight. Sharing the anchorage were the 74-gun guardships the *Terrible*, the *Egmont*, the *Royal Oak* and the *Lenox* – a stirring sight for the young Robert, for these were line-of-battle ships, Britain's first defence against enemy fleets.

The next few days brought a quickening of tempo as the ship was thoroughly cleaned, her decks holystoned white, her brass polished, and all made ready aloft in anticipation of the arrival of the man in whose 'care' Robert had been placed. On 19 May, Commodore Moly-neux Shuldham, the newly appointed Governor of Newfoundland, along with his staff and retinue of thirty persons, were rowed out to the ship. As Shuldham's boat came alongside, the *Panther*'s crew lined her side-deck and the governor stepped aboard to the screech-ing whistle of the pipes and the salutes of the assembled officers and midshipmen. A thirteen-gun salute thundered out from the *Panther*. The commodore's broad pennant was broken out at the masthead as the ship's captain, Cornthwaite Ommaney, welcomed his superior on board. Meanwhile, the answering concussions of the reciprocal salutes rolled over the water as the other ships at anchor responded to the solemnity of the event. It is unlikely that at this moment Shuldham paid any attention to his new midshipman. Whatever conventions governed his conduct ashore towards the grandson of a duke, naval rank always took precedence over social rank on board a man-of-war. Having agreed to undertake the patronage of Lord Robert Manners, Shuldham no longer had a duty towards him, at least until the lad had proved himself – and there was no guarantee of that.

Finally, on 20 May 1772, the anchor was weighed and the *Panther* made sail towards the English Channel. At last, Robert was at sea for the first time. Passing through St Helens Road and rounding the eastern end of the Isle of Wight brought the shock to his body that accompanies the first hours on a moving ship. If Shuldham's arrival had lifted his spirits, now came the full reality of his new way of life. The heave of the deck beneath his feet, the sting of cold rain on his face and the wind-ache that accompanies the duty of staring at the horizon looking for 'strange sail' were unfamiliar to him. So, too, were the arcane orders that set the seamen scampering about the decks and taking to the dizzyingly high rigging. He would have found most of the language incomprehensible and confusing. What, he must have wondered, was meant by 'ease the topping lift on the spanker boom'? And then, if his stomach was queasy like his father's always had been, he would barely have eaten and drunk, at least for a couple of days.

'Sketch between decks', May 1775, depicting a ship's cockpit, the home of the midshipmen. One of those shown here may be Lord Charles FitzGerald, later to be one of Robert's rivals for promotion (see page 213).

There was little consolation below decks, where the stink of un-washed humanity, the wretched feeling of seasickness and the onset of loneliness would likely have kept him awake as much as the unfamiliar creaking of the ship's timbers and the snores of sleeping men in their swaying hammocks. After four hours he was woken – probably just as he was dropping asleep – for his turn on duty. Placed in one of two 'watches', each comprising some 200 men, he took his turn to be on deck to trim sails, pump the bilges and generally 'work the ship'. His body – unfamiliar with such physical exertion – had to endure the routines, which continued relentlessly night and day; nothing stood in their way, and no amount of a young lad's exhaustion and misery could have allowed him to miss his watch.

This was the start for him, for perhaps years to come, of time measured with a sandglass and arranged into four-hour blocks, with two-hour 'dog-watches' in the late afternoon to alternate daily the hours each watch was on deck. A sequence of bell-ringing every half hour marked the passage of time: 'eight bells' meant one watch could go wearily below to grab some sleep, provided there was no call for all hands on deck, while the other watch stumbled bleary-eyed to the darkness of the upper deck, the only light being the 'glim' in the bin-nacle illuminating the magnetic compass that kept the *Panther* upon her appointed course.

*

The weather had been moderate, with thick fog patches, when the *Panther* set off, but as she headed down-Channel towards the open Atlantic in late May, the wind picked up from the north-west, soon rising to 'hard gales' with a 'great swell' rolling in from the west, as the ship's sailing master recorded in his log. Though tired and hungry, Robert would have had to face the fearful task of going aloft for the first time while the ship was moving; as a future officer, he would not be considered proficient without confidence in the aerial world above the solid hull. If he was lucky, an old sailor would have taken a shine to him and helped him in his first terrifying venture onto a yard-arm, perhaps to take in sail in a sudden squall, white knuckles on his small hands gripping the tarred rigging as he climbed, the ship plunging and gently rolling, with nothing but his own strength to keep him from

falling. Then, he would have to step gingerly along the footrope swaying under the yard, moving outwards until only the crests of the waves
were below him and, as soon as he had caught his breath, lean over
the yard in a line with other men, balancing precariously while using
both hands to struggle with the heavy canvas. Although falls from the
rigging were surprisingly rare at the time, they could be fatal, whether
one fell to the deck or into the sea. A ship sailing at perhaps 5 or 6 knots
would soon leave a boy behind; he would likely be drowned or impossible to find by the time the boats had been unlashed and launched.

Exhausted, and with feet firmly back on the deck, once his stomach
had settled Robert could expect the standard daily rations of bread or
hard-tack biscuit and salted beef or pork, along with 'small-beer' (i.e.,
weak beer) in considerable quantities, fresh water being difficult to
keep 'sweet' at sea. Away from land, fruit and vegetables soon ran out
or went rotten in the salt-laden air. It was a harsh transition from his
childhood fare with oranges, lemons, strawberries, cucumbers and the
like on a regular basis. Being a wealthy boy, Lord Robert would have
brought his own luxuries to tide him over for a while, but these, often
shared with messmates, must have soon disappeared. He would not
have been underfed, but it was not unknown for hungry boys to brave
the bitter-tasting weevils in the biscuit and even the more decayed version of the same, containing 'large white maggots with black heads
[which] were fat and cold to the taste, but not bitter'.[3]

Yet any despair would soon have given way to elation, when, early in
the passage, the training began for what Robert truly came to sea for:
to learn to fight. In Newfoundland, the *Panther* might have to fire at
French and Spanish vessels to chase them off the fishing grounds, and
her crew had to be prepared. Reminders of this prospect came when
occasional 'strange sail' were spotted on the horizon, some of them
coming within hailing distance. Observing the conventions of the
time, the *Panther* saluted a Dutch ship-of-war with nine guns, seven
being received in reply, then soon afterwards hove-to and 'spoke with
the Mars, East Indiaman, 6 months out from Bengal'. A few days later,
a passing vessel told them of a 'pirate' in the 'Gulf of Florida' that
had taken three West Indiamen from London, an affront that must
have caused a frisson of excitement, hinting at the possibility of action,
despite their distance from that area.

Transforming a disparate crew into an effective fighting force was not just about firing guns, but also about courage, discipline and teamwork. This was impressed on the minds of the *Panther*'s newcomers for the first time on 8 June 1772 as Captain Ommaney read out to the assembled ship's company the Royal Navy's disciplinary code enshrined in the *Articles of War*. He was required to do this by regulation, at the start of a voyage and after Divine Service every Sunday. One can imagine the quickening of the boy's heartbeat as he heard how those who did not do their 'utmost to take or destroy every ship which it shall be his duty to engage' could be hanged or shot. Unnervingly, most of the *Articles* governing various aspects of misconduct at sea, from mutiny to running a ship upon the rocks, might result in the death sentence. Even, as Captain Ommaney read out, 'the unnatural and detestable sin of buggery and sodomy with man or beast' would be 'punished with death'.

Of course, less extreme punishments existed too: insolence, disobedience and derelictions of duty, such as dozing on watch – which endangered the safety of the ship – would attract a variety of sanctions. 'Young gentlemen' such as Robert would not be flogged at the gratings for these offences, as the common seamen were, but instead were bent over the breech of a gun and caned – 'kissing the gunner's daughter' – or sent to the masthead alone for several hours.

And then came the thrilling aspect: for the ship's company frequently 'exercised the great guns and small arms' during the passage to Newfoundland. Robert had spent many hours as a child with his brother Charles using flintlock sporting guns and had learned to fence, so he would have acquitted himself well with the cutlass and musket, and with pistols loosed off at empty wine bottles dangling from an upper-yard.

The *Panther*'s main armament was, by contrast, new to him. Brought to 'general quarters', the gun-crews practised firing the cannon usually in quiet weather, on a target at sea – an empty cask thrown overboard. He must master the complex procedures of an eighteenth-century muzzle-loading gun as the men worked to improve their speed of operation, since a rapid rate of fire yielded a powerful psychological effect on an enemy. Repeating the drills also helped to guard against accidents. Men's feet – for the seamen were invariably bare-footed at sea – could be crushed as the guns recoiled, and exploding barrels were not unknown.

Captain Ommaney, overseeing the activities from the quarterdeck, might use new and inexperienced midshipmen to relay messages to the lieutenants who commanded the gun-batteries, and being a 'doggy' was probably Robert's first experience of going to general quarters aboard the *Panther*. Here would be a chance to make an impression, for it is inconceivable that Commodore Shuldham would not have come on deck to observe, out of professional curiosity, how Captain Ommaney and his ship's company conducted themselves. Later, Robert would practise being stationed with the lieutenants by the guns or in the 'fighting-tops', the platforms at the head of the lower masts where a small detachment of seamen and marines armed with muskets could pick off the officers on the decks of an enemy vessel.

Through these manoeuvres, Robert was rapidly introduced to the business of leading the older men, though with a confidence long nurtured by giving instructions to servants, this would have come more naturally to him than to others. Yet it remained to be seen whether he would abuse his authority and follow the example of other midshipmen who let power go to their heads, becoming tyrants over the older seamen. His character would be demonstrated in other ways too, for as a 'young gentleman' he would sometimes have dined with the captain, usually on Sundays after Divine Service, or with the commissioned officers in their wardroom. This provided a welcome respite from the ship's normal unappetizing fare, for captains had their own cooks and usually had a few luxuries to hand; but these occasions also tested both a young man's manners and his head. For he would be expected to drink like a gentleman, while his conversation and his intellect – and hence his potential – were revealed to his seniors.

Then, back with his messmates, there was fun to be had. In the short, afternoon dog-watches it was customary for the midshipmen and the seamen to have some free time for exercise and leisure. Robert had a 'reserved' and 'amiable' nature, but was also given to 'frolicsome moods' and had not been above getting into trouble in his childhood. Mischievous pranks on board, such as sending newcomers to 'go and hear the dogfish bark', were usually harmless, but attracted informal punishments like a bucket of sea-water over the head or down the victim's sleeve.

During the passage, the wind rose frequently to 'hard gales', on one occasion tearing sails from their yards. The thrashing, uncontrolled canvas must have been a frightening sight for a boy not accustomed to such a scene. When the wind eased off, to encourage confidence aloft, the four 'middies' were allowed to 'skylark'. Leaving their smart uniforms for use in port and wearing instead the seamen's favoured style of dress – the cropped jacket and trousers – they would climb to the top of the masts some 180 feet above the waterline. Once their initial fear had been overcome, few lads were daunted by the prospect of going aloft, and in daylight and clement weather the maze above their heads may have proved inviting, not least because it allowed them fresh air and some limited freedom away from the smelly accommodation of their quarters. Gaining familiarity with the immense complexities of the rigging and sails, Robert would no longer have been mystified by the order to 'ease the topping lift on the spanker boom'. He would have quickly realized, too, that cutting a dash aloft was the best way of both establishing one's place in the pecking-order of the cockpit and of engaging the attention of one of the officers.

If the boys presumed their days of formal schooling were over, they were wrong, for the *Panther*, being the Newfoundland governor's ship, boasted schoolmaster David Conway on her books. Each day, weather permitting, this worthy was supposed to instruct Robert and his young

Hands aloft on a yard, taking in sail.

messmates in the mysteries of trigonometry and the calculus, as well as encouraging them to learn French and pursue an enthusiasm for the classics. But Robert, already well-versed in these subjects, was more likely to have been excited by learning how to keep track of the ship's position in the vast, grey Atlantic Ocean, with only the sun, moon and stars as distinguishing features. He would have been taught to master the taking of 'observations' – measuring the angle of elevation of a celestial body above the horizon – and the subsequent well-established calculations to determine latitude, and been introduced to the more complex and erratic calculations of 'lunar distances' to find longitude. Then he was no doubt, over dinner, drawn into discussions as to whether the marine chronometer, or sea-clock, could offer an alternative solution to the unsolved problem of the day: how to keep accurate time at sea to produce the most reliable way of finding longitude.[4] Without a chronometer, navigation in the North Atlantic was a fine art, for celestial bodies were frequently obscured by cloudy skies. Captain Ommaney and his sailing master, Mr Edward Haddock, used the technique of 'parallel sailing': staying as close as they could to the 47th Parallel – the latitude of St John's, Newfoundland – by means of 'observations' when possible, the compass and a knotted line to measure speed through the water.

As the *Panther* reached the point of convergence of the warm Gulf Stream with the colder Labrador Current, south-east of Newfoundland, she ran into heavy fog. Icebergs loomed out of the mist, surely an extraordinary sight for new boys like Robert, even if he had seen paintings of them at home. Among the 'isles of ice from all points of the compass' that Haddock noted in his log, the crew began to check the depth of water regularly with a 120-foot lead-line. The first indication of their approach to their destination would be the shallow, sandy-bottomed fishing ground of the Grand Banks, wherein lay the low and dangerous sandbar of Sable Island. 'Armed' with tallow in its hollow base, the lead attached to the end of the line could pick up a sample of the sea-bed, enabling the proximity of land to be determined by the nature of the bottom and the depth of water.

With some of the seamen 'swinging the lead', Haddock observed that '36 isles [of ice]' could be seen from the deck and '46 from the masthead' as the *Panther*'s crew cautiously brought their ship in, among the rocky bays of the Newfoundland coast. On 22 June 1772, after a month at sea, they arrived off the harbour of St John's and entered the narrow entrance under the loom of Signal Hill on the north shore, with Fort Amherst to the south. The fortifications here, like those at Portsmouth, were for Robert another reminder of his father: they too had been strengthened during Lord Granby's tenure as Britain's Master General of the Ordnance. Within the harbour lay the 16-gun *Nautilus*, the 20-gun *Alborough* and the 14-gun *Otter* riding to their anchors. As the *Panther* approached them and dropped her own 'best bower', the thunder of saluting guns echoed around the heights. Thirteen blanks fired from each of the ships marked the arrival of Commodore Shuldham as Newfoundland's governor.

Typically for the area, gales, rain and a shroud of thick fog set in. Some of the ship's company, including a marine, were given a dozen lashes for the various offences of 'drunkenness', 'neglect of duty', 'gaming', 'disobedience' and 'profaneness'. By now, it was clear to the men that Captain Ommaney was a martinet; but extremes of punishment would not have surprised Robert after his schooling at Eton.

The relief of a safe landfall gave the boy a moment to think of home. Not wishing to worry his grandmother, Charlotte Somerset, he held back on describing to her the discomforts of the voyage; but to Thomas Thoroton, secretary to the Duke of Rutland at Belvoir Castle, he let down his guard and admitted the experience had not been easy. The letters arrived home in mid-August 1772, and Thoroton, excited to hear from Robert but lacking the boy's sensitivity, forwarded them on to Charlotte. She relayed to Robert's brother Charles on 20 August that: 'I find by Bob's letter to Mr Thoroton that he has had a pretty sharp specimen of a seafaring life… Thoroton sent me the letter [Bob] wrote with a full account of the Dreadful Storm they were in of which he made no mention to me believing very justly that it would affect me more than his loving Friends at the Castle.' However, the old lady had confidence in her younger grandson and his future prospects: 'According to my Notion of Bob he will persist which if he does he will be Considerable at Sea.' Other than being sometimes 'frolicsome', the boy had rarely been any trouble to her – unlike Charles.

★

From an early age, Robert's strong sense of duty and military-mind-edness were noted, traits credited to his Norman ancestry. He was certainly aware that his Manners forebears – the de Manières – had arrived in the north of England in the eleventh century and that by the fourteenth century had built Etal Castle in Northumberland to defend English borders against the Scots. They had also defended Norham Castle on behalf of the bishops of Durham, thus holding positions of trust in the eyes of the monarch. Robert also knew of another notable ancestor, Robert de Todeni, who had been one of William the Con-queror's greatest barons as well as his standard-bearer at the Battle of Hastings in 1066. Todeni had been granted land across eleven English counties, on which he built the castle that came to be known as 'Belvoir'.

The Manners family had been elevated socially around 1490, when George Manners married Anne St Leger, a niece of Edward IV and Richard III, thus admitting the family into royal circles. A most fortu-itous inheritance then ensued. George's mother was Eleanor de Ros of Belvoir; when her heirless brother died in 1508, which was after her own death, it was with George that the name of Manners and the castle of Belvoir were united.[5]

Possibly as a 'bribe' for loyalty from this now influential and landed family, in 1525 Henry VIII then bestowed upon George and Anne's son, Thomas Manners, the hereditary title of Earl of Rutland, and later the posts of Warden of the East, West and Middle Marches and Steward of Sherwood Forest. Nine generations of earls through two centuries would thereafter see the family become one of the wealth-iest in England.

The Manners' most critical social advance came, however, in 1703, when the 9th Earl was created 1st Duke of Rutland by Queen Anne. Nominally, this was reward for having supported the Glorious Revo-lution and Protestant accession of William III to the English throne in 1688, but a less glamorous story has been handed down through the generations: that the ambitious mother-in-law of the 9th Earl's eldest son wanted her daughter to be a duchess rather than a countess, so she persuaded Queen Anne to bestow the title. Nevertheless, the Rutland dukedom lay at the very top of the social ladder, second only to the king himself. There were just twenty-five non-royal and royal dukes in the country.

Conscious of this esteemed ancestry, Robert entered the navy as a grandson of the 3rd Duke, imbued with a family pride symbolized by the peacock in the Manners' crest and their motto *Pour Y Parvenir* – 'to attain one's object'. A string of subsidiary and courtesy titles also highlighted their rank, accompanied by confusing name changes: an eldest son might start his life as Lord Roos (derived from 'Ros') when a grandson and indirect heir, then become Marquis of Granby when direct heir, before ending up as Duke of Rutland.[6]

Yet, the Manners were not of the arrogant, ruthless ilk – they tended to be generous, retiring country-lovers, conducting themselves with discretion rather than causing a stir as political movers and shakers. It was said that the 1st Duke had not even especially wanted his new title. While successive earls and dukes of Rutland had generally favoured limiting monarchical authority, at the same time they had been dutiful, avoiding taking sides where possible. They had even evolved a tradition whereby the father on his deathbed would call his sons to him and tell them they must be willing to raise a regiment at their own expense if the defence of the country required it and must only accept posts offered by the crown for duty, not personal profit. In common with other noble families, the eldest son would inherit the title by custom and the lion's share of property and wealth by settlement, in order to keep the estate intact and attached to the family name. Meanwhile, younger brothers might receive an allowance and some property that was 'entailed' (to use for their lifetime, but which they could not sell), but were expected to embark on a profession of service – not of trade – and use it to establish their own household.

Such younger brothers were, though, unlikely to choose the navy. With their experience of hunting and shooting on country estates, they were generally better suited to army life and its pecking order of regimental prestige. Another weighty reason that deterred them from serving at sea was typified by the attitude of Robert's grand-mother, widow of the 6th Duke of Somerset and the daughter of an earl. Charlotte Somerset had not wanted her younger grandson to join the ranks of naval officers, for she considered them socially inferior. While respecting their seamanship, she thought them 'idle', possibly because battle-action was infrequent. At the root of her prejudice was the notion that schoolmasters were not present in all naval vessels and that most officers thus missed out on a formal education, having joined the service at a very young age to gain maximum sea-time and experience. The rough-mannered 'tarry-breeks' figure of the 'tarpaulin' officer was inimical to the self-image and aspirations of families like hers. She would also have considered that the business of learning how to handle, navigate, manage and – eventually – command a ship, let alone a squadron or a fleet, simply took too long. Looking askance at the drudgery and poor prospects of the sea-service, to say nothing of the obligatory six years' sea-time needed to obtain commissioned rank, Charlotte had hoped Robert would instead take the easier and more congenial route of purchasing a commission in the army. Or, if not the army, utilize family connections to seek a route into politics or the Church.

But the boy had disregarded her wishes, and now he found himself surrounded by midshipmen and commissioned officers drawn from the poorer gentry and from professional naval families. It is true that the number of well-educated and well-connected naval officers was increasing, as wartime successes and vast fortunes earned by capturing enemy ships – 'prize money' – attracted aristocratic younger sons to the sea service. Nevertheless, despite the occasional presence of noblemen's offspring, such as lieutenants the Honourable James Luttrell and Charles Powell Hamilton serving with him in the *Panther*, Robert still remained an oddity. With genteel manners, a rounded education, an ability to speak French and a penchant for reading Plato and Aristotle in his spare time, he stood out in the navy – as according to a later description, 'a character totally unknown here'.

In this position, Robert faced a rude awakening, not only in the physical hardships of shipboard life, but in its meritocratic nature. It mattered whether the commander of an expensive ship-of-war with its complement of several hundred valuable men was competent. Though most successful naval commanders had used 'interest' along the way, generally their careers had been glittering because they had also deserved their promotions. They, in turn, were sceptical about aristocratic boys, even if wooed by their status and connections; one young hopeful was described as 'well-bred, [as] gentlemanly a young man as can be, and I dare say an excellent fox-hunter, for he seems skilful in horses, dogs, foxes and such animals. But unluckily... these are branches of knowledge not very useful at sea, we do not profit by them off Ushant.'[7]

Boys such as Robert often joined with an innate sense of entitlement, and they could be a 'damnable nuisance', becoming foolhardy or too distracted by a parallel political career to take their shipboard responsibilities seriously. Robert was potentially no different in this respect. From a childhood spent on the grand fox-hunting estate of Belvoir Castle, and even though driven to embark on life in an unfamiliar environment, he retained the inborn expectation of rapid preferment and access to the potential rewards of honour, glory and prize-money. He was bred to believe his connections would override the personal battles that lay within the Georgian navy of the 1770s and leave him well placed for any battles that lay without.

For Robert, though, such inherited assumptions were tempered by a hard-nosed awareness that obtaining promotions might, in reality, not be so easy. And so his outward confidence masked an underlying humility and reserve. He knew that he was going to have to use his inner resources and work hard to impress his superiors for he did not have the network of 'interest' that should have been available to him. Lord Robert Manners was an orphan and could not turn to his famous father for help, while his ageing grandfather, the duke, had little concern for his grandson's naval career. His best living connection was his charming but wayward brother Charles.

Charles Manners was the young man to whom Charlotte Somerset – after voicing her confidence that Robert would 'persist' and be 'Considerable at Sea' – said: 'I hope & believe you will be so at Land if you don't run into Party but be always your own man.' In truth, she was worried about her eldest grandson. The eighteen-year-old seemed to lack direction and focus, in contrast to the discipline Robert was learning at sea. In an age when landowners addicted to gambling might lose their estates on the throw of a dice, she fretted as to whether Charles would be able to uphold the family title which he stood to inherit. Furthermore, the government's disastrous policies towards the thirteen American colonies appeared to be giving rise to disturbing political turmoil, and only time would tell if the older boy could be relied upon to help his younger brother in the fierce struggles that might lie ahead.

While her two grandsons unknowingly stood upon the threshold of the world's first modern revolution, their lives had already been far from straightforward.

2

'Going at it bald-headed'

September 1750 to October 1770

'Going at it bald-headed'

The marriage of Charles and Robert Manners' parents had been a 'mighty topic of conversation'.[1] In the summer of 1750, their father John Manners, Marquis of Granby, moved his lover and three illegitimate children out of his London home to make way for a wife. For some time, the hard-drinking Granby had been searching for a suitable spouse, preferably a wealthy heiress, fuelling the pen of social gossip Horace Walpole:

> We picked up Lord Granby, arrived very drunk from Jenny's Whim [tavern in Pimlico], where... he had dined with Lady Fanny and left her and eight other women and four men playing at brag. He... made over his honourable love upon any terms to poor Miss Beauclerc who is very modest, and did not know at all what to do with his whispers or his hands. He then addressed himself to Miss Sparre, who was very well disposed to receive both; but the tide of champagne turned, [and] he hiccupped at the reflection [of marrying her].[2]

By September 1750, having ejected his lover, 'Mrs' Mompesson, the twenty-nine-year-old Granby had decided upon the Lady Fanny. She was Frances Seymour, the twenty-two-year-old daughter of Charles Seymour, 6th Duke of Somerset, and tongues wagged hard as to how much she brought to the match: their marriage settlement ran to 246 sheepskins-worth of parchment on which to record the detail.

As heir to the 3rd Duke of Rutland, Lord Granby could expect to inherit vast wealth, including the magnificent estate of Belvoir Castle.

In the meantime, his allowance was not enough for a flamboyant life-style, so he had borrowed heavily against his future inheritance and now hoped to gain from his new wife who, unusually for a woman at the time, owned land and property. Yet, as it turned out, Frances fell short of being the unencumbered heiress of Granby's desire, for she also had large debts, neither of them being able to 'conceive of a use to money but to give it away'. 'Don't you like this English management?' Walpole commented drily. 'Two of the greatest fortunes meeting and setting out in poverty and want.'[3]

Aside from being heir to a duke, the Marquis of Granby was not a man who would easily have escaped attention. Charismatic, robust and generous to a fault, he was a skilled horseman who had, during the military conflicts of the 1740s, gained a reputation as a brave and talented soldier. He was also a hard drinker and a gambler. 'Lord Granby, when not engaged in war or hunting,' one later observer remarked, 'seems like many other active spirits, to have been apt to get into mischief. [He] was a convivial soul and he flinched no more from the bottle than he did from the foe.'[4] Bald by the age of twenty-five, he chose not to wear a hat or wig, for which he was considered somewhat vulgar, and Horace Walpole thought that at times he behaved like a drunken lout. Nevertheless, the Duke of Rutland had supposedly taught his son and heir 'never to do, or suffer, a bad deed', and Granby's charity, within his own lifetime, would become legendary. An annual subscription to the Lock Hospital – which specialized in treating venereal diseases and printed at the top of its receipts 'Go and Sin no more' – was just one example of the many ventures he supported.

In contrast, little is known of his wife's character, though she appeared to be musical since she played the harpsichord. A contemporary described her as 'a well-natured, vain, weak, inoffensive person'.[5] She certainly possessed a fragile constitution, and her childhood had been blighted by constant colds and indispositions of one sort or another, during which her mother Charlotte, Duchess of Somerset, had nursed her assiduously. 'Yesterday at five o'clock in the afternoon I gave Lady Frances the quarter of an ounce of oxymes squills,' wrote Charlotte to her doctor, referring to an expectorant made from vinegar, honey and the red-rooted squill, or sea-onion. '[B]ut between

London   1753   Bro.t over —— 1913 7 6½

Supra for several Acc.ts brought over ——— 105 – –

June 15 1753   Paid a Benefaction for enlarging the building of the } 10. 10. –
Lock Hospital

Paid William Rose for playing upon the Birth } 1. 11. 6
Pays in London

16   Paid a Night Nurse for Lady Frances for three } 3. 3. –
Months Attendance

Gave to the Poor at the Door when your Lordship } 1. 6. –
left London

21   Paid Lord Guernseys Coachman & Postillion —— – 15. 6

July 2   Paid Will Manby Sen.r a bill of Particulars .. 6. 8. 6

Feby 20   Paid a Christmas Box bill by particulars 8. 7. –

March 19 1754   D.o Nurse Tyson for attending her Ladyship } 10. 10. –
on M.r Charles Manners

Paid the Clerk of S.t Georges Hanover Square }
D.o Trebecks Fee for Registring M.r Charles — } 1. 6. –
Manners 1. 1. Clerk for his Attendance .5.t }

—————— 148 17 6

Car.r forwards —— 2062 5 – ½

twelve & one she had so violent a fit of coughing I thought she would have puked[,] but she did not & this morning had two stools both much loaded with phlegm, she has now drank asses milk in a morning above these two months.'[6] As Frances began to bear children in 1751, her deliveries were often difficult and she was prescribed such remedies as 'the blood and liver of a freshly slaughtered lamb'.

In an age when love was largely irrelevant to patrician matches, it was said that Granby and his wife adored each other – even the waspish Walpole thought them happy – and within eight years of their marriage, they had produced seven children. An heir John, with the courtesy title of Lord Roos, arrived in 1751, followed two years later by a girl named Frances. On 27 February 1754, another boy was born, named simply Charles, after his Somerset grandfather. Three other daughters died in infancy. Robert Albinine Manners, their youngest child, was born on 6 February 1758 at the family's London house in Albemarle Street, off Piccadilly, causing Granby's clerk Mr Hempsall to add a note to his accounts: 'Paid Dr Trebeck for registering Master Robert Manners in the parish of St George's, Hanover Square: £1 1s.' Indeed, Hempsall listed the expenses incurred to pay all those attending Robert's birth – the doctors, midwives, nurses and a wet nurse – totalling more than £80, almost three times the sum Granby's father was paying annually to rent seven acres of land in Knightsbridge. At a time of high infant mortality, when diseases like smallpox ravaged every class of society, those who could afford it were willing to pay handsomely to promote the survival of children and protect their family dynasty. This time, the new baby was strong and healthy, and Granby now had an 'heir and two spares'.

The four surviving children, John, Frances, Charles and Robert, were cared for by nurses and tutors, the first adults with whom they probably had their most significant bonds. It was still fashionable for noble families to encourage children to grow up quickly by leaving them in the care of others, though this child-rearing style also helped to guard against the emotional destruction caused by the high infant mortality. Parents were absent much of the time, following the call of politics and society, frequenting fashionable salons, soirées, dinners and dances, while leaving their little ones in the hands of nurses, nannies and tutors.

Yet the baby Robert, in the first years of his life, saw even less of

London 1757 Bro* over — 3962 16 7

Physicians Fees &c

9 May 57	Paid Nurse Denman for attending Lady Frances in the small Pox	10.10...
17 Sept	Paid D* Mevrick for attending Lord Roos —	5.5...
21 Dec*	Paid D* Heberden for Ditto.	3.3...
7 March	Paid D* Hunter for attending Lady Granby's lying in of Master Rob* Manners.	31.10...
	Paid M* Blackwell Midwife for Ditto.	31.10...
	Paid Nurse Tyson for Ditto.	10.10...
19	Paid Ditto for two weeks additional attendance	4.4...

Payments of Interest &c

Family accounts 1757–8, showing some expenses relating to Robert's birth.

their father than the others had done in their early years. For in 1758, Lord Granby, when his youngest boy was just five months old, disappeared off to war. With no intention of remaining idle while waiting for his inheritance, the thirty-seven-year-old answered the call of military duty.

*

A childhood spent fox-hunting on the Belvoir estate had prepared Granby well as a soldier, and his skill as a rider and an eye finely tuned to tracking down a quarry first coming to the fore in the 1745, during the Jacobite Rebellion led by 'Bonnie Prince Charlie' – that doomed attempt to topple the Hanoverian monarchy and restore the Stuarts. Then, in the wars with France and Spain in the 1740s, his obvious ability and courage attracted the notice of high command and built him a loyal following. Now, in the spring of 1758, he was appointed to lead a crack cavalry regiment, the Royal Horse Guards, better known as

the 'Blues'. Two years earlier, a fragile peace had given way to open
warfare with France over the borders between French Canada and the
thirteen British colonies in North America. Thus had begun the Seven
Years' War between the imperial powers, whose competing interests
had overflowed back into Europe; and British and Prussian troops had
been unable to stop the French from targeting Hanover – the German
territory abutting the North Sea, over which Britain's Georgian mon-
archs were hereditary electoral princes.

It was the task of the Blues, along with other British regiments under
the overall command of the Prussian Prince Ferdinand of Brunswick,
now to recover Hanover. King George II needed some persuading that
Granby was the right man to lead the Royal Horse Guards, regarding
him as 'a sot, a bully, that does nothing but drink and quarrel'.[7] But
Granby was otherwise so popular that upon the announcement of his
colonelcy, no less than fifty-two young officers applied to serve as his
aide-de-camp, a number that – even in those days of interest and preferment – was considered remarkable. He selected the young Charles
Cornwallis, whose title at the time was Viscount Brome.

After gathering horses and equipment, much of it paid for out of
his own pocket, Granby embarked for Germany in July 1758, suffering
his habitual seasickness on the rough crossing. Robert, being but a
tiny baby, would not have noticed his departure, but the older children were aware of a flurry of preparations, including the despatch
of some greyhounds and the marquis's favourite chargers, Dormouse
and Windsor. Now, in the absence of their father, there followed a
tense period of waiting for news and for letters, during which time the
children could intuit the anxiety felt by their mother and their now
widowed grandmother, the Duchess of Somerset, who stood by to
help with them. Granby arrived in Germany to find voracious sickness
among the troops already out there: the British commander, the Duke
of Marlborough, soon died, leaving Lord George Sackville to take his
place, with Granby second in command of the British forces as well
as commander of the Blues. In an age when common disease was still
a greater danger than infrequent battle for those on campaign, the
letters written home on Granby's behalf by his army chaplain, Bennet
Storer, were eagerly anticipated, for they reported almost obsessively
on Granby's health – 'Lord Granby is well', 'Lord Granby is troubled

with a rash' – alternately allaying or increasing the marchioness's apprehension.

Then, the following year, came the sudden start of Granby's fame, a reputation that would forever have a hold over the lives of his children. When Prince Ferdinand's Hanoverian forces, of which the British detachment formed a part, prevailed over the French at Minden, on 1 August 1759, the victory was surrounded by controversy. It was bruited abroad that Sackville had misconducted himself, to such an extent that he was accused of cowardice. It was said that he had deliberately delayed sending the cavalry forward in support of the infantry as they gallantly attacked the enemy, thereby missing an opportunity to annihilate the French army. With Sackville publicly disgraced, British public opinion – never very bothered about the facts – credited Granby with the infantry's success at Minden, even though the Blues had not taken part in the action on the day. 'Granby, who is the Mob's hero… has defeated the French!' commented an astonished Horace Walpole. 'The foreign gazettes I suppose will give this victory to Prince Ferdinand but the mob of London, whom I have just this minute left, and who know best, assure me that it is all their own Marquis's doing!'[8] In the wake of Sackville's disgrace came Granby's opportunity: he was now appointed commander-in-chief of the British forces in Germany.

As the year progressed, the British were increasingly euphoric: victory – on a colossal scale – was in the air. Minden was but part of the *annus mirabilis* of 1759. British arms had made gains in India, Admiral Boscawen had scored a notable success over the French off the Portuguese coast, and General Wolfe had died wresting Quebec – and Canada – from the French in September. Then, as the year drew to its end, Admiral Hawke, in the gathering darkness of a winter afternoon on 20 November, chased a French fleet under Admiral de Conflans into Quiberon Bay on a dangerous south Brittany coast. Amid strong gales, and with no chance of escape, the French were defeated, removing the threat of any invasion of Britain's coasts.

Yet, these successes did not bring the longed-for peace. Granby's service continued, while for the family the national mood was utterly eclipsed by personal tragedy. Early in the New Year of 1760, the delicate Marchioness of Granby fell ill, and on 26 January 'a St Anthony's Fire struck in, and seized her brain'. She died, aged thirty-two, of the

acute streptococcal skin infection erysipelas. Typical of his brand of
Anglicanism, the army chaplain Bennet Storer both broke the news
to Granby and tried to reassure those at home: 'The death of the best
of women... in whose loss the best of men is made miserable. Tho'
nothing can as you well know, surpass Lord Granby's tenderness and
feeling, yet I flatter myself his Lordship's natural fortitude and resolution will not fail him in so severe a tryal.'

Taking leave of absence, Granby came home for a few weeks to see
his children and his mother-in-law, the dowager Duchess of Somerset,
who had taken them into her care. But he found it hard to face 'so
distressful a meeting' and soon returned to the field. But then came a
further blow. Frances's death was followed five months later on 2 June
by that of his heir, the nine-year-old Lord Roos. The poor boy perished
of 'pernicious worms', possibly picked up from one of the family's
many dogs.

Whatever Granby's inner feelings over this second tragedy, relief
came in the peremptory call of duty: in spite of, or because of, his
grief, he led a ferocious cavalry charge in Germany against the flower
of the French army, at Warburg, on 31 July 1760. During a complex
manoeuvre, the exhausted British infantry were unable to advance
through the marshy ground in the heat, and Prince Ferdinand ordered
Granby to advance with twenty-two squadrons of cavalry supported
by artillery. Granby's force moved forwards at a trot with the artillery closed up. Pausing to redeploy and unlimber the guns, he told his
trumpeter to sound the charge. At the head of the Blues, the marquis
led a furious charge, repeatedly breaking the French line and scattering
a mixed rabble of 20,000 horse, foot and artillery who 'threw down
their arms and splashed frantically through the fords... Thus brilliantly
ended the action of Warburg.'[9]

Granby had taken post 'well in front of all', and in the fury of the
advance he lost his hat and wig, leaving his hairless pate gleaming in
the sun. According to an officer in the Prussian army, Granby 'had
his hat blown off, a big bald circle in his head rendering the loss more
conspicuous. But he never minded; stormed still on, bare bald headed
among the helmets and sabres.'[10] The action restored the reputation
of the cavalry after its inactivity at Minden, giving rise to the expression 'going at it bald-headed'.

None of this glorious achievement compensated Granby for his double personal loss, as observed by those closest to him. 'I pray God preserve you the two charming boys which are left,' wrote his friend the Duke of Newcastle.

★

When Charles's and Robert's mother had died, it was not their paternal grandfather who stepped in to look after them and their sister Frances. For the sixty-two-year-old Duke of Rutland was an ailing, distant figure, absorbed in his own second family of illegitimate children by his mistress 'Mrs' Drake.

Instead it was their maternal grandmother, the dowager Duchess of Somerset, who took them into her permanent care. Although she was herself now sixty-seven, Charlotte Somerset had more than enough strength of character to be a surrogate mother. Born in 1693 the daughter of Daniel Finch, 2nd Earl of Nottingham and 7th Earl of Winchelsea, she had grown up at Burley-on-the-Hill, not far from Belvoir Castle, and was married at thirty-two to Charles Seymour, the 'Proud Duke' of Somerset, who was almost double her age. He lived at Petworth House, which he had inherited from his first wife, Elizabeth Percy, and his pride and pomposity were legendary. On Charlotte tapping him with her fan to gain his attention, he rounded on her: 'Madam, my first duchess was a Percy, and she never took such a liberty.'[11] Although Charlotte appeared never to criticize her husband, whom she nursed with some devotion – treating him with such curious nostrums as 'powder of crab's eyes' and 'black wool dipped in oil of vipers'[12] – Somerset left her almost nothing on his death in 1748. This may have been because his Percy grandson and heir had died in 1744, and he blamed Charlotte for producing only two daughters and no additional male heir. Be that as it may, her Manners grandsons, Charles and Robert, were to become the sons she never had.

The three children went to live with Charlotte in her London homes of Sutton Court in Chiswick and Hill Street in Mayfair. That the elderly lady had a strong sense of morality combined with a tender love for her young charges was evident in her letters to their father. Her grandchildren, already familiar with her presence and their parents' absence, and possessing the innate resilience of the young, recovered their spirits enough to be cheeky to Mr Palmer, their tutor. Charlotte told Granby that she responded by threatening them with 'an instrument of government', which had the desired effect, after which things went on 'mighty well'. But later in 1760, she nervously told Granby that 'Master Robert was on Tuesday afternoon taken with a feverish disorder'. The doctor thought it might be chickenpox, but Charlotte rather hoped it would prove to be smallpox because 'whatever tis there's no signs of there being many [spots] & it would be a happiness to have that distemper over with him & no danger of communicating it to the others, they are all kept from him & were so from the first day he was taken ill'. In the event, Robert's disorder proved 'nothing more than a Tooth with the addition of a Cold'.

However, Lord Granby, out in the field, though spared from losing another son, was to suffer further heartbreak. The marquis had, from the first, acknowledged the offspring of his liaison with Mrs Mompesson preceding his marriage to Frances Seymour. His illegitimate children George, Anne and Elizabeth had taken the family name of Manners, were educated appropriately, and socialized with his legitimate children. In 1761, the twelve-year-old Elizabeth died. Bennet Storer dutifully relayed Granby's condolences to Mrs Mompesson amid the pressure of war ('Lord Granby is this moment gone out to throw some shells into Gudenberg'). Then in 1762, his own much-loved younger brother, Lord Robert Manners-Sutton, died in England from an illness.[13] Granby himself was dangerously ill at the time, and Bennet Storer delayed telling him until he was better, for fear the shock would kill him.

At last, in March 1763, Granby was reunited with his family, after the Seven Years' War had concluded with the Treaty of Paris, of 10 February. Hanover, Canada, Florida, trading posts in the East Indies, four additional valuable West Indian sugar-islands and the North American colonial borders were secured, while the Grand Banks fishing rights were claimed within Britain's empire at the expense of France and Spain. Although this success was credited largely to the political war leadership of the elder William Pitt, Lord Granby returned to England as one of the most famous men in the country. While he was undoubtedly a man of military talent, his reputation was exaggerated by public acclaim, for, being subordinate to Prince Ferdinand of Brunswick, he had not been tested in *overall* command. The real source of his popularity was not his talent and courage, but his generosity and concern for his men, most unusual for the time. Known as the 'mob's hero' and 'father of the army', his conduct in this regard was epitomized by Edward Penny's painting *The Marquis of Granby Relieving a Sick Soldier*. Prints of this image, along with verses written in his honour, rolled off the presses, outselling even prints of Benjamin West's *Death of General Wolfe*, while Granby's friend Sir Joshua Reynolds painted several life-size portraits of him, depicting his distinctive bald head. One evening in London, as Granby entered the Theatre Royal in Drury Lane, the audience stopped the performance, and clamoured for the 'Marquis of Granby's March'; at a birthday party for the king at Northumberland House in the Strand, as Granby entered the grounds, illuminated by thousands of lamps, the band stopped and instead struck up Handel's 'See the Conquering Hero Comes'. Wherever he went, Granby was celebrated and cheered. 'The British Hero' by Richard Rolt was written in his honour and set to music by William Boyce; another song, containing the refrain 'Granby O, gen'rous Granby O!', was a favourite with many around the country who had heard from discharged soldiers about his willingness to share their hardships and dangers.

Granby's consideration for his soldiers continued after their campaigning together, and he provided for wounded warrant officers, many of whom established public houses named after him. The inn-signs invariably showed the marquis bald-headed, an allusion to both his habitual appearance and to his wigless and dazzling charge at Warburg. More than two centuries later, in the 1980s, there were still around a thousand 'Marquis of Granby' pubs in England.[14] And to this day, the Blues, now the Blues and Royals, is the only regiment of the British army that is permitted to salute without wearing headgear. Some soldiers became his loyal personal servants, including John Notzell, a Swiss Hussar who had been Granby's batman on campaign, and John Glover, a sergeant who became a valet.

*

Granby's return to England did not mean that, initially, his sons saw much more of him. Naturally enough, Charles's life was completely changed by the death of elder brother John, Lord Roos, for he was now Granby's heir and had been sent off to board at Eton College in March 1762. It was, according to his grandmother, not too soon, for Charlotte had shrewdly observed that 'M[aste]r Charles... is extremely addicted to yawning and has rather a dislike to looking upon a Book but whenever he does give himself the trouble tis with good success for he catches quick & retains long... he complains that he is no sooner dropt asleep than he is awakened again to go to his Book.' On 16 April 1763, just weeks after Granby returned from his five years in Germany, Robert followed his indolent brother to boarding school, ending the only period in which the two boys were ever apart during their early childhood. Their sister Frances, however, remained living with Charlotte, and she may have seen more of their father.

Robert was just five years old when, with John Glover in attendance, the family carriage first brought him to his new school. The sight of Eton's imposing buildings looming out of a 'dreary swamp' of water-meadows on the north bank of the Thames, with the ramparts of Windsor Castle rising in the distance beyond, must have been daunting for the small boy, who throughout his father's long absence had not left London. Robert was unusually young to be starting at the school, even for a time when little thought was given to the sensibilities of children; but it may well have been at his own request, for he would have felt his separation from Charles acutely. Had the family not endured so many untimely deaths, the boys' schooling would certainly have been different, for Granby had not intended to send son John to Eton until he was twelve. Most of the boys there were aged between nine and sixteen.

Whether this early disruption of Robert's childhood bonds with nannies and others with whom he had become familiar was voluntary or not, his arrival at Eton threw him into an intimacy with his brother, despite an age gap of four years. It created not a gulf between them, but a profound and lasting connection. At first, Charles would have been able to care to some extent for Robert, protecting him from the worst vicissitudes of life at Eton. The older boy had already been there a year and could help the younger through the first frightening days at the bottom of a strange and abrasive new social order; but the school and its tough environment, which was intended to foster independence, would induce two very different – though deeply affectionate – characters.

And Eton *was* tough. Granby's friend the elder Pitt remarked that he had 'scarce observed a boy who was not cowed for life at Eton: that a public school might suit a boy of turbulent, forward disposition, but it would not do where there was any gentleness'.[15] Flogging was routine, fagging – younger boys acting as personal servants for older boys – was expected, homosexuality was quietly tolerated even though it was illegal, and other 'amusements' indulged in by the boys included bull-baiting and cock-fighting, the 'pelting of Greek scholars' on their way to class and 'booking' boys for farting.[16]

Then, as now, Eton was one of the foremost schools of choice for members of Britain's social elite. Yet, it offered prospects to more than just the upper echelons of society. In fact, it had originally been founded, by King Henry VI in 1440, to provide education for poor boys. 'Oppidans' – the sons of noblemen and wealthy merchants – paid fees that funded the free education of up to seventy poor but clever boys: the 'Collegers'. Although the class divide was rigorous and the poor boys slept in the 'Long Chamber', separate from the Oppidans' boarding houses, nevertheless the sons of bakers, grocers, tea-dealers, ballet-masters, shipwrights, apothecaries, drapers, cheesemongers, bricklayers and many other trades were thrown together in lessons with the sons of dukes, earls and gentlemen.[17]

Charles and Robert boarded just across the road from College Chapel in Manor House, one of thirteen houses run by female Dames or male Domines for the Oppidans. Their house lay under the watchful eye of Mrs Young, the best known of the eighteenth-century Dames, and it accommodated many of the best-connected boys. The older boys tended to rule the boarding houses in the place of adults. At night in particular, there was no proper adult supervision. The potential for abuse, by flogging or otherwise, was notorious. Though buggery was in theory punishable by death, it was viewed among adolescent boys to some extent as a 'phase'; rather, it was masturbation that attracted the greatest stigma. A pamphlet first distributed in London in 1716, and attributed to Dutch theologian Dr Balthasar Bekker, remained compulsory reading for schoolboys and their masters throughout the eighteenth century. It was titled, in full, *Onania, or, The Heinous Sin of Self-Pollution, And All Its Frightful Consequences, in Both Sexes, Considered: With Spiritual and Physical Advice To Those Who Have Already Injured Themselves By This Abominable Practice*. With many boys having to

share beds, the concern was that they would 'pollute' each other and
that masturbation, mutual or otherwise, would 'weaken the boy and
ruin the man'.[18] It was a paradox that society condemned this, while
openly acknowledging the licentious sexual practices that Charles and
Robert could observe in their own family.

Dr Edward Barnard was headmaster at the time of the Manners
boys' arrival and had been so since 1754. Under him, the school pros-
pered, its pupils increasing from 300 to 500 boys. Barnard had followed
the disastrous Dr Dampier, 'who believed that respect, Latin, and even
Greek could be driven into boys with a birch'.[19] Barnard was not such
a flogger, preferring to punish with his cutting wit; but he was not
keen on long hair and was said to have lopped off a boy's pigtail with
a 'greasy commons knife'.[20]

In 1765, Dr Barnard became Eton's Provost – chairman of the
governors and appointed by the crown – with Dr Foster becoming
headmaster in his place. Foster did not share Barnard's lenient attitude to flogging, but Charles seemed to stay on the right side of him.
Responding to his grandmother's stern lectures, Charles assured her
that: 'Dr Foster has approved of me vastly & has given me a very good
caracter & I hope I shall prove a very good man & be of very great

*Lower School at Eton remains largely unchanged from the 1760s. Groups of desks faced in
different directions, so a variety of classes could be taught simultaneously.*

service to my King & Country & better satisfaction of my all [*sic*] relations of my family & friends & other people, & contribute to lengthen
& make your life happy & not to bring you by my wickedness & folly
with sorrow to the grave... I am Dear Grandmama your most loving
affectionate Son.'

From a distance, Charlotte Somerset, concerned for her small boys
in this harsh environment, fussed over them, sending treats, books and
pocket money – along with continued reminders to behave themselves.
As time went on, and as Charles seemed to thrive, a little cheekiness
crept into his letters to her:

> Dear Grandmama, I was very sorry to hear you was not well, and
> very glad to Hear you are very well again the Pears are very fine
> flavoured, they were a little bruised in comming, you ought to
> Have packed them up in trays. I gave some to some Boys they said
> they were the best they ever tasted. I should be glad you would
> send me some more, & another Ham, the last was extremely
> good... I hope you think my writing is a little improved... Bob
> joins with me in Duty to you & Love to Sister & tell Her I shall
> write to Her in a Day or two...

She replied with a swipe at how quickly he consumed whatever she
sent: 'I have order'd you some Tea and Chocolate which as you say
won't last for Ever but give me leave to say has made a quicker Exit
than usual... My love to Bob.'

The school, set at the end of a high-street of shops running towards
Windsor Bridge, included an ancient chapel and cloisters. The 'Lower
School' for younger boys and the 'Upper School' for older boys were
situated around a spacious, open courtyard. Masters were few and the
classes large, consisting of up to sixty boys each, with groups of desks
facing in different directions to enable a variety of lessons to be taught
simultaneously in the barn-like rooms. With so many boys gathered
together under one roof, the repetition and rote-learning created a din,
increasing when inattentive scholars burst into songs and choruses,
which were often obscene. Discipline, when it was imposed by the
praeposters or prefects, was arbitrary and brutish.

Notwithstanding the lack of masters to teach it, the pupils' syllabus
was rigorously classical and very demanding. It was centred on the

works of Homer, Virgil and Horace and would play a part in shaping the boys' outlook and giving them a frame of reference for their public behaviour, such as the fable of Hercules faced with choosing between Pleasure and Virtue, as well as practical skills including persuasive oratory and elegant writing. As the boys became competent in Latin and Greek, they were taught to imitate classical verse and rhetoric, to write with comedy and wit, and to excel in the reduction of an argument or idea into a pithy closing comment or 'joke'.[21] However, they also learned arithmetic, algebra, geometry and geography, and for those with 'gentle' pretensions and the necessary money, French lessons, dancing and fencing were available. Then, apart from the formal lessons, prayers, roll-calls and the like, the boys in the Upper School were required to produce extra work in their free time.

Both Charles and Robert were assisted by a schoolmaster named John Ekins, whom the boys adopted as their personal tutor; he helped to make up for the deficiencies of the school's actual teaching. Despite his inherent laziness, Charles proved a good classical scholar with an aptitude for writing verse and doggerel. Several of his creations survive, such as a ditty for his bookish friend Thomas Grenville entitled *Donarem pateras*, meaning literally 'I would give bowls...' and inspired by Horace's ode of the same name, implying that poetry is worth more than fine gifts.[22]

> Dear Thomas prithee condescend
> To take these volumes from a friend
> Goblets with gold & jewels rough
> And seals I'd give, & jewels enough,
> With every other precious antique
> To make a virtuoso frantick;
> Pictures & marble busts in plenty
> *Crumenâ non deficiente* [if money was no object]
> But books, friend Tom, I'd have you know it
> Are the fit present from a Poet
> So don't despise my gift, but take it
> With the same friendly warmth I make it.

Even the youngest boys attended classes from eight in the morning to six at night on Mondays, Wednesdays and Fridays, with Tuesdays and

Thursday afternoons off for games such as the Wall Game (unique to Eton and involving a ball and scrumming against a wall), football, cricket and fives. Besides these formal sports, they found time for other more dubious-sounding activities such as 'hunt the dark lanthorn', 'puss-in the corner', 'steal-baggage' and 'sliding down the sides of the stairs from the cloysters to the college kitchen'.[23] Boys being boys and the age being louche, Eton schoolboys also indulged in betting, drinking, wenching and the persecution of animals.

One of the school's greatest attractions for parents was the chance it provided for their sons to make contacts that would stand them in good stead in later life. A handful of boys even came over from North America, for some colonists considered that it was preferable to send their boys to England on a ship with a cargo of tobacco than to subject them to a rudimentary local education.

For Charles in particular, friendships forged at Eton would prove enduring as the boys grew together into classical scholars and seasoned drinkers. Along with Thomas Grenville and his brother George, others who became life-long friends were the clever Alleyne FitzHerbert from Tissington Hall, Derbyshire, whose father owned plantations in Jamaica and Barbados, and who was 'the best of his year on the examination';[24] a boy named Daniel Pulteney, who seized this opportunity to strike an acquaintanceship with a future Duke of Rutland; and two sons of the Earl of Harrington: Lord Petersham and Henry Fitzroy Stanhope.

The insular academic institution with its arcane traditions lay cheek-by-jowl with the town, enabling the friends to frequent the coffee-houses and shops of Eton High Street and experience 'the bawdy low-comedy of the Christopher Inn and its rumoured brothel'.[25] They bought oysters – the cheap fast food of the day – and lived off credit, as did so many others at that time. Their fellows were referred to by nicknames such as 'Snowball', 'Teapot', 'Woglog' and 'Mother', and similarly disrespectful sobriquets were applied to the masters; the former headmaster had been called 'Perny-pojax Dampier' and Charles and Robert's own tutor was known as 'Buck Ekins'.[26]

Of course many other contemporaries, while not being friends of the Manners boys as such, would also remain in their lives as public figures. Of particular note was Charles James Fox, described by the elder Pitt as having been brought up 'without the least regard to morality and with such extravagant vulgar indulgence that the great change which has taken place among our youth has been dated from the time of his son's going to Eton'.[27] In 1764, when the young Fox was fifteen, his father took him away from Eton for four months and encouraged him into all kinds of exploits in Paris and elsewhere. When he returned, he was thought by the masters to be 'a thoroughly bad character';[28] he was flogged, but the boys just laughed at him. By the time Fox left Eton, the ridicule and the floggings were said to have reformed his character. While that was not entirely true, and he would remain debauched and flamboyant, ahead of him lay a high-profile political career in defiant opposition to the government.

As a ducal heir, Charles seems to have flourished during his time at Eton, and does not appear to have attracted any of the sanctions beyond flogging, such as being locked in isolation or physically maimed. Robert, harder-working than the lazy Charles, leaves no trace of his particular friendships at that time, and the brothers may have simply shared the same friends. However, his exposure to flogging would stand him in good stead for life in the navy, for it was said that midshipmen with a boarding-school background coped better than those unaccustomed to arbitrary physical punishment. (Yet it also appears that the school may have fostered in the boy a distaste for corporal punishment, for he would later come up with an ingenious alternative.)

Eton boys did openly rebel against the severity of punishments, sometimes creating a state of near-anarchy in an institution staffed by an insufficient number of masters. And Charles and Robert joined in at least one of the school's 'rebellions' of the period, when, in November 1768, a dispute arose over the privileges between prefects and assistant-masters. The brothers, along with 160 other boys, marched to Maidenhead, throwing their schoolbooks into the river as they crossed Windsor Bridge – except for Thomas Grenville, who characteristically would not part with his Homer. But after collectively spending more than £50 at an inn, on beer, wine, dinner and cards, their stand against authority ran out of ideas. Most of the miscreants returned to the school next morning, but some of the more wilful and high-bred boys set off for London, Charles and Robert among them.

Lord Harrington would only speak to his son Lord Petersham at the door, ordering him to return immediately to Eton. 'Sir,' responded Petersham, 'consider I shall be damned if I do.' To which his father responded: 'And I will be damned if you don't.' Displaying the wit Eton encouraged, the son riposted: 'Yes my Lord, but you will be damned whether I do or not.'

There was a similar encounter between the Manners boys and their father at about the same moment. Already warned of the revolt, Lord Granby had pretended to be surprised when they arrived on his doorstep. 'Well, boys, what brought you here?' he asked on their being admitted to his presence. 'We have left Eton,' they replied.

'So I perceive.'

'Oh, we have all been used so ill. Dr Foster has driven the scholars away – and we have done as the rest – and so have come home.'

'Very well, very well,' responded their father with every appearance of his customary easy-going generosity, 'and you would like to go to the play this evening, hey boys?'

'Oh, yes, you are very good, sir.'

'Yes, you shall go there tonight for your own pleasure,' affirmed the marquis, 'and tomorrow shall return to Dr Foster and be flogged for mine.'

And, as the story has it, Granby kept his word and sent the boys back to school to be soundly thrashed.[29]

★

Over the years following his return from Germany, Lord Granby had managed to spend time with his boys whenever he could, during their holidays. On these occasions he could provide them with an education entirely different from the classical rigour on offer at Eton. It was at Christmas 1764 that the brothers travelled with him together for the first time to Belvoir Castle – their induction to the country seat of their grandfather and the place that defined them as a family. It was the six-year-old Robert's first visit to the splendid estate, and the impact upon him must have been considerable. The ten-year-old Charles was most likely impressed too, for he had not been there since he was a baby and he was now in line to inherit it. The castle stood 450 feet above sea level, and so powerful was its presence that it was said the eye was 'drawn to it from almost every point of the compass'. It stood where the boys' Norman ancestor Robert de Todeni had originally built a fortification named *Belle Voir*, 'beautiful view' – until Saxon resentment had caused the repudiation of the French name, with the spelling converted to 'Belvoir' and pronunciation to 'beaver'.

The 'castle' that the boys knew was the third to have been built on the site, the first and second having been badly damaged in the Wars of the Roses and the Civil War respectively. Designed by John Webb, a pupil of Inigo Jones, and completed in 1668, it had four flat-roofed wings set around an open courtyard. More of a large house than a fortress, its walls were draughty and crumbling and its windows rattled in the wind. The living rooms were on the upper floor, from where the views were magnificent. Their own bedrooms looked inwards over the courtyard and a well, but their father's bedroom, the Great Yellow Room, looked northwards out over the open Lincolnshire landscape. In their family wing, the Drawing Room contained cases of miniatures, including images of their dead mother. The ducal bedrooms and dressing rooms were in the north-west corner, next to the 'Musick Room' and 'The Best Dining Room'. Although it fell short of the Baroque or Palladian grandeur of the great homes of other aristocrats, Belvoir was loved by the Manners family.

As the boys explored the great chambers and galleries, adorned with portraits, they were followed by the eyes of past kings and generations of ancestors, some in armour and others in sumptuous robes, captured by distinguished artists. Graceful ladies also stared down upon them, in elegant poses and dressed in the highest fashions of their day. Here were Jeremiah Van der Eyden's paintings of the nine earls of Rutland, along with depictions by other artists of the Rutland countesses, and of the three dukes of Rutland and their duchesses too. Such display of prestige cannot fail to have impressed on the boys their sense of being among the 'first families of the kingdom'. The Evidence Room, on the castle's ground floor, held manuscripts dating back centuries, from which the brothers could trace their descent from Belvoir's early lords, the Albini and de Ros barons, who sought to limit King John's powers by compelling him to put his seal to Magna Carta in 1215, right through to the activities of their more recent forebears. Quickly, they would have become aware that the Manners were among those 'Whig' families with vast country estates who wished to bind the monarch to the rule of law and Parliament, and in so doing to protect their land and property from high taxation and crown confiscation.

At a time when some Whigs were beginning to consider the countryside dull compared with London, Charles and Robert became imbued with the Manners' long-standing passion for Belvoir and its rolling green pastures and woodland. The brothers learned to hunt the fox, a relatively new sport which their father and grandfather followed enthusiastically, maintaining at Belvoir one of the finest packs of foxhounds in England. When the elderly duke was in residence he would sometimes, in a reflective mood, regale them with stories of exploits chasing the fox. Granby himself kept his own pack at Croxton Park, a few miles from the castle, and the boys often stayed in the hunting lodge there.

Through the Belvoir Hunt, the two brothers could witness the 'royal dukes, the wits, the dandies and the statesmen of the day', rubbing shoulders with Lincolnshire yeomen and squires to positive effect. This happy interaction of different classes 'may be traced to the fact of the hounds being owned by a family which in the town represented the country and to the country brought the refinements of the town'.[30] They also learnt to enjoy other pursuits, such as the shooting of rabbits and game-birds, and trout fishing near Haddon Hall – the Derbyshire property acquired via the romantic elopement of John Manners and Dorothy Vernon in 1563. At Christmas 1765, the eleven-year-old Charles was given his own shotgun, manufactured by gunsmith Edward Newton in the nearby town of Grantham; the following year, an impatient Robert, unwilling to wait another three years, received his own weapon.

Over the winter sporting season, Belvoir Castle came alive with guests who danced, dined and gambled late into the night, consuming more than 300 eggs a day, 3,000 pints of beer a week, and enjoying such luxuries as pineapples grown in hot dung-pits on the estate. Stilton cheese, which originated from Melton Mowbray, a few miles from the castle, was a favourite offering at table; in 1724 Daniel Defoe had noted it came 'with the mites, or maggots round it, so thick, that they bring a spoon with them for you to eat the mites with, as you do the cheese'.[31] Such conditioning perhaps inured the teenaged Robert to the occasional maggots in the midshipmen's fare aboard the *Panther*.

Beyond such home-grown delicacies, Belvoir's guests also enjoyed the benefits of Britain's world trade that had been secured by victory in the Seven Years' War. Spices and tea came from the East Indies, whence came also live turtles, carried from tropical waters, 'turned-turtle' onto their backs and hydrated with doses of sea-water, ending their days as soup served from the castle's copper cauldrons. Among the other exotica, as noted in castle accounts, were oranges and lemons from the Mediterranean, wine from South Africa, arrack from India, sugar and rum from Barbados and snuff made from Virginian tobacco. The Manners family were not colonial plantation-owners, but they knew people who were and they – like all of Georgian society – unashamedly enjoyed the end-products of slavery.

The workings of the Belvoir estate depended on the employment of a multitude of contractors and at least fifty permanent staff, who cooked and cleaned for the family, saddled the horses, fed the foxhounds, mowed the lawns, caught moles, gathered acorns and cared for Granby's favourite pointer dogs, Ralpho, Pero and Flora. The boys were familiar with the butcher Mark Balls, the rabbit-monger Mr Bones, Sam Buckle the saddler and Mr Memory the grocer, and of course the indispensable valet John Glover, the clerk John Hempsall, who managed Lord Granby's accounts, and John Notzell the manservant. Indeed, the castle's Cellar Books reveal that Charles and Robert, while on holiday at Belvoir, were exposed to a range of people there, and not just the social elite. A number of curates, apothecaries and professional men were among the most regular visitors, valued for their friendship and services, while occasional guests included military men such as Charles, Viscount Brome (by now Earl Cornwallis), who had been Granby's *aide-de-camp* in the Seven Years War, and the tall, taciturn Howe brothers, distant relations from neighbouring Langar Hall. William was a general, but the dark-visaged, blue-uniformed Richard, Earl Howe, was not only a post-captain in the Royal Navy but had also commanded the *Magnanime* and led Hawke's fleet in its pell-mell pursuit of de Conflans at Quiberon Bay in 1759.[32]

Thus, although Lord Granby was absent for a large part of his boys' childhoods, and despite the early loss of their mother, Charles's and Robert's formative years came to be enriched by their father's generosity and easy-going way of life, wide-ranging friendships, and his tolerance of the extended family. In the diverse fold of visitors to Belvoir were several cousins – as well as a few more born out of wedlock, treated as equals in all but inheritance rights – and various other children who were recipients of charity. Charles and Robert's close circle included the curate's son Edmund 'Mun' Stevens, whom Granby had funded to attend Eton; Evelyn Sutton, the illegitimate son of Granby's dearly beloved but now deceased brother; and the two surviving half-siblings, George and Anne Manners, born to Mrs Mompesson. And when the duke was in residence at Belvoir, the unorthodox arrangements entailed such bizarre anomalies as Rutland's mistress, Mrs Drake, dining at the table while her brother attended to the duke as his valet. *Town and Country Magazine* reported: 'There is indeed a whimsical hospitality that reigns throughout the family; while the menial servants are dwelling in plenty below stairs, the upper domestics are reclining in luxury in the offices and their master is assisting at the convivial board of the most elevated nobility surrounded by bastards.'[33] Curiously though, the brothers' sister Frances appeared to lead a separate life and did not often join this *mêlée*. It is not known how much time Granby spent with his legitimate daughter, who attended a good school in London and otherwise remained living with Charlotte Somerset.

Besides at Christmas, the brothers visited Belvoir at Easter and in the summer, and sometimes also travelled a further 120 miles to Granby's favourite seaside resort of Scarborough. The Yorkshire fishing port was famous for its annual forty-five-day fair, which attracted people from all over Europe. It was popular with the aristocracy for bathing and spa-water, and the boys may well have seen their father jump naked from a boat to swim in the sea, as was the fashion of the era. In 1768, Scarborough also provided the Parliamentary constituency into which their half-brother George was installed, at vast expense.

At other times they stayed at Cheveley Park, a property that Charles owned since it was settled on him via his late mother's inheritance from her father. Here, Granby bred racehorses, and with late summer visits to Newmarket, 'a short chaise ride' away, he introduced his sons to horse-racing and to his habit of betting. An inveterate gambler, Granby rarely, unfortunately, seemed to win anything.

The marquis himself spent much of the spring and early summer in London, to attend Parliament and the social gatherings held in the grand houses of the aristocracy. He no longer owned a house in Albemarle Street, instead residing for some of the time at his father's property, Rutland House, in Knightsbridge. This locality was still set among green fields, though construction was creeping steadily westwards from the centre of London. The 7 acres that the Duke of Rutland rented – which today are buried under brick and tarmac close to Harrods – contained orchards, stables, paddocks, a vinery, a dairy, brewhouses and 'fowl-houses'. It was no coincidence that the house that the duke chose to build here, in the early 1750s, resembled the hunting lodge he had erected in the 1720s at Croxton Park, near Belvoir Castle, with a central building between two outlying wings connected by colonnades. He did not care much for city life, but as he now spent much of the year in London, the rural location outside the city suited him. Rutland House was close to the termination of the Great West Road, the main route connecting London, Bath and Bristol. The road was so deep in mud that in places it was almost impassable, and so thief-infested that it was patrolled by cavalry at night. As evening drew on, those on foot bound west for the village of Kensington used to pause at Hyde Park Corner until a sufficient number were collected to brave the dark stretch of road. A bell was rung as the party started off to alert any further lone travellers in need of a convoy. For those bound east, Rutland House was one of the last buildings on the road before reaching the city, and to those who regularly passed, the jack-boots and leather fire buckets hanging beneath the colonnades were a pleasing sign that their journey was nearly over.[34]

The duke – who in his youth had been an enthusiastic collector of art, patron of the arts and dutiful statesman, said to have a voracious sexual appetite – now lived at Rutland House quietly with Mrs Drake. He travelled less frequently and was increasingly disengaged with public life. For his grandsons, though, visiting Rutland House in the holidays allowed them to mingle with generals, admirals and politicians, with literary and artistic luminaries, with dazzling ladies – indeed, with all the glittering panoply of London's high society, and its seedier side, too. They quite possibly heard the quip about their grandfather and one of his earlier mistresses. One evening at the theatre, when the actress Peg Woffington was performing, an adventurous member of the pit had called out: 'Whom did you sleep with last night Peggy?' She came forward instantly, rapping back: 'Manners you dog!'[35]

★

Throughout all this time, Charlotte Somerset was keeping a close and observant eye on her grandchildren. Whether the brothers suffered emotionally from not having their birth mother present in their lives can only be guessed at, for the dead were soon dropped from mention in all correspondence, almost as if they had never existed. Occasionally, Charlotte would send them a picture of their mother, but without any revealing comments. In any case, even if Charles did hold memories, Robert could not have remembered her and only knew what she looked like from portraits and the miniatures at Belvoir Castle. With early death so common, even among the aristocracy who could afford better medical care and the new, but risky, smallpox inoculation, incomplete family units were relatively normal. Granby himself, who had lost his own mother early in life, would have been aware of the need for a certain emotional pragmatism. However, his wife's death can be said to have impacted the boys in at least one significant way. The greatest female influence on them became that of their grandmother.

Staunch, moral and upright, yet also tender and humorous, Charlotte Somerset was of a different character to their spendthrift mother (of whom not much is known). She entered wholeheartedly into the maternal role, ordering books, organizing their breeches and stockings, shoes and jackets, so they could look 'Sunday-best' all week at Eton – for there was then no school uniform – and undertaking numerous random tasks such as, on one occasion, repairing Charles's watch, the return of which he peremptorily demanded ('Pray send my little watch as soon as possible I am very impatient for it… I like it vastly.')

Charlotte's concern and care were unremitting, especially when the boys were on holiday with their father, for she was aware of the *laissez-faire*, even irresponsible, side of her son-in-law's nature, and she pulled them up short when good fox-hunting weather caused them to be late back to school. Although Granby could (as the Eton rebellion showed) have his boys flogged, his kind disposition meant that he generally applied a soft touch, and she felt impelled to watch out for incorrect behaviour. 'I hope your Pa has interest Enough with you to make you forbear y[ou]r vile practise of picking y[ou]r nose for if you should Continue it you'll bring a humor that will not Easily be got the better of,' she told Charles. And it is unlikely that Lord (or the late Lady) Granby would have issued quite the same sort of warning as Charlotte did on reading some 'saucy letters' in the press: 'I immediately Concluded it was the style of one of the Expelled reprobates or one that ought to be so,' she wrote, adding: 'I hope my Dear Bob will take Warning & never follow the bad Example of these Worthless Young Creatures who so long as they are Wicked must be Unhappy.'

Above all, though, the old lady wished to prevent her grandsons from copying their father's obvious inability to manage his money and from falling into the Eton boys' ruinous habit of shopping on account at their parents' expense. Yet, although she constantly chastised Charles for his 'extravagance' and 'way of going on' by purchasing new suits 'for one single day's wear', Charlotte seemed unable to resist his growing charm and confidence in his position as an heir, sometimes softening her admonishments with wry humour. During one holiday when the boys were at Belvoir, she told Charles in response to his plea for help with a costume so he could attend a masquerade with his father that: 'For me to choose a [Spanish] Dress for you [is] the most ignorant in all the modern follies of any Creature Upon the face of the Earth & consequently left it to your Sister & your Taylor to settle... So my Dear Charles having nothing to add upon this important subject will only Desire my Respects to the Duke of Rutland affectionate compliments to Lord Granby & Bob... your very affectionate Grandmother (but very Unskilful in Masquerades).' Even so, she could not quite bring herself to leave it all to him, for: 'To shew you how

An extract from a letter from Charlotte Somerset to Charles, 1769.

Expedite I am in Executing your Commissions I send you the Enclosed packet of all the Smart Colors in Harris's shop.' She added: 'If you Choose red which will certainly be the Smartest[,] either the Scarlet or changeable pink will differ from all your Forerunners. I have one objection to a Colored Cap because it may be supposed you will sweat (far be it for me to add stink) & in that Case the original Color of the Cap will soon be much Changed.'

However, her despair set in as an increasingly dark cloud gathered over their lives. It had begun on Granby's return from Germany, at which time he had been courted to join the government: it was said that a messenger with an offer of employment waited at every corner of his homeward journey. But Granby was not keen to accept. Aside from a dislike for the ministers of the new young king, George III (who had succeeded to the throne in the middle of the Seven Years' War), he had no taste for the expedient alliances indulged in by Britain's feuding governing families. Although he supported the Whig interest, the Manners family tradition was not to take sides openly, and rather leave room for tactical manoeuvre; it was even said that their ancestors never wrote anything down that might incriminate them. It was a disposition that had saved family members from execution on a number of occasions. Lord Granby embodied this wariness; temperamentally more suited to the battle and hunting fields, he was indecisive and procrastinating in the political sphere. He intensely disliked public speaking; indeed, he was said to 'tremble like a woman' at the prospect, and although for many years he had held an elected seat in the House of Commons, first for Grantham, then for Cambridgeshire, he had refrained from voicing judgements of others. His short, infrequent utterances in the House had largely concerned the improvement of roads, but they were thought to be full of common sense and tolerance.

He did not fend off the courting for long, and by 14 May 1763 had reluctantly accepted a non-political post, as Master General of the Ordnance; but the timing was bad. The marquis found himself surrounded by tremendous instability, as colleagues – many of them his relatives and personal friends – vied for positions under the new king. Then, as the decade progressed, they argued over the American colonists' refusal to pay for their defence during the Seven Years' War. In attempting to tax the colonists, the government had infringed the

Whigs' concept of 'liberty', which spilled over into a wider debate.

Valued by the king for his popularity, Granby remained in post throughout the various short-lived governments of the 1760s, tending to his responsibilities: supplying artillery, small arms and munitions to the army, and the maintenance and improvements of coastal fortresses as far afield as Africa and India required dedicated work somewhat distanced from the political whirl. But in 1766, he was also made commander-in-chief of the British army, placing him at the very centre of affairs, under the political leadership of his friend the elder Pitt, now 1st Earl of Chatham, along with Augustus FitzRoy, 3rd Duke of Grafton. Public confidence in Granby, based on his past reputation, was expressed in a patriotic quatrain in the *London Chronicle* of 29 August 1766:

> In spite of haughty Bourbon's union,
> Or supercilious Rome's communion,
> Shou'd they dare brave us we'd soon at 'em,
> Inspired by Grafton, Granby, Chatham.

Torn between conflicting loyalties, the marquis attempted to stay out of ministerial wrangling as the dispute between the British government and the American colonies grew more bitter. In 1768, after a two-year ministry, Chatham, who was broadly sympathetic to the colonists, resigned, leaving Grafton to take over the leadership. Early the following year, an anonymous and vitriolic critic who signed himself 'Junius' began to attack Grafton's administration in the *Public Advertiser*. Accusing the government of violating Englishmen's constitutional rights and liberties, Junius also implicated the commander-in-chief. Still popular with the public, Granby should have shrugged this off, but an old friend, Sir William Draper, ineptly tried to defend him, conceding that the convivial and famously hard-drinking Granby was open to imposition by unscrupulous associates. Junius pounced: 'It is you Sir William Draper, you have taken pains to represent your friend in the character of a drunken landlord who deals out his promises as liberally as his liquor.'[36]

Then, at the close of the decade, Granby was faced with a decision whether to support Parliament's expulsion of radical MP John Wilkes, and Junius made further stinging personal attacks. Wilkes, a Member for Middlesex, was a fearlessly outspoken libertarian, who had made an enemy of other politicians both by his criticism and his rabble-rousing. Cross-eyed and unprepossessing, Wilkes was also formidably intelligent, and when Parliament demanded his expulsion on grounds of seditious and obscene libels, he fought for the rights of those who had voted him in. Initially, Granby sided with the minority who supported Wilkes, believing that expelling an elected Member was – according to his Whig precepts of liberty – a gross abuse of power. However, Granby's innate distaste for the man overcame his principles, and he was persuaded to change his mind and side with Parliament. Junius grabbed the moment and thundered: 'Does [Granby] not at this moment give up all character and dignity as a gentleman in receding from his own repeated declarations in favour of Mr Wilkes?'[37] Hurt by this attack, Granby then made yet another *volte-face* and decided to join with Lord Chatham, who had come back into the political arena and who supported Wilkes. Thus, after spending Christmas 1769 with Charles and Robert at Belvoir, Granby returned to London in the new year of 1770, and on 9 January he withdrew his support for Wilkes's expulsion. Eight days later, against the will of the king, he resigned from his posts of commander-in-chief and Master General of the Ordnance. Charles and Robert, not in any way shielded from the events, were sent to London from Belvoir by their grandfather with a message for Chatham to say that the Duke of Rutland was 'in raptures at the part Lord Granby has taken'. In Rutland's Whiggish view, Granby's resignation showed loyalty to the cause of liberty.

For his family, by contrast, Granby's efforts to follow his conscience brought tragic consequences. Bereft of public office, salaries and perquisites, Granby was now confronted with rising financial problems. He remarked one day, when his clerk John Hempsall sent him £100, that it had arrived 'not before it was wanted'. His home in Albemarle Street had been sold to raise funds, but he had still been living beyond his means and taking advantage of the credit boom of the late 1760s, and many of his creditors now called in their loans. Although he had some rental income from property entailed on him and from his wife's properties, such as Cheveley, now owned by Charles, inheritance law forbade him to trade them. He did sell some land he managed to extract out of the arrangements – but it was not enough.

Ale Drank 7 Hhds Rem.d 7 Hhds
Small Beer Drank 5 Hhds Rem.d 24 Hhds
Wax Candles Burnt 8 pounes Rem.d 3 Doz:
Com.o Candles Burnt 5 Doz: Rem.d 14 Doz.
This Account Ends Munday Oct.r 27 1755
Account of Wines at Belvoir to Oct.r 27: 1755

	1	Burgundy	8	4
	2	Claret	26	3
	3	Redport	10	10
	4	Lisbon	26	10
	5	Medeara	3	11
	6	Sweetmountain	4	7
	7	Mountain	1	7
	8	Rhenish	1	11
this L.d Granbys	9	Old Hock	—	1
	10	Sheney	2	1
	11	Luceda	1	11
	12	Cyprus	—	2
	13	S.r Robert Sutton D.o	—	2
	14	Tent	—	9
this L.d Granbys	15	Hermatage	—	10
	16	Mum	2	7
this L.d Granbys	17	Arrack	—	11
	18	Rum Shrub	—	5
this L.d Granbys	19	Burgundy	—	9
this L.d Granbys	20	Champaign	—	11
	21	Rum	1	11
	22	Brandy	1	6
Barbados Drams		Cetron water in Pints	1	2	9
		Tansey water in Pints	1	—	1
		Mint water in Pints	—	—	9
		Usquebaugh in Pints	2	—	11

A Belvoir Castle cellar book dating from 1755, showing
Lord Granby's consumption of wines and spirits.

Always an indulgent man, Granby had not built up all the debt purely for himself; even Horace Walpole, who for unknown reasons disliked him, found generosity 'not only innate' in Lord Granby's breast, but 'never corrupted there'.[38] Numerous examples of his kindness to others were recorded by Hempsall, not least his contributions to the Marine Society's scheme started in 1756 to recruit boys from poor backgrounds for the navy and give them a respected career; or paying for surgery for a little girl run over by a coach; or funding tutors so that the Belvoir stable boys could learn to read and write. His charity was said to be 'of the rare order which thinketh no evil and which relieved misery as soon as witnessed without demanding certificates of character, marriage lines or the profession of any prescribed orthodoxy of belief'.[39]

A further drain was his attendance to the 'Rutland interest' in several constituencies in addition to Scarborough and difficulties in his family's pocket borough of Bramber.[40] However, the financial effect of electioneering combined with his generosity and gambling – not to mention maintaining his own set of foxhounds at Belvoir and a stable of 'running horses' at Cheveley, and his heavy, habitual drinking and a laxity in ordering his affairs – began to depress him. Pride forbade him from asking his father for help, for the old duke had told him: 'I must deal openly with you, and plainly tell you, that I have done all I can for you, and must now turn my thoughts to providing for others. Keep this in mind, that your future ease and happiness in great measure depend upon the resolution you take.'

Granby was unable to overcome his propensity to procrastination, and his dark mood spilled over into his family. Charles, now nearly fifteen, and Robert, eleven, who had witnessed their father ascend to celebrated war hero and prominent politician, and now descend to stand on the edge of bankruptcy, were continually lectured by an anxious Charlotte Somerset to refrain from following his dissolute behaviour. Meanwhile, Granby's sense of impotence was increased by being out of office during the international crisis of 1770, when Spain attempted to lay claim to the sovereignty of the Falkland Islands, which even caused Charles to talk of following in his father's military footsteps. The army and navy were put on a war footing, prompting Charlotte to write, in a letter to her grandson that: 'As to War I believe tis not much to be fear'd but should it happen & your Father not have the Command, there will be but poor Work made of it & Even if he has I don't think he will need your assistance & therefore I should hope you would bend your thoughts to serve your Country with your Head & not with your arms.'

In the autumn of 1770, the boys returned to Eton, leaving their father in Scarborough, where he had gone to support his candidate for a by-election for the constituency's other seat (there being two seats per constituency in those days). Granby was accompanied by his chaplain Bennet Storer and his loyal manservant John Notzell. The marquis grew unwell, complaining of pains in his chest and calling for his doctor. At about four o'clock on the afternoon of Thursday 18 October, Storer heard a curious rapping from the room above. He ran up the stairs and to his 'inexpressible horror' saw Granby speechless and in convulsions. The former soldier did not recover. John Manners, Marquis of Granby, died aged forty-nine, with Notzell, a reminder of happier days, by his side. Dr Mounsey pronounced the fatal seizure to be caused by 'an attack of gout in the stomach'.

The Marquis of Granby was buried at the family church in Bottes-ford, near Belvoir, there to lie among his ancestors, his wife, his son Lord Roos and his little daughter Elizabeth. Although, in his final years, the committed soldier had proved a poor administrator, his popularity with the general public remained until his death and long beyond. 'It is impossible to pretend to describe the distress of the whole country,' observed a family friend. 'Every place you passed thro' in tears!' Lord Chatham told the Duke of Rutland: 'The loss to England is indeed irreparable.' The *Gentleman's Magazine* expressed the nation's reaction:

> What conquests now will Britain boast
> Or where display her banners?
> Alas! In Granby she has lost
> True Courage and Good Manners.

In one man was combined the irresistible seductions of excess along with the stern call of public duty. In his shadow, Charles and Robert would come to act out these extremes of Georgian high life.

3

'Granby's sons'

NOVEMBER 1770 TO APRIL 1775

'Granby's Sons'

The Manners boys were at Eton when they received the news of their father's death, and their lives were thrown into turmoil: Charles was now in line to become the 4th Duke of Rutland instead of the 5th. Aged sixteen, he was suddenly Marquis of Granby in his father's place, though his grandmother said wistfully that: 'Grievous very Grievous it is that it should have devolv'd upon you in the way it has.' Few could bring themselves to call him 'Lord Granby' for many months. But still he received a stream of letters, as attention centred on him as the direct ducal heir. His grandfather's secretary Thomas Thoroton wrote to say: 'I must tell you, that the eyes of all your father's friends will be turned to you,' adding, 'my dear Lord, I hope soon to have the happiness of embracing you and dear Bob.' Twelve-year-old Robert received little attention in comparison – not entirely forgotten, but tacked on to the end of letters to Charles almost as an afterthought.

The grief and worry caused by Granby's death then intensified, because it seemed for a time that the boys' grandfather, now aged seventy-four, would not long survive the shock of losing the twelfth of fifteen children born to him. Rutland was devastated at the death of 'his darling son' and heir, and friends observed how he fell 'into a sudden melancholy and for three weeks appeared to… be petrified'. With Belvoir Castle 'the headquarters of misery and dejection' and Rutland's household concerned with 'easing the most bitter sensations of this miserable family', his close circle rallied round. Yet, despite their efforts to 'divert the duke's gloomy thoughts', it seemed that 'every day [brought] somewhat or other to cast clouds over us'.

By now, the elderly Rutland was showing symptoms of what was probably Parkinson's disease. Politically unambitious, and devoted to his estate and his quiet country life with his mistress, Mrs Drake, who became his life-long companion after his duchess died young, he remained an aloof and somewhat confusing figure to the two brothers. Although Horace Walpole, more sympathetic to the father than the son, alluded to the duke as a 'nobleman of great worth and goodness', and most people considered him 'warm, open, and benevolent… [letting] you into a free communication', there was another side to Rutland. As family friend Levett Blackborne described, his mood could 'in an instant (on being pressed to something against its bent) cloud itself into form and reserve [that] effectually *freezes* and even petrifies an assailant'. Something of his mood-swings now afflicted him, for, to everyone's astonishment, in mid-November his grief 'suddenly wore off'. In the words of a contemporary, within a few days, 'his Grace seemed no longer to recollect "What a son he had lost!"… The papers have reduced him to death's door: on the contrary he [is] better than ever I remember.' Some attributed his apparent recovery to the wisdom of age; others to a pragmatic stoicism in the face of adversity.

At the same time, Rutland took on a stubborn demeanour. As condolences poured in and his secretary's table lay 'covered with letters' of genuine sympathy and opportunistic flattery, there were also dozens of letters from people left in dire circumstances by the loss of Granby's benefaction. The most pressing were from creditors demanding repayment. Granby's debts amounted to £60,000, which, by the standards of the day, was not an outrageous figure though a very sizeable sum. But his saleable assets were calculated at £23,000, leaving as much as £37,000 to find. 'The multitude of distressful applications tortured [Thoroton] to the soul', but the duke blocked him from dealing with them. Reneging on an earlier undertaking to honour his son's debts, with a 'characteristic aversion to trouble' Rutland took on 'a settled and confirmed resolution never to meddle with the administration' of his son's affairs.

The old man's intransigence extended to his grandchildren. For reasons known only to himself, but perhaps because he thought they would fritter money away like their father, he simply refused to give them the allowances provided for in their parents' marriage settlement. As soon as they were able to get away from Eton for the Christmas holidays, Charles and Robert went to Belvoir to formally ask the duke to be their guardian and for the money to which they were entitled. Their presence brought cheer amid the gloom, and the household was sad when they returned to school; but the boys' request failed to move Rutland. Nevertheless, Charles pledged to Thoroton and others of the duke's associates that when he came of age he would pay off everything his father owed, 'though he should live upon a crust from 21 to 61'.

Thereafter it was clear that Rutland had no wish to interest himself in his grandchildren's complex affairs. Although still a minor, Charles had access to the rental income from the Somerset properties settled on him, in which Robert also had a share, but the inheritance was entangled with that of their aunt Charlotte, Countess of Aylesford. In the face of Rutland's obduracy, his associates were left to manage these assets, as well as the sale of scores of horses, hounds and other items to ease the pressure from Granby's creditors. Charlotte Somerset also stepped in; she herself was now seventy-seven, but did not demur from taking on the substantial workload of managing the Somerset settlement on behalf of Charles, Robert and Frances. She took on this burden because she did not trust the duke's close circle, particularly his second family. In her view, they were more concerned to 'aggrandise' themselves and their illegitimate children – 'spurious slips', as she called them, 'that Solomon says shall take no roots'. She believed that the Manners side of the family and their satraps – including the Thorotons – were neglecting the welfare of the legitimate children. She also heartily disapproved of her son-in-law's former lover and the children that the liaison had spawned, but on this occasion acceded that Mrs Mompesson and daughter Anne Manners should continue to have an annuity so as 'not to starve [and to] live Decently in some part of England at less Expense & hazards than going abroad which is a wild project for two helpless women'. However, she was unimpressed by what she observed as the duplicity of Granby's clerk: 'Poor Mr Hempsall who apprehended Starving has owned he has £6,000 & tis pretty Confidently asserted he has more than Double that & a House at Newark of his own Building ready to receive him.' Meanwhile, the old marquis's personal servants, Glover and Notzell, were kept in the family's employ.

The brothers, who still had the emotional support of each other, displayed remarkable stoicism in the face of their father's death and grandfather's neglect. Granby's early demise meant that both boys gained the premature status of ducal sons – rather than grandsons – and that Robert could now use the title 'Lord'. Charles, the responsibilities of adulthood suddenly thrust upon him, seemed to step directly into his father's boots. Picking up on Granby's political connections, he immediately tried (albeit unsuccessfully) to arrange a meeting with Lord Chatham, as well as involving himself in his father's electoral interests at Scarborough and at Bramber.

While the new young marquis seemed to charm everyone he met, his grandmother was worried. She was already aware of his habit at Eton of running up debts, which she had told him was 'worse than robbing upon the highway'. She warned: 'At the rate you are going on you will spend your fortune before you come to it.' She found him a slack correspondent, too. And he was cheeky as well as indolent. In a letter to Thomas Thoroton, he described how 'to use a splendid expression, I had the Honour of a Conference with Mr Ambler, who I was afterwards informed, for I dozed the whole time, Held forth for two hours with all the Heavy & Dull perplexity of a Lawyer. He seems particularly Happy in communicating His own dull soporifick faculties.'

Robert was less of a worry to his grandmother. Mindful of his position as a younger son, he had worked hard. As a family associate, Richard Watson, later noted in his 'Anecdotes of Lord Robert Manners', he 'acquired a very competent knowledge of the classics; the taste for the fine writers of antiquity, which he there imbibed never forsook him, for it was his constant practice to employ a part of his leisure in perusing the most admired of their works. It was [also] observed that his mind was active, bold and enterprising, and his genius wholly military.'[1] Such virtues, however, did not render him immune from grandmotherly scrutiny: 'I thank Bob for the promise of writing next post but shall more if he performs it.'

In many ways, Charlotte continued to treat the brothers as children, sending them 'sweetmeats' and clothes. She worried that they would

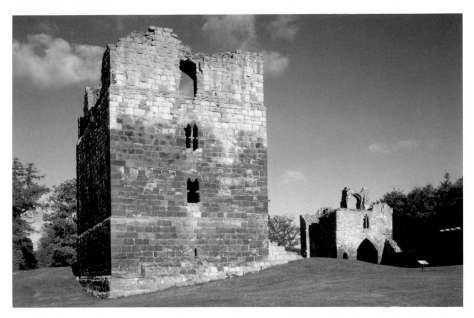

1. The Manners family was probably granted the manor of Etal in Northumberland after the Norman Conquest. Robert Manners built the castle in the fourteenth century in a strategic position by a ford over the River Till. The family ceded the lands to the crown in the sixteenth century. Etal castle is now owned by Lord Joicey and administered by English Heritage.

2. *A view of Belvoir Castle from the South West with Belvoir Hunt in Full Cry*, 1730, by Thomas Badeslade. This was the third Belvoir Castle to stand on the site since the Conquest. It was designed by John Webb, a pupil of Inigo Jones, and completed in 1668. From 1801 it was gradually rebuilt to create the fourth castle. The painting shows the layout of the seventeenth-century formal gardens and the statues, by Caius Cibber, positioned along the driveway.

3. John Manners, 3rd Duke of Rutland (1696–1779), paternal
grandfather to Charles and Robert Manners, in a miniature by
C.F. Zincke, signed and dated 1722. This portrait was probably
painted to celebrate his being made a Knight of the Garter,
a year after he inherited the dukedom in 1721.

4. Charlotte Finch, 6th Duchess of Somerset (1693–73), maternal grandmother
of Charles and Robert Manners, as portrayed by Thomas Hudson.

5. Rutland House in Knightsbridge was built by the 3rd Duke of Rutland in the 1750s, and occupied by the descendants of his union with his mistress, 'Mrs' Drake, until 1835. Eventually the house was knocked down but the properties now on the site – overlooking Hyde Park – are named Rutland Gate.

6. The twenty-year-old John Manners, Marquis of Granby (1721–70), by Jean-Etienne Liotard. This is a rare portrait of Granby with hair. Bald by the age of twenty-five, he seldom wore a wig thereafter.

7. Frances Seymour, Marchioness of Granby (1728–60), by Joshua Reynolds. She was eldest daughter of the 6th Duke of Somerset and Charlotte Finch, and mother to Charles and Robert Manners.

8. A miniature of John Manners, Marquis of Granby,
aged about forty, by Henry Spicer.

9. Spurs worn by the Marquis of Granby during the Seven Years' War. The more elaborate
examples (*top right*) were purchased on campaign in Germany. The pocket watch
may have been the one Robert had with him on the *Resolution* when he was
wounded, which was returned to Belvoir after his death.

10. John Manners, Marquis of Granby, portrayed by Sir Joshua Reynolds, in the uniform of the Royal Horse Guards (the Blues).

11. A print of Edward Penny's *The Marquis of Granby relieving a Sick Soldier*, originally painted *c*.1765. Granby's popular heroism was celebrated in prints, coins and a variety of memorabilia.

12. John Manners, Lord Roos (1751–60), in an anonymous portrait. Older brother to Charles and Robert Manners, John Manners died aged just nine, probably of 'pernicious worms', leaving Charles to inherit the dukedom.

13. Cheveley Park, near Newmarket, by Jan Siberechts, 1671. Originally bought by the 6th Duke of Somerset, Cheveley Park was settled on his grandson Charles, 4th Duke of Rutland, via Charles's late mother's inheritance from her father. The house remained in the possession of the Manners family until 1892.

14. Newmarket Heath in the 1730s, by Peter Tillemans. The Manners family frequented the horse races here, for Newmarket was just 'a short chaise ride' from their property of Cheveley Park.

15. An English man-of-war entering Portsmouth Harbour, by Dominic Serres (1722–93). The anchorage at Spithead, where Robert spent many winter months as a midshipman in the *Panther,* can be seen in the distance.

fall into bad company and run 'into Mad Politicks nor yet into the more Mad Follies & Extravagances of this Unhappy age'. She admonished Charles for his terrible handwriting, and was shocked that he was still procrastinating over negotiating with Rutland for money. In late November 1770, she again took up her pen: 'I am sorry to find you so dilatory, affairs of Consequence ought never to be delayed,' she scolded, '& sure tis of some Consequence to know what may be allotted for your own maintenance, what for your Brother & what for your Sister.' She was unable to obtain from the duke the £300 she was normally given at Christmas to buy presents for them and could not make do from her own slender resources: 'Meat & Drink I can & always will give your Sister[,] Yourself & Brother whenever you come to me but Shoes & Stockings there must be some provision for.'

When Rutland returned to Knightsbridge at the end of February 1771, Charlotte went to see him to try to wrest the children's allowances from him. She took the boys' sister Frances with her, hoping that the family resemblance with Lord Granby would stir 'tender emotions' in the old man; but it was to no avail. 'Surrounded with Dogs & Thorotons,' as Charlotte noted disparagingly, he would not speak 'one single word of any affairs relating either to [Charles], Brother or Sister'. As time went on, her concern led her to become Charles's legal guardian, 'having before my Eyes the Example of your Grand Father whose great Caution for fear of being Entangled with the administration during the whole half year of being Guardian remained in a total Inaction not a little Detrimental to your affairs'. In so doing, she was able to draw funds from Rutland's bank on behalf of Charles. Robert, on the other hand, retained his grandfather as his guardian, although Charlotte Somerset still looked after him, keeping a special purse from which to pay his bills. Something of her burden seemed likely to be soon eased, for by now the eighteen-year-old Frances was being courted by George Carpenter, 2nd Earl of Tyrconnel, who offered the prospect of a good marriage.

Charlotte's assumption of Charles's guardianship was to cause the elderly lady much stress. She was even expected to help with his growing political interest in Scarborough and Bramber, though she retorted that 'he might just as reasonably have Expected from me a Solution of a Problem in Euclid as any determination relating to those boroughs'.

Charlotte was, however, indomitable in the face of these predicaments. She wisely enlisted the assistance of her own family, foremost among them her sister's husband, William Murray, 1st Earl of Mansfield and Lord Chief Justice of the King's Bench, who had already acted for the family as a trustee for the marriages of Charlotte's two daughters. For once, Charles's reaction gratified her. 'Tis a present pleasure that you are so Desirous to have Lord Mansfield's Directions[;] better you cannot have.' Someone else she trusted was Joseph Hill, a lawyer whom the boys had come to know at Eton; he would in time prove a sound choice.[2] But despite her efforts, Charlotte was unable to master Charles's spending habits. He was not only running up debts for his own luxuries, but was also showing signs of his father's generosity of spirit, for he defended and gave money to a boy called Charles Cropley, who was being picked on by other boys.

Charles was settling nicely into the lifestyle of heir to a dukedom and was thoroughly enjoying Eton, which was often the case for the best-connected boys. As a 'duke's son', he was given the honour of holding up the king's train at the Knight of the Garter installation of 25 July 1771, at Windsor. It was the heir who was the important one; no provision was made for the younger brother to be part of the event, and had it not been for their grandmother's thoughtfulness ('My Blessing to Bob tell him I shall get him a Ticket for he must see this Splendid Show'), Robert might not have been able to attend at all. The ceremony took place in St George's Chapel next to Windsor Castle, just across the river from Eton. Charles and Robert were certainly aware that within the chapel was the Rutland Chantry containing the elegant effigies of George Manners and Anne St Leger, whose fifteenth-century marriage had elevated the family into royal circles. On the floor of the Chapter House was the tomb of Henry VIII, to whom the family owed its earldom from 1525; and alongside Henry lay the body of his favourite wife, Jane Seymour, an ancestor of Charles and Robert's maternal grandfather Charles Seymour, the 6th Duke of Somerset. The Chapter House was lined with brass stall-plates showing the names of the knights over the centuries – including the current Duke of Rutland and at least twelve other ancestors. As the ceremony took place, each new knight or their proxy was introduced to the king. One in particular would have interested Charles and

Robert: Prince Ferdinand of Brunswick – on whom the honour had first been informally conferred by Lord Granby in a tent in Germany, during the Seven Years' War. The whole Garter event reinforced the brothers' sense of belonging to one of England's first families.

★

In the winter of 1771, Charles made the decision to leave Eton and attend Cambridge University. He dragged the moment out, drawing a wry rebuke from his grandmother: 'I confess you have not overcharged me with letters of late but as I am willing to hope you are always better Employed I don't complain. I am glad to find you have thoughts of leaving Eton[;] I began to apprehend you would take up your residence there for life. Your Comparison of quitting it with the same reluctance that the Ladies do their looking glass is strong Especially where the Paintpot is upon the dressing Table…' Charles finally went up to Cambridge in November 1771, taking his Eton tutor John Ekins with him and acquiring – perhaps to the relief of Charlotte Somerset – a new influence in the form of the highly academic Richard Watson: a professor of chemistry, a fellow of the Royal Society, and the university's Regius Professor of Divinity.

Before heading to Cambridge, Charles went to Bath to honour an Eton custom by sitting for a 'leaving portrait' to present to the school's provost, Dr Barnard. For this task he had selected the distinguished artist Thomas Gainsborough. While in that city, Charles also sat for the fashionable pastel artist Hugh Douglas Hamilton, from whom he had commissioned some signature small oval portraits of himself and of Robert, sister Frances and Eton school-friend Daniel Pulteney.[3] Although she disapproved of this extravagance, Charlotte cared for her grandson too much not to support him, and she was now left with the inconvenience of chasing up Hamilton, whom she considered most slack and 'a sad dog'. When she visited the artist at his lodgings, she was met at the door by a 'dirty drossel' who pretended he was not at home, so Charlotte 'heartily scolded' her, then castigated Hamilton in a letter to Charles ('He is as Obstinate as a mule & now when I do trudge after him is not visible [&] he has not so much altered the color of Bob's cloathes nor done any one thing you ordered'). She then turned on her grandson: 'What with Pictures[,] presents & such like

Expenses we shall outrun your Vast Maintenance which will neither be
for your Credit nor Mine... Unless you will restrain your Extravagancy
I must give up the Guardian Ship for tis utterly Impossible for me to
hold it.' By now, Charlotte had extracted additional income from the
Somerset settlement, but it seemed this only increased Charles's expenditure. She warned him that 'Dreadfull Consequences must ensue'
from being profligate, a reference to the early death of his father. Charlotte's concern also reflected a growing credit crisis among the wealthy
elite. The father of his Eton friend Alleyne FitzHerbert was suffering
severe depression, and he would commit suicide in January 1772 after
failing plantations in Barbados and Jamaica left him with an untenable
burden of debt. Even the income of Charles's grandfather – normally
more than £25,000 per year – was uncertain, for Rutland was having
trouble collecting rent from his tenants.

While Charles started at Cambridge, Robert spent the winter of
1771–2 at Belvoir, to talk with their grandfather – who was still his
guardian and looked fondly on him despite the usual detachment –
and decide what to do with his life. The obvious choice was to join
the army, which the rest of his circle fully expected him to do. But the
result of his ponderings was a resolution to remove himself from any
necessity to rely upon the intransigent old duke. And he knew from
his father's experiences that substantial sums would be required to purchase regimental commissions and maintain the military lifestyle, so
this option would only be possible if he went cap-in-hand to his grandfather. There was, however, a most attractive alternative: the Royal
Navy. The sea-service required no commissions to be purchased and
even provided free accommodation and training. It could also enable
him to avoid accusations of hanging on to the coat-tails of a famous
father, especially should he not live up to expectations.

The navy had, in fact, already been growing in Robert's consciousness throughout his young life. But ironically it was Charles, in the
days before he became Granby's heir, who had first been lured by the
thrill of great sea battles: Admiral Hawke's destruction of the French
fleet at Quiberon Bay during the *annus mirabilis* of 1759 had caught
the imagination of the little five-year-old boy. He had scrawled in
pencil, then carefully traced over his words in ink, and sent the result
to Hawke:

Sir Edward Hawke

I hear you have beat the French fleet when they were coming to kill us and that one of your captains twirled a French ship round till it sunk. I wish you was come home, for I intend to go to sea if you will take me with you.

I am Lord Granby['s] second son

Charles Manners[4]

Hawke's spectacular victory inspired prints and popular songs, the most enduring of which was David Garrick's patriotic 'Heart of Oak', its music composed by William Boyce. It complemented the already popular 'Rule, Britannia!', written by James Thomson and set to music by Thomas Arne as part of the masque *Alfred*.[5] Such patriotism served to foster in the public consciousness – as well as in little boys – the potential of the navy to aggrandise the nation.

As they grew older, Charles and Robert would have learned that their father's friend, the 1st Earl of Chatham, was the prominent war leader who had turned the myth of British sea power into a reality. The victories of the Seven Years' War had brought mastery of the oceans. The navy was, consequently, essential for acquiring and protecting overseas territories and ensuring the safe shipping of such lucrative commodities as rum, sugar, tobacco, spices, coffee and tea, which the boys saw many times on the table at Belvoir. They were aware, too, of those individuals who had distinguished themselves in the process, men who had then drifted in and out of the boys' lives during school holidays: Richard Howe and his dashing role at Quiberon Bay, William Cornwallis (brother of Granby's *aide-de-camp*), and the Affleck brothers, Edmund and Phillip, whose family rented some Manners land in Suffolk, were all names they knew. They had even, playing around one holiday, broken the nose of George Cockburn, who at the time was Comptroller of the Navy as well as Granby's candidate for a Scarborough by-election. They would have known, too, that in 1770 the mobilization of Britain's navy had played a significant role in over-awing a Spain attempting to establish sovereignty over the Falkland Islands.

Such factors meant that the sea now seemed a vehicle for eighteenth-century notions of honourable fulfilment: a reputation might be made in action upon the quarterdeck as surely as it might be made upon a horse on a field of battle. Officers fortunate enough to have high command in a fleet action might even be rewarded with a title. The fate of the unfortunate Admiral Byng, who 'failed to do his utmost' to prevent the loss of Minorca in 1756 and was executed *pour encourager les autres*, meant that an atmosphere of aversion to cowardice prevailed.[6] Although Lord George Sackville, the 'Coward of Minden', had survived his disgrace, his obloquy was not forgotten.

Moreover, this was still a palpable age of discovery. In 1772, Captain James Cook set off on his second world voyage, this time on the collier brig *Resolution*, which, as Robert may well have been aware, started its life as the *Marquis of Granby* (built by a Hull businessman who may well have known Robert's father through family connections).[7] And at social gatherings, once the cloth had been drawn after dinner, gentlemen debated the utility of new navigational instruments, while Robert's grandfather and father were almost certainly among the 'lords and dukes' and other notables such as William Stukeley and Benjamin Franklin who had knocked on John Harrison's door to view the marine chronometers the clockmaker hoped would solve the longitude problem.[8]

Thus, the allure of the Royal Navy to a young mind was potent; and it was increasingly attractive to a growing number of the younger sons of the nobility. Robert was not the only one of his essentially army family to be seduced by the navy's growing prestige, and he may well have been influenced by his cousins. Evelyn Sutton, who spent many holidays with the boys at Belvoir, and the Finch brothers, sons of their aunt the Countess of Aylesford, had all chosen to serve at sea.[9] It is possible, too, that Robert was aware his ancestry was not entirely devoid of naval connection. Among Belvoir's bevy of red-coated military forebears staring down at him from their portraits, in the Evidence Room was an ancient charter and wax seal depicting a ship. As long ago as 1464, one Sir Robert Manners of Etal had been deputy to the Lord Admiral of England. Then, on the ancestral tombs at the local church of Bottesford, an intriguing inscription described how the 6th Earl of Rutland (in an earlier creation) had been appointed an admiral in 1623, and, according to his charter, had been ordered to 'pursue, burn, spoil, kill and destroy' the enemy fleet. These posts were essentially political rather than truly seafaring, but nevertheless were spurs to a boy's imagination.

Yet, as tempting as opportunities for honour and titles undoubtedly were, and notwithstanding an urge for independence from his grandfather, there was also a genuinely practical – and possibly over-riding – reason for Robert's desire to join the navy. While Charles would inherit Belvoir and most of its income, the younger boy would have to find his own way of augmenting his allowance if he wanted to establish his own household and live in style. His inherited allowance via his parents' marriage settlement was £600 a year, and in due course he would also receive £12,250 in cash, which would be released from his mother's settlement when he turned twenty-one. His grandmother described this fortune as 'moderate', so he did not have to take a profession *solely* to earn an income, for at the time a 'gentleman' could get by on about £300. But Robert was no mere gentleman. He was Granby's son, and he expected more.

Naval incomes were not the solution in themselves, for as a midshipman he would receive only around a shilling a month, and as a post-captain he could anticipate an income of £200 per annum (as half-pay in peacetime), though this doubled in wartime. The key lay in prize-money. If a British man-of-war captured an enemy vessel, everyone on board shared its value, on a sliding scale from the captain downwards, once the Prize Court had declared the ship a legal seizure. Officers could dream of 'a landed estate gained in an afternoon'. It was said that Vice Admiral Augustus Keppel had earned £25,000 of prize-money during the Seven Years' War, freeing him from the unpleasant consequences of being a younger son whose father had been ruined by extravagance. This was a powerful example for a young man in Robert's situation, for Keppel was another of Granby's associates. If Robert joined the navy in peacetime, he might – with influence and string-pulling – make post-captain before a new war broke out. And if he did so, promotion was thereafter guaranteed by seniority. If he lived long enough he would progressively fill dead men's shoes and reach flag-rank; an admiral – even one on half-pay – enjoyed a decent salary.

In short, these inducements together exerted a strong influence on the youthful Robert Manners, enough to persuade him, as Shakespeare put it, to seek 'the bubble reputation / Even in the cannon's mouth'.

Indeed, even the possibility of death would barely have deterred him. It would have to be, of course, a glorious death in action, at the moment of victory; but an alternative need not yet be contemplated.

Into these heady thoughts another practical consideration intruded: Robert would have to move quickly. The minimum age for making lieutenant was twenty, so if he joined at fourteen he would be the right age after serving the six years of sea-time necessary to apply for a commission. At that time, boys were taken on at the discretion of captains and flag-officers, and Commodore Molyneux Shuldham was willing to take a son of Lord Granby with him in the *Panther*. It was probably the most prestigious posting available at that time, given the vessel's attachment to Shuldham as the Governor of Newfoundland. For his part, the commodore would have taken on the risk of an aristocratic lad in return for the connections and interest he might thereby secure. Moreover, cruising on the Grand Banks offered Robert the best way of learning his profession rapidly in the 'nursery of seamen' – so named not just as a training ground for future officers but also for the skilled fishermen who became useful seamen when impressed into the Royal Navy in times of war.

Charles's new tutor at Cambridge, Richard Watson, said of Robert:

> At the age of fourteen his entreaties overcame the fond apprehensions of his aged grandfather the Duke of Rutland, and he obtained his permission to follow the bent of his disposition, by entering into a profession as full of danger and of honour. Judging that the glory and the security of England depended chiefly on her naval force he chose that line in preference to the land service to which it might have been expected that he would have had an hereditary bias from the circumstance of his father having long commanded the army of Great Britain with singular reputation.

So it was that by April 1772, Robert was stepping out of his carriage at Portsmouth and – like Hercules, choosing to take the hand of Virtue – was about to follow a difficult path that might lead to greater gain.

*

Charlotte Somerset, given her condescension towards sea officers, was not impressed with her younger grandson's choice of career. But she was delighted that he came to see her before leaving for Portsmouth, telling Charles that he 'came in pure hungry [&] much mortified he could not Call upon you at Cambridge but being saddled with two Thorotons [it] was not in his power'. Always mindful of their intimacy, she told the older boy on 2 April 1772: 'Your Grand Father consents Bob comes hither tomorrow & goes on shipboard some day next week so that I beg you would come hither without delay that you may not miss seeing him before he goes.' Thus, she enabled the boys to have their last painful parting before embarking upon their different directions. She also remarked that: 'Your Sister missed seeing him... had she known of his being here I am apt think she would not have danced [at the club] very light... [I] may venture to say you have a true share of her love.'

Charles had settled quickly into his new life at Trinity College, Cambridge. In the aftermath of Granby's association with John Wilkes's expulsion from Parliament, the young marquis was busy exploring Whig notions of liberty and studying the works of the seventeenth-century philosopher John Locke, encouraged by his new tutor. 'Make Bacon, then and Locke, and why should I not add that sweet child of nature Shakespeare, your chief companions through life,' opined Watson; 'let them be ever upon your table, and when you have an hour to spare from business or pleasure, spend it with them and I will answer for their giving you entertainment and instruction as long as you live.' His encouragement regarding Locke found an immediate response in the young Whig. Besides the philosopher's cogent arguments that protection of individuals' rights to 'life, liberty and property' was the basis of legitimate government, he had also spoken against flogging children and forcing them to grow up too quickly, which may well have appealed to Charles. The marquis asked his grandmother to send him three volumes of Locke's works. 'My Dear Child,' wrote Charlotte in reply, 'I give you abundance of thanks for your kind letter & the more because it was legible.'

But Charles could hardly now be considered much of a 'child'. Even before leaving Eton, he had seduced a shopkeeper's daughter; and now he was courting scandal, being credited with writing pamphlets about the freedom of the individual, the mortality of the soul and – even worse – in defence of modern adultery.[10] Among his surviving notes from that time are lists of 'Books I mean to read on government: Locke, Machiavelli, Raleigh', along with history books he thought would help him 'write speeches on different subjects' and 'definitions' such as 'Knowledge is the perception of the connection & agreement, or the disagreement & repugnancy of any of our ideas.'

Preoccupied by his studies, Charles neglected his grandmother, who was clearly irritated by his lack of correspondence. 'Tho you have no just Claim to a letter from me Nevertheless as I write to Bob (who by the by has wrote to me) I will not refuse you a Word or two least you shall take miff... If you have not yet bestowed one line upon Poor Bob I entreat you would for I love to have people happy.' She feared the worst for her grandson: 'My Dear Charles... When I reflect how very swiftly the time draws on for your Coming Upon the Stage of the World[,] Fears & Anxiety well nigh over set me... God almighty has Blessed you with a Good Head & a Good Heart[;] make use of the one that Treacherous and Cunning people may not abuse of the other.' In her view, 'You must turn out either Surprisingly Good or remarkably the Contrary for your Composition allows of no medium.' But behind all her remonstrations and admonitions lay a profound tenderness: 'Could you Inspect my Heart you would there find in Indelible Characters the most unfeigned & ardent Wishes for your Welfare in this world.'

Charles spent late July and August 1772 in France. He eschewed stretching a grand tour further afield for – even if others saw him as wayward – he himself felt the pressure to maintain the family's political connections now that his father was dead. His half-brother George, MP for Scarborough, had died in June, and Charles had involved himself in funding the subsequent by-election (much to his grandmother's irritation) before heading to the Continent. During his few weeks away, Charlotte's letters became increasingly despondent, now that all her grandchildren had flown the nest. (Frances was married on 9 July 1772 to Lord Tyrconnel.) 'Nothing Contributes more to health than Ease of Mind so I do assure you nothing can more Contribute to my Ease of Mind than your good Behaviour,' she wrote, pleading with Charles to avoid the 'Detestable Company of 'Profligate Wretches' and 'Frothy vain pretenders to Wit'. By early October 1772, Charlotte was weakened by a violent and painful attack of a 'Dangerous Illness'.

Nevertheless, news from Charles brought 'great pleasure that you are not Enamoured with that Sink of Wickedness Paris... I applaud your resolution to come back an Englishman & take nothing from the French except their language.' She added: 'I have not heard from Bob since you went[;] he certainly wrote to you at the same time,' and begged Charles to come home. 'I long to see you,' she concluded plaintively. Charles obeyed her wishes and returned to England in time for the autumn term at Cambridge.

*

The following month, Robert also returned to England when, on 21 November, the *Panther* anchored at Spithead. Robert's induction into the Royal Navy had, in truth, been disappointing. It seemed that the Newfoundland station was hardly the exciting 'nursery of seamen' he had hoped for. The *Panther* had lain mostly at anchor in St John's for over four months. On a rare cruise to some outlying islands, in company with the *Nautilus* and *Placentia*, the ships chased a few foreign vessels away from the fisheries, again passing 'large isles of ice' on returning to St John's. The main excitement had been an altercation with some French fishermen who tried to build stages and cure fish in Port Bonavista, beyond the southern limit of that part of Newfoundland where the French, by treaty, were allowed to operate. Otherwise, to break the monotony, Robert had taken advantage of the practice whereby midshipmen were temporarily transferred to more active vessels, joining Captain James Hawker in the frigate *Alborough*. During his brief sojourn, he befriended a boy named Robert Home, who had run away to sea. Good at drawing, Home produced a picture of Robert in his uniform and gave it to Captain Hawker, little knowing it would resurface many years later, when it was presented to the family in 1809.[11]

By early November 1772, the *Panther* was under orders to embark Commodore Shuldham and carry him home before the Atlantic winter weather endangered the crossing. Hastened by following winds, the passage lasted just two weeks. At Spithead, the ship lay surrounded by bum-boats and invaded by wives, sweethearts and whores, while the *Panther*'s crew was busy making good the ravages of the passage. Robert was unable to obtain leave to visit Charles in Cambridge, which he wanted to do. In fact, he was so busy on the ship that he barely had time to keep in touch even with his grandmother; he was still unable to join Charles for Christmas with the old duke.

On 23 December 1772, Charlotte Somerset wrote to Charles: 'I received a Hare and Partridge from Belvoir for which pray return my thanks… I as yet hear no more of Bob.' She had investigated the possibility of Robert attending the Naval Academy at Portsmouth, where, with fees as much as Eton's, wealthy boys could study navigation in lieu of serving sea-time. She thought he should attend the academy so as to avoid 'any Idle habits but get all possible Instruction in the Profession he has chosen in which I hope he will make a respectable Figure and likewise some addition to his Moderate Fortune'. Another letter followed on 28 December, in which Charlotte told Charles that she would:

> … send Bob as soon as I can get hold of him & pray (if you can get permission), bring him back with you that he may go to the academy… Wearied out with Expectation of him from Day to Day I send John Glover to Portsmouth to fetch him. If he should be come away I shall not fail to send him to Belvoir as soon as John Glover returns. Respects to the Duke and Compliments to Mr Thoroton & his Family from your truly affectionate Grand Mother and zealous Friend C Somerset.

It was the last letter she ever wrote to Charles. Trying to bring the brothers together after Christmas was Charlotte Somerset's final act of kindness towards her grandsons. A few days later, on 3 January 1773, at the age of almost eighty, she died, to be buried under her pew in St Nicholas's Church near her home at Chiswick. In her home was found a purse containing £40 12s, the balance of Robert's allowance after she had paid the last of his Eton bills. Her death was a profound loss for the boys. 'Ah she has gone, & with her all is fled', wrote Charles, moved to express his grief in verse:

> Yes dearest friend & parent t'was from you
> The choicest blessings of my life I drew
> Your kind maternal hand was stretched to save

My earliest years for ever from the Grave
And through the slippery paths of heedless youth
Guided my untaught soul to heaven & truth.
Oh if in future times some virtuous ray
Gleam on my breast, & brighten into day
Then let me tell with pride thy glorious name
And boast to Thee I owe whate'er I am.

Less than two years after their father's demise, there was now no immediate family member demonstrably engaged with the welfare of the brothers and their sister. And although Charles's lines acknowledged his grandmother's efforts to shape his character, it was still an open question as to whether the young man, soon to turn nineteen, would heed her words and moderate his behaviour and spending.

However, his lust for life soon prevailed once again, as it had after the death of his father; but along with it came a deepening sense of obligation to maintain the political interests of his family, now that he felt even more alone with this charge. He could at least call on a significant guiding hand in the form of his great-uncle by marriage, Lord Mansfield. The Lord Chief Justice dominated the world of law in eighteenth-century Britain and had set in motion a significant step towards the abolition of slavery when, in 1772, he ruled that the holding of slaves within England and Wales was illegal.[12] He loved his wife – Charlotte's sister – but they had no children. One of his own wards was Dido Elizabeth Belle, the mulatto daughter of his nephew Captain Sir John Lindsay, who had sired the girl with an African slave and brought her to England in 1765 to entrust her to Mansfield's care. Although busy with matters of state, the judge always found time for family, and especially so for the nephew of his much-loved wife.

But Charles, heeding his grandmother's entreaties to 'always be your own man', initially eschewed advice from his great-uncle. Instead, he took advantage of a privilege available only to the sons of aristocrats, and graduated with a 'Nobleman's MA' without having to pass examinations. Then, in the autumn of 1774, aged only twenty, he stood as a candidate for Member of Parliament for Cambridge University.[13] He won his seat in the House of Commons unopposed. To do so under-age was unusual; and it was a significant step not only for Charles, for his success could also benefit his brother.

*

Robert would, by now, have been thoroughly pleased to find himself with such a well-placed connection in Parliament. After just two years of service he was yearning to become a commissioned lieutenant. With his father dead and his grandfather showing no further interest in his career, Charles could prove to be key to advancement. Although the Royal Navy was a more meritocratic service than the army, it was still a Georgian institution that functioned on 'interest', and no ambitious young officer could afford to ignore the potential of political clout.

Following the death of his grandmother, Robert had remained on the Newfoundland station, disregarding her wish that he attend the Naval Academy at Portsmouth. He encountered some familiar faces when his first-cousins Seymour and William Clement Finch, a midshipman and lieutenant respectively, joined him in the *Panther*. But other than during the bi-annual transatlantic crossings, the *Panther* spent little time at sea. This was a disappointment to Robert, especially when wardroom chatter cited such adventures as Captain Constantine Phipps's 1773 expedition towards the North Pole while trialling a copy of a John Harrison marine chronometer. Robert might even have heard that a midshipman exactly his age, named Horatio Nelson, took part in this voyage. However, if he felt envy, he would have had little time to dwell on it, for the *Panther*'s crew were never suffered to remain idle. Constant manoeuvres and drills familiarized Robert with the business of being a sea-officer; and at least he was involved in testing a 'Foxon's Perpetual Log', a newly invented device that would replace the knotted line for measuring a ship's speed through the water.

By 1774 Robert, now aged sixteen, was proving to be compassionate by nature, like his father. He had not worked out his frustration on his subordinates or become a tyrant of the lower-deck; instead, he had adapted well enough to the arduous, cold and wet shipboard life. He even now had an affinity for the service, which had found its way into his heart despite the disappointments, discovering that sense of belonging that creates loyalty and overcomes homesickness and

loneliness. In short, he had discovered a meaning for his life underpinned by the routines and regularity of shipboard duty. 'From his first
entrance into the navy he became the favourite of his superior officers,
and by his courage and adroitness in the discharge of his duties of the
inferior stations, excited, in all who knew him, the strongest expectations that [he] would excel in the highest situations of his profession,'
wrote Richard Watson. He was, however, not entirely a paragon. Now
that his brother was in Parliament, the 'amiable' boy was also developing a touch of arrogance in his manner, confident in an innate sense
of entitlement conditioned by his aristocratic childhood. Surrounded
by officers obsessed with their 'prospects', and with peacetime berths
being limited, he threw himself wholeheartedly into the era's relentless focus on professional advancement and seeking out 'interest' to
help wherever possible. But, while officers with poor chances enthusiastically joined the traditional toast to the 'next war', Robert, with his
social superiority *and* a brother in Parliament to support him, could
see no reason why he should not achieve swift preferment.

★

Yet, in 1774 the brothers stood on the verge of momentous events
that would force them, at their young ages, into soul-searching choices
between pleasure and virtue, self-interest and duty, and between factions and opinions in a divided nation – choices that would test their
loyalties, and could even threaten the affinity between them.

They had unwittingly observed the crisis unfolding when they
were children, while their father was drawn into the political ferment
of the 1760s. Government ministers, most notably Granby's friend
George Grenville, had tried to strengthen British administration of
the thirteen American colonies and, via the Sugar Act of 1764 and the
Stamp Act of 1765, to make the colonists contribute to the cost of their
defence during the Seven Years' War. The constitutional arrangement
between Parliament and the colonies had long been loosely defined,
resulting in the colonists establishing their own assemblies, which had
become their sole means of voting for revenues. Under the slogan of
'no taxation without representation' – for no MPs sat in the House
of Commons on their behalf – they fiercely objected to Parliament's
attempts to tax them. The 2nd Marquis of Rockingham – Granby's

friend, hunting partner and a nephew of Charlotte Somerset – led the government for a brief spell in 1765–6 and repealed the Stamp Act, assisted by the Pennsylvanian politician and polymath Benjamin Franklin, then a colonial agent and spokesman for American interests in England. However, Rockingham fell short of appeasing the colonists because Parliament enacted the Declaratory Act – insisting on Parliamentary sovereignty over the colonies 'in all cases whatsoever'.

By the 1770s, Britain's relationship with America had not recovered. Now, many of the colonists considered that their own assemblies would better protect their rights as individuals. In addition, Parliament had been further discredited as a representative institution by the 'arbitrary' act of expelling Wilkes as an elected Member in the late 1760s. The Wilkes affair had contributed to the crisis, reinforcing a view that Parliament was becoming a more dangerous 'ruler' than the king and his ministers. The colonists questioned whether their lives, liberty and property should be at the mercy of a body of men living 3,000 miles away and preoccupied with British concerns.

This perspective was not sufficiently understood by those governing Britain, who persisted with the view that imposing Parliamentary authority was paramount. While Robert had been (literally) learning the ropes and Charles studying Locke, both were also aware of the reports of riots, outrages and affronts to British authority carried out by American colonists. Most notable were the assault on Lieutenant Dudingston, of the revenue schooner *Gaspée*, by a party of Rhode Islanders in June 1772, and the seizing and dumping of British East India Company cargoes of tea in Boston harbour – the 'Boston Tea Party' – in December 1773.[14] By now, a number of colonists talked of independence from Parliament (though at this time still maintaining allegiance to the crown), and in 1774 the First Continental Congress assembled at Philadelphia. Americans had outgrown their status as dependent colonists; they were now communities with economic needs beyond acting as mere suppliers to the mother country, and they wanted to work together to run their own affairs.

Colonial resistance intensified as Parliament passed, with an overwhelming majority, the bills that resulted in the so-called 'Coercive Acts' of 1774 – known in America as the Intolerable Acts – which aimed to punish Massachusetts and Boston particularly (for the tea dumping). Although some failed attempts to conciliate were made, by the New Year of 1775 British troops had been despatched to North America to restore order, sanctioned by George III, who had come to see forceful persuasion as the only way of bringing the colonists to heel. This was followed up with the adoption of the draconian Restraining Acts, demanding that the colonies trade only with Britain and thus denying American goods their continental European markets.

If America was in turmoil, Britain too seemed to be approaching a nation in crisis. Many who regarded themselves politically as Whigs were distinctly uneasy with the robust positions taken by the predominantly Tory administration of Lord North, the prime minister. 'It is but too visible, from the rash measures pursued by the ministers of your government here in England,' remarked the MP Temple Luttrell, older brother of James (Robert's lieutenant in the *Panther*), 'and from the temper and situation of your American colonies, that a civil war will be inevitable.'

Early in 1775, as the *Panther* lay at anchor at Spithead, divisive opinions were infiltrating the commissioned ranks. In Parliament as well, Whig officers of both the navy and the army pronounced that they would not wish to serve against the colonists, their fellow countrymen. Robert's family friend the Honourable Augustus Keppel was one such man. And his distant relation Vice Admiral Richard Howe said an officer could have no more painful a struggle 'as that between his duty as an officer, and his duty as a man'; but then he admitted that 'however he suffered, if commanded, his duty was to serve... [though] if it was left to his choice, he certainly should decline to serve'.

Robert, who turned seventeen in February 1775, would have to decide whether his loyalties lay with his career or with his familial politics. The New England Restraining Act had excluded the northern American colonists' vessels from the Grand Banks fishery, a move that meant the Newfoundland station could become more exciting for the midshipman. Meanwhile, Shuldham's governorship had been terminated, and he was appointed instead naval commander-in-chief on the North American station. Either way, whether remaining in the *Panther* or going with Shuldham, Robert might have to serve against the colonists.

In England, Charles was provided with some diversion from such weighty political matters when, at twenty-one, he came of age in February 1775. 'The Day was observed at Grantham by ringing of Bells, Bonefires, and other Demonstrations of Joy. An Ox was roasted whole; at night some grand Fireworks were played off, and the Town illuminated,' reported the *Stamford Mercury*, adding that 'the Inhabitants appearing emulous to shew their Respect on this Occasion, to a Gentleman of such promising Abilities; and who is likely to be an Ornament to his Country.' But the young Parliamentarian was aware that he was now expected to prove his worth, as he considered whether to support government policy or instead back the small but influential group of politicians – mainly Whigs – who were speaking out in the spirit of John Locke against the taxation and coercion of 'fellow countrymen'. These men were proposing conciliatory measures, which they hoped would appease the colonists who would then drop their claims for independence.

Charles had, for some time, been attending passionate debates in the tiny House of Commons. The chamber – formerly St Stephen's Chapel within the Palace of Westminster – was only 58 feet long and 33 feet wide. Owing to the arrangement of the inward-facing pews, the Members, roughly dividing themselves into factions, sat opposite one another, the aisle between them (it was said) being slightly greater than the width of two extended sword-arms. There was insufficient seating for all 558 Members. To rise and vote, by walking through one of the lobbies, was to run the risk of standing for the rest of the day. However, at that time politics was still a part-time occupation for most MPs, and over-crowding usually only happened at times of national crises.

By his own admission, Charles had 'entered [those] walls with prejudices against the system [the] administration was pursuing'. Although imbued with the Whig philosophy to reject taxation and violence, true to family form he thought 'it was but justice to hear the arguments that might be urged on both sides, to compare those arguments, and draw [his] opinion from that comparison'. The majority of Members supported the government's advocacy of vigorous measures against the colonists. William Innes summed up the opinions of many during one debate in November 1775:

The grand claim of the Americans is liberty; but it appears to me absurd to say, that a people who import slaves and are despotic over them, nay, many of whom draw their sustenance from the very bosom of slavery, have a right to the freedom which the inhabitants of this country enjoy... Don't grant them liberty but let England rule them properly... I hope and trust, the ministry will continue firm, and that after ages shall not be able to say, that in the days of our most gracious sovereign, George the Third, America was lost to England. Let us be steady in pursuing the interests of this country but at the same time merciful and forgiving... Your naval power is great; your resources for military men, while you have riches, are immense; but above all, your cause is just: be not afraid; Heaven will support you.

By the time Innes made this speech, Charles knew where he stood. In March 1775, the House of Commons had debated a bill to restrain the commerce of the southern colonies, which made up Charles's mind. Attending the third reading of the bill, on 5 April 1775, he was moved to overcome an inherited lack of self-confidence in public speaking. He stood up, the twenty-one-year-old Marquis of Granby, to deliver his maiden speech to many who remembered his late father. 'I rise to trouble the House,' said Charles, 'with a few words on the bill now before it. I had sat, Sir, during the course of two divisions, without taking any part; even so much as giving a silent vote on the American question.' Gaining confidence, he continued: 'As to the bill... I think it in every respect too arbitrary, too oppressive, and so totally founded on principles of resentment, that I am exceedingly happy at having this public opportunity of bearing my testimony against it, in the strongest manner I am able. In God's name what language are you now holding out to America!'

Charles declared the present 'methods' to be detrimental to any kind of reconciliation, and he likened efforts to force the Americans to obedience to 'a ruffian... when he forcibly enters my house, and with a dagger at my throat or a pistol at my breast makes me seal deeds which will convey to him my estate and property'. He said it was not the land he was interested in but only the principles of liberty in men, asking how could forcing a man to give up his possessions

Marquis of Granby

THE
Parliamentary Register.

NUMBER XXI.
(Or NUMBER IX. of the Second Session.)

CONTENTS.

HOUSE of LORDS.

LONDON:
Printed for J. ALMON, opposite Burlington-House, Piccadilly.
M,DCC,LXXVI.
[Price One Shilling.]

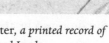

Charles subscribed to J. Almon's Parliamentary Register, *a printed record of Parliamentary debates in the Commons and Lords.*

because he had rebelled in the cause of liberty bring peace and loyalty
to the world? 'I have a very clear, a very adequate idea of rebellion, at
least according to my own principles; and those are the principles on
which the [Glorious] Revolution was founded. It is not against whom
a war is directed, but it is the justice of that war that does, or does not,
constitute rebellion.' He added:

> From the fullest conviction of my soul, I disclaim every idea both
> of policy and right internally to tax America. I disavow the whole
> system. It is commended in iniquity; it is pursued with resent-
> ment; and can terminate in nothing but blood. Under whatsoever
> shape in future it may be revived by whomsoever produced and
> supported it shall from me, meet the most constant, determined,
> and invariable opposition.

Charles sat down to Whig cheers. His speech excited gossip and discussion even in the provinces; indeed, his friend Daniel Pulteney, visiting
Cambridge at the time, remarked that he did not even need to order
'Almon's collection of debates at the coffee house' – referring to the
new *Parliamentary Register*, the forerunner of *Hansard* – for it was
printed in the local newspapers.[15]

But nothing Charles said made any difference. The government
continued on its path, and his prediction was correct. Although many
politicians had ridiculed the idea that a British army would encounter
significant resistance from the colonists, the skirmishes of Lexington
and Concord two weeks later, on 19 April 1775, were followed by the
more serious engagement of Bunker Hill in June. The rousing of the
adjacent countryside trapped British troops in Boston. The commander-
in-chief, General Thomas Gage, wrote home with a warning of dire
consequences: 'These people show a spirit and conduct against us they
never showed against the French... a rage and enthusiasm as great as
ever people were possessed of and you must proceed in earnest or give
the business up.'[16]

Charles Manners had placed himself firmly with the minority who
opposed the war. Admirable though this was from a moral point of
view, in doing so he threatened to blight his brother's career.

4

'A place without honour, profit or pleasure'

'A place without honour, profit or pleasure'

O n a hazy summer's day in late June 1775, the frigate *Enterprize* slipped her London moorings on the Thames at Deptford, set her topsails and proceeded downstream with the ebb tide, passing as she did so the rolling green hills of Greenwich Park on the south bank. Lord Robert Manners, aboard as a midshipman, could see against the skyline the Royal Observatory, founded a century earlier for research to improve navigation and to 'find the so-much desired longitude of places'. A little later, he passed the Royal Arsenal at Woolwich, which had once been part of his father's fiefdom as Master General of the Ordnance. Then, as the shore fell away beyond the marshes of Kent and Essex, the *Enterprize* set her lower sails to make her way through the channels that threaded among the shallows of the outer Thames Estuary. The vessel was guided by beacons placed carefully by Trinity House, a body charged with the safe navigation of the Thames since Tudor times. Finally, she reached the open sea, doubling North Foreland with its lighthouse, squaring away past the white cliffs of Dover and heading down the Channel, accompanied by summer thunderstorms. By 9 July, the *Enterprize* was at anchor at Spithead. There, her captain, Sir Thomas Rich, awaited his orders from the politicians and officers who made up the Board of Admiralty, the navy's highest command.

The now seventeen-year-old Robert was also hoping for news. A few weeks earlier, with the prospect of war looming, he had been so desperate to secure a lieutenancy that he ignored the possibility that rapid promotion might be denied him – because his brother had spoken so eloquently against the government's colonial policies in April. There was no point in turning to his uninterested grandfather for help, so he had asked Charles to solicit for him a lieutenant's commission after just three years of service. The two young men, in a kind of naive hopefulness combined with a sense of entitlement and pride as 'Granby's sons', simply tried to shorten the six years Robert must otherwise endure in limbo as Mr Midshipman Manners. Charles agreed to go straight to the top and approach the Earl of Sandwich, the First Lord of the Admiralty, whose decision it would ultimately be. This was a bold move – for the old Lord Granby and Sandwich had not got on.

While awaiting the answer, Robert was not insensitive to the precariousness of his position and the need to 'cut a figure', to attract the notice of the Admiralty by securing the commendation of a captain, or better still a flag-officer. In peacetime, this could only be achieved by demonstrating outstanding ability in seamanship or administration; but for a young man prepared to risk his life in battle and distinguish himself in action, war might offer a quicker route to a lieutenant's commission than 'interest'. Yet, gallantry might require serving against the 'British' colonists in America. He would do it if commanded, but it was not his choice. However, on this occasion, luck was on his side. Having obtained his release from Captain Ommaney of the *Panther*, he found a ship that was not heading for America but still might offer a chance of action. The British intelligence network had hinted at the possibility of trouble in the Western Mediterranean, with rumours of a Spanish mobilization to recover Gibraltar – the coveted gateway to the Mediterranean. British possession of this 'barren rock' (as a friend of Charles described it), obtained in 1713 at the Treaty of Utrecht after the War of the Spanish Succession, was a red rag to the Spanish bull. It was possible that with the British distracted in North America, Madrid might well act. To go to the assistance of Gibraltar would suit Robert admirably: it would mean he could delay choosing between familial politics and his profession, for serving against the old enemy of Spain was perfectly acceptable for those who preferred not to fight compatriots in America.

A midshipman's berth on the 28-gun frigate *Enterprize* bound for Gibraltar was thus Robert's choice, and he was able to persuade

Captain Rich to take him. A smaller vessel than the *Panther*, with a ship's company of 200 officers and crew plus 50 marines, the *Enterprize* was a most versatile man-of-war. Frigates were used as convoy escorts, as cruisers sent to observe an enemy coast and to prey on enemy trade, and as despatch vessels and the 'eyes' of the battle fleet. If, and when, that fleet came to action, the frigates sailed parallel to the line of battle, clear of the gun-smoke, repeating the admiral's signals for all to see. Some of these functions might admirably suit Robert's ambitions. A product of a ship-building programme introduced by Lord Sandwich, the *Enterprize* had been built at Deptford, nearly 50 miles from the open sea, and launched the previous year. Some considerable effort was still required to complete her fitting out before setting off to Portsmouth.

On arrival at Spithead, in early July, Robert received no news of the longed-for lieutenancy and so threw himself into his duties as a senior midshipman, preparing for a 'cruise' to the Mediterranean. While the ship lay at anchor, he would undoubtedly have been sent away in the boats as the last of the stores and victuals were taken on board. It was now that the officers sent their last letters ashore, a task they would have entrusted to the midshipmen. Robert would not have left the *Enterprize* without a warning from the 1st lieutenant to guard his men well, for the seamen at the oars might seize any opportunity to desert if they had been pressed or were in the navy against their will. The distractions of the area were also legendary. On the eastern side of the harbour, beyond the dockyard walls and among the dwellings of labourers, lay the taverns and brothels, the assembly rooms and respectable coaching inns – running the whole gamut of Georgian society, and providing a potent lure for naval men. On the western side, where many of the seamen's families lived, was Gosport, a small town said to have 'a full share of the vices of Portsmouth, polluted by the fortunes of sailors and the extravagances of harlots'.[1] Within Gosport lay Haslar Creek, with a Royal Naval Hospital built beside it – said to be the origin of the expression 'up the creek without a paddle', applied to those who would die there and thus never return.

Whether or not Robert had indulged himself with the women referred to variously as 'Portsmouth brutes' or 'Spithead nymphs'[2] during the many winter months when the *Panther* lay off the harbour entrance is unknown; but now his duties precluded any amorous distractions. This was a marked contrast with his brother.

*

Charles, for all his bold words to the House of Commons, did not back them up with action. For now, politics was swept aside by beauty in the shape of Lady Mary Isabella Somerset. Charles's need for love and young female company after a childhood somewhat starved of it distracted him from political duties, for the lady suited him perfectly. Not only was she extremely beautiful, but she was also aristocratic and possessed a keen artistic knowledge, which chimed with Charles's inclinations. Her only fault, if it can be considered so, was that her family was Tory in political sympathy.

Mary Isabella, the only surviving one of five daughters of the late Charles Somerset, 4th Duke of Beaufort, from Badminton House in Gloucestershire, was a young woman whose beauty was much admired. She had spark too, for unusually she liked to hold the reins in her phaeton, a practice her mother thought 'rather hazardous but to you, you say it does not appear so'. Since October 1771, Mary Isabella had been living in Europe with her mother and an orphaned niece, Elizabeth Compton. The two young women had studied the riches of Italy under the guidance of an Italian tutor, Signor Lorenzo Pignotti, and according to Mary Isabella's diary they had seen electrical experiments conducted by Signora Laura Bassi and met the castrato singer Farinelli. And as ladies of 'fashion', clothes and hats were as interesting to them as culture; on returning to England in the autumn of 1774, Mary Isabella noted that they wore 'pea-green' riding habits while driving through Windsor Great Park, and professed to be sorry there were not more people about to admire them. On that same day her diary contains a detailed description of a visit to Windsor Castle and St George's Chapel, where she remarked on the tomb of 'one of the Granby family', meaning the effigies of George Manners and Anne St Leger in the Rutland Chantry.

Mary Isabella's mother then set about arranging for her daughter to meet the current scion of 'the Granby family'. Already a passionate collector of art, Charles was impressed not only by Mary Isabella's aesthetic appreciation, but by the fact that her father had been a patron of Canaletto. As further proof of her artistic credentials, one of her relations had been married to Thomas Gainsborough, the artist for whom Charles had sat after leaving Eton. Happily – in contrast with the arranged marriages of their parents' generation – the couple by all accounts seem to have genuinely fallen in love, and in early July 1775, now that Charles had come of age, he proposed to her. Eager not to pressurize her into marriage, he nervously and humbly told her: 'You stand as free and unrestrained in relation to acceptance or rejection, as you did before I had the honour of your acquaintance.' To his delight, she agreed to his proposal.

A euphoric Charles relayed the news to his old Cambridge tutor, Richard Watson, admitting that he had 'formed a Tory connexion', but assuring him that 'Whig principles are too firmly riveted in me ever to be removed'. He thanked Watson 'for making me study Locke; while I exist, those tenets, which are so attentive to the natural rights of mankind, shall ever be the guide and direction of my actions'. Watson replied that he must be 'a Whig in domestic as well as political life, and the best part of Whiggism is, that it will neither suffer nor exact domination'.[3]

Charles now had a less pleasant task, for he had to visit the elderly duke at Belvoir to discuss the terms of the marriage settlement. For once, he was not dilatory over his correspondence. 'As we parted,' he told Mary Isabella, 'a separation which I think was rather tender, I cannot help returning you my sincerest and most affectionate thanks for your ten thousand kind letters.' To Charles, his fiancée's letters expressed 'an attachment so firm that it is beyond the power of human reduction to dissolve it', and he responded with his own heightened sense of love's rapture:

> But whither does my frantic imagination carry me? Does not my pen flow beyond truth? And is not this a mere reverie? Yes! It is at present a reverie! But I must conclude as it is now late at night, and I am just stepping into bed, but were I stepping into my grave and calling my creator as a witness to the truth of my affection I

could not with more sincerity assure [you] of the zeal and ardour
with which my attached and affectionate heart burns for you.
Adieu my dearest Lady Mary, love me and prove it by taking care
of yourself. I am everlastingly yours…

★

So absorbed was Charles with Mary Isabella that he almost neglected
his brother. When, that deliriously happy summer, he remembered to
approach Lord Sandwich to request Robert's commission, it was too
late to do much good. In mid-July 1775, the *Enterprize* had departed
from Spithead. Running into a hard gale from the south, Captain Rich
had then put into Falmouth, Cornwall. Here, while waiting for fair
winds to cross the Channel and the Bay of Biscay, Robert would have
witnessed the arrival of the mail packets, blown in by the southerly
gale, for Falmouth was home of the Post Office Packet Service. Its
little ships maintained diplomatic, commercial and private communications with Lisbon, Gibraltar, the West Indies and North America.

The *Enterprize* was trapped in Carrick Roads, the broad estuary of
the River Fal, for a week waiting for the gale to ease, during which
time Rich kept his men occupied by painting 'the ships sides with
varnish of pine'. In his few idle moments, Robert's thoughts were of
money and how he was going to have access to it abroad. His bank
account had been receiving monthly payments of £52 10s from his
grandfather, which made up the annual £600 allowance and were a
welcome addition to his meagre midshipman's pay. As probably the
wealthiest midshipman in the cockpit mess, Robert was to become
noted for his generosity.

The wind came fair at the end of July, and the *Enterprize* finally
weighed her anchor. Crossing the Bay of Biscay, she was off Cape
Finisterre on 4 August when Robert began a letter to Charles:

> You should have heard from me long [before] had not I believed
> your attention had been taken up about more material objects
> than reading or answering my letters. Only should you have a
> moment free from raving about Lady M[ary] S[omerset] & con-
> templating on her beauties I should be much obliged to you if
> you return and answer to the few lines I shall now send you.

He needed Charles to do something else for him even more pressing than obtaining a commission. 'There is one thing about which I should be much obliged to you if you would speak to my Grandfather. It is with respect to an allowance to fix some way for me to draw for money.' At this moment, he did not have time to finish the letter. The ship had picked up the prevailing northerly wind, reaching Lisbon on 6 August after a good passage of nine days. This was Robert's first visit to a beautiful European city with narrow streets, red-tiled roofs and vast and ancient cathedrals, which lay under a hot sun. Despite the extensive damage done by the catastrophic earthquake in 1755, Lisbon, with its mixture of old and new, was a fascinating contrast to Newfoundland's dreary ice, gales and fog.

Leaving Lisbon, the frigate rounded Cape St Vincent and set sail for the Strait of Gibraltar, whereupon her crew beheld the thrilling sight of Spanish men-of-war, a whole squadron of them, whose menace was palpable. Robert had never seen a potential enemy fleet before, and he sensed the frisson that ran through the men as Captain Rich was called to the quarterdeck and all off-duty officers and midshipmen crowded the rail, full of curiosity. But excitement was tinged with disappointment, for in Lisbon they had learned the Spanish navy had indeed been mobilized, but not for any attack on Gibraltar; instead, a massive amphibious assault had been launched against Algiers, from where Barbary corsairs operated under the protection of the Ottoman *dey* (or *bey*).

Shortly after seeing the Spanish ships, on 23 August 1775 the *Enterprize* sailed into Gibraltar Bay and made her way towards the anchorage in the shadow of the prominent rock, while firing a fifteen-gun salute in honour of the governor, Edward Cornwallis, uncle to Charles Cornwallis. Once the ship was safely moored, her crew were piped to witness a punishment – Seaman Samuel Bright was flogged for having fallen asleep on watch – after which the men were sent about their 'normal' duties. Unenthusiastically, Robert added another few lines to his unfinished letter: 'We see daily numbers of Spanish men of war passing thro' the straits returning from their late expedition at Algiers where they lost nearly 6 thousand men among whom were a great number of the 1st rank.' He suspected that the news would already be known in England via the intelligence network and gazettes, so there was little point in enlarging. Despite employing nearly fifty ships and more than twenty thousand troops, the Spanish expedition had failed.

The *Enterprize* now came under the orders of the commander-in-chief of the Mediterranean station, Vice Admiral Man, who flew his flag aboard the sixty-gun *Medway*. Also present in Man's squadron were the *Levant* and the *Alarm*, and all four ships were variously deployed in the Strait and beyond to protect British merchantmen from the Barbary pirates who preyed on Christians and sold them into slavery. Although his sea-time had increased, the expectant Robert was not impressed by the station. At the end of September, he added in a petulant tone to his still unsent letter that: 'I have now been 6 weeks at Gibraltar & it is without exception the dullest & most disagreeable place I ever was at. I have been but 3 times ashore & do not intend to go again, so I shall have a pretty long confinement aboard as we shall stay till November.' Finally signing and sealing his missive, he put it aboard a Falmouth Packet. If he expected good news by return of post – the quickness of communications being the one advantage Gibraltar had to offer him – he was to be disappointed. Back in England, a different note, dated 8 September 1775, had reached Charles. It was from the First Lord of the Admiralty.

Lord Sandwich had not been prepared to make an exception for Robert. Beset by such applications from all and sundry, he generally adhered to the rules that gave him a defence against all the pressing demands for promotion and which helped reduce the possibility of incompetence among officers. The six-year rule was a useful excuse to say 'no' to such aristocratic pretentions – especially emanating from a member of a prominent Whig family (and the son of a man Sandwich had disliked) after just three years of service.

Having failed to procure what would have amounted to a considerable favour, Charles could do no more for his brother. He turned, instead, to another fruitless endeavour: extracting from his grandfather a sum of money sufficient to set him up prior to his marriage. For help, he looked to his uncle, Lord Mansfield, but even the Lord Chief Justice's exceptional legal mind was stumped by Rutland's obduracy. The duke had tied up his estate so comprehensively that Mansfield told Charles that the duke's attitude must be 'a matter of great consequence to you for the rest of your life, it incapacitates you from paying

Hinchingbrook Sept: 8. 1775

My Lord

Your Lordships may be assured that I am thoroughly disposed to shew every civility & to give every assistance in my power to Mr Manners, but he cannot according to the fundamental rules of the Navy be made a Lieutenant till he has served six years, & passed an examination. I have the honour to be

Your Lordships
most obedient
& most humble servant
Sandwich

A letter of 8 September 1775 from Lord Sandwich to Charles,
in which he declines to promote Robert to lieutenant.

your father's meritorious debts'. Nevertheless, some astute advice from Mansfield rescued Charles from a disastrous confrontation with his grandfather. Charles was lucky, in that Mary Isabella agreed to a minimal settlement on the proviso that it would be reviewed immediately after the duke died. The meagre terms of the document did not require 246 sheepskins, unlike the settlement of his parents.

The couple wed on 28 December 1775. Lady Katherine Pelham, the duke's sister, told the new Lady Granby on that day that: 'I have earnestly wished Lord Granby's happiness, & it is with infinite satisfaction that I have all the reason in the world to believe you will make those wishes successful.'

★

Robert, meanwhile, had not found much in the way of happiness. Thwarted by Sandwich's negative response and with duty preventing him from returning home for the wedding, he spent Christmas aboard his ship getting boisterously drunk in 'Bacchanalian madness'. Such necessary excesses made the monotony of cruising and convoying between Gibraltar and Lisbon tolerable, for the stultifying routines of the ship were not easily borne by a lively and frustrated young mind. Occasional events brightened his days: a strange sail on the horizon or a school of dolphins gambolling under the bow, dinner with the captain, and on one occasion a spectacular eclipse of the moon. Otherwise, Robert was bored, and the only fun to be had was that created by the men themselves, with jigs and reels and the sounds of fiddle, fife and drum an important part of life aboard naval ships.

Then, towards the end of March 1776, came dramatic change, and the news must have swept the ship like wildfire. Captain Rich received orders that they were to 'burn, sink and destroy American ships'. In defiance of the British government, the Second Continental Congress at Philadelphia had had the effrontery to empower colonial privateers to operate against British trade. Worse still, the Congress had established a new fleet, to be known as the Continental Navy. Rich and his officers must have read this with a growing sense of outrage: this was not merely rebellion, it was treason! But as soon as the fury had subsided, the wardroom must have crackled with the sudden consolations of the situation. A maritime war – the 'next war' of their Saturday toasts – meant opportunity for action, for distinction, and for prizes. And, although on the Gibraltar station they had nothing to fear from the Continental Navy, the chance of seizing a rebel-commissioned privateer or, better still, a fat American merchantman bringing goods from the colonies to the Mediterranean, enlivened everyone. Regardless of private thoughts about Americans as fellow countrymen, for the first time in Robert's career prize-money was a real prospect. On 24 March, in anticipation of such good fortune, the ship's sailing master, Alex Gatt, recorded in his log that they 'manned and armed the longboat ready to cruise against the Americans'. The boat was fitted with a small carronade which could be used as an auxiliary to the frigate herself, and a day later they put to sea.

The *Enterprize* now chased every strange sail in sight, firing at them to make them heave-to so men could board and 'examine' them. Most of the vessels were European, but on 30 April Robert witnessed for the first time the taking of a prize. Gatt's log recorded that they 'took a ship from Pennsylvania and put an officer and 10 men aboard to take her into Gibraltar'.

The new situation did not suit everyone. While war offered prospects to midshipmen and officers, some of the seamen and landsmen were less enthusiastic. A man-of-war commissioned in peacetime offered some prospect of a return home; war meant indefinite service. That said, the *Enterprize* seemed a reasonably happy ship with a minimum of flogging, and what there was (as in Seaman Bright's case) was incurred by egregious conduct. But other ships suffered some trouble. Captain Hay of the *Alarm* caught three men attempting to desert in Gibraltar. On 3 September 1776 they were court-martialled and sentenced to 300 lashes each by means of a 'flogging round the fleet' – the severest punishment short of hanging. It was intended as an example to all. The men were tied to a wooden tripod erected in one of the *Alarm*'s boats, and this was then pulled around all the men-of-war lying in the anchorage. The crew of each was mustered 'to witness punishment', lining the rails and the rigging as the *Alarm*'s boat drew up alongside, whereupon lashes were laid 'on the beare back of them', as Gatt wrote in his log, until the full sentence had been carried out. Afterwards, the wretched victims' torsos were said to resemble scorched and blackened meat. To further prevent trouble, the three men were then sent

to serve in different ships, the *Enterprize* receiving Robert Williams. A
few days later, he died of his wounds and was buried at sea.

While Lord Robert was compelled to witness this grisly scene, and
though he would have appreciated the necessity for discipline, it only
reinforced his sense of compassion. But with Williams soon dead, the
incident was put to the back of his mind, like so many individual tragedies at sea. Robert was also distracted by another financial problem.
Although he had been able to obtain money from his grandfather
while in Gibraltar with which to buy food to supplement his rations,
he now required extra funds, as his frigate had been despatched by
Vice Admiral Man upon a more extensive cruise, and the 'young gentlemen' aboard hoped to have the chance to take some leave from
the ship and travel ashore. Captain Rich had received orders to sail
the *Enterprize* to North Africa upon a diplomatic mission, after which
he was to proceed to Leghorn (Livorno) on the north-west coast of
Italy. Before the frigate left Gibraltar, Robert was advised by letter
that Messrs Herries & Co. had received £200 from the Duke of Rutland upon which Robert could draw 'circular notes', an early form of
traveller's cheques designed to assist the aristocracy on their travels.

The first port of call was Minorca, which had been returned to the
British by the peace treaty of 1763. Upon arrival in mid-September
1776, a ferocious gale prevented the *Enterprize* from passing through
the narrow entrance, flanked by high cliffs, into the enclosed harbour of Port Mahon, and Rich was obliged to drop the anchor; but it
dragged, and the ship would have ran upon the rocks had it not been
for some local fishermen who towed her through, and on into the
harbour past Quarantine Island and 'Bloody Island' with its recently
rebuilt naval hospital, to the British naval base on Saffron Island (Isla
Pinto). Once again, the fortifications that Robert could see about him
had been part of his late father's responsibility as Master General of
the Ordnance. Perhaps his thoughts also turned to the tragic Admiral
Byng, for the old Marquis of Granby had been one of those who tried
to save the officer from execution after his role in the loss of Minorca
in 1756.

For a whole month, the *Enterprize*'s crew prepared for the voyage
to North Africa. The gale that had greeted their arrival marked the
onset of winter, which could be as unpleasant in the Mediterranean

as in the Atlantic. The fierce winds drove up short, steep seas, requiring the closing-off of all ventilation below decks and consigning the ship's company to the miseries of damp and foul air. Even in the shelter of Port Mahon, the work of refitting and refreshing all the tiers of water-barrels was bedevilled by the thunder, lightning and pouring rain. Finally they were ready and on 15 November a pilot was embarked; he was employed for his local knowledge and would assist them in their safe approach and entry into Tripoli, on the Libyan part of the Barbary Coast. The passage, in predictably boisterous weather across the Sicilian Narrows, occupied two weeks, but in due course the ramparts of Tripoli lay before them as they closed the coast.

One of the oldest ports in the Mediterranean, having been established by the Phoenicians seven centuries before Christ, Tripoli's natural harbour was flanked on the western shore by a small peninsula but exposed to northerly winds. On the ship's approach, the pilot turned out to be of no use and was 'suspended from his duty', for Captain Rich considered the man 'did not know what he was doing'. Now the burden fell upon Gatt the master. As the *Enterprize* made her slow and stately entrance under the cannon of the huge castle, her large ensign fluttering at her mizzen peak, an eleven-gun salute thundered out. Its reverberations from the stone ramparts were augmented by the answering concussions of the reply. Once the ship was safely anchored, a boat commanded by a lieutenant was swung out, lowered and immediately sent ashore to bring the British consul on board, so that Captain Rich could confer with him.

Tripoli was one of three semi-independent *pashaliks* within the Ottoman Empire, with which Britain, along with France and several other countries, had treaties intended to protect their trade from the freebooting Barbary corsairs.[4] These pirates had for centuries preyed on the merchant shipping of northern Europe as it sought to acquire the riches available at the Ottoman ports of the Levant, chiefly Smyrna (Izmir). Great Britain, like the other treaty-holders, maintained a consul in Tripoli, and a British man-of-war visited the place annually to 'show-the-flag' and demonstrate the puissance of the mighty King George III of Great Britain and Ireland. Sir Thomas Rich had been tasked to convey despatches to and from the consul, and, in the consul's presence, to enjoy an audience with the *pasha* (or *bashaw*). Among the matters to be explained to him and his *vizier*, or chief minister, was the new status of any merchant ships owned by the rebellious Americans. But, attempts to involve the Barbary corsairs and the *pasha* in the destruction of rebel trade – among the objectives of Rich's visit – failed; American ships, far from being fair game, continued for the time being to be protected by the *pasha*'s treaty with France.

Despite this impasse, during Rich's delicate mission the protocols were observed assiduously by both sides. Thus, although December brought 'fresh gales and a great sea from the north' causing the *Enterprize* to roll and pitch at her anchor, as evidence of the *pasha*'s good faith the ship was occasionally provided with a whole 'day's provisions', consisting of 'bread, bullocks and vegetables of various kinds'. From time to time a boat was sent ashore to fetch fresh water. For the most part, the crew were kept busy keeping the ship spick-and-span, for she was on show and visited by the *vizier* and the Venetian consul. On these occasions a detachment of marines was paraded and the ship's hands put through various manoeuvres to impress the visitor with the professional ability of the Royal Navy. Rich entertained his guests, too.

However, there was to be no Bacchanalian Christmas for Robert and his shipmates that year, for on Christmas Eve 1776, as noted in the ship's log, Rich 'parted of the *Bashaw* for the last time about the business that he came here of', and orders were given to prepare for departure. A few days later on 29 December, after receiving several packages destined for the 'Emperor of Morocco's son', the *Enterprize* weighed her anchor and departed straight out into the teeth of a north-westerly gale. With reduced canvas and her yards braced hard against the catharpings, the frigate was pressed over at an angle as she clawed her way to windward, pitching into the waves, her decks constantly swept by a stinging spray. She covered a mere 277 nautical miles in eleven days, which amounted to just 1 nautical mile per hour, as Gatt carefully calculated. In those high winds and steep seas, the frigate suffered immensely: sails were torn, masts were split by the bucking of the ship, and the rigging was severely strained. The stormy conditions demanded the utmost from the ship's company. Pumping the ingress of sea-water out became a long and tedious ordeal, while aloft, and in spite of the gale, sails had to be replaced and every remedy, howsoever temporary, had to be made. Battened down below or battered by the elements above, Robert and the other 'young gentlemen' would not have been exempt from these exertions. In such a situation, the only relief came with a brief respite in a hammock, or from the extra – and encouraging – rations of grog ordered by Captain Rich.

Fortunately, nothing lasts forever, and by 9 January 1777 the men found themselves anchored off the *pashalik* of Tunis, where they were to stay for almost a month. Here, Sir Thomas Rich repeated his diplomacy, and his ship's company, having repaired the ravages of the gale as best they could, spent time painting cannon-shot and polishing brass so that the *Enterprize* was restored to the smart appearance she had exhibited at Tripoli. While the rest of the crew set-to, Rich permitted Robert and some others to abandon their duties for a time and visit the ruins of Carthage, which lay on the north-western side of Tunis Bay.

Carthage had been considered by Aristotle as having one of the best governed populations in the Mediterranean world. Also one of the most powerful cities, it grew to rival Rome until it was eventually conquered to become the fourth city of the Roman Empire. Though not on the usual trail of any grand tour – the Barbary Coast being notorious for bubonic plague and other unpleasant infections, not to mention the pirates – Carthage figured strongly in the European imagination as a place of interest and antiquity. The little party from the *Enterprize* visited the Temple of Water and the two great reservoirs where Robert – able to indulge his keen interest in the classical world – observed that 'almost all the walls are left entire'. He found the aqueduct, which brought in water from Zowan, 60 miles away, 'a most astonishing work', and, on counting the 230 arches that stretched across the plain of Zama, he further concluded that it was 'an almost entire one worthy of the people who constructed it'. Using his trigonometrical skills, he measured each arch at '17 feet in space & 120 in height' and thought it all a 'glorious sight demonstrating its former magnificence'.

Robert was less impressed by the locals, even though 'they were indeed civil enough to us, & generally are so to the English, for whom they profess a great friendship & I believe do esteem more than any other Christian power'. He would later write in a letter home that although 'they would cheat & rob you ... they would not spit at you or perhaps murther you as you walk along, which they will do in several

other parts, & this they look upon as the highest proof of their moderation & urbanity'. In a tone reminiscent of his grandmother's wry
humour, he observed that 'notwithstanding a few of these kind of
inconveniences I could readily have stayed there sometime longer'.

On 6 February 1777, sixteen live bullocks were lifted aboard the *Enterprize* to provide fresh meat, and the ship departed for Minorca, taking
just five days to make the passage. Entering Port Mahon, the vessel had
to be secured off Quarantine Island for three days. Having come from
plague-ridden North Africa, the crew were obliged to endure this short
hiatus. But once formal clearance had been obtained, Captain Rich
then proceeded directly towards Leghorn, where the *Enterprize* arrived
on 4 March. A free port in the Grand Duchy of Tuscany, Leghorn was
open to the shipping of all nations; it was a most important centre of
trade, and one with which the English had enjoyed commerce for over
a century. A long-established expatriate British community lived there
to facilitate commerce, and British merchant ships were among the
many that filled the busy harbour. One of the tasks of Vice Admiral
Man's squadron, the *Enterprize* included, was to provide protection to
the ships in the convoys back and forth through the Strait of Gibraltar.

To Robert, Leghorn was an interesting contrast to Carthage, alive
and thriving, with its teeming bridges and narrow lanes, its grand
noblemen's *palazzos* and the dense network of canals that linked its
many warehouses to the port itself. Once again, the 'young gentlemen' obtained leave of absence to travel – to see the Leaning Tower
of Pisa, before moving on to visit Pistoria, Lucca and Florence, with
Robert's circular notes from Herries proving useful for paying their
way. Such opportunities for travel, without a tutor at one's heels, was
an attraction for young men in the navy. Indeed, at least one busy officer was known to have seduced 'princesses, marchesas, countesses, a
Portuguese royal Duchess, the wife of the Doge of Genoa, and several
nuns' while serving in the Mediterranean.[5]

By mid-April 1777, on their return passage to rejoin Man's flag at
Gibraltar, they fell in with another gale, 'a great sea from the south-
west carried away the foretopmast'. As before, the crew had to clear
away the wreckage with its tangle of rigging, torn sails and splintered
wood, replacing the broken spar from the limited stock of spares they
carried on board. It was such tasks, routinely undertaken, that made

the British fleet a highly efficient machine, for there were no teachers
of seamanship superior to sea-time and experience. In due course, the
packages the *Enterprize* was carrying for the Emperor of Morocco's
son were transferred to the *Alarm*, which lay in Gibraltar Bay, while the
ship's company continued to make good the ravages of their recent
passage.

★

It was now almost two years since Robert had last seen any of his family. He could not have known that in the autumn of 1776, 'at half after
five o'clock this afternoon, September 28th[,] a little dear girl (with
black eyes) came crying into the world'. His new sister-in-law Mary
Isabella had given birth to a daughter named Elizabeth. Nor did he
know the details about some scandalous indiscretions committed by
his sister Frances, even if gossip had filtered into the Gibraltar newspapers. There were no letters awaiting him on the 'barren rock' to
rectify this lack of family contact. In fact, he was not forgotten, but,
unknown to him, correspondence had gone astray.

For all Lord Robert's largesse to his messmates of the *Enterprize*'s
cockpit, his natural aloofness and reserve (and his ducal connections)
conferred all but impenetrable barriers to close friendship. Having had
an education beyond the majority of his shipmates must have also
imposed its own frustrations. He must have longed to know what
Charles thought of the American colonists' Declaration of Independence of July 1776, as news of it passed through the fleet. He might
even have noticed that one signatory had attended Eton while the
brothers were there: Thomas Lynch. Such worldliness and precocity
would have inclined him more to the lieutenants, whose commissioned ranks he so wished to join and whose society he had penetrated
in discussions about their sight-seeing excursions on the Barbary Coast
and in Italy. Throughout the *Enterprize*'s cruise in the Mediterranean,
Sir Thomas Rich – who in common with all post-captains entertained
his midshipmen and officers to dinner, if only to discover what made
them tick – had recognized some of the young man's potential. By
now, Robert had become a competent seaman, willing and able to
accept responsibility and possessing a natural air of command. As a
result, Rich and his 1st lieutenant had allowed Robert to assume some

of the duties of a commissioned officer. But Robert's ambition was still unrealized; 'acting-up' gained him experience and brought his commander's good opinion, but it was still dependent on favour. It was not the same as a confirmed commission.

However, he must have been stirred afresh by the electrifying news that now came aboard, for the Comte de Vergennes, chief minister to King Louis XVI of France, had agreed to send military aid to the American rebels. Moreover, Louis had ordered the French navy onto a war footing. For some time the French had been supplying the rebels with arms, a covert initiative that was an open secret in London and brought fears that France would try to exploit America's revolutionary war to seek revenge for territorial losses in the Seven Years' War. But the supplying of guns and ammunition, which had to run the gauntlet of the Royal Navy's cruisers off the American coast, was one thing; the mobilization of the French navy, which had been almost entirely reorganized and consisted of some of the finest men-of-war then in existence, was quite another. If France was to enter the war, there would be an end to delicate consciences, no holding back over fighting as there had been over engaging the American rebels. The prospects for ambitious naval officers would now surely improve, especially if Spain were to follow in France's footsteps. The two Bourbon nations would certainly wish to capture valuable sugar islands and might even attempt to invade British shores.

Yet, while officers expressed their innate confidence in the Royal Navy with enthusiastic toasts to 'the next war', inwardly they knew that the jostling for commissions would be intense, and they each had their own personal considerations, too. A nagging anxiety gripped Robert. His request for promotion to lieutenant had been turned down, and the Gibraltar station had proved not merely dull and disagreeable but had not met his expectations. For the sake of maintaining personal honour, the age required of a young man in Robert's position to prove his courage and conduct – which meant finding 'the best possible ship on the best possible station'.[6] Tedious, unspectacular duty was to be rejected by men of standing as a matter of principle. Despite Captain Rich's encouragement, Robert was thoroughly disillusioned; he remained nothing more than a midshipman. He had so far, it seemed, been cheated of his 'moment'. It would not be long before he would turn twenty and complete his six years of service, and it must be time, he thought, to return home and try again for a lieutenancy, for the *Enterprize* could do nothing further for him. Perhaps, too, there was a girl in Portsmouth he was longing to see.

In early May 1777, the *Enterprize* sailed with yet another convoy, Rich's orders being to accompany the merchantmen north as far as the latitude of Cape Finisterre. From here, the convoy would be seen back to England by escorts from the Channel Fleet. For Robert this was a further blow, meaning the *Enterprize* would have to return to Gibraltar. However, a month later, just before parting with the convoy off Finisterre, Robert found a moment to dash off a letter to his grandfather's secretary, Thoroton. The missive bore the ink-blots and scrawled script of a hasty composition written in the midst of an Atlantic swell. '*Enterprize* at Sea June 3rd Latt: 42° 00' Long: 16° 20' Cape Finisterre E by N 110 leagues,' Robert began:

> I resume my pen to enquire after you all, & to desire a more regular correspondence in which you have certainly failed extremely, for in summing up accounts, I find I am so great a Creditor, that you can never make up the balance at least without the danger of injuring your fingers. I therefore forgive you the present debt provided you will make more regular payments in future.

He hurriedly described to Thoroton the 'delightful territories of Italy' and the rather more qualified chance he had been given to see the 'inhospitable deserts of Lybia, having stay'd at Tripoli 7 weeks (nearly an age in that country, & amongst those people)'; he summed up Tunis, 'which, saving the present inhabitants, who deserve & have the same mean character of its ancient ones, is the first country in the world'. But such observations were not his main reason for writing. Knowing that Thoroton had the duke's ear, he ran on: 'You must know that I have almost served the stated time as Midshipman & would now write to ask my Grandfather's pleasure concerning my stay here whether he would have me remain or come home.' Still short of his majority, the nineteen-year-old Robert was dutifully requesting Rutland's permission to leave his attachment to Captain Rich. He concluded: 'We are now giving [the merchant masters] their final orders therefore I must take leave… I am in a great hurry forgive faults & read it if you can.'

With that, he scattered sand over the paper to dry the ink, sealed his letter, dashed on deck and slipped it into the *Enterprize*'s mail bag as it was sent over to a homeward-bound merchant ship.

It must have been with wistful feelings that Robert watched the convoy disappear over the northern horizon as the *Enterprize* headed back to the south to resume her tedious and unappetizing duties. But then, on 24 July 1777, they captured an American merchant ship, 'a schooner from Salem to Bilbao', and 'put a midshipman and seven men aboard to navigate her'. Disappointingly, it was not Robert who was entrusted with this important task. Keeping their prize in company, they soon afterwards fell in with a French vessel, whereupon Captain Rich adopted a common and legal *ruse de guerre*. Both the schooner and the *Enterprize* hoisted the new ensign of the American Continental Congress, one of which had been purloined from the schooner's flag-locker. This enabled them to close with the Frenchman, and the three ships hove-to for their captains to confer. Thinking he was talking to Americans, the French captain was free with his gossip, telling of 'warlike preparations' at Toulon and the fitting out of a large armament there. He was bound for Brest and was afraid that war would be declared even before he got there.

Robert informed Charles that 'this news we got by the advantage of wearing American colours', but in truth his glee was half-hearted. More than ever he wanted to return home and seek a commission by whatever means was at his disposal. There was no word from his grandfather when the *Enterprize* returned to Gibraltar; but to Robert's delight, in August 1777 a letter arrived from Charles, which had been written and posted months before but had come by a circuitous route. It provided a great fillip to Robert's flagging spirits, and he replied: 'I will not attempt to describe the joy your letter has given me, it greatly overbalances & makes an ample recompense for my pain in not having heard from you before.' If Charles had mentioned their sister Frances, Robert did not refer to it. On family matters, he replied only how happy he was to hear about his new niece Elizabeth, whose pet-name was 'Diddle', along with a flattering intimation that he stood high in the opinion of the respected Lord Mansfield: 'I thank you for the good opinion you have of me; as to your wishes & Lord Mansfield's predictions time must shew & my actions alone declare I hope I shall fulfil

them, it is & always will be my constant endeavour to merit them.'
The long overdue letter also charged Robert – too late – with assessing, on his visit to Italy, some Poussin paintings which Charles wished
to acquire.

Hearing from Charles made up Robert's mind in August 1777 to
return home by hook-or-by-crook, to see his family and to try for promotion. Now that he had proved his abilities as an acting lieutenant,
'all my naval friends especially the Captain have advised & even push'd
me to it some time since', he told Charles, 'as really this is a place
without, honour, profit or pleasure'. Rich's release was gratifying; it
meant he might leave the *Enterprize* with no ill-feelings or charges of
arrogance. Gaining the Duke of Rutland's permission was now of
diminished importance, for, as Robert declared to Charles, 'I intend
no longer to defer the pleasure of seeing you', despite the possible
hazards of capture, or as he put it, of 'being in an unfriendly way taken
by your Friends' – an allusion to the fact that Charles had connections
among the French aristocracy. By deciding to return home, perhaps his
run of bad cards would end.

Robert completed his letter with a flourish that Charles cannot have
failed to be touched by, even allowing for the forms of the age:

> Now my Dearest Brother these few lines principally are to assure
> you that you have [delighted] me by giving your hand to so ami-
> able & illustrious a person [as Mary Isabella] [and] to assure you
> with desiring my most unfeigned love & wishes to my dear sister
> in law that may heaven shower down on your health & happiness
> & all its choicest blessings is the sincere wish & constant prayer
> My Dearest Brother your most affectionate & truly loving Robt:
> Manners.

He was writing to a man whose experiences during the long period
of separation between them could hardly have been more different.

5

'These are the times that try men's souls'

1775 TO SPRING 1778

'These are the times that try men's souls'

By the summer of 1777, it had been more than two years since the Manners brothers had last seen each other. While Robert had been enduring the rigours of shipboard life, Charles had launched himself headlong into the fashionable lifestyle of high-society Whigs. Country sports, theatre, concerts, dining, intellectual interests, gambling and gossip filled his colourful days, luring him away from obligations and duty. He did not forget his younger brother, but in his own ways he was certainly *busy*.

In contrast to Robert's nomadic existence at sea, Charles was enjoying the stability of marriage and fatherhood. The young Marquis and Marchioness of Granby made a striking couple: he had grown into a charming, handsome, extravagant *bon viveur*, while she was a leader of high fashion with its elegant gowns, elaborate wigs and stunning hats that were sometimes so tall that the wearer had to sit on the floor of her carriage. Charles could be proud of a wife thought by some to be 'the most beautiful woman in England',[1] while the memoirist Nathaniel Wraxall described how 'grace itself formed her limbs, and accompanied her movements, [a] faultless sample of female loveliness'.[2] Others said she had 'a delicacy and cultivation of mind rarely to be found'.[3]

Funded by an allowance from the Duke of Rutland and rental income from the Duke of Somerset settlement, Charles and Mary Isabella passed the time with their daughter 'Diddle' in the manner of the old Lord Granby with his children. They travelled to Cheveley Park to bet on the races at Newmarket, visited Belvoir to shoot and hunt, and made excursions to Scarborough's seaside, for Charles said he thought 'an annual ducking there... of no disservice to [one's] health'. Charles was not such an accomplished rider as his father, but unlike some of the other Whig grandees he remained passionate about country pursuits.

Naturally, the young couple spent the spring and early summer in London for the social season, where they leased 16 Arlington Street in Mayfair. While in the metropolis they would have spent time apart, not only because Charles had political matters to attend to, but also because it was accepted that women could go out to public events and private evening parties without their husbands. For some women, this meant opportunities to develop friendships with men that could lead to affairs, though this would have been unlikely in Charles's marriage at this stage: Mary Isabella, as a young wife, was at least expected to produce a legitimate male heir before becoming too wayward.

They could not, however, entirely escape salacious interest in the Manners' personal lives. The brothers' sister Frances had always appeared to have lived a separate life, about which almost nothing is known, though her affection for Charles and Robert was evident in their grandmother's letters. But now, in the spring of 1776, her fourth year as the Countess of Tyrconnel, she became an object of public attention when her coach-footman witnessed her regularly meeting the sportsman, artist and politician Charles Loraine Smith in London parks. She would give him a lift back to his lodgings. It was said that she drove miles out of her way to drop other guests off first so she could be alone with him, and the pair sometimes stayed in her coach until two o'clock in the morning. Then, on 13 July 1776, she sent the porter away from her London home in Hanover Square, supposedly on an errand, but when he returned she was nowhere to be found. Frances had eloped. It was thoroughly embarrassing for all concerned. Her husband, tracking her down at some lodgings, offered to overlook what had happened, hoping to avert a worse scandal; but she refused to come home, and was rumoured to be pregnant by her lover.

Even within the tolerance and libertinism of Whig society, Charles, as a man with public obligations, could not be seen to approve of what Frances had done. For one thing, her first child, a son, had been still-born in April 1773, and since then she had not provided Tyrconnel with an heir, thereby putting family inheritance arrangements at risk. For another, she had generated gossip for the newspaper columnists in an age when access to print was burgeoning, even in the provinces, and publishers eager for profit found the private lives of the aristocracy a guaranteed seller. Despite the nation's growing sexual freedoms, the public still expected the aristocracy to behave in ways that lent credibility to their status as the leaders of society.

No evidence exists that Charles made an effort to support his sister. Instead, he appeared to focus on his own interests. As with most Whigs, the pursuit of pleasure was a serious matter. Charles prided himself, for example, on his patronage of the arts, an occupation that took up time and energy; and, like other noblemen, he consumed large quantities of claret instead of (the potentially unsafe) water and went to considerable lengths to have well-stocked cellars, using diplomats abroad to help source exotic liquors. Music was an important part of aristocratic life, and during the couple's visits to Rutland House, in Knightsbridge, they could enjoy the distinguished violin playing of Giovanni Stefano Carbonelli (also employed by the family

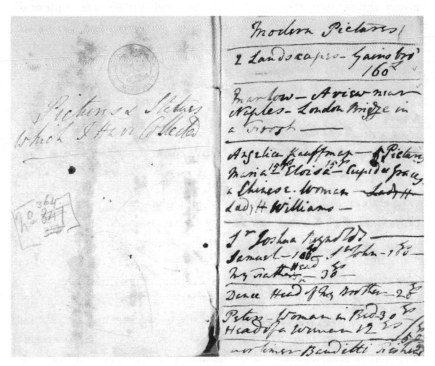

Charles's little book listing 'Pictures & Statues Which I Have Collected'.

as a vintner): he arranged a continuous musical programme for the duke, who was a committed patron of the opera.[4]

Both Charles's Somerset and Rutland grandfathers had been avid collectors of paintings, responsible for large and significant collections at Petworth House and at Belvoir, and old Rutland was an accomplished artist in his own right. In the 1750s, he had commissioned the building of the external picture gallery, adjoining the south wing of Belvoir Castle, to house his acquisitions. By now the duke, elderly and ailing, had somewhat lost interest; but Charles had taken up the mantle and seemed to have inherited his grandfather's eye for paintings that might prove valuable for future generations. He was also capitalizing on the old Lord Granby's friendship with Sir Joshua Reynolds, the doyen of the art world and President of the Royal Academy. With Reynolds' friendship and advice, the young marquis was starting to make some astute purchases.

Charles's approach to collecting ranged from acquiring contemporary masterpieces by continental artists, such as the Swiss painter Angelica Kauffman, to supporting the growing interest in British artists such as William Marlow, Richard Cosway and George Stubbs. He commissioned two superbly executed portraits of his favourite dogs, Turk and Crab, from Stubbs, who for a time lived in Lincolnshire, not far from Belvoir. His collecting also reflected his strong interest in the family's history and its long association with dissent from crown authority: he commissioned paintings of the early 'Albini' lords of Belvoir and of the 'signing' of Magna Carta – the document that the disaffected American colonists were now proclaiming as 'the great Charter and Fountain of English Liberty'.[5] He also had the sculptor Joseph Nollekens create busts of not only his father, but also of Oliver Cromwell and William III, the latter representing the Glorious Revolution of 1688 and the idea that a monarch would never be able to rule again without Parliament.

Predictably, Charles's interests and lifestyle resulted in his living above his means, on top of which his father's debts were still a burden. His late grandmother would no doubt have been horrified, though both Lord Mansfield and Joseph Hill remained on hand to advise and assist where they could. His Cambridge tutor Richard Watson also stayed in contact, attempting to fill the moral void left by Charlotte

Somerset. Like her, he had observed the struggle in Charles's soul. 'Persevere, I beg of you, in the resolution of doing something for yourself,' wrote Watson, 'your ancestors have left you rank and fortune; these will procure you that respect from the world, which other men with difficulty obtain, by personal merit. But if to these you add your own endeavours to become good, and wise, and great, then will you deserve the approbation of men of sense.'[6]

Watson advised Charles to spend more time reading rather than idle his time away like other 'men of fashion', and to be like those who 'have the courage to abridge their pleasures for the improvement of their minds'. But he cautioned Charles to be discriminating:

> ... some books are to be tasted or read in part only; some to be swallowed or read wholly; and some to be digested or read with great diligence or well considered... You can no more have an intimacy with all books than with all men and one should take the best of both kinds for one's peculiar friends... thus with books as

Richard Watson, tutor to Charles, family friend, and later Bishop of Llandaff.

with men, a few friends stand us in better stead than a multitude
of folks we know little of.[7]

Choosing friends was no easy task for Charles, for men in his position
were always courted by those who stood to gain by acquaintanceship.
In a society characterized by the upward cultivation of 'interest' and
the downward dispensing of patronage, Charles's entitlement came
with obligations that required shrewdness on his part in the judgement
of men, and the ability to distinguish the capable from the opportunist,
the useful from the mere hanger-on. However, as Charlotte Somerset
had perceived with clarity, Charles's ability to select his friends wisely
was variable; in particular, his kind and generous disposition rendered
him vulnerable to those who made a show of solicitude. Although he
had genuine friends, such as Alleyne FitzHerbert, a rising star in the
diplomatic world, he had others like Daniel Pulteney, who, while an
entertaining character and sometimes useful, came to be a drain on
Charles's patronage and goodwill. Its significance was not yet apparent, but he also had a deepening friendship with Lord Chatham's son,
the younger William Pitt, whose arrival at Cambridge in 1773 had led
Charles to seek him out – an action that would profoundly influence
both their lives. Charles and William were connected by politics, but
they had something else in common: both had ambitious younger
brothers serving in the Royal Navy.

Convivial places for Charles to meet his friends were the London
gentlemen's clubs situated between the Houses of Parliament at
Westminster and the Mayfair residences: Boodle's and Almack's in
Pall Mall, and White's in Mayfair. (A little later, these establishments
all moved to St James's Street.) Conversation, culinary delicacies and
excessive drinking were integral to life at the clubs, while gambling
was especially rife, for the aristocracy were obsessed with dice and
card games, many of the players suffering breathtaking losses. They
bet on all sorts of things: who would be the next prime minister, or
who might be hanged next. Charles was a member of Almack's (soon
to be renamed Brooks's), having been proposed in 1775 by his father's
old friend Sir William Draper. Also a member was his bibliophile Eton
friend, Thomas Grenville. Almack's had by now become a gathering
place for verbose Whigs, with one *Parliamentary Register* recording

that 'the members pay more than six pence a piece for their supper; and as to talking, Lord how they do talk! They talk bawdy, my Lords, and sometimes heterodoxy, but not blasphemy; no, not so bad as that neither; but they talk what is worse than all, they talk politics.'

★

In the summer of 1776, while Frances was travelling miles to spend time alone with her lover, and Robert was chasing American prizes off the coasts of Spain and Portugal, there was certainly much for Charles to discuss with his Whig friends when it came to politics. The *London Gazette* was the first publication to print the American Declaration of Independence in its edition of Saturday, 10 August 1776. Initially, limited space was given to it because public interest was diverted by scandal – the trials of the Duchess of Kingston for bigamy, and of the actor Samuel Foote for sexual assault.[8] Both trials contributed to the unease about the country's seemingly increasing decadence. But those who noticed the Declaration, and who thought about it, could see that the colonists were not only repudiating the authority of Parliament for threatening the individual's rights to 'Life, Liberty and the pursuit of Happiness', but were now also talking of severing allegiance to the British crown and pressing instead to become a republic. King George III, convinced that force was the only solution, had become an object of colonial vilification; he appeared to have cast himself in the role of 'tyrant'. Inspired by the anti-monarchist sentiment of Thomas Paine's pamphlet *Common Sense* – that the king should be the servant of the people, not their master, and that having no monarch would be preferable to having a repressive one – the authors of the Declaration adopted Paine's reasoning: 'We have it in our power to build the world over again.'

Yet for Charles and a number of the Whigs, their concern was about far more than the colonists' attitude to king and Parliament; it lay much closer to home. Could their own 'natural right', as they perceived it, to govern through hereditary seats in the House of Lords and control over many of the seats in the Commons be under threat? Could the king's hard line against the colonists reflect an increasing royal authority in Britain, at the expense of the British people's own 'life, liberty and property'?

In truth, at that moment George III was not the tyrant that the colonists portrayed. His sanctioning of the use of force was to uphold Parliamentary sovereignty over the colonies, rather than to enforce his own will. He was no domestic despot either, for, though he could choose his Cabinet ministers, in order to be effective they needed the approval of both Houses of Parliament. Nevertheless, in the Lords more than half of the 150 peers were 'King's Friends', making it impossible for those with opposing views to win debates in a vote. With political parties in the modern sense not yet in existence, the king's power base came from those who received patronage from the crown and from those loosely referred to as 'Tories', who agreed the king had the right to choose and control his ministers provided Parliament approved of his choices. George III also had on his side the 'independent gentlemen' who would form allegiances when it suited them, but who usually supported the government.

For a number of Whigs, the king's selection of ministers was highly questionable. It would not have been lost on Charles that the Secretary of State for the American Department was the 'Coward of Minden', the once-disgraced Lord George Sackville who had, thanks to a twist of fortune, acquired a new name – Lord George Germain – and gained favour with the monarch. Appointed in 1775, Germain now held a significant and influential post driving military strategy in North America, and though generally able (Minden aside) and experienced, he was not widely liked and was often at loggerheads with Lord Sandwich, the Cabinet member representing the navy. The king kept Germain in post because he firmly supported the use of force and believed the colonists' will to fight was fragile. Equally, Lord North, the prime minister, was a target for the Whigs' disapproval.[9] Initially attempting conciliation in the early stages of the war, he now accepted that a military solution was required to maintain Parliamentary sovereignty over the colonies; but he was proving a vacillating leader in a time of crisis. Despite this, the king kept him in post because his talent for finance and ability to deflect political attacks with intelligent humour meant that he could hold the respect of the majority in both Houses. But a minority of voices, such as the Whigs at Almack's club, continued to 'abuse the Minister at a great rate; they say he has ruined the resources, and blasted the national honour of the country'.

Now that the colonists were accusing George III of tyranny, political voices in Britain were thrown into ferocious debate. The Whigs contended that Parliament should select and control the ministers as a defence against royal abuse of power. But it was no simple matter for anyone to take a stance against the king, his ministers and his 'Friends'. Charles may have been sufficiently moved, back in April 1775, to state 'from the fullest conviction' of his soul that he would meet government policy towards the rebellious Americans with the 'most constant, determined, and invariable opposition'; but in doing so he had risked being accused of treason – a highly serious and consequential allegation. The idea of a *formal* opposition to the monarch and his ministry did not exist, and the small but vociferous group of Whigs taking a stiffening stand against the war risked punishment if they appeared to align themselves with the rebels currently in arms against the crown. When, in 1776, Charles's free-thinking ex-tutor produced *The Principles of the Revolution Vindicated*, he gave lasting offence at court, even though the 'Revolution' of the title was that of 1688. But Watson's radical egalitarianism was evident in his first sentence. 'Mankind,' he wrote, 'may be considered as one great aggregate of equal and independent individuals... we are all sprung from the same stock, born into the world under the same natural advantages.' He claimed that he was simply defending British freedoms, but his words were interpreted by many as a bold support of the American rebels. Whatever his precise intentions, Watson would later attribute his lack of career progress to this publication, and from this moment on he would fall back on the patronage of his old pupil, Charles.

For Charles, it was not only a matter of appearing traitorous: he also had to decide where his loyalties lay even within his own circle, a matter complicated by its interbred nature. 'Damn the Whigs,' it was said, 'they're all cousins.'[10] The 'opposition', such as it was, was not united, its factions agreeing only that taxation of America was an abuse of power and that the colonies should be retained at all costs but without resorting to violence. Otherwise, pressures and contradictions abounded everywhere. Charles's relative Lord Mansfield, although a Tory, was Whig-like in his support of individual freedom; and in dealing with the legality of aspects of liberty such as slavery and press-ganging for the navy, his arguments repeatedly reflected Locke's espousal of political freedom, religious toleration and economic individualism. Yet, Mansfield was also closely involved in running the government as an adviser to George III, and fiercely opposed the demands of the American colonists, counselling the king to treat them as rebels and traitors.

Mansfield had hoped to influence his young nephew and was disappointed when Charles chose to align himself with Lord Chatham. That talented statesman, credited with the great victory and territorial gains of the Seven Years' War, was aged sixty-eight in 1776. He had no wish to see the American colonies lost to Britain, believing them to be 'the great source of all our wealth and power'.[11] But he was the only British politician prepared to limit the sovereignty of Parliament in order to avoid violence. Charles had long admired Chatham, having been heavily influenced by the old Lord Granby's association with him, and this was the reason he had sought out friendship with Chatham's son at Cambridge. A further incentive to follow the small but influential group of 'Chathamites' was that they included William Petty, 2nd Earl of Shelburne, whose hero and patron during the Seven Years' War had been Charles's father.

However, Charles was also courted by Charles Watson-Wentworth, 2nd Marquis of Rockingham, who was now aged forty-six. Here again was a family connection, for Rockingham's mother was Mary Finch, another sister of Charlotte Somerset, and he himself had been a friend and hunting partner of the old Marquis of Granby. The 'Rockinghamites' favoured avoiding force by granting constitutional rights to the colonists, but in the context of maintaining the sovereignty of Parliament over the colonies 'in all cases whatsoever', for they were perceived as indispensable to Britain's position as a great power. Though mindful of not appearing traitorous, those who privately hoped America would win did so in the context of the struggle between liberty and the crown, rather than from a true desire to see the colonies become an independent republic. This group had some intellectual weight behind it: Charles's once wayward and now corpulent Eton contemporary, Charles James Fox, had risen from the opposition benches to deliver witty, blistering and eloquent diatribes more than 200 times between 1768 and 1774. Equally brilliant was Lord Rockingham's secretary and his spokesman in the Commons: the

Irishman Edmund Burke, one of the greatest political thinkers of the era, who fought a life-long struggle against the abuse of power.

Charles, shy about speaking in the presence of such distinguished orators (despite his magnificent maiden speech, which had earned Whig praise and plaudits), found himself in a quagmire of competing friendships, points-of-view, interests and inclinations. His now-disgraced friend Watson was a staunch and outspoken Whig; his mentor Lord Mansfield was a political rival to his idol Lord Chatham; his wife had Tory affiliations; he himself was a Whig torn between his country estate and the temptations of court favour; he also had a younger brother in the navy who stood to gain financially from war; and still ringing in his ears were the words of Charlotte Somerset: 'I hope you will always Consider yourself as your own man & not be Guided by a Patriotic Finger held up nor yet intimidated by a Ministerial Nod.' The world of high politics was damnably confusing. In the face of the many competing claims on their loyalties over the centuries, it was little wonder that his ancestors reputedly lacked political ambition and tried to avoid taking sides.

As time went by, the bright lustre of Charles's political promise began to dim as his commitment proved inconsistent. His natural indolence and procrastination prevailed, as he chose to observe from the sidelines and eschew hard work or regular attendance in the Commons. Unless one was a minister, the very part-time nature of political life opened the door to distractions, and Charles was a man easily distracted. Art collecting, *soirées*, gambling, and – when in the country – hunting, shooting and fishing all reinforced the emerging view others had of him, of being an 'idle' fellow. He was not that different from many other Whigs in this respect, a perception that damaged their collective reputation as politicians. Charles had an unfortunate tendency to be *intellectually* lazy, with a dislike of the preparation required to make Parliamentary speeches. He had made one impassioned maiden speech, touched as it was by the risk of royal disapprobation: surely that was enough? What more could he do?

Then again, it was also impossible to know how events would evolve in America and whose point of view would be vindicated. The sting of the Declaration of Independence was offset shortly afterwards, in August 1776, by news that General William Howe, supported by his brother Richard's naval fleet, had succeeded in capturing New York and Manhattan. The Howes had reluctantly agreed to serve in America – only on the condition they could also act as peace envoys, though in this respect they were unsuccessful. But in spite of capturing New York, William's military achievements were controversial, for he seemed to have missed several opportunities to ensnare George Washington, who had emerged as the leading American general, appointed by the Second Continental Congress as commander-in-chief of the Continental Army. Described by British commanders in the field as 'the old fox', Washington was a man whose wily qualities were not yet obvious to the government in London. With New York firmly in British hands – as it would remain until the very end of the war – Lord North and his ministers remained hopeful that British might and military professionalism, backed up by the sea power of the Royal Navy, would ultimately prevail.

For a time, this viewpoint seemed to be reinforced by the economic difficulties of the rebels and a general falling-off in morale in both the Congress and the Continental Army. The nadir in rebel fortunes found expression in the pen of Thomas Paine, who was now serving as a volunteer *aide-de-camp* to Major-General Nathanael Greene, Washington's most able subordinate field officer. In a series of tracts entitled *The Crisis*, Paine sought to raise the spirits of the depressed soldiers, beginning with the ringing words 'These are the times that try men's souls' and going on to spur them to greater efforts: 'The summer soldier and the sunshine patriot will, in this crisis, shrink from the service of his country... Tyranny, like Hell, is not easily conquered; yet we have this consolation with us, that the harder the conflict, the more glorious the triumph.'

The run of British successes was undermined at the very end of December 1776, when Washington achieved victories at Trenton and Princeton, inflicting heavy casualties. No one could yet know this would prove a turning point for the rebels, for again, back in Britain, the sting was offset by another illusory success: General Charles Lee, Washington's second-in-command, was captured on 13 December 1776 at Basking Ridge, still in his dressing gown, by a troop of cavalry commanded by the dashing Colonel Banastre Tarleton. Lee was taken to New York as a prisoner. He was heard to remark that 'no-one will be free on the earth and a dark cloud of slavery has covered the whole globe', according to a letter to Charles from Thomas Thoroton junior, son of the old duke's secretary, whose regiment was guarding Lee. The younger Thoroton was able to offer further sidelights on the captive general: 'Lee is at times, very spirited, writes a great deal, and afterwards burns it.' He described how Lee was surprised both to find so many 'gentlemen' among the British soldiers and that they could supply him with something as learned to read as a volume of Tacitus' *History*.

While the British government remained optimistic about American events, Whig hopes of using conciliation to bring about an early end to the war were faltering. The year of 1776 was already a low point for the political opposition, for they had failed to win the support of the British public. Despite the intellect of some of their members, the Whigs could not accept that the American rebels preferred their own interpretations of traditional liberties to those proffered in Britain. In effect, the opposition attacked government policy without producing any real solution of their own that might allay the crisis, and thus they laid themselves open to the charge of engaging in factious quibbling rather than constructive argument. Until the latter part of the war, its British opponents were not coherent, effective or popular. And now, with the capture of New York and then of Charles Lee, it seemed that the government would be vindicated and British military force could win over a 'Foe whom it is plain you can beat, whenever you set yourselves heartily about it'.[12]

The Marquis of Rockingham, however, remained adamant that conciliation was still needed and its pursuit a worthy cause. In gathering all about him who might help change government policy, he turned to the son of his old friend, the late Marquis of Granby. Rockingham now began to exert considerable pressure on Charles, for if he would turn up and vote with the opposition, the young Marquis of Granby could bring like-minded friends and extended family to do likewise. Rockingham wrote a stream of letters trying to persuade Charles to continue the vehement opposition he had so ably expressed in his maiden speech. On one occasion he waited at home all day for Charles, who had promised to call round but then simply failed to show up. Rockingham implored Charles in late October

1776 not to desist from voting with the opposition, saying if he did: 'It would be a horrid damp to all our friends, who rejoiced so sincerely in the expectation of your being the mover of this important & decisive business... My good dear Lord, do not decline this business – on which the hereafter fate of this country may depend.' Professing to be 'now quite exhausted' with his efforts to stir up the opposition, Rockingham, in letter after letter, all but begged Charles to pull his weight: 'The same load is laid upon me. I feel my inability to execute as well as it ought to be, but I find I must.'

Rockingham was, like Charles, a 'high Whig' of vast estates, whose home in South Yorkshire – Wentworth Woodhouse – had more than 300 rooms and the longest country-house façade in Europe. His ministry of the 1760s was said to have been composed mainly of his friends from the turf, 'persons called from the stud into the state, and transformed miraculously out of jockies into ministers'.[13] Yet, though a loyal man who could inspire devotion and reconcile individuals, he never united all those who claimed the label 'Whig'. Charles, though friendly with Rockingham and sharing his interests in hunting and the turf, and patronizing such artists as Stubbs and Gainsborough, was still aligned with Lord Chatham, who at this time was not so active on the political scene. Deliberately standing aloof to show his allegiance, and not wishing to engage fully in the political process in the face of such overwhelming responsibility, Charles resisted Rockingham's pleas.

He was also no doubt further confused by reports he was receiving from the frontline in America. His close family friend Edmund Stevens – the curate's son known as 'Mun' whose Eton fees old Lord Granby had paid – had departed with his regiment in the spring of 1776. Mun had arrived in New York in time to hear reports of George Washington, on the verge of quitting it, threatening to 'lay that beautiful city to ashes'. His letters to Charles were informative; they also supported a growing view, shared even by the Howe brothers, that the rebels were so intent on independence that there was little choice but to intensify military operations *à outrance* or submit to the ambitions of the colonials and grant them independence.

Mun wrote regularly despite the difficult conditions in which he found himself on campaign. 'I am only in a fly tent, and have neither bed, chair, or table; therefore excuse this scrawl, for I have scribbled it upon my knee.' In this war that, in many respects, was one waged *between* Americans, often dividing families, he went on to describe what he called the Patriot rebels' 'barbarous acts of tyranny' inflicted on their fellow countrymen, the Loyalists, who had 'declined entering into their wretched designs and infamous machinations... Many of the worthiest and most respectable men are kept chained down to the ground with scarce victuals to eat, or any change of linen.' Mun knew that his letters might be opened *en route* and had to be careful in what he wrote (and he did not, for example, describe any of the atrocities which were known to have been enacted by British soldiers against the rebels); but his insights must have been a source of further confusion for the indecisive Charles, enmeshed as he was in the contesting arguments.

Knowing that Charles would be interested in his father's old friends, Mun added that General Howe was 'beloved to a great degree by his army' and that Charles Cornwallis, the late Lord Granby's *aide-de-camp* now serving in America, also stood 'in high estimation'. Perhaps it was a relief to Charles Manners to reach the lighter matters at the end of one letter: 'If you have any good ale do send me out a barrel... A Stilton cheese or two and some Cotham Cheeses would be very acceptable.' Presumably the Stiltons were despatched, complete with their maggots.

Mun also asked Charles whether he had 'heard lately of that dear boy Bob'. It was Robert who represented perhaps Charles's greatest dilemma, for to wholeheartedly support those who wished to end the war as rapidly as possible would certainly blight Robert's chances of the rapid promotion and prize-money of which he dreamed.

In the event, Charles prevaricated, the Rockinghamites lost heart, and, though some people remarked that the numerals of the New Year in 1777 bore the ghastly appearance of a row of gallows, the British government awaited with optimism the successful outcome of a grand strategic plan: to divide the rebels by driving a wedge between New England and the middle and southern colonies. General John Burgoyne was to lead a large invasion army southwards from Canada, hoping to meet a similar force marching northwards from New

York City. Even the Whigs grew optimistic: at Almack's club, in June, a 50-guinea bet was placed that the war would be over within two years and that America would remain a colony.[14]

★

While Britain waited for news, Charles typically had other distractions. He could not ignore the worsening plight of his sister, whose marriage, by the spring of 1777, was heading for a divorce, which at that time could only be enabled by an Act of Parliament. Most of the leading daily papers such as the *St James Chronicle*, the *Morning Post* and the *Morning Chronicle*[15] carried regular reports on the Tyrconnel Divorce Bill until it went through in May. But Charles's correspondence of the time was filled with more pleasing matters. Alleyne FitzHerbert, his clever fellow Etonian, had by early 1777 secured a diplomatic post at Brussels in the Austrian Netherlands, and Charles asked him to organize the purchase of a quantity of Tokay, a sweet wine from Hungary. He also asked FitzHerbert to look out for suitable art purchases in conjunction with James Byres, an art dealer based in Rome, whom Mary Isabella had encountered during her Italian travels. Through FitzHerbert and Byres, Charles learned of a series of paintings by Nicholas Poussin that might come up for sale, the *Seven Sacraments*. Executed between 1637 and 1640, they now hung in Rome's Boccapaduli Palace, where they had become required viewing in any gentleman's grand tour.

To Charles's mind, the *Seven Sacraments* were a highly desirable purchase. But he was not the only one who admired them. In March 1777, FitzHerbert had told Charles that having informed Sir Joshua Reynolds of the possibility of their sale, the artist was 'in raptures at the intelligence and persisted in his former opinion that these pictures (besides being a great national object, and consequently worthy of your Lordship's publick spirit) would be, at even 12000 crowns, a most desirable and advantageous purchase… and that in short if you should decline taking them he should be exceedingly happy to buy them himself'. FitzHerbert suggested that Charles should trust Mr Byres and instruct him to bid for them.

Knowing that brother Robert at some stage was heading to Italy, having helped him procure the funds for travelling via Herries & Co.'s circular notes, Charles wrote in April 1777 to ask his brother to visit

Rome and send his opinion on the *Seven Sacraments*. This was the letter that reached Robert too late, only after he had returned to Gibraltar, disillusioned and resolving to return home. In the younger man's eventual reply he regretted being unable to oblige: 'Two of the officers who went [to Rome] saw the same subject not in the Palazzio [*sic*] del Paduli, but in the one of the Palazii [*sic*] di Colonna which were very fine, but not having received your letter till now, I have made no other enquiries & fear I shall not be able, as I intend no longer to defer the pleasure of seeing you.'

In any case, by then there was no point in Robert looking at the Poussins even if he had been able to, for Charles had learned from Byres that Pope Pius VI had forbidden the removal of the pictures from Rome. There was nothing more to be done, and Charles had to accept disappointment – for the time being.

Robert left the *Enterprize* in the autumn of 1777 and made it safely home to England for the longed-for reunion with Charles, there to learn about the indiscretions of their sister Frances. These took yet another turn for the worse in October. Without the family's knowledge, she had suffered a miscarriage (unless the rumours of her pregnancy had been false all along), thrown over her lover Smith and then married the Honourable Philip Leslie, younger brother of a man who had a controversial claim to the title of 'Lord Newark'. The Earl of Mansfield wrote from his home at Kenwood to Charles on 29 October: 'It is bad, thank God it is no worse... I see in the papers they have been married at Canterbury, which I think very likely, because a gentleman who was with me last night when I received the letter said that he, Philip the husband, was in town yesterday sennight [a week ago].' Frances's conduct was sufficient to secure her isolation. In contrast to the affection prevailing between the two brothers, from this time onwards Charles and Robert ostracized their sister, though she continued to receive her due allowance from their parents' marriage settlement along with a tight-fisted second marriage settlement from their grandfather.

★

As Frances's reputation sank, better news arrived from across the Atlantic. William Howe had succeeded in occupying Philadelphia, after beating back Washington at the Battle of Brandywine on 11

September 1777. Yet, despite British feelings of elation at dispossessing the Americans of their seat of the First and Second Continental Congresses, this was scarcely a great victory, for Washington was still at large, and Howe had in fact merely secured winter quarters for his army. Charles, though, felt suddenly motivated to take a more active role at Westminster, following the lead of Lord Chatham who had decided at this moment to re-engage with the political scene. Robert could now observe his brother's attachment to Chatham and his developing friendship with the earl's oldest two sons, John and William Pitt; and Robert was also soon to cross paths – if he had not already – with the youngest son, James Charles Pitt, also a naval midshipman.

Lord Chatham was also corresponding more cordially with Rockingham. Indeed, the prospect of political union between them was growing, as they concurred the war should end before it was too late and before Britain was compelled to recognize the thirteen colonies as an independent nation. Charles was sufficiently stirred by the apparent reconciliation between them to attend the House of Commons and even to make his second-ever speech. On 28 November 1777, he moved the same amendment as did Chatham in the Lords. Describing the war as 'unnatural', Charles insisted that it would only bring calamities upon both Britain and its rebellious colonies, and that the groundwork for an agreement should be laid immediately. He said that the 'point of the sword' had not brought peace and the present moment of continued uncertainty over the success of arms was 'a most proper time for attempting to effect [peace] by a measure of cordiality'. He asked permission to read the amendment, which was 'to advise His Majesty to adopt some measures for accommodating the differences with America by treaty [and] to agree to a cessation of all hostilities; at the same time to assure His Majesty of the determination of his Commons to co-operate with him in every measure that contributed to the re-establishment of peace.' Although the motion failed, by 243 votes to 86, Charles was subsequently regarded by Lord North and others as a potential intermediary in any ministerial overtures to the opposition.

We do not know whether Lord Robert Manners squeezed into the Strangers' Gallery of the Commons to hear his brother; but several men who were there complemented Charles's oratory. The Scots-born

George Johnstone, a post-captain in the Royal Navy and sitting Member for Appleby (in Westmorland) wrote on 29 November: 'I regard your Lordship as a singular example of magnanimity in the present scenes of dissipation, and I consider you like Hercules struggling between Virtue and Pleasure.' Encouraging Charles to speak again, to overcome his phobia of public speaking through practice, he laboured his point. 'I am certain you have all the requirements to become one of the best speakers in the House,' he wrote in flattering tones. 'The manner excellent and manly. The modesty which you dread most captivating. The tones of voice charming and distinct. The argument neat and to the point.' It is hard to judge with hindsight whether Charles spoke so well, for it was in the interests of many to persuade a future powerful duke to attend Parliament more frequently – and Johnstone was an inveterate currier of favour.

There was also praise from Thomas Townshend, a supporter of Chatham, who congratulated Charles 'upon your appearance the first day... you showed the House what you could do, when you come to be in a habit of speaking to them'. He, too, encouraged Charles to speak again, assuring him that with practice he would be very good. But the young marquis was not to be won over. He failed to attend Parliament the following day, drawing a rebuke from Johnstone, who conveyed a vivid image of the verbal sparring Charles had missed:

> I was sorry you did not come to the House the second day. It was by far the best I have seen in the House of Commons. Conway spoke from the heart... Burke attacked Wedderburn with repeated flashes of wit like the forked glare of lightning in a thunder storm under the line. He was shrivelled under it like a blooming tree after a hurricane. [William] Adam spoke wildly, Fox flew at him and overturned both him and his arguments.

Meanwhile, Rockingham never gave up on Charles: 'It has been determined that a motion is to be made in both Houses of Parliament,' he wrote to him with heavy emphasis, 'for fixing a day for taking the state of the nation into consideration,' and he hoped 'your Lordship will be in Town for that day,' adding: 'I had the pleasure of a long & very satisfactory conversation on Saturday last with L[ord] Chatham.' But just days later, the prospect of reconciliation in the opposition ranks was shattered when news of catastrophe reached English shores on 3 December. General Burgoyne had, on 17 October, surrendered his entire army of 6,200 soldiers 9 miles south of Saratoga.[16] The grand strategic plan to seal off New England and divide the rebels had failed. William Howe, in redirecting his own forces the previous month for the taking of Philadelphia, had in fact thus failed to link up with Burgoyne's army marching south. At the same time, Sir Henry Clinton, left in command of New York, had hardly stirred from that city. Isolated, and with supplies and ammunition almost exhausted, Burgoyne found himself trapped by superior rebel forces and was compelled to offer his sword to General Horatio Gates to 'avoid the unnecessary effusion of blood'.

This was a decisive and highly consequential victory for the rebels and a mighty blow to British prestige. The calamity rocked both North's ministry and the opposition. Charles heard from Mun Stevens, who wrote from Philadelphia that 'the probability of conquering [the rebels]... in our present situation appears to me (but this my dear Lord is only for your private ear) altogether chimerical... I never could speak my mind so freely to you before because I never had an opportunity till now of having a letter conveyed to you with safety.'

The Battle of Saratoga destroyed the reconciliation between Chatham and Rockingham, for it brought about a substantial realignment in attitudes towards the colonial crisis. Whigs began to accept the concept of American independence from the British Parliament, though they still hoped to retain some kind of constitutional or imperial connection. Chatham, however, supported by Lord Shelburne, remained unshakeable in his view that the loss of the colonies would expose Britain to a resurgent France.

Happily for Charles, a charming distraction arrived in the form of a baby son. On 4 January 1778, an heir, John Henry Manners, was born. The joy could be shared with the infant's Uncle Robert, who had already been able to form a bond with his fifteen-month-old niece 'Diddle' since his return to England. As for the boy's father, not only was Charles relieved to have an heir, but he threw over preoccupations with the tiresome rebellion across the Atlantic and that same month, at an auction at Christie's, splashed out £211 1s on the purchase of an extremely rare, full-length portrait of Henry VIII, created in the

sixteenth century by Holbein the Younger's circle and based on the artist's great wall-painting of the Tudor royal family in Whitehall Palace.
It was that monarch who had created the first Earl of Rutland in 1525,
and perhaps the arrival of little Lord Roos inspired Charles in his purchase, for the painting added lustre to other reminders of the family's
legacy already in his possession. In the middle of the nation's political
crisis, Charles was appearing to be, as Edmund Burke described the
Whig grandees, one of 'the great oaks that shade a country, and per-
petuate [their] benefits from generation to generation'.

Yet, it would be impossible for Charles to stay diverted for long,
for Saratoga was accompanied by other dramatic developments. The
previous month, the Moroccan sultan, Muhammad III, for whose son
the *Enterprize* had borne presents from Tripoli, had included 'United
States of America' in a list of countries to which Morocco's ports were
open, thus becoming the first nation to publicly recognize the colonists' independence. But this diplomatic flourish by an African despot
paled in significance compared to a threat closer to home. Perceiving
in Burgoyne's defeat a fatal weakening of Great Britain, France also
formally recognized the United States, on 6 February 1778. Thanks
to Congress's envoys, led by Benjamin Franklin, this recognition
was accompanied by a Franco-American Treaty of Alliance. France
could now seek reprisals from its defeat in the Seven Years' War and
openly supply in abundance the arms and money that had hitherto
been covertly provided to assist the American rebels. Shaken by this
dreadful news, which would transform the nature of the conflict, the
Rockingham Whigs prepared a motion for withdrawing the troops
from America, in an effort to prevent war with France.

The prime minister, Lord North, tried to resign – and also to draw
Lord Chatham back into the ministry to manage the war. Even Charles
was caught up in the bickering. North took advantage of the young
marquis as a potential intermediary, sending him to call on Chatham at
home, in Hayes, to convince him that the Rockinghamites would support him if he took office. But the king did not want Chatham in the
ministry and would not budge: 'I am extremely indifferent,' he wrote,
'whether Lord Granby goes or does not go with the abject message of
the Rockingham party this day to Hayes; I will certainly send none to
that place.'[17] North remained in post.

On 7 April 1778, the Whig Duke of Richmond laid bare the truth of the situation as he saw it, in a motion in the House of Lords. In his speech he told his fellow peers that as the rebel Americans could not be defeated, they were already effectively independent and that recognition of this was no more than plain common sense. Britain, he pronounced, could not fight a war against America and France at the same time.

Meanwhile Charles had been seeking Chatham's knowledge and advice. By now, the great man was often too unwell to reply to Charles's letters, with Lady Chatham writing in his stead. Still, the earl summoned the strength to attend the House to make known how he felt: that he could not contemplate the loss of the North American colonies which he had been instrumental in securing during the Seven Years' War. He rose from his seat to counter Richmond's notion of a fait accompli and appealed to his fellow peers to resist Whig proposals and refuse independence to America. Spectators were permitted in the Lords, and Chatham's three sons John, William and James Charles Pitt – the last recently made a lieutenant – were there to support him; but the young Marquis of Granby, Chatham's friend and protégé, was characteristically absent. With a cool irony, Charles Francis Greville, the antiquarian, collector and politician, remarked to Charles that evening: 'I know you are interested in the event of this day's debate. I almost expected it would have secured to us the pleasure of Lady Granbys & of your company.' His next words were sombre:

I now do not regret that you did not attend the H. of Lords as you avoided a very affecting scene which I saw. The D[uke] of R[ichmond] had made his motion. Ld Chatham had answered him & opposed it. He reminded us of the spirit of his country & of its former glory. He treated the idea of submitting to the insults of France as pusillanimous & independence of America not to be admitted at any rate. He spoke about 10 minutes. The D. of Richmond replied & near the conclusion my eyes were on Lord Chatham. I thought he attempted to rise and was feeling in his pocket when to my surprise he fell back in a fit. The House was full and was cleared. He was removed to one of the committee or dressing rooms & the House adjourned for a little.

The ailing Chatham was carried out and taken home to Hayes the following day. He never recovered. Although the young William Pitt asked Charles to visit his father as a 'mark of your attachment to him and of your attention to his family', the marquis did not make the effort, even though Chatham lingered on for over a month. News of his death, on 11 May 1778, fell on the nation as relations with the French grew ever more hostile. Even the many critics of Chatham felt the loss, for there was no man in government who possessed his qualities as a war-leader. Charles Greville further remarked that: 'The minds of individuals are like the nation or like the army in America or like our resources, all capable of great exertions but [descending] into distraction and despondency for want of a leader in whose honesty and spirit the nation can confide.' In a complete change of tone, he then added: 'I should have written to L[ad]y G[ranby] to wish her joy of her star... the opportunity of purchasing diamonds will be frequent as what is once set as a fashion whether it be a knot under the chin or under the ear it will certainly be followed by some.'

Greville apologized for this flippant remark following such a serious subject, but said he was attempting to remain light-hearted, which he believed to be a 'prudent' strategy in the face of yet more bad news: for the threat to England itself was suddenly made manifest, not immediately by the French but rather in the name of the rebel Americans. With a small squadron of privateers provided and fitted-out in France, at French expense, the renegade Scotsman John Paul Jones, who had joined the American cause, descended on the coasts of Cumbria, Kirkcudbright and Wigton in April 1778. After terrorizing White-haven – then a busy port – Jones went on to harry British shipping in a series of depredations, petty enough in themselves, but sufficient to highlight the dangers of economic warfare and stoke fears of invasion.

The result was a stiffening of the national backbone. The traditional means of self-defence, the county militias raised by ballot and commanded by noblemen with homes in the county, were galvanized into action across the entire country. Charles's uncle Lord George Manners-Sutton was responsible for the Nottinghamshire militia, his cousin the Earl of Winchelsea for the Rutlandshire, and his brother-in-law the Duke of Beaufort for the Monmouthshire, while the Duke of Devonshire called out the Derbyshire, and Sir James Lowther the Westmorland militias. The majority of these forces gathered at two main encampments, at Coxheath in Kent and Warley in Essex. Thousands of men trained and slept in primitive conditions, with no sanitary arrangements.

Charles, whose family had long been associated with command of the Leicestershire Militia, was ordered to go with the men to Liverpool, south of Whitehaven, in case John Paul Jones returned or any bold French corsair followed his example. This was an occupation he relished far more than sitting in on Parliamentary debates, for he could don a uniform in emulation of his famous father. Moreover, his commission as a king's officer in command of a county militia came automatically, in contrast to poor Robert's frustrated attempts at promotion. Charles could also take his wife with him, though he planned to leave the baby John Henry in the care of Mary Isabella's mother, the Dowager Duchess of Beaufort.

Now that war with France was almost inevitable, an immense pressure would come to bear on the nation's resources, especially on its manpower. Much of the British army was in North America, but conflict with France would open new theatres of operations – amid the lucrative sugar islands of the Caribbean, for example, where garrisons would require immediate reinforcement, to say nothing of other British outposts such as Gibraltar, or in India, where the French had been competing with the British for years and would be sure to seize on any weakening of imperial defences. Then there was the necessity of protecting the fleets of merchant vessels around the globe, as well as the convoying of troop- and supply-ships and, of course, the defence of the home coast from invasion. To place Britain on such a war footing required an augmentation of the Royal Navy. This responsibility fell upon the Earl of Sandwich in his capacity as First Lord of the Admiralty. He and his colleagues, both in Cabinet and on the Admiralty Board, had to consider another factor: the risk of Spain joining in to seek redress for its own losses of the Seven Years' War. The British fleet would not be able, numerically, to match a combined Franco-Spanish fleet.

At least the prospect of war with France now brought back into the fold those naval officers who were disinclined to serve against their 'fellow-countrymen' in America. George Johnstone summed up the transformed circumstances as he told Members of the Commons that:

As long as the war was a war upon the rights of Americans and upon the liberties and privileges they were entitled to as British subjects, he was determined to decline his most favourite pursuit, that of his [naval] profession, but as soon as France interfered in the contest the nature of it was totally changed. It was not now a war with America but a war with France... the object of which [is] the destruction of England.

Johnstone made his point at a telling moment – on 19 April 1778, the third anniversary of the Battle of Lexington, whose 'first shot' was now truly being heard around the world.

★

For Lord Robert Manners, qualms about serving against the Americans had apparently evaporated in the face of his frustrated ambitions. He was so desperate to find a station with 'honour' that at some point during the winter of 1777–8 he had accepted the opportunity to sail with John Byron's squadron and take up a vacancy in Admiral James Gambier's ship in North America. (Gambier had been, for years, a sycophant of the Manners family.) But once again Robert was to be disappointed for Byron's orders changed and there was no prospect of a passage out. Instead, it seems he spent time with Charles and the family at Belvoir while also travelling to see childhood friends at Scarborough, where he is also thought to have made himself useful to the rapidly expanding Royal Navy by offering his services to the Regulating Captain in charge of the Impress Service, an officer busy pressing fishermen for His Majesty's service: unemployed naval officers were, in effect, happy to connive in this state-sponsored kidnapping of reluctant and hapless victims.

Then, in the new year of 1778, for the first time Charles's Whig connections played into Robert's hands. Another naval officer who had recently agreed to return to active service was the Honourable Augustus Keppel. A Whig and – as a son of the Earl of Albemarle – the scion of a noble house, Keppel fell within the ambit of Robert and Charles, having also been a friend of Lord Granby. He was a familiar figure in London society and was acquainted with a number of Charles's circle, including Sir Joshua Reynolds, whom he had taken to sea in 1749.

Keppel had – unusual even for a naval officer serving in Parliament – become very political, one of Rockingham's right-hand men, and so far had refused to serve.

Keppel now allowed Robert to be entered in the muster book of a ship in Portsmouth so he could include this as sea-time towards his lieutenant's examination, for which he would be eligible in April 1778. As an admiral, Keppel could take midshipmen onto his books at his discretion, although Lord Sandwich knew, and in this instance disapproved of it, for if Robert was not aboard then it was 'false muster'.[18] But the admiral could not offer Robert a confirmed lieutenancy – for this was the First Lord's domain – so instead he most likely pressed hard for a vacancy to be found for the young man. Keppel was known to have plagued Sandwich with incessant demands for promotions for his friends.

By April 1778, Robert was back in Portsmouth, living aboard the ship in which he had been mustered. There, he was so busy that Charles Greville, on a visit to the fleet, remarked to Charles that: 'I attempted in vain to see your brother altho I saw his shipmates.' Within a short time Robert stood before a panel of experienced officers for his examination – and almost six years to the day after first going to sea, received his commission. Now he was no longer Mr Midshipman, but rather Lieutenant Lord Robert Manners of His Britannic Majesty's Royal Navy. His run of bad cards at last seemed to be ending. War with France would mean that honour – and a greater share of prize-money – could be within his grasp.

6

'The oak of old England'

Spring 1778 to August 1778

'The oak of old England'

I n late April 1778, a fleet was gathering at Portsmouth unlike anything Robert had seen before. Described by Charles Greville as 'the glorious sight of 31 ships of the line at Spithead', the anchorage was now crowded with 74-gun ships, in contrast to the handful of guardships normally stationed there. Anticipation rippled through the thousands of assembling sailors, for rumours spoke of the imminent arrival of one of the Royal Navy's only three 'first-rates' – a three-decked ship carrying a hundred guns or more. Greville, for one, was keen to 'encourage patriotic croaking until the Victory arrives at Spithead'.

The *Victory* had been ordered in 1758, the year of Robert's birth, built at Chatham and launched in 1765. She was the finest creation of naval architect Sir Thomas Slade, who, starting out as a shipwright in the Royal Dockyards had, in 1755, been appointed Surveyor of the Navy. His unmatched genius went on to dominate ship designs of the latter part of the century and to produce vessels admirably suited to British strategic requirements. Now, the *Victory* was at last being 'brought forward out of ordinary' after lying unused on the River Medway for thirteen years. The commissioning of a first-rate vessel was an indication of the gravity of the situation facing the country, for the *Victory* was to be the flagship of the senior admiral commanding Great Britain's chief line of defence: the Channel Fleet.

On 13 May 1778, the massive ship arrived at Spithead under the temporary command of Sir John Lindsay, Lord Mansfield's nephew. This was also a significant moment for Robert personally, for on this same day was dated his commission as 6th lieutenant in the 90-gun *Ocean*. He was to serve under the command of Vice Admiral Sir Hugh Palliser, a 'King's Friend', who had for some years sat on Lord Sandwich's Board of Admiralty. Palliser agreed to take Robert in his ship probably to oblige Lord Sandwich, who was under considerable pressure to find a vacancy for the newly made lieutenant, but it may also have been because he had other connections with the Manners family. Palliser was a Member of Parliament for Robert's childhood haunt of Scarborough, where the other seat was held by the Earl of Tyrconnel, still loyal to the family despite his divorce from the now ostracized Frances.

With the *Ocean*, Palliser and Robert were under orders to join forces with the *Victory* and the Channel Fleet, in order to guard the English Channel by cruising off the Île d'Ouessant – or 'Ushant' to generations of British tars. From the waters around this north-western finger of continental Europe, they could keep watch on the French fleet at Brest, ready to fall on it should it venture out – whether for an attempted invasion of England, or bound for North America or the West Indies, or to raid Britain's rich trade with India and the Far East.

The man appointed by George III to command the Channel Fleet from the quarterdeck of the *Victory* was none other than Admiral Augustus Keppel. Although an experienced officer, he had never before commanded a large fleet and had not been to sea for fifteen years, having refused to serve against the Americans. However, his name had continued to rise by seniority on the list of flag-officers, reaching the status of full admiral in late January 1778, when the prospect of war with France prompted his return to sea. Lord Sandwich, with a limited flag list to choose from for major commands, recognized that Keppel was popular with the general public and acknowledged that his strong association with the political opposition should not prevent his being selected as commander-in-chief of the Channel Fleet. In any case, this critical appointment, unlike the North American station, in theory transcended political differences.

Supporting Keppel as subordinate admirals were the Whig Sir Robert Harland and the Tory Palliser, with both of whom he enjoyed a good professional friendship. John Jervis, a later First Lord of the

Admiralty but at this time a post-captain, regarded the appointments with some satisfaction: 'They are tough fellows and will do well,' he wrote to Sir Henry Clinton.[1]

★

The gathering ships that Robert now observed at Spithead may have been a magnificent sight, but the Royal Navy suffered a significant, 'crippling disadvantage'. Keppel had arrived in Portsmouth in March 1778 expecting to see, according to rumours and the assurances of Sandwich, a strong and well-appointed fleet. He was to be disappointed. His correspondence with Sandwich at this time was littered with lamentations, as he considered himself in the 'most anxious and critical situation that ever an officer who had character to preserve was placed in'. Specifically, he found 'only six ships-of-the-line' that were in a fit condition to go to sea. And even these, he remarked, 'on reviewing them with a seaman's eye they gave me no pleasure'.[2]

In the preceding years, Lord Sandwich had failed to persuade his Cabinet colleagues to mobilize full naval strength, because the suppression of the rebel American colonists had been seen mainly as a land-war, with the navy performing a supporting role. Although Sandwich had set in place a new ship-building programme in the early 1770s, the escalation of the war to include France required a rapid 'armament'. The solution was to commission ships such as the *Victory*, whose build had been initiated during the Seven Years' War. Many of those men-of-war had been hurriedly constructed of unseasoned oak sourced in Stettin and Danzig (Gdansk) rather than the oak of the English woodlands that was – at least in the popular imagination – regarded as the essence of the navy's protective strength: Britain's 'wooden-walls'. Sandwich's Board of Admiralty ordered a number of these ships to be brought out 'of ordinary' – to be fitted-out, manned and sent post-haste to join the Channel Fleet.

Given his anti-government disposition, Keppel had some reason to exaggerate the poor state of the ships he found at Spithead; but certainly they left a good deal to be desired, and so too did their manning, for they were mostly well short of the established complements needed for efficient fighting. Also lying offshore was a large West India convoy of 200 ships, some of which had been idly waiting for three months, their departure delayed because the men-of-war assigned to escort them were short of men. This was serious, for the British sugar islands had been cut off from their traditional food supplies, which used to come from the American colonies, creating a famine that the convoy was supposed to alleviate.

Robert's new ship, the *Ocean*, had, like the *Victory*, been ordered in 1758 and came from the drawing board of Sir Thomas Slade. But Robert, in parting company with his previous ship the *Enterprize*, had left behind the compactness of a frigate as well as its dash and *élan*. The *Ocean* by contrast, being a 'second-rate' ship of three decks and ninety guns, was slow and lumbering and consequently more difficult to handle. She had double the number of people aboard – if fully manned a complement of 750 men – and her captain, John Laforey, was a seasoned and experienced officer who had been a post-captain for twenty years. However, on 24 April 1778, with a greater pomp than had greeted Molyneux Shuldham aboard the *Panther*, Vice Admiral Palliser had arrived on board, his flag being hoisted as the guns roared out their salute. Robert now had the satisfaction of serving directly under both a captain of distinction and a flag-officer. His fortunes had taken a turn for the better – though the complications of politics might yet blight him, and he would have to conduct himself with some circumspection.

As Robert settled in, he had the assistance of the faithful John Glover to organize his additional personal effects, including a new uniform. It was the only familial contact he could find time for amid the bustle of preparation, for he had to put off a proposed visit from his 'dearest brother' Charles because, as he hastily scribbled, 'we are taken up in changing ships and much engaged in preparing the ship I am now on board. Therefore I would wish you to defer it till after next Monday... Make someone write a day or two before you come down to John Glover, as I shall be on board.'

The regulation of the *Ocean* was vastly more complex than anything that Robert had yet encountered. As a junior commissioned officer, he would have found himself much put-upon, at the beck and call of anyone senior to himself. Although he would command a division of guns in action and would be the second officer of a watch at sea, for now there were a thousand and one mundane jobs to attend to. There was the loading of stores to be supervised; sails and rigging to be checked; the crew's battle stations to be drawn-up, posted and rehearsed; and small books of flag signals to be copied out carefully and prepared for each officer. And as if all these practicalities were not enough, there were also the all-important forms and ceremonies to be observed, which the Georgian navy considered essential to its tradition and discipline. Then, Robert would also have found himself taking his turn as 'officer-of-the-deck', obliged to hang about the quarterdeck with his telescope and a brace of midshipmen, watching the *Victory*'s rigging for flag signals from the commander-in-chief, Keppel.

No doubt far less dull to a hot-blooded twenty-year-old was his duty to ensure that only legitimate 'wives and sweethearts' came on board, in an effort to forestall the arguably necessary invasion of prostitutes. He was also supposed to check that visiting traders and usurers were licensed, and to keep an eye on the marine sentries. They were tasked with restricting illegal smuggling-in of liquor and preventing desertions facilitated by the bum-boats that flocked among the men-of-war, for no ship could afford to lose crew.

Beset by a dizzying list of duties, obligations and courtesies, Robert's own preferences and desires had to be put aside. No wonder he could not be hospitable towards Charles; besides, what would Charles, the elegant sophisticate, aesthete and ducal scion, make of all this organized confusion? In Robert's eyes, his brother was 'not seaman enough to understand'.

In the wardroom – after the grubby cloth had been drawn and the sentries posted for the night, and after the duty officer had departed for his station wrapped up in his cloak against the dew of the evening – commissioned officers left to the bottle could revert to speculation and gossip – 'scuttlebutt', as the seamen called it. Ruminations on their own futures and chances were a constant obsession, but there was much to discuss, too, about what lay ahead for the Channel Fleet.

No one among them would have been in any doubt about their chief objective: to at least neutralize the French fleet lying in Brest if they could not bring it to action and defeat it. They knew they faced in the French navy – the Marine Royale – a formidable fighting force, strengthened and reorganized since its defeat in the Seven Years' War.

The Minister of the Marine Royale, the Duc de Choiseul, had both money at his disposal and the invaluable services of brilliant and innovative *constructeurs*, a new breed of ship-designers who brought to the French shipyards early scientific attempts to understand hydrostatics and stability. Many French vessels now tended to be longer, narrower and faster sailers than their British counterparts. Other crucial differences existed too. The manning of French ships reflected a less random method than the British expedient of impressment, and the French officer corps was divided into two strands, *les officiers bleu*, who were men from seafaring families and who largely occupied the technical, lower ranks, and *les officiers rouge*, all aristocrats, men bred to arms but with an emphasis on service at sea, producing an able elite. The French aristocracy was larger than the British equivalent, and anyone born into a high-class family had elevated rank in the Marine Royale and an expectation of privilege, in contrast to the Royal Navy's relative meritocracy. The absence of an expanding French middle class ensured that a gulf existed between the two classes of officers, with the lower unable to rise beyond a certain level.

The Marine Royale may have been a daunting opponent, but there was no sense of inferiority among the officers and seamen of the British fleet now gathering. Its ships were of more robust build and its crews were fitter, having spent longer periods at sea after the Seven Years' War, exerting the nation's sea power. And, as Robert had learned on his first transatlantic passage in the *Panther*, the British emphasis on gunnery practice produced superior teamwork for firing formidable broadsides; while supporting this savage advantage lay a superior victualling system, better on-board health and a general ability 'to keep the sea'. When it came to it, the men would fight furiously too, not only to work off a good deal of suppressed libido but because wise captains kept their men fortified with frequent doses of alcohol: it made them passive and active by turns, and the trick was to rouse them at the right moment.

By 31 May 1778, Keppel's Channel Fleet was assembled at St Helens Road: around thirty first-, second- and third-rate ships riding to their anchors, with accompanying cruisers, chiefly frigates, to act as eyes and ears. They formed a community of men and ships, thrown together for now but each with different fortunes ahead. Robert knew a good number among the vessels and their companies. The *Terrible* had been at Spithead when he had first arrived there in 1772. His cousin Evelyn Sutton, with whom he had spent many Christmas holidays at Belvoir, had command of the frigate *Proserpine*, while James Charles Pitt was a lieutenant aboard the 74-gun *Robuste* and Sir John Lindsay had transferred to the 90-gun *Prince George*. Constantine Phipps, now 2nd Baron Mulgrave and a Lord of the Admiralty, was aboard the 74-gun *Courageux* – captured French vessels usually retained their names, thought to serve as a form of intimidation – and being a Yorkshireman had with him the men from Scarborough whom Robert may have helped press into service. One man elsewhere was Mulgrave's midshipman from his 1773 Arctic adventure – Horatio Nelson – who was now a lieutenant chasing American privateers in the West Indies. Also absent from British waters was Vice Admiral Richard 'Black Dick' Howe, who was still in North America.

The attention of the entire country was upon this grand armament, the chief bulwark against the French. Charles Greville expressed something of this when he wrote to Charles Manners with a hint of uncertainty but a good deal of expectation. 'I cannot give you the satisfaction of hearing that the [British] fleet has left St Helens. You have looked often and with anxiety to the clouds in hopes that Keppel or a detachment from the fleet should rouse the spirit of the country and make us feel once more that we are a nation.'

By now, the speculation was not only about the enemy fleet at Brest, for – as Robert could recall when the *Enterprize* tricked a French merchantman into divulging secrets – another fleet was fitting out in Toulon. Intelligence suggested it might soon depart, but British naval resources were stretched too thinly to be able to stop it from leaving the Mediterranean. Once in the Atlantic, the fleet could serve any of France's strategic objectives – whether they be to invade England, or sail westwards to capture Britain's sugar islands, or assist the rebel colonists. Fears were confirmed by 5 June, with the news that the Toulon fleet – comprising twelve ships of the line and four frigates, commanded by the Comte d'Estaing – had left the Mediterranean. Evelyn Sutton in the *Proserpine* trailed the French admiral for almost 300 miles out in the Atlantic to determine his destination, and Sutton's theory was supported by intelligence from the *Enterprize*, arriving from the

Mediterranean: that d'Estaing was steering for North America. The news rang alarm bells in the Admiralty. Nervous that Admiral Howe's small fleet at New York would be overwhelmed, the Board set the Channel Fleet a-buzz with orders for thirteen ships of the line to be detached to chase the French. Four days later, a hurriedly assembled squadron set off westwards, under 'Foul-Weather Jack' – Vice Admiral John Byron, who seemed plagued by encounters with rough seas.

Splitting the Channel Fleet, however, created a dangerous gap in Britain's home defences. Lord Sandwich had long argued with Lord Germain that more ships should be available in home waters; he had only got his way with the entry of France into the war. But detaching Byron's ships annulled his hard-won advantage, and Keppel now feared being outnumbered by the French fleet at Brest. The loss of men was serious, too, prompting an embargo upon all merchant shipping and the imposition of a 'hot press'. The measures were so rigorous that even the market-boats between Portsmouth and the Isle of Wight were kept in harbour. The ports were scoured for seamen, who were forcibly clapped under the gratings of the press-tenders and sent off to Spithead to be bent to the will of the king's service. Drafts of angry, demoralized and resentful seamen and landsmen arrived aboard the *Ocean* and her sister ships, to be flogged, cajoled or led to their duty by young men like Robert Manners.

★

At the end of May 1778, Robert had told Charles that 'there seems little appearance of our leaving this place'. But only three days after Byron's departure on 9 June, Keppel, with twenty-one ships of the line remaining to him, ordered his fleet to weigh anchor. Throwing out a cloud of frigates ahead, Keppel made his way to the westward with orders to cruise off Brest, to prevent any further French ships from Toulon linking up with the twenty ships of the line thought to be fitted out at Brest, and to attack any that they might encounter.

Hearts raced in the Channel Fleet when, on 17 June, two French frigates were sighted, the *Licorne* and *Pallas*. Keppel sent two British frigates to capture them and prevent their carrying news of his position to Brest. That same day, the French frigate *Belle Poule* was also sighted, and ordered to heave-to. The French captain refused to comply, and a sharp action ensued involving the British frigate *Arethusa*. The *Belle Poule* escaped capture, though their spat was significant in other ways: it represented the first shots fired in anger, and thus formalized the start of the new war with France. From papers taken from the captured frigates, Keppel learned that the fleet at Brest now numbered thirty-two vessels, considerably larger than the Channel Fleet – intelligence that rattled him. On 21 June, his fleet turned for home, Keppel invoking the clause in his orders that allowed him to retire to the shelter of the Isle of Wight if he was confronted by a superior force.

The return of Keppel's ships after so short and unsatisfactory a cruise caused consternation. There was fear in London that an unexpected convoy arriving from the West Indies convoy was now inadequately protected, and the government was inundated with complaints from the influential merchants – the 'West India Interest' – upon whose support much of the war-effort depended. The country had looked forward, with much expectation, to an outstanding success at sea to bolster its morale after the calamity of Saratoga on land; but it seemed that Keppel's fleet had come home with its tail between its legs. This

Admiral Augustus Keppel, 1st Viscount Keppel (1725–86):
portrait bust by Guiseppe Ceracchi (1779) at Belvoir Castle.

general ill-feeling was deepened by the newspapers, which inveighed against the ministry and mooted the possibility of a French invasion. With war now on the doorstep and 'a *Gazette* every morning at breakfast', tension was growing between the different interests.[3]

Taking up the anchorage once again at St Helens Road, Keppel demanded further reinforcements, while the ships' companies waited in suspense in windless and hazy conditions. An air of foreboding prevailed, which was not conducive to good order: two members of the *Ocean*'s company were punished for being mutinous. Gradually, more ships arrived from the Medway, bringing Keppel's fleet closer to parity with the French. One of these was the brand-new 90-gun second-rate *Formidable*, into which Sir Hugh Palliser shifted his flag. Seeing their admiral departing to another ship must have been something of a dampener to the inhabitants of the *Ocean*'s wardroom.

For Robert and his fellow officers, returning to the anchorage meant exposure to the political turmoil and to the glare of the nation's hope invested in them. At the same time, each man also had his private concerns to catch up on. Robert learned that his sister-in-law had miscarried, five months after the birth of John Henry, and that his niece 'Diddle' was dangerously ill following an inoculation against smallpox. At this time, Charles and his wife were at Cheveley, preparing to go to Liverpool with the Leicestershire Militia, and John Henry, 'Lord Roos', had been placed in the care of Mary Isabella's mother and her niece, Elizabeth Compton, with whom she had travelled extensively in Italy. It was an arrangement that appeared to work, for Elizabeth told her aunt: 'Roos I am sure knows me already and is really fond of us both, now when one says "Roos kiss me", he directly puts out his dear little head and does nothing but crow, laugh and jumps.' The trio were staying in Brighton, from where Elizabeth wrote regularly, dreading her aunt's departure to Liverpool, which she considered 'the other end of the world from us', and wishing instead that 'the miserable nasty Lord Amherst' would send them 'to Bristol instead of Liverpool', concluding 'it really is horrid'.

Like other women of her class, Elizabeth spent her days absorbed in 'genteel' pursuits such as embroidery, sharing the details with Mary Isabella: 'Lady Katherine Pelham insisted upon my giving her that frightful scarlet and blue purse[,] however I intend to work her a most magnificent one by next winter.' Yet she was aware of the national mood and would walk or ride to a 'sea seat' on the cliffs each day to observe any ships going by. The news had reached her at Brighton that the Channel Fleet was waiting at St Helens ready to set sail again, and, though she could not see it from so far to the east, she looked for the ships on the horizon and echoed many when she remarked to Mary Isabella: 'I think it is dreadful that Admiral Keppel and the sailors go out so desperate, for the French can never conquer them, so that they might be rather cooler.' Still, she was worried for Robert and other serving family members: 'It is really dreadful to think so many must infallibly fall, we really talk of nothing but your family and the fleet and we constantly drink their success in every undertaking and your healths first and then the fleet in bumpers.'

★

Elizabeth could not know that on the very day she was writing this, 8 July, the French fleet was sailing out of Brest: thirty-two ships of the line commanded by Vice Admiral Comte d'Orvilliers. However, the intelligence soon reached England, along with the detail that a French aristocrat well known to the British aristocracy, the Duc de Chartres, was aboard one of the ships. The following day, Keppel in the *Victory* – with twenty-nine other British ships of the line – departed from St Helens. Although Keppel's fleet was outnumbered, it was thought that several of d'Orvilliers's ships were smaller men-of-war and thus that the combined power of the British ships' gunfire would 'throw a greater weight of metal'. Keppel was determined to force an action on the French – if only he could find them.

The news of the second departure of the Channel Fleet reignited hopes of a swift and decisive victory. But, as the 'excessively hot' days passed with the constant threat of thunderstorms, no word of any action came ashore with Keppel's dispatches. Elizabeth Compton, looking out to sea in vain for a sign of the fleet, told Mary Isabella on 22 July that 'our toast was, that the French fleet with M. de Chartres may be towing into Portsmouth Harbour and that success may always attend the British fleet'. Then, with nothing else of substance to report, she flitted back to more frivolous concerns: 'the sea looked quite desolate yesterday. I bathed this morning[,] there was quite an assembly[,]

I shall have my [bathing] machine on Tuesday I saw it today and it is indeed very comfortable… I think a buff satin petticoat with a purple fringe would be very pretty with my shawl, do you my dear girl?' She added some fulsome praise of John Henry: 'Your angelic little boy is a great comfort to me… he has been saying mama mama bababa all the morning and is in perfect health, good humour and spirits.'

While Elizabeth and Mary Isabella exchanged charming pleasantries, and Diddle's recovery was assured, Robert and his fellows were in a grimmer situation. The knowledge that the French were at sea sharpened their mood, and they had Keppel's new 'order of battle' for his expanded fleet to consider. Robert would at last see in practice what he had learned only in theory for the past six years. Each line-of-battle ship was allocated a station in the van (front), centre or rear division of a 'line ahead' – which meant that they would lie roughly two-tenths of a nautical mile apart in a bow-to-stern configuration. A fleet of thirty ships could thus be strung out over 5 miles. A line that was formed in this way protected the vulnerable ends of each vessel while presenting the maximum number of guns to fire broadsides at the enemy, who was expected to pass in a parallel line going in the opposite direction.

Lieutenant Manners had been diligent in his studies, and in common with his fellow officers he was familiar with *The General Printed Sailing and Fighting Instructions*, which had been largely unchanged for almost a hundred years. To these, most flag-officers added handwritten 'Additional Instructions', containing their own modifications to suit the varying circumstances they considered might apply. Robert would have appreciated that the *Instructions* allowed little room for individual initiative; even though the traditional line ahead tended to produce inconclusive results. Decisive actions were usually brought about only by overwhelming superiority, hence Keppel's previous unwillingness to meet an enemy force a third larger than his own. Unorthodox manoeuvres (such as Hawke's at Quiberon Bay in 1759) were considered acceptable only in exceptional circumstances, when some condition favoured a sudden departure from convention.

In any case, once an action had begun, attention would be fully absorbed by the extraordinary co-ordination required to manoeuvre these great ships in company and to maintain station under sail. Vital to success were the skill and fighting spirit of individual captains and their sailing-masters, all of which hinged upon their collective coolness under fire. As a general rule, the larger the ship, the more difficult she was to handle, and the three-decked first-rate vessels were notoriously mule-headed – though there were exceptions like the *Victory* herself, which was said by her admirers to behave like a frigate. Such manoeuvrable ships of the line were rare, however, and collisions were not uncommon, especially once masts and sails had been shot away or the concussion of hundreds of cannon had destroyed a light breeze so that ships drifted aimlessly, becalmed.

Then, there was the additional complication of needing enough hands to fire the guns as well as to handle the sails. The favoured, but by no means standard, tactic of the French was to engage from the downwind (leeward) side of the opponent, aiming their guns high as they fired bar- and chain-shot, to disable the rigging of the enemy ships and make them unmanageable. In contrast, the British preferred the upwind (windward) position so they could fire low and land cannon balls 'between wind and water' to smash the hulls of the enemy, kill as many enemy sailors as possible and board the ship when the moment was right. Aggressive British tactics were, to some extent, spurred on by the thought of prize-money. The ideal action consisted of beating a target ship into quick submission and compelling her to strike her colours to be taken 'in prize', which could happen in single-ship duels or in the heat and thunder of a fleet action. But victory was never certain, and much depended upon the relative positions of the fleets, the strength of the wind and the prevailing sea conditions.

Amid such exacting circumstances, Robert, as a lieutenant, would be one of the officers supervising the gun-decks; but he might also have to stand a turn on the quarterdeck with a brace of midshipmen with codebooks, to read, decipher and acknowledge signals from the commander-in-chief's flagship – signals such as 'form line of battle', 'general chase', 'the fleet will tack in succession' or 'engage the enemy more closely'. The ultimate flag signal was the 'striking' – the hauling down – of the ship's ensign or colours to signify surrender. Although signals were not yet standardized, a remarkably sophisticated system existed, which comprised gunfire, lanterns and flags. The *Ocean* herself had over thirty flag-halyards, comprising nearly 6,000 feet of rope with which to hoist flags in different combinations. But even with the

provision of frigates stationed at intervals to repeat signals, the successful transmission of alterations to a battle-plan during action might
be well-nigh impossible. Flags obscured by gun-smoke, or hanging
limp in calm or wet weather, led to uncertainty and confusion; and
yet accurate observation of signals was vital, for those captains who
failed to respond adequately might risk professional humiliation or
even the firing squad.

As the prospect of putting long years of study into practice now ran
in Robert's mind, Keppel's fleet of thirty line-of-battle ships, including
seven three-deckers, proceeded in search of d'Orvilliers. The summer
weather made its own unseasonal contributions. For two miserable
weeks, thunder and lightning, fog and drizzling rain alternated with
gales and squalls. Frigates were sent to scout in different directions,
but there was no knowing where, or even whether, they would find
the enemy fleet. And then, on 23 July, about 100 miles west of Ushant,
excitement rippled through the ships' companies as a large group of
strange sails came in sight through the murk. Soon, thirty-two ships
came into view. D'Orvilliers had been found.

It was too late in the day to force an action, so Keppel kept his fleet
facing south-west during the night, with the wind from the west-north-
west. Using deep-sea lead-lines armed with tallow, which revealed
some 500 feet of water below them and a sea-bed of coarse sand and
broken shells, the ships' sailing masters could ascertain their rough
location in relation to the coast. The following morning, as first light
dawned, they realized the French fleet had sailed straight past them in
the dark of night and now had the windward position; but were cut
off from Brest, except for two vessels which remained to leeward and
which promptly made off in the direction of their base-port.

The British lookouts soon saw the *Victory* hoist the signal for the
fleet to form the line of battle. This meant they now had to manoeuvre into their prescribed stations within the three divisions each of
ten sail of the line. Keppel, as commander-in-chief, took the middle
position of the centre division. He was also an 'Admiral of the Blue',
which referred to his seniority relative to the Royal Navy's tripartite
hierarchy, expressed in colours rising from blue through white to red
within each rank of rear, vice and full admiral. Thus, he flew a blue
flag from the *Victory*'s mainmast, with each of the other ships of the

centre flying blue ensigns from their mizzen peaks to indicate they were in his division. Commanding the van was 'Vice Admiral of the Red', Sir Robert Harland, whose red flag flew from the foremast of the 90-gun Queen, while 'Vice Admiral of the Blue', Sir Hugh Palliser, being more junior, commanded the rear division and flew his blue flag from the foremast of the *Formidable*.

The *Formidable* took the middle position of the rear ten ships; ahead of her was Captain Alexander Hood in the *Robuste*, with Lieutenant James Charles Pitt aboard, and behind her was the *Ocean*, making Robert's ship the fifth from the very tail of the British formation. A ship called the *America* was in the line behind Robert, with a Lieutenant Thomas Foley aboard (a man destined for a distinguished career), followed by Captain Bickerton in the *Terrible* and Captain Allen in the *Egmont*. All flew blue ensigns to show they were under Palliser's flag.

Out on the unengaged side of the British line were the fleet's six cruisers – two small fire-ships and four frigates, including two sixth-rate 28-gun frigates the *Proserpine* and the *Fox*, commanded by Evelyn Sutton and Thomas Windsor respectively – stationed ready to relay signals within the fleet.

Their French adversaries, also in three divisions, included in the centre (white division) the 110-gun *Bretagne* (Comte d'Orvilliers's ship) with the 90-gun *Ville de Paris* (under the Marquis de Guichen) and the 74-gun *Fendant* (under the Marquis de Vaudrieul). The van (white and blue division) was commanded by the Comte du Chaffault in the 80-gun *Couronne*, while in the rear (blue division) was the Duc de Chartres in the 80-gun *Saint-Esprit*. In a 74-gun ship also named *Robuste* was the Comte de Grasse, who would loom large in the French – and British – naval story, and in Robert's as well.

As acknowledgements of Keppel's signal to form the line ran up the flag-halyards and the marine drummer on each ship beat his snare drum to send the ships' companies to battle stations, each man-of-war was transformed. With a quickening of heartbeats, seamen removed the bulkheads normally subdividing the lower decks. Some of these were hinged wooden panels, others no more than canvas screens, but their absence revealed the ships for what they really were: great floating batteries, their now unimpeded decks lined with cannon. The *Ocean's* upper deck bore fifteen 12-pounders on each side, her middle gun-deck

ORDER OF BATTLE, as it stood 27th July 1778.

LINE OF BATTLE, 27th July 1778.

The Monarch to lead with the Starboard, and the Ramillies with the Larboard Tacks on board.

Frigates.	Rates.	Ships.	Commanders.	Guns	Men.	Division.
	3	Monarch,	Captain Rowley,	74	600	
		Hector,	Sir John Hamilton, Bart.	74	600	
		Centaur,	Captain Cosby,	74	600	
		Exeter,	Captain Nott,	64	500	
	2	Duke,	Captain Brereton,	90	750	
		Queen,	Sir Robert Harland, Bart. } Captain Prescott,	90	772	Vice-Admiral of the Red.
Fox, 28 Guns,	3	Shrewsbury,	Captain Ross,	74	600	
		Cumberland,	Captain Peyton,	74	600	
		Berwick,	Hon. Keith Stewart,	74	600	
		Stirling Castle,	Sir Charles Douglas, Bart.	64	500	
		Courageux,	Right Hon. Lord Mulgrave,	74	600	
		Thunderer,	Hon. Captain Walsingham,	74	600	
		Vigilant,	Captain Kingsmill	64	500	
	2	Sandwich,	Captain Edwards,	90	750	
	3	Valiant,	Hon. John Leveson Gower,	74	650	
Arethusa, } to repeat 32 Guns, } Signals,	1	VICTORY,	Hon. AUGUSTUS KEPPEL, Rear Admiral Campbell, 1st Captain to the Admiral, Captain Faulknor,	100	894	Admiral of the Blue and Commander in Chief, &c.
Proserpine, 28 G.	3	Foudroyant,	Captain Jervis,	80	650	
	2	Prince George,	Sir John Lindsay, K. B.	90	750	
Vulcan, } Fire- Pluto, } ships,	3	Bienfaisant,	Captain Macbride,	64	500	
		Vengeance,	Captain Clements,	74	600	
		Worcester,	Captain Robinson,	64	500	
		Elizabeth,	Hon. Frederick Maitland,	74	600	
		Defiance,	Captain Goodall,	64	500	
		Robuste,	Captain Hood,	74	600	
Milford, 28 Guns,	2	Formidable,	Sir Hugh Palliser, Bart. } Captain Bazeley,	90	772	Vice-Admiral of the Blue.
		Ocean,	Captain Laforey,	90	750	
	3	America,	Right Hon. Lord Longford,	64	500	
		Terrible,	Sir Richard Bickerton, Bart.	74	600	
		Egmont,	Captain Allen,	74	600	
		Ramillies,	Captain Digby,	74	600	

A contemporary copy of Admiral Keppel's order of battle, 27 July 1778.

fifteen 18-pounders and her lower gun-deck fourteen 32-pounders. She could, in total, throw a broadside of 900 pounds of iron – even more, if the guns were double-shotted with two cannon balls in each barrel for maximum effect at close range.

For protection, nets were spread to prevent damaged spars from falling onto the men below, and boats were put over the side to clear the decks and reduce the risk of wounding sailors through wood splinters. Precautions against fire were taken by strewing the decks with wet sand and by rigging wet blankets, cloths and frieze screens around the hatchways, while the galley fire was doused. Eventually came the thunderous rumble as the great guns, charged and shotted, were run out through the gun-ports as Keppel's fleet bared its teeth.

A strange silence then fell upon each ship as the hands waited at their stations. On deck and aloft, men watched for orders to brace the yards and trim the sails, while others with small-arms, led by a midshipman, were stationed up the masts, ready to pick off enemy officers. On the upper-deck the marines were lined up beside the hammock nettings, their muskets loaded and primed. The captain, 1st lieutenant and master strode the quarter deck, keeping their eyes on the progress of the ship and their attention on maintaining her station; accompanying them were the signalling party plus a midshipman or two to act as runners ('doggies'). On the lower gun-decks stood the lieutenants including Robert, each standing behind his division of guns, his sword drawn, while the gun-crews knelt alongside their pieces. Even lower in the ship, below the waterline in the cockpit, the surgeon and his mates prepared for the gruesome task that lay ahead; and in the ship's very bowels was the gunner in his felt shoes, positioned within the copper-lined magazine, making up cartridges and passing them through the heavy felt curtains to the boys – the 'powder monkeys' – who stood ready with their wooden boxes to carry them to the guns.

★

Such an anticipatory state on that day should have led to the opening of fire and the culmination of the disciplined 'exercises with the great guns'. But what transpired was a complete damp-squib: Keppel's attempts to bring the French to battle by sending after the two retreating frigates failed to tempt d'Orvilliers to engage. For three days

thereafter, Keppel pursued the French fleet in wet and squally conditions, watching for a chance to force them into battle. The two fleets
manoeuvred in sight of each other, but the wariness of the French
admiral baffled his antagonist's efforts to sail within range, and all the
while their crews kept at general quarters. With the ships still cleared
for action, men slept beside their guns, ate cold food and lent a hand
on deck or aloft if occasion demanded.

As dawn broke on Monday 27 July, Captain Laforey in the *Ocean*
observed that the French fleet, which now appeared to number
twenty-seven sails, still showed no more intention of battle. By this
time, the two fleets were about 6 miles apart, both heading north with
the wind from the south-west. However, d'Orvilliers's ships were in
line ahead, while Keppel's three divisions were at that moment in a
rough line abreast. Harland's van lay spread out for 4 miles to port of
the *Victory*, and Palliser's rear extended 3 miles to starboard. Thus the
British fleet effectively formed the horizontal of a capital 'L', while the
French formed the vertical ascender.

In his efforts to bring the French into action, Keppel was not over-fin-
icky about the British formation. He kept the signal for 'general chase'
flying, confident that he could count on his captains to form the line
ahead as best they could if and when the enemy could be engaged.
Even so, several of the slower sailers among Palliser's rear division
were falling astern, and at five o'clock in the morning the *Victory* signalled that seven of Palliser's 74-gun ships – faster than the heavier
Formidable and *Ocean* – should make more sail and press ahead ready to
support the centre if an opportunity for action arose. As the remainder
of Palliser's division tried to catch up, Laforey in the *Ocean* judiciously
ordered the serving of wine to his men, the ship having run out of
small-beer. Meanwhile, low, heavy clouds began to obscure the French
fleet from view.

The morning wore on ponderously, and at around eleven o'clock,
after a thick shower of squally rain had hidden for forty-five minutes
the movement of the opponents from each other, the visibility cleared
to reveal the two fleets now in a position to form their lines and pass
in opposite directions. The French, in the windward position and still
heading roughly north, jostled into a ragged line, having reversed their

order so that their rear was now their van. The British van and centre, now heading southwards in the less-favoured leeward position, were in a similarly disordered configuration. Their station-keeping was hindered by the squalls and wind shifts, so much so that the hoisting of battle-ensigns was delayed – these being large and expensive, and therefore held in reserve given the conditions. The ships in the rear had muddled their stations in the line and were somewhat detached, but, owing to Keppel's signal to chase, were still in a good position to thwart d'Orvilliers's line of advance. Keppel now hoisted the signal for action, as prescribed in the *Fighting Instructions*: 'As soon as the admiral shall hoist a red flag on the flagstaff at the foretopmast-head, every ship in the fleet is to use their utmost endeavour to engage the enemy, in the order the admiral has prescribed unto them.' As the large flag rose up the *Victory*'s halyards and the signal was repeated by the accompanying frigates and the flagships of Harland and Palliser, a cheer accompanied the bright flutter of newly-hoisted blue and red battle-ensigns, presenting a contrast to the plain white of the ensigns flown by the French (in this pre-revolutionary Bourbon period).

The two fleets surged towards each other: but the leading ships of Harland's van barely came within range before they had passed by the enemy van. By about noon, the *Victory* herself was at last close enough to open fire on the *Bretagne* and then on the *Ville de Paris*. The other ships of the centre division were now in range too; at one moment the British *Courageux*, with the impressed Scarborough fishermen among her company, appeared to be on a collision course with a French ship. 'Never fear,' said her captain, Lord Mulgrave, directing the master to stand on; 'give him the stem; the oak of old England will be too hard for the Frenchman.'[4] It was said the French ship bore away in fear, while the British van and centre rapidly passed the main enemy formation, leaving Palliser's rear division, the *Ocean* amongst them, to run the gauntlet and take the brunt of the French punishment.

As 6th lieutenant, Robert shared command of the lower-deck gun batteries with the 2nd lieutenant, supported by a brace of master's mates and a couple of midshipmen. At first, the two officers peered from an open gun-port to gauge the progress of events. Their men were quiet and ready at their loaded pieces, the decks beneath their feet wet and sanded, their heads bound with kerchiefs to stop the sweat running into their eyes and to prevent their eardrums from being perforated by the concussion. The guns were traversed with handspikes, ready to open fire with one shattering, simultaneous and demoralizing broadside when the word came. Robert and the other lieutenants conferred, passing their instructions to the gun-captains who waited, with smoking linstocks, as the tension mounted. The guns were double-shotted for maximum effect.

When the crucial order came and action was joined, the *Ocean*'s gun-crews plied their monstrous artillery with all the vigour they could muster, under the bellowed encouragement of their officers. The lower decks became a living hell of cacophonous noise and reverberation, the huge guns rumbling as they were driven backwards by the recoil, the smoke from their muzzles filling the now-reeking air. Gun-captains shouted as their crews went through the routine of worming, sponging and loading cartridge and ball, then hauling the monstrous pieces back up to the gun-ports as fast as they could to inflict the maximum punishment upon the passing enemy. After the first broadside, it was up to the lieutenants to make the best use of the opportunity – letting the faster crews fire as effectively as possible, or reining them in to fire in subdivisions, while keeping an eye on the supply of powder and shot. They dragged men hit by splinters, or with bare toes crushed under a recoiling gun-carriage, out of the way, and sent for middies to help with the wounded. Amid such noise, smoke and the flare of detonation, the gun-deck grew darker and men became automata, in thrall to the drills they had so often practised.

The *Ocean* lay in a tight position ahead of the *Formidable* and astern of the *Egmont*. Robert would hardly have been aware on his lower deck that the ship could barely hold her station, Captain Laforey later remarking: 'The distance between [the *Formidable* and the *Egmont*] was so short that it was with difficulty I could keep betwixt them to engage without firing upon them, and I was once very near on board the *Egmont*' – he almost ran into her stern. Indeed, the position of the *Ocean* forced the *Formidable* to 'back her mizzen topsail' – the nearest a sailing-ship could do by way of braking her forward motion. This caused the next ship astern, the 74-gun *Elizabeth*, to sheer away as she, in turn, almost ran into Palliser's flagship. Simultaneously, the *Formidable*'s Captain Bazely was obliged 'to bear up to one of the enemy's ships' to avoid a collision, the two passing so close that the Frenchman's bowsprit was within a few feet of the flagship's huge main topsail.

The closing of the two fleets, so ponderous at first, seemed to accelerate with the diminishing distance between them, giving the gunners – kept for so long in suspense – only a few minutes to wreak whatever havoc was possible. Nor were the French idle. They poured bar-shot, chain-shot and 'langridge' – metal cases filled with ragged pieces of scrap iron – towards the British sails and rigging. But since the French ships lay to windward, many of their projectiles flew low, causing hull damage among Palliser's rear division.

The action was brief, confused and much hampered by smoke, for the captains feared aiming at the wrong ships. The *Ocean* ceased firing around one-thirty in the afternoon as she had now passed the French fleet. Her foretopmast had been badly splintered by 'double-headed shot', and in her wake a number of other ships, their rigging crippled by the French, were no longer in the line, their crews frantically 'knotting and splicing' to repair the damage. Near to the *Ocean* lay the *Terrible*, leaking badly with 'five holes shot between wind and water'.

Meanwhile to the south, anticipating Keppel's wishes, Harland had turned the van of the Channel Fleet northwards in the wake of the French, while Keppel's centre followed suit. But the *Victory*'s rigging was so cut up that valuable time and ground were lost in the manoeuvres. By the time she was heading in the right direction, it was two o'clock in the afternoon and the British were in such disarray that Keppel hauled down the signal for close action and re-hoisted the order for forming the line of battle.

With the enemy now out of range, the priority was for Keppel to re-form and concentrate his fleet, for it seemed d'Orvilliers might return and close in to snatch a victory over the British. Keppel, informed of the French manoeuvres by lookouts, kept the line-of-battle signal flying but then turned his own ship, the *Victory*, back round to the southwards. His intention was to draw the fleet together to protect a group of five still-disabled men-of-war to the south-east, the loss of which would be catastrophic. Meanwhile he ordered Sir Robert

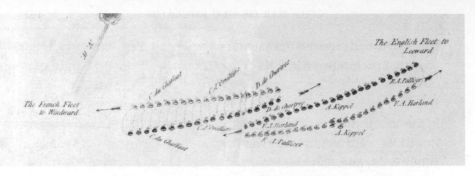

A contemporary depiction of manoeuvres at the Battle of Ushant, 27 July 1778.

Harland's van to cover the rear until Palliser's ships, now some way to the north-west, could make sail and follow the *Victory*. The British fleet's situation was critical, though the French were not yet pressing the feared attack. At about five o'clock, Keppel ordered Harland to resume his station ahead and despatched the frigate *Fox* to summon Palliser to assume his position in the rear of the fleet with all despatch.

Yet, what happened next caused great confusion among the whole fleet, not least among the ships of the rear division. Palliser ignored the message, making no move to obey. Robert, along with all those in the *Ocean*, had seen Keppel's signal for the line, but protocol dictated they wait for a signal from their own divisional commander – which never came. By seven o'clock that evening, a frustrated Keppel went to the unusual expedient of individually summoning each of the other ships in Palliser's division by its number to join his flag, even though, with the deteriorating light, d'Orvilliers had still not pressed home his advantage. At twilight, Palliser's ships, including the *Ocean*, deserted him and took station astern of the *Victory*, as the onset of night drew a veil over the darkening sea. Beset by 'fresh gales' which were 'squally with rain most part of the night and exceeding dark', those aboard the *Ocean* struggled manfully to repair their ship while keeping station astern of the *Victory*'s lanterns.

Everyone expected to re-engage at dawn. But to their 'great surprise, at daylight… found the whole French fleet had stole away under cover of a dark night, except three sail which remained in sight and immediately crowded all the sail they could to the southward'. Far away in the south-east quarter, the rest of the fleet was just visible, but Keppel's ships were in no condition to pursue. It was clear that the enemy, though they had failed to press matters when they had an advantage, had received the least damage from the encounter and had acquitted themselves admirably – to the dismay of the British.

★

In the aftermath of battle, Keppel took his battered fleet to the closest Royal Dockyard on England's south coast, reaching Plymouth Sound by 31 July. A day later, Charles Manners' friend Antony Lucas thoughtfully sent a few lines to Belvoir – where the marquis had stopped briefly *en route* to Liverpool – relating what he knew of the battle, including that 133 British sailors had been killed. His understanding was still somewhat muddled. Lucas was unaware that Robert had been caught in the heaviest action in the rear division, instead telling Charles: 'Knowing of your anxiety for Mr Manners, I should have been happy to have sent you further particulars but I hope you may rest easy on his account, as it appears the engagement was with Harland's [van] division.' To Charles's profound relief, he received shortly afterwards a letter from Robert himself. Given that the battle had been the newly made lieutenant's first fleet action, Robert was oddly low-key about it, though it was soon clear why: it had, truth be told, been a disappointment:

> My dear Brother, The fleet is just arrived tho' not in a very good condition, but as the purpose of this letter is only to express my hopes that you are well & to inform you that I am so. I shall refer you to Ad. Keppels letter for the particulars of the engagement. I shall only say that we have not brought in Monsr de Chartres & it was more a skirmish than an action... We find the people at this place [Plymouth] highly exasperated against us for not doing more. I wait impatiently for a letter from you, direct to me *Ocean* Plymouth. Pray give my love and compliments to L^y Granby. I will take an opportunity of informing you more of the matter. I am your affectionate Brother Robt: Manners

The Marquis of Rockingham was also thinking of Charles's affection for Robert when he told him he had heard from one of the captains that 'your brother is very well'. However, unsurprisingly his letter continued in a political vein: 'The French ships were well beat tho' we have no trophies. The ministers and publick are dispirited because they expected that we were at least to take half of the French fleet.'

Despite the consternation that met the returning fleet, in the days following it was agreed that the navy had done all it could. Rockingham told Charles that 'all the seafolks who know the circumstances are all satisfied that our friend Admiral Keppel has acted with great ability and great spirit'. There were no calls for Keppel to be court-martialled in the manner of Admiral Byng, especially as it transpired that d'Orvilliers's reticence in pressing his advantage reflected instructions from France's foreign minister, the Comte de Vergennes, to avoid action if possible and focus on protecting commercial shipping in European waters, so as to preserve the French sail of the line for future ambitions. (The French, at this time, regarded completion of a mission as more important than battle or victory, and fought only if it was necessary to attain the object of an operation.) In turn, Keppel praised his men and officers on their conduct, and, with considerable forbearance, he did not challenge Palliser as to why he had ignored the signals and thus prevented the fleet from renewing the action.

Antony Lucas may have been wrong in thinking Harland's division had been in the thick of the fighting, but he had been correct about the number of men lost, to which he might have added a further 373 wounded. Although French casualties were heavier, at 161 killed and 513 wounded, the French fleet had inflicted greater damage. So, though strategically indecisive, the Battle of Ushant – as it became known – proved a moral victory for the French, for d'Orvilliers's better-prepared fleet had humiliated Britain's hastily assembled foremost defensive asset. In Britain, the national situation appeared little improved. All energies at Plymouth were thus employed in refitting the fleet for sea, for it was essential that the English Channel was not left unguarded for long. Keppel and Palliser worked around the clock to hurry repairs, though both were ill at the time and were quarrelling over logistical matters.

Among the officers and men involved in the 'skirmish', there were many stories of individual courage and disaster; but as so often was the case, one man's loss tended to be another's gain. An enquiry into the conduct of Captain William Brereton of the *Duke* deprived him of his command, not for 'behaving ill' on 27 July but for getting drunk on the 26th and 28th. His dismissal opened the way for a reassignment of officers. Robert was now transferred to the *Victory*, as the ship's

6th lieutenant. Further detail was relayed to Charles, on 14 September 1778, by Thomas Thoroton:

> This day Captn Berkeley (lately lieutenant on board the *Victory* but now made Captain by the dismission of Captn Brereton) arrived in town. He left Adm: Keppel & the whole fleet consisting of 33 ships of the line all in perfect health & spirits cruising off the Lizard. He particularly told Betty Neale that he left your Brother [Robert] in perfect health on board the *Victory* where he succeeds him as Lieutenant. They have heard no tidings of the French fleet tho' they have cruised far to the westward to find them out. This is all the news that I have been able to learn shou'd a *Gazette* come out tonight or tomorrow you shall have it.

The next big news, when it came, was utterly unexpected. Both Charles and Robert Manners, already absorbed in their separate ways in Britain's struggle to preserve its empire, were to find themselves caught up in one of the Royal Navy's most damaging and notorious feuds.

7

'Prodigious bickerings'

SEPTEMBER 1778 TO MAY 1779

A letter from Robert to Charles, 11 September 1778,
when the former was serving in the Victory.

'Prodigious Bickerings'

'*Victory* at Sea 11th Sept: … My dearest Brother… You see by the representation that I am at present in the *Victory*,' wrote Robert to Charles in the early autumn of 1778. 'I quitted the *Ocean* last Monday fortnight. We expect to see the French Fleet very soon, if they are at sea.' In the preceding days, Admiral Keppel had pushed his men hard to repair their ships, intending to search for d'Orvilliers off Brest, claiming that: 'If I see the French fleet and we don't fight close, it shall be their fault and not mine.'[1] The British fleet eventually left Plymouth on 22 August 1778.

Robert's prospects had taken a turn for the better with his transfer to the *Victory*. He was now right at the heart of the Channel Fleet, and coming directly under the eye of the commander-in-chief could be a decided advantage. He was in good professional company, too. The *Victory*'s captain, Jonathan Faulknor, had a distinguished record, while Keppel's 'Captain of the Fleet' – effectively his chief-of-staff – was Rear Admiral John Campbell, a navigational specialist involved in the development of a most significant instrument: the sextant.

The fleet was now up to thirty-three ships of the line, with Sir Robert Harland remaining as second in command and Palliser third. Robert did not yet know it, but Palliser's earlier decision to shift his flag from the *Ocean* to the *Formidable* would play in his favour too, for it had removed Robert from any obligations to a man who espoused political views opposite to his own, a circumstance that was to have an added piquancy in the months to come.

As they cruised in the waters around Ushant, some days brought hard gales, others no wind at all and fog so thick that Keppel ordered a signal gun to be fired every half hour to keep the fleet together. From time to time, the line of battle was formed when strange sails were seen on the horizon, and frigates were sent to intercept them. Several French merchantmen were seized in this way, which pleased Robert for he now could claim a lieutenant's share of prize-money, though his portion was yet small.

The boisterous weather brought damage aloft, according to the sailing master's log: spars broke and sails tore on an almost daily basis. Below, water leaks destroyed both stored food and gunpowder. No fresh stores were received from land, and the men were soon suffering from scurvy. Robert noted in his own lieutenant's log that they 'Serv'd the ship's company an allowance of grogg' in an attempt to keep up morale. But the men were disgruntled, and most days saw the call for 'all hands to witness punishment', when one seaman or another was given a dozen lashes for 'drunkenness and mutiny'. One of the *Victory*'s marines, Bartholomew Little, became so dispirited as to end his own life by jumping overboard.

The cruise was a failure. Although the French fleet was known to be at sea, it was actually far to the south of Keppel's station, d'Orvilliers being concerned with protecting trade rather than risking his fleet in battle. By October 1778, with the ships and men in poor condition and winter approaching, Keppel grew despondent and reluctantly admitted he could no longer keep his vessels at sea. Poor morale affected the entire fleet, and both Keppel and Palliser were unwell. Deeply disappointed by the elusiveness of the French, the Channel Fleet turned for home.

There, things did not improve, for gloomy news awaited them. On 27 October 1778, as the *Victory* and the other ships arrived at Spithead, her master noted in his log: 'Joined riding here Lord Howe in His Majesty's ship *Eagle*.' 'Black Dick' had arrived back from North America after resigning his command. With an inferior squadron, he had repelled an attack at New York from Comte d'Estaing with no help from 'Foul-Weather Jack' Byron, whose squadron of thirteen men-of-war arrived too late after being scattered and damaged by a hard gale in the mid-Atlantic. Howe was now thoroughly disillusioned with the war and did not feel he could continue at sea so long as Lord Sandwich remained First Lord of the Admiralty, for he blamed Sandwich for the debacle with d'Estaing. General Sir William Howe had also resigned his command; the brothers were frustrated by the failure of their missions as peace commissioners, and, in William's case, by his inability to defeat Washington.

Yet, this news was vastly overshadowed by a great surprise of more direct consequence for the Channel Fleet. Nearly three months after the Battle of Ushant, on 15 October, a mischievous letter had appeared in the Whig *General Advertiser and Morning Intelligencer* blaming Palliser for Keppel's failure to renew the attack on the French fleet during that encounter. Rumours circulated that the letter had been instigated by Keppel, who, while publicly praising his officers, had privately criticized Palliser for ignoring the signal to engage, and who accused him of throwing victory away by his insubordination. There appeared to be no evidence that Keppel knew about the letter in advance; but with its publication, the two admirals were galvanized into action: both hauled down their flags and came ashore. Robert gave his perspective to Charles on 30 October 1778:

> Our admiral [Keppel] set off for town this morning & I fear will resign if not well receiv'd... Sir Hugh Palliser is gone up to London highly exasperated at a letter which appear'd in one of the daily papers reflecting severely on his conduct during the action. He talks of clearing his character in a public manner & insists on laying the whole affair before Parliament... If anything now happens here I will let you know.

As the admirals stormed off to London, Robert wistfully told his brother: 'I am sorry to find you are still at Liverpool as I had hopes of seeing you, which now will be rather difficult as I cannot possibly be absent from the ship more than 4 or 5 days & that must be secretly.' He thought he would soon be away to sea again. 'The Fleet and particularly the *Victory* is ordered to be fitted immediately which has the appearance of our making another cruize this winter a thing from which I cannot perceive that any good can result.' In his view, the ships would be damaged by winter weather, leaving the French 'safe in their port ready to take possession of the seas, when [we] are incapable of assisting [our fleet] and affording the country or trade any protection.' It was fair evidence of the morale of the Channel Fleet

that autumn, coming as it did from an intelligent and keen young officer. And there was more bad news from the other side of the Atlantic:
'You have heard I suppose,' Robert wrote, 'that Dominica is taken [by
the French], & that probably Tobago will fall soon. I believe the news
to be authentic.'

To this unhappy situation was added an ill-concealed personal gripe.
Their cousin William Clement Finch had, Robert had heard, 'taken
a prize his share of which will amount to about [£]62,000 a fortune
quickly made with little trouble as he did not fire above 3 or 4 guns.
[And] it was not 3 months ago that he took another that will bring him
in 12 or [£]15,000.' These were prodigious sums of money and must
have stung Robert with acute envy, for his share of prize-money from
the *Victory* would eventually amount to a mere £56 1s 6d – though of
course in other ways he was far from being a pauper.

Trapped at Spithead, Robert longed to hear from his brother, urging
'Give me an answer to this letter soon' or gently upbraiding him with
comments like: 'I fear my former letters have not reach'd you as I have
not receiv'd any answer.' Charles had certainly received them but was,
as usual, absorbed in his own interests. For while Robert had failed so
far to haul in significant prize-money, Charles and his wife were, by
contrast, proving adept at *spending* money.

*

The Marchioness of Granby had accompanied her husband as he
travelled to take up his militia responsibilities, arriving in the north-
west of England by early August 1778. The pair were staying – having
eschewed life in a tent – at Eaton Hall, the stately home of Baron
Grosvenor, about 30 miles south of Liverpool.[2]

A woman of the marchioness's position was supposed to be mostly
concerned with hats and embroidery, but Mary Isabella was among a
number of upper-class women drawn by the politics of the time into
breaking with tradition and actively supporting their husbands' duties.
Georgiana, Duchess of Devonshire, had become a notable campaigner
for the Whig opposition, while Mary Isabella, though from a Tory family, gained a favourable reputation as a political hostess. She was said
to be much duller in conversation than the outspoken Georgiana; and
the diarist Fanny Burney later recorded in 'Two celebrated Duchesses

discussed' that Dr Johnson thought Mary Isabella 'very weak and silly, as he knew that she endured being admired to her face, and complimented perpetually, both upon her beauty and her dress'.[3] However, perhaps her 'dullness' was to some extent on account of her carrying herself with more temperance than Georgiana, for it was also said she had a combination of looks, charm, determined nature and 'impeccable conduct', which won her the approval of such stern critics of 'political women' as the writers Horace Walpole and Nathaniel Wraxall.[4]

Georgiana went with her husband, the Duke of Devonshire, to the militia encampment at Coxheath, and, enthralled by the spectacle of thousands of men mobilizing for war, she paraded regularly through the camp to lend patriotic support, inspiring other women to do the same. Mary Isabella, meanwhile, became popular in Liverpool, prompting a tribute in verse from *Williamson's Advertiser* (23 October 1778):

> In beauteous Granby nature sure design'd
> The fairest form to clothe the sweetest mind:
> She joins in Granby, courteous, great and good,
> The brightest virtues with the noblest blood
> And from her heart, so generous and humane,
> Impels benevolence through every vein.[5]

She was even investing her own cash in the fitting out of privateers to be sent to capture French merchant ships – as part of the response to the enemy's use of corsairs in the war on trade. In conjunction with a Mr Nicholas Ashton from Liverpool and with her husband Charles, Mary Isabella had shares in two privateers, the *Lady Granby* of 45 tons, and the *Marchioness of Granby* of 260 tons, which were successful in seizing several French merchantmen. She inspired 'Several ladies of the first rank' to follow her example, so that a number of privateers were 'sent to sea against our perfidious enemies merely by British pin-money'.[6]

Meanwhile, although the couple had Diddle with them, the eight-month-old John Henry was still with Mary Isabella's mother, the Dowager Duchess of Beaufort. The infant appeared to be strong, for the duchess informed Mary Isabella that: 'Your sweet boy is thank God perfectly well: he has been eating thin chicken broth with approbation;

he looks quite jolly... We have had three charming days and today
is like summer glowing with the heat of Virgo.' The duchess also
expressed concern that: 'Lord Granby is not quite well; he is no doubt
perplexed and seized about his regiment.'

In truth, Charles was more troubled about his finances than anything
else. On his way to Liverpool he had stopped at Belvoir to persuade
his grandfather to pay off one of his debts; thereafter began a stream
of letters to his lawyer Joseph Hill chasing up loans and urging him
to 'recollect I am much pressed for money'. Charles hoped that Lady
Mary Duncan was not calling in her £10,000 loan (the terms for which
involved repaying her with £900 a year for life), and if not, then could
she let him have another £10,000? His letters reveal a situation of
considerable complexity: all kinds of loans of different amounts from
various sources, a situation made more confused by Charles's own
somewhat disorganized mind, with important documents 'somehow
mislaid'. One of his scribbled tottings-up on a random slip of paper
show outgoings amounting to £32,000, including £8,500 of 'gaming
debts' and £695 for the annual lease of his London house in Arlington
Street; it also indicates that he had managed to borrow £14,000 from
friends and family, of which £3,000 came from his younger brother
Robert – who must have been saving for the previous few years – and
£3,000 from Sir Joshua Reynolds.

Charles was borrowing all this money against his future inheritance. On visiting his grandfather at Belvoir in August, he found the
duke in deteriorating health and declaring that he would 'spend the
remainder of his days at Knightsbridge'. Charles desired a 'private
word' with Hill for 'the most efficacious mode of securing [Rutland's]
effects in case of his death and my absence'. Joseph Hill had agreed not
to charge the marquis for his services until the duke died – amounting to a seven-year bill of £1,542 17s 10d. That figure was dwarfed
by Charles's debts, which stood in total at £25,469 11s 11d. Echoing
the old Lord Granby, he instructed Hill to find him some money 'the
sooner the better'.

*

At Spithead, Robert had returned to his ship and to the dark mood of
the Channel Fleet after a trip ashore to meet with Joseph Hill, who

paid him £300 – possibly the annual repayment for his £3,000 loan to Charles.

Contrary to Robert's expectation, the fleet did not return to sea at the end of October. Aboard the *Victory*, a few men attempted to desert or resorted to 'suttling' – getting drunk on black-market alcohol smuggled aboard from bum-boats. Together with the other lieutenants, Robert strove to keep the crew occupied with repairing, replacing used stores and victuals, refilling fresh-water barrels, and even noted in his log the 'unhanging' of the ship's rudder to be sent ashore for repairs. An important task was cleaning the shingle ballast, which became wet and foul at the bottom of the ship, generating noxious gases – not least because men may have found the shingle more inviting than the ship's 'seats of ease', exposed to the weather at the head of the ship, though the practice was strictly forbidden.[7]

The admirals, meanwhile, were in the throes of a bitter dispute that was rapidly escalating into the political sphere. Palliser had furiously demanded that Keppel publish a denial of the newspaper accusations – which Keppel declined to do for political motives: he was becoming most useful to those who wanted to discredit the ministry. When Parliament met on 26 November, Horace Walpole described how 'prodigious bickerings' permeated both Houses, as the two admirals clashed in the Commons. Palliser, of humble background, was tired of what he considered to be ill-informed and unmerited criticism from the aristocratic Keppel and his supporters. On 9 December, he demanded a court martial, accusing Keppel of being pusillanimous in the way he had gone into battle at Ushant, and charging him with 'misconduct and neglect of duty'. Palliser's demand put Sandwich in an awkward position. If he supported the court-martial, he would seem to be attacking Keppel and thus incur the wrath of his supporters, the Whigs; if he suppressed it, it would seem he was sheltering Palliser, the Tories and the King's Friends. In the event, Sandwich chose to examine the conduct of Keppel as commander-in-chief – and authorized the court-martial.

This turn of events caused general amazement in London and consternation in the fleet, for Keppel was thought to have acted with some toleration – even 'culpable forbearance' in the view of some – in not criticizing Palliser straight after the battle. 'The disgust of the major and better part of the marine [the Royal Navy] is not easily expressed,'[8] remarked Edmund Burke. The service split into two factions, for and against Palliser, and the dispute raged as much in the wardrooms of the fleet as in the London salons, and with the bitterness of a vendetta. Since Sandwich's family name was Montagu, Keppel's supporters were dubbed 'Capulets'. Thus, at the height of the struggle with France and America, whose outcome was so dependent on the navy, the service was beset by a political feud difficult to comprehend today. It was more than a personality clash between two admirals; it became a conduit for opposition attacks on the government. And looming over it was the pallid spectre of Admiral Byng. Would Keppel, if judged guilty, receive the same fate? Some thought it likely, for Keppel had sat on the court-martial that had condemned Byng to be shot. Death already hung in the air for the Channel Fleet, which, just after Christmas 1778, witnessed the execution of one David Cane for the murder of a seaman named Michael Cavenard, aboard the *Worcester*.

The court-martial of Augustus Keppel began at Portsmouth on 7 January 1779. It should have been held on board ship, but a special Act of Parliament had been passed for the court to sit on shore because of Keppel's ill health. Taking advantage of this extraordinary proceeding, all the leading members of the Rockinghamites and many of their wives travelled down to Portsmouth to support their naval hero. 'The Dukes of Cumberland, Richmond and Bolton are here,' wrote the judge advocate, George Jackson, to Lord Sandwich. Even Charles was there, having obtained leave of absence from his militia. Jackson continued: 'The Marquises of Rockingham and Granby; Lord Effingham; Lieut-Gen Keppel [William Keppel, younger brother of Augustus] and Mr Burke; I do not know if Dunning is; I could see Mr Lee.'[9] Robert, having served in Palliser's division at the battle, was due to be called as a witness – although he intended to give evidence in favour of Admiral Keppel, his family's friend. He was fortunate that Palliser had transferred to the *Formidable* before the Battle of Ushant, otherwise his loyalties might have been torn.

This 'strange-managed dispute between the two Admirals' as the king described it brought Parliamentary business to a standstill. 'Everything awaits the determination of the court martial,' remarked Horace Walpole, 'even France and America seem to lie upon their oars till the oracle at Portsmouth has pronounced'.[10] Meanwhile, Rockingham and his followers, along with the townspeople of Portsmouth and any curious gentry with the leisure to attend, packed the court to clap and cheer everything said in Keppel's favour and to deprecate Palliser. The politicians whipped up sentiment for a man who might very well be on trial for his life, and 'tears were shed, witnesses were hissed, the Deity was invoked'.[11] Such reactions may have influenced the proceedings, the prosecution in particular finding it 'no joke to be hissed by a court full of dukes, marquises and earls'.[12]

There followed the giving of evidence from a succession of witnesses whose cross-examinations showed how hard it was to remember what happened, even with the help of logbooks. The squally weather, gun-smoke and the preoccupations of the day in both fighting and repairing damage caused a confusion in eyewitness accounts, everyone appearing to have observed the course of events differently. The complexities of the flag signals and their timing, the precipitate nature of the action, and the partial viewpoints made it difficult for the court to follow the train of events with certainty. Evidence included such mystifying (to many) descriptions as:

> At 3 h 30 min. flag union and blue, with a red cross at the mizen peak; no time mentioned when hauled down. Three h. 15 min. pendant yellow mizen top-mast head, hauled down 33 min. after four; pendant white 3 h. 50 min. mizen-top sail yard hauled down 32 min after five; 33 min. after four, flag striped blue and white main-top mast head; hauled down at 24 min. past four; at 37 min. past four, flag Spanish ensign main-top gallant mast head, no time when hauled down...[13]

Witnesses were careful how they expressed themselves. Apart from the intimidating atmosphere of the court, in a trial with such overt political implications their own futures were at stake, and many, including Robert, had already decided how their evidence would be coloured. However, the consensus of most who were called upon to speak was that the commander-in-chief had made every endeavour to re-engage, and that Palliser had ignored the signal to re-form the line by taking his station independently of the fleet's rear. Palliser himself said his ship was damaged and he could not comply with the signal to engage, though he had failed to acquaint Keppel of this at the time.

Rumours circulated around Portsmouth that the relevant pages from the *Formidable*'s logbook had been torn out and destroyed. Such was the paranoia that when one morning a man approached Captain John Carter Allen with a banknote drawn anonymously for £1,000, an outraged Allen locked the importunate fellow in a room, threatening him with a pair of pistols until he disclosed where the money came from. It turned out it was from an admiring lady who wished to help Allen pay off his debts, rather than a bribe for Allen to give evidence against Keppel. Allen, who had been captain of the *Egmont* – the ship ahead of the *Ocean* – was regarded as a most honourable man and had been called as a witness by Palliser.

With its talk of 'larboard tacks', 'lee and weather bows' and 'bow-and-quarter lines', the trial was all too much for the easily bored Charles. He thought his leave of absence from his militia could be better spent at Cheveley. Indeed, he had already left by the time Captain Allen took the stand on Saturday, 16 January 1779, one among the twenty-eight post-captains called to testify. Despite his having been in Palliser's rear division, Allen gave evidence in favour of Keppel. The following day, Robert wrote to Charles that Allen had spoken 'full as concise & precise and as much in favour of Admiral Keppel as Captain Windsor'. Both Allen's and Windsor's evidence was important, the latter's because he had been sent by Keppel in his frigate, the *Fox*, to summon Palliser to join the line of battle. Crucially, Windsor said that he had not been asked by Palliser to inform Keppel that the *Formidable* was badly damaged.

Several of the captains of Palliser's division stood by him out of loyalty or political faction; but Robert's captain, John Laforey, did not. On 4 February 1779, he contradicted a claim made by Palliser's defence, that the signal for re-forming the line of battle had not been seen in the *Formidable*. Captain Laforey told the court it had been clearly observed aboard the *Ocean*, lying close by, adding some further technical details that weakened Palliser's case, before declaring clearly for the commander-in-chief. 'Admiral Keppel,' he affirmed, 'had left no means unaffected to bring the French to action, or to continue it afterwards.' Then, irritated by the rambling proceedings, he pointedly added that the question for the court was 'whether the Admiral [Keppel] did his duty, or whether he neglected his duty; whether he disgraced the British fleet, or whether he run away? – I will sit here if necessary to the day of resurrection to hear what the Prosecutor [Palliser] says or the Prisoner [Keppel], but keep to the point.'

On Sunday, 7 February, Robert was able to tell Charles that: 'I have not yet heard when I am to be call'd. I trust now there will be no occasion.' He was right. The trial had swung in Keppel's favour, winning him much wider fame than his naval exploits had ever done. 'He is grown at least one foot in stature and very little less eloquent than Mr Burke,' Lord John Cavendish said waspishly. 'So many pleasing circumstances attend this attack on him it is very far from being a matter to be lamented.'[14]

Finally, on the morning of Thursday, 11 February, the Honourable Augustus Keppel was acquitted. At one o'clock, the Marquis of Rockingham, who always wrote the time on his letters, sent a note to let Charles know, emphasizing the important message: 'The accusation was unanimously voted malicious and illfounded.' A procession formed around Keppel, his supporters wearing light blue ribbons with his name in gold letters, and he was marched through the streets of Portsmouth behind a band playing 'See the Conquering Hero Comes'. 'The whole concourse and ladies from the windows supplied the vocal part and the crowd closed each period of the harmony with a choral cheer… it is impossible to paint the joy that possessed every face.'[15]

For Keppel, this was a spectacular vindication. News of the acquittal reached London that evening, where the Rockinghamites were ready with a general 'illumination', as the usually dark streets shone from the celebratory lamps that they placed in their windows. It was a warm night, and people took to the streets to express their relief at the outcome of this *cause célèbre*. A mob quickly formed, tearing down the gates of the Admiralty and roaming the city, gleefully breaking the windows of government ministers' houses. Palliser was even in fear of his life; his house in Pall Mall was looted and his furniture burnt in St James's Square. Lord Germain had all his doors and windows battered in, and the prime ministerial residence of 10 Downing Street was saved only by the reading of the Riot Act and the prompt intervention of a company of Foot Guards.

On 12 February, Keppel hoisted his flag once again aboard the *Victory*. On the same day in the House of Commons, Colonel Isaac Barré carried a motion thanking him for defending the kingdom; four days later, Rockingham moved a similar resolution in the Lords, and Keppel was presented with the Freedom of London, the parchment laid in a box of heart-of-oak.

As for Palliser, he was a few weeks later acquitted of misconduct, the court having found him to have acted 'in many instances' in a 'highly exemplary and meritorious' way; but he was also shamed by the court for not having communicated the *Formidable*'s damage to Keppel, which he might have done via the *Fox* or some other means. Less public attention accompanied this trial, for most people thought the man had already suffered enough. But Palliser never again served at sea.

★

While the Keppel–Palliser affair had been dragging on, Charles and his family remained at Cheveley, where they had all gone down with sore throats, bringing him little sympathy from relations. His aunt, Lady Katherine Pelham, told him: 'I verily believe you to have very few faults. Sorry I am to hear you guilty of the bad one of keeping intolerable hours, which will undoubtedly hurt both yours and Lady Granby's health.' No doubt his late nights were spent mostly gambling, though he did have some serious matters to attend to. Charles now informed Joseph Hill that he intended to emulate what his father had done before him and sell land that was not historically attached to the family inheritance, and that this 'financial business would prevent him from being at the next meeting of gentlemen'.

The minor affliction of Charles's ailment appears to have been well advertised. From Liverpool, Nicholas Ashton wrote on 12 February 1779 with unctuous irony: 'My dear Lord... [I] heartily rejoice that you with Lady Granby and the young lady are recovered from that alarming complaint of a sore throat... this complaint seems to have been general through the Kingdom but I do not hear of it being fatal except in a very few instances'. But Ashton was mainly writing to relate 'a disagreeable piece of news'. The privateer the *Marchioness of Granby* had been captured and taken into Brest. Nevertheless, Ashton sounded slightly relieved. Her crew had been on the way to causing a 'national disturbance' for they had been attacking neutral Dutch vessels, despite having orders to the contrary. 'With so mad a set of men on board there was no knowing what mischief they might have done,' he opined. He also informed the marquis that the sloop *Lady Granby* had gone missing, news that Charles relayed to a family agent, Mr Uppleby: 'my privateer has been absurd' and that there could be £6,000 to pay in damages, the insurance having just run out. 'It is very unfortunate,' remarked Charles with dry understatement.

Nicholas Ashton added at the bottom of his letter: 'I sincerely hope the news you send me of a change of the First Lord of the Admiralty and secretary of the American Department [Germain] may be so and that Lord Howe may succeed Lord Sandwich.' The Keppel–Palliser affair was being seized on by the opposition to try to bring down ministers and replace them with those sympathetic to their cause. Even the king admitted that perhaps Lord Sandwich, who might have prevented the entire affair, should go. In Brooks's club – the former Almack's – Charles James Fox bet George Hanger 10 guineas that Sandwich would not still be First Lord one calendar month after the court-martial.[16]

The opposition grabbed the chance to attack Lord North too, exploiting the disagreements between him, Sandwich and Germain. Since France's entry into the war, and in the light of emerging intelligence that Spain was on the edge of an alliance with France, and that their fleets combined would outnumber the Royal Navy, the prime minister had become even more indecisive – and even more persistent in his efforts to resign. North had an awkward, ungainly appearance, with heavy eyelids that fell over prominent eyes, giving him a sleepy look; but his jovial manner, self-deprecating wit, profound knowledge and a gifted ability to match and deflect the brilliant speeches of the opposition meant that he retained his popularity in both Houses. These qualities, combined with his especial skill in raising capital (he introduced competitive tendering for loans to his government), ensured that the king kept him in post.

Yet the Marquis of Rockingham remained determined to keep up the pressure. Turning his attention to a motion that Charles James Fox planned to put before the House of Commons on Monday, 8 March 1779, Rockingham made it his goal to persuade as many people as possible to turn up and vote with the opposition. Fox intended to attempt to force a vote of no confidence in the government on the grounds that North was incompetent and had misled the public into thinking his ministry could handle the war. News of the motion rapidly circulated, attracting a number of prominent figures, including Admiral Keppel and Lord Howe, both of whom stayed in town specially over that weekend, in order to vote.

Once again, Rockingham was irritated that Charles was not in London and was unlikely to be there for Monday's debate. The older man was working round the clock, always writing the time on his letters as if to prove it, and on 'Friday night 12 o'clock' of 5 March he dashed off an exasperated summons to Charles at Cheveley, asking him to 'forego the gratification of lesser pleasures, when perhaps you might by giving them up, for a few days, really afford most useful and honourable service to your country'. Charles's absence from the Commons would, he said, be 'much regretted by <u>your friends</u>, & is even a matter of Triumph amongst others, who I am sure, you would by no means wish to please. The destruction of the [ministry] & more particularly <u>the admiralty</u>, you have every reason both <u>Publick</u> and <u>Private</u> (if you think for a moment) to be desirous of accomplishing.' Thus, Rockingham made oblique allusion to the possible benefits for Charles's brother of ousting Lord Sandwich, for a new First Lord might offer Robert a favourable commission. 'Many of our friends,' Rockingham went on, 'insist that we have a very good chance of having even larger numbers on Monday than we had on the former day, and perhaps the disarray among the enemy may reduce their numbers.'

As usual, Charles's reasons for not being present in Parliament were numerous; but, other than being busy, the most cogent one was that the opposition minority had little chance of winning a vote, so what was the point? There were a number of Whigs who did not like seeing their true weakness exposed in Parliamentary divisions, so they preferred to stay away. They 'will be found at the hazard-table', observed Horace Walpole tartly, 'instead of at the plough'.[17] In any case, it was still the hunting season, and Charles, again like other Whigs, might be plagued with illness but at 'the sound of a fox-horn... experienced miraculous cures'. Rockingham, however, was not deterred: 'Your Lordship's absence also occasions the absence of Mr Sutton and as I hear, also, of Mr Thoroton,' he told Charles, 'but I assure you the two or three votes more or less would not make me write so pressingly to you, if I did not think that it is not a pleasant thing that maintaining and professing the good principles which you do, you should nevertheless appear for a moment to be inattentive in your exertions at their most critical time.' Rockingham could scarcely have been more stinging, plucking at the young Marquis of Granby's conscience, but to little avail.

The tiny House of Commons was packed when Fox rose to make his motion at half past four that Monday afternoon on 8 March. 'Ignorant or treacherous ministers had imperceptibly dragged or rather allured this infatuated country to the very verge of destruction,' he began, alleging that Lord Sandwich had broken his word that he would provide adequate ships for the Channel Fleet and thus was no longer worthy of public confidence. He poured scorn on how he thought Sandwich would try to justify himself: 'I was not the author of the American war,' Fox said in mimicry. 'America rebelled. I am not answerable for the events of the French war; it was the perfidy of France that made the kingdom abet our rebellious subjects. I did not encourage the Bostonians to destroy the tea, nor to rise, nor to fight to declare themselves independent.'

Next, Fox tore into Lord North, alluding to the prime minister's habit of entering the Commons immediately after an audience with the king, wearing court-dress and the blue ribbon of the Order of the Garter:

> When the first disturbances relative to the destruction of the tea sent to America broke out in that country [and] the people did not submit [to the Boston Port Bill], the noble lord in the blue ribbon said 'Send a few regiments, and force the Port-Bill down the throats of the discontented and mutinous with powder and ball'. That recipe not proving efficacious says the noble Lord 'We will hold out terms to them' which gave birth to his Lordship's celebrated conciliatory proposition. [This] was treated with the contempt and derision which it merited. The noble Lord finding himself baffled in all his plans, at length grew disgusted and angry and [tried] to bully and deceive, to cheat and frighten. The people of America had too much good sense and resolution to submit to either.

One of the opposition's principal arguments was that the Channel Fleet was unprepared and outnumbered and that the money raised for the fleet had been squandered – circumstances especially worrying if

Spain were to join the war. 'When Keppel went out in June,' continued Fox, referring to events leading to the action of Ushant, 'the British fleet was... not equal to [that of] France alone, let alone Spain as well and having a force in America and the Mediterranean at the same time. In 1756, the first year of the previous war, there were eighty-nine ships of the line, yet in this first year of war with France the navy could not cobble together more than forty-two.'

Lord Mulgrave, who commanded the *Courageux* during that battle, sat in the Commons (rather than the Lord, being a peer of Ireland), in the role of the Admiralty's spokesman. He responded stoutly that ship numbers were *not* less than they were in 1756 and that the British force was *not* inferior to the French. He rejected accusations of incompetence in not sending Byron's ships out quickly enough to help Lord Howe (who had to face the enemy outnumbered), and he explained the actions of the Admiralty Board in not wanting to leave Britain's coast weakly defended. He would therefore 'give his hearty negative to the motion'.

Lord Howe, another peer of Ireland, rose in the Commons to second Fox's motion. He said he 'had been deceived into command, deceived while he retained it, he was tired and disgusted in America and would have resigned his command and returned had he not wanted to abandon his post in the face of a superior enemy but Mr Byron's arrival had given him the opportunity'. Howe was followed in the chamber by Keppel, who pronounced himself astonished that Mulgrave could assert that the French fleet was inferior when 'it was notorious all over Europe' that d'Orvilliers had sailed from Brest with thirty-two ships of the line. 'Was his squadron suddenly created?' he asked, with rhetorical flourish. He went on to affirm the shortage of British ships and the deficiency in their condition. 'On the whole he pronounced the admiralty-board totally negligent, misinformed and every way unequal to the administration of the naval affairs of this country,' reported the *Parliamentary Register*. It was a damning indictment from two influential sea-officers; and it was followed by a succession of ministers and MPs who 'walked over this beaten field', all with different opinions on the numbers of ships the British and French actually had and whether public money voted for the navy had, or had not, been wasted.

Eventually it was Rockingham's spokesman, Edmund Burke, who

brought the debate to a head by addressing the prospect that Britain's naval assets could not match the combined fleets of France and Spain. He rose from the opposition benches and likened the behaviour of the government to two men wearing cloaks who had stolen a piece of meat. 'They pass it dexterously to each other as they are searched, denying all culpability.' So he would put the question 'fairly and roundly to ministers – was the state of the navy – supposing that Spain should decide to join in – able to cope with the united force of the House of Bourbon?' At one o'clock in the morning, the House divided: 'the ayes 174; the noes 246'. Fox's motion of no confidence had failed by seventy-two votes. Had Charles attended with his friends and relatives, the opposition would still not have won; but the vote was close enough to alarm the ministry.

★

As the 'prodigious bickerings' continued apace in Parliament, Robert found himself in a fleet in poor shape. Desertion and indiscipline among the ships' companies had increased in the absence of their admirals and captains, who attended Keppel's court-martial and then Parliament, while the officers were deeply divided among themselves. As the aftermath rumbled on, many captains who supported Keppel, and even some moderates who had taken no part in the affair, threw up their commands, declaring that they could not serve under an Admiralty that had permitted such groundless charges to be advanced against one of its senior flag-officers. Among them was Captain Sir John Lindsay, Lord Mansfield's nephew. Such was the rancour caused that Lieutenant James Charles Pitt was removed from the *Robuste* by family influence after it was said that the vessel's captain, Alexander Hood, had tampered with the ship's log in support of Palliser.

Despite the controversy over Lord Sandwich's conduct, he continued to be retained by the king as First Lord. It was then confirmed that Keppel had resigned out of principle, taking with him the *Victory*'s Captain Faulknor. In fact, the Keppel–Palliser affair left the Channel Fleet – though not the whole navy – badly disunited for 1779. It was not forgotten on quarterdecks for many years.

Robert did not follow the lead of the dissident captains. He remained determined to serve, and on 16 February 1779 had even moved up a step, becoming the *Victory*'s 5th lieutenant. Perhaps he believed in the sentiment of Welbore Ellis, who told the Commons: 'History tells us we do not strike our decisive blows till towards the close of the war. So if there is weakness in the navy at the start of the war it must be an inherent fault in our constitution, not with the present management. We have repeated often that our first efforts are weak and feeble and later counter balanced by strength and vigour.'

The sabre-rattling of the opposition was obscuring much of what the navy was actually achieving, such as Admiral Barrington's capture of the island of St Lucia the previous December. It was also shrouding the simple truth that meeting the navy's requirements took time. Wood had to be seasoned, with much of it brought from the Baltic, and ships took at least three years to build. It was not possible to fill, in a week, an arsenal with powder when saltpetre came from Bengal. Patience was needed.

Naval defence also aspired to secrecy. Lord Sandwich had himself insisted on not declaring overall ship numbers, to try to prevent intelligence from filtering through to the enemy. But averting leaks was difficult. France maintained a spy-ring in Britain, run from the embassy in London, which picked up scraps of information in a wide variety of ways. These formed the basis of the detailed tables of British naval strength, together with the exact location of ships, maintained by the French ministry throughout the 1760s and 1770s. For its part, Britain secured naval intelligence both indirectly, from an agency run from the Dutch republic, and directly through the reports of strategically placed diplomats such as Alleyne FitzHerbert, who often relayed his messages via a secret code, and through captains in both the merchant navy and the fighting fleet. The result was that each side knew, with surprising accuracy, the state of its enemy's naval power and its own superiority – or inferiority – at sea, even if the detail was not admitted in Parliament.

Discretion was also sought regarding some significant innovations. The Royal Navy had been initially reluctant to adopt the new short-range lightweight 'carronade' guns, but Sandwich – through the administration of Charles Middleton as 'Comptroller of the Navy' – had them mounted on several ships in place of the light guns at the bow and stern with great success. He also reintroduced 'coppering' – sheathing the ships with copper below the waterline to protect timbers from the depredations of the voracious 'ship-worm', *teredo navalis*, which had a penchant for boring into oak. Coppering also discouraged marine growth, thereby enabling ships to sail faster and to require less frequent docking for cleaning. Early experiments in the technique had failed, owing to the electrolytic corrosion of adjacent iron fastenings; but though a fully effective solution had not yet been found, Sandwich insisted that coppering of the entire fleet should go ahead – and at that moment, as the opposition thundered in Parliament over the First Lord's 'incompetence', the 74-gun *Terrible* and *Resolution* were undergoing the process at Portsmouth in case they were to be sent to the West Indies, where ship-worm was at its worst. Meanwhile, the more enlightened naval officers understood that an insistence on copper sheathing, despite its problems and considerable cost, could contribute to achieving superiority over the French.

In early March 1779, the *Victory* was ordered into dry-dock to have her bottom scraped clean of marine growth. She was not at this time coppered, the priority then being given to ships destined for foreign service, and she would go on to wait some years for her turn. Nevertheless, her dry docking hindered Robert's plans for heading up to London, and he was compelled to inform Charles in a letter of 11 March that 'the presence of all the Officers being necessary, I am prevented from seeing you in town as I intended'. The letter suggested his brother's rate of correspondence had not improved, for Robert continued: 'I saw Captain [Evelyn] Sutton the other day who told me that Roos was quite recovered, which (except one letter I received from Mr Thoroton two months ago, & the seeing *your* name once or twice in the newspapers) is all that I have heard of you since your departure from this place.'

Thinking of Charles's connections, Robert asked his brother if he knew who would take command of the Channel Fleet when the campaigning season opened. Indeed, the disruption caused by the Keppel–Palliser incident was such as to revive Robert's hopes of further promotion, for a change of ministers might improve the prospects for Whiggish officers. Although his ideal was to obtain a direct step to post-captain, which meant command of a ship of twenty guns or more, he recognized that an acceptable interim commission would be

the lesser rank of 'master and commander' of a smaller vessel. Robert
told his brother that 'I have wish'd to speak to you [for] some time' on
this matter, but had 'delayed writing on a supposition of seeing you
before this'. He was now 'afraid that will be impossible until the ship
goes out of the harbour which will not be this month unless something very extraordinary should happen'. He went on to say that if
he were to be made a master and commander immediately, he might
thereby be high enough on the list to become a post-captain should a
change in the ministry and at the Admiralty take place. He explained
that Keppel could not help him, for the admiral's priority was for
lieutenants who had been in the *Victory* on that fateful day of 27 July
1778. Robert pleaded for Charles to help, pressing him hard: 'I wish
you would consider this[,] at least let me know your opinion of it as
I assure you it is of great consequence.'

By 18 March 1779, Robert had discovered who was to be appointed
the new commander-in-chief of the Channel Fleet. In the wake of
the resignations, Sandwich had been obliged to scrape the barrel for
a replacement. He chose the ailing Admiral Sir Charles Hardy, who,
ashore for nearly twenty years, had been asked to come out of retirement. Hardy, a veteran of Quiberon Bay in 1759, was a well-connected
officer and an effective manager of people, able to mediate to some
extent between the factions; but, as the Duke of Richmond pointed
out in Parliament, he had arrived 'at a period of life little calculated for
the performance of active service'.

Robert had no desire to remain a lowly 5th lieutenant under Hardy
in the *Victory*. By 1 April, he had resigned his commission and was on
half-pay, his cousin Seymour Finch taking his place on board. Later,
so that he could get paid, Robert submitted his log to the Admiralty
office with a note from Captain Faulknor: 'These are to certify the
Right Honourable the Lords Commissioners of the Admiralty that the
Hon'ble Robert Manners served as Sixth Lieutenant under my command, on board His Majesty's Ship the *Victory*... during which time he
complied with the General Printed Instructions.'[18]

Realizing he could not rely upon assistance from his brother, and
despite the fact that the 'Parliament Pack was in full cry after Sandwich',[19] Robert had decided to take the bold step of seeking the ear of
the First Lord himself for a new posting. He was, at least, successful in

persuading Sandwich to grant him a meeting. Standing before such a powerful man of his father's generation, the ambitious second son of Lord Granby now asked boldly for a post-captaincy in a 74-gun line-of-battle ship that would be close to the heart of any action. Sandwich, though he had disliked Granby, 'promised' that he would oblige – or so it seemed to the determined young nobleman. After Robert had departed, Sandwich drew his appointment book towards him and wrote in the column headed 'Recommended By' the word 'Himself'.[20] Robert was not unusual in seeking out the First Lord in person; but he was unusual in making such a bold move when most of his friends were in opposition. Such was his resolve to succeed.

Just then, the First Lord was struck by a personal tragedy. Sandwich, a patron of Handel, had a mistress called Martha Ray who was celebrated for her renditions of 'I Know that My Redeemer Liveth'. On 7 April 1779, shortly after Robert's visit, she was brutally murdered by a jealous suitor. But Sandwich's state of mourning did not diminish the Rockinghamites' attacks, which went beyond the political and into the personal. Opponents accused him of degeneracy – the innovation of the eponymous 'sandwich' supposedly a by-product of his late-night gambling – and they disparaged his association with the notorious Hell-fire Club, its members thought to be high-society rakes engaged in immoral acts. They lampooned him with the nickname of 'Jemmy Twitcher', likening his conduct to the betrayer of Macheath in John Gay's pungent satire *The Beggar's Opera*, and even suggested that he should be hanged for mismanagement of the navy. Keppel's engagement off Ushant should have ended in triumph, said his critics; Sandwich had neglected 'that very fleet, which was then known to be the only safety of these kingdoms, and our only dependence', asserted the Earl of Bristol, 'that very fleet which was to protect us from the trump'd up report of an invasion; that blown up bubble (pardon the expression my lords) to draw the attention of the people from their more immediate misfortunes'.

There was no let-up for Sandwich: on 19 April, less than two weeks after Martha's murder, Charles James Fox rose in the Commons to make a motion for the removal of the First Lord of the Admiralty from his office. On this occasion, Fox purported to be attacking the management of the navy rather than the war with America. He laughed, he told the House, at the 'pompous accounts' of successes that made their way into the *London Gazette*, and said they were of little consequence when it was considered how dearly they were purchased, when so many of the triumphant troops were, in fact, dead or dying in military hospitals. The victories, he pointed out, were nearly as costly as the defeats. Fox claimed not to be in any faction, but rather to speak only for the good of the country and for recovering the nation's former power, reputation and glory.

Once again, Lord Mulgrave spoke in defence of Sandwich: 'When he came to the presidency at the Admiralty there was not a year's timber in any one of our yards, no stores in our arsenals and the whole navy in a perishing state. The noble lord, by his activity and sagacity, had entirely altered the case,' for by importing foreign supplies there was now 'at least timber enough for three years' consumption in every one of our yards'. To these defences of the First Lord, Mulgrave added that: 'Our arsenals were also full of stores; our navy had a great[er] number of large ships than ever, and it was not only in a respectable but in a more flourishing and better state than ever.' In his opinion, there was 'not a more able, active, or knowing minister than the present First Lord of the Admiralty, nor one who deserved better of his country'. Mulgrave was supported by Captain Walsingham, who defended the use of Stettin oak, saying that though the quality varied, the greater part of it was equal to English oak and 'like [Lord Sandwich's] heart, was sound and incorrupt, notwithstanding all the misrepresentations that had gone forth to the contrary'.

After this warming reassurance, the House divided – the ayes 118 and the noes 221 – and Fox again lost his motion in the Commons, while Sandwich retained his place at the Admiralty. Things were not boding well for the opposition; there had been in excess of a hundred fewer members in the chamber than on the occasion of the earlier motion of no confidence in North's ministry. The majority of Members in both Houses of Parliament continued to support the government. The impending entry of Spain into the war, the threat of an invasion, the dire state of affairs in North America, the French threat to the West Indies, the vulnerability of trade with India and the lack of available troops all made it inconceivable to the majority of 'independents' that the ship of state should be rocked. This was Britannia *contra mundum*, and the persistently oppositional stance of the Whigs seemed to be verging on the treasonable.

Heedlessly, Fox returned to the fray just ten days later, now attacking Lord George Germain and other ministers over their conduct in waging war with the American Congress. On 29 April, he rose to argue that the thirteen colonies of North America were already lost. The cost of this fiasco had been £40 million and the squandering of 30,000 lives, he said. The persistence of the government in continuing the war with America put him in mind of two lines from an old song:

> You know you are in the right,
> I think you are in the wrong.

For all Fox's rhetoric, the government still clung on, and both Sandwich and Germain remained in their posts, Lord North arguing that their dismissal would amount to a vote of no confidence in his ministry.

*

We cannot be sure, but it is unlikely that the Marquis of Granby was in Parliament to listen to Fox's latest blast.[21] On that same day, the marchioness gave birth to another daughter, Katherine, and Mary Isabella liked her husband to be present when each of their children was born.

A month later, Charles had yet another reason to be distracted, this time by an event that would profoundly change the personal lives of the Manners brothers. On the morning of Monday, 30 May 1779, he dipped his pen into ink and hurriedly scrawled a note to Joseph Hill, who was out of town: 'The Duke died last night[.] I wish you would come up to London and to my house.' The eighty-two-year-old Rutland, having outlived twelve of his fifteen children, had passed away at Rutland House in Knightsbridge on 29 May. He was buried at Bottesford Church on Saturday, 12 June – and at last Charles assumed the dukedom.

8

'An extreme hard case'

JUNE TO DECEMBER 1779

'An extreme hard case'

The new Duke of Rutland was twenty-five years old, affable and kind, a little portly and increasingly inclined to excess in drink and gambling. Although he was always well intentioned in his public life, and would henceforth assume his hereditary ducal seat in the House of Lords, Charles still lacked drive to engage publicly in political debate. Besides, he now had much else to absorb his slightly chaotic mind. He was the new owner of not only Belvoir Castle, but also Cheveley Park in Cambridgeshire, Haddon Hall in Derbyshire and around 150,000 acres of land across several counties, which by now brought in some £35,000 a year. By custom, it now fell to him to keep the land, property and title attached to the name of Manners, and not to lose them through treason, poor political alliances – or an unlucky throw of the dice.

Charles, like others of his social group, had a strong sense of his heritage, but it appears to have been intensified by losing so many family members in early life. Soon after inheriting the dukedom, he updated the family's genealogical tree. No one had bothered to do this over the previous three generations, even though it was not only symbolic of pride in family ancestry, but essential to helping define inheritance arrangements and establish contingencies in the event of disruption of the line.

His country estate, like those of other Whigs, induced a profound emotional response in Charles. Belvoir Castle itself was in a somewhat poor condition when the old duke died, including its interior. 'In the whole house, there is no furniture (pictures excepted) that a broker would think worth the carrying away,' wrote a visitor, 'nor one chair, table, carpet or curtain of use or comfort!' The same visitor asserted that Charles 'instead of refitting, repairing, and such like necessary and honourable works, laid about him, like a dragon to buy pictures (a finishing not a commencing taste); and in truth he did that with judgement'.[1] But Charles eschewed piecemeal repairs to Belvoir in favour of something altogether grander. He decided to engage Lancelot 'Capability' Brown to draw up plans to remodel the draughty, damp old castle and to redesign the landscape into Brown's style of 'natural' woodland and lakes. It was no surprise that the designer should be Charles's choice, for this 'omnipotent magician', as the poet William Cowper described him, had worked for a number of noble families wishing to develop their country properties as visible symbols of privilege and status. His clients had already included Charles's maternal grandfather, the 6th Duke of Somerset at Petworth House, and Mary Isabella's father, the 4th Duke of Beaufort at Badminton. Now that Charles had an heir – little Lord Roos was a year old – there was another generation for which to create a more splendid Belvoir, a vision that went far beyond what Charles's father had attempted by way of planting trees with imported Canadian seeds. Charles had another connection with Brown, having been at Eton with Brown's sons (one of whom, naval officer John 'Jack' Brown, had served in the *Nautilus* on the Newfoundland squadron with Lord Robert).[2]

Charles's land ownership around the castle was surprisingly patchy, owing to William the Conqueror's original dispersed grants, which were intended to prevent local alliances between rebellious nobles. Charles now pursued the idea of selling some outlying properties and land, not just to raise capital for his lifestyle but also to find the means to purchase land within 10 miles of the castle and thereby create a more consolidated basis for Brown's plans. But all of this would challenge the new duke, for sorting out its complexity was hard for a man driven more by emotion and desires than by business sense.

For the Belvoir inheritance, Charles was obliged to abide by time-honoured trust law, with its settlements and entail, the objective of which was not only to keep land and property attached to the family name, but also to deter profligate sons from ravaging the family fortunes. The Somerset inheritance, however, was still shared with his aunt Charlotte Aylesford, and with Robert and sister Frances. In 1779, Charles pursued an Act of Parliament to disentangle all these claims and enable him to extract sellable land out of the arrangements and to have more control over providing for those dependent on him. Most pressing was the rewriting of his will and marriage settlement to provide pin-money for Mary Isabella and allowances for his children; and he hoped now to be able to pay off his own, and the remainder of his father's, debts.

But Charles was also generous and loyal, and there was sentiment and affection in his financial arrangements, not merely adherence to the customs of noble families. He continued sustaining 'inherited' connections such as with his father's lover Mrs Mompesson, who lived in a decent house near Lincoln Cathedral with a £400 annuity; and he provided continued employment for the Swiss hussar and loyal servant John Notzell. Perhaps fortunately, he did not have to consider his grandfather's mistress: the old duke had left the lease of Rutland House in Knightsbridge to Mrs Drake and her family, where their descendents continued to live until 1835.[3] (Charles himself continued to inhabit 16 Arlington Street in Mayfair.) The new duke attempted also to assist his close friend the younger William Pitt, who, though short of money, was trying – if unsuccessfully – to secure the Cambridge University Parliamentary seat now left vacant by Charles's elevation to the Lords.

*

As a duke, Charles was in a position to give a considerable financial leg-up to his beloved brother. The change in their circumstances, in the spring of 1779, had come at a rare moment when they could spend time together, Robert being ashore in London on half-pay. The naval lieutenant was now twenty-one years of age. He was described by Richard Watson as nearly 6 feet in height, 'justly proportioned and made for strength [as well as] activity. His countenance was to the general degree beautiful without being feminine, his eyes were large, very dark and full of fire or of softness according to the particular sensations which at the moment influenced his mind. His complexion inclined to brown with a great deal of colour.' Possessing a wry wit, he 'loved society and was very convivial', yet also had a 'grave and reserved' side. Watson described a young man who:

> … never spoke his opinion but on the surest grounds, and seldom
> but in company of his friends, except for the sake of justice and
> truth. He had a generosity which could never refuse relief to any
> object of compassion which claimed his benevolence. He had a
> clear comprehension and sound judgement, was versed in almost
> every kind of reading and perfectly master of the most approved
> treatises on the subject of his own profession. In short he seemed
> to be deficient in no one qualification requisite to render him the
> best possible friend and one of the greatest and most able officers.

Watson's fulsome panegyric did, however, fail to point out Robert's
faults. The younger Manners was quickly bored, easily irritated and
quite capable of carrying himself with a touch of arrogance.

For Robert, the early summer of 1779, when he was on half-pay with
no commission, was also a brief time in which he was able to enjoy
London's cosmopolitan culture and was noted among his contemporaries for his sense of fashion. He could afford to, for he was now a
wealthy man. Although a full lieutenant's pay was just 5 shillings a
day – or about £100 a year – on old Rutland's death, Charles more than
tripled Robert's annual allowance to £2,100; there were few lieutenants then in the navy receiving such an income. Robert also extracted
the £8,250, with interest, from the inheritance he shared with his Aunt
Charlotte. He prudently added this capital to his account in the bank
of Messrs Snow & Denne, no doubt dreaming of one day purchasing
his own land and property. He also appointed the agents Ommaney &
Page to handle any future prize-money.

It was almost certainly now that he sat for the artist Richard
Cosway, who painted two miniatures, and for Nathaniel Dance (later
Dance-Holland) who produced two paintings; and possibly also for
both the sculptor Joseph Nollekens and the artist Benjamin Wilson,
though they may have created their works after Robert's death. Robert
enjoyed music, and now was his chance to visit London's theatres and
opera houses, and to attend church services, for he was known to have
had an interest in religion.[4] We do also know that Robert was busy
running up bills for some rather expensive strawberries. The favoured
variety was a newly cultivated cross between a Chilean and North
American plant, held to be an erotic symbol and an aphrodisiac. But

what appealed to him most – the strawberries themselves, the servant Elizabeth Neale who delivered them, or another lady with whom he may have shared them – can only be guessed at.

While Charles and Robert could spend time together and strengthen their bond, they continued to drift apart from their sister. Frances was now living in Boulogne, in northern France, where her husband had a wine business; but they had fallen on hard times. Perhaps the brothers' hard-heartedness was more to do with public appearance than private feeling, for both of them were so generous-minded in other ways. In fact, Charles did oblige 'my ~~unfortunate~~ sister' (either he or Hill later crossed out the adjective) with a much improved financial arrangement from the one she had received from their grandfather; and he included provision in his rewritten will for her new-born son, whom Hill referred to as 'Poor Little Leslie'. Still, the coldness in the brothers' communications prevailed. Frances later wrote, with sadness, that Charles did not seem to wish to hear from her.

Whatever Charles and Robert truly thought of Frances, her situation could not be put to the backs of their minds in 1779. In that year, the full forty-page transcript of her divorce case was published in the sensationalist compendium *Trials for Adultery, or, The History of Divorces*.[5] Produced for amusement and titillation, this publication was so popular that it ran to seven volumes. There for all to see, in the first volume, were the lurid details of what servants said they had seen Frances doing on a 'sopha' with her lover. It caused embarrassment for the family all over again. Uncomfortably for Charles, when he eventually took up his seat in the House of Lords, he would have to sit through debates on an anti-adultery bill attempting to curb the 'problem' of adultery and divorce that was thought to be threatening the structure of English society, by undermining marriage as the stable foundation of hereditary land ownership and power. Members in both Houses debated whether such bills would relieve the 'suffering of cartloads of women' and whether the Marriage Act of 1753 had caused an increase in divorces. One Member blamed the perfidious French, who 'had contributed not a little to [divorce] by the introduction of their *petit maitres* fidlers and dancing masters who had been allowed to teach our wives and misses to *allmandi* and to twist and turn them about at their pleasure'. For some Members, the adultery question was more

*Breaking the enemy line, from Robert's own copy of
Paul Hoste's* L'Art des armées navales *(1697).*

important even than 'peace or war, or any constitutional question'.[6]

In London, Robert was not so preoccupied with the city's temptations as to be distracted from his resolve to make 'a name and figure'
in the navy. Although he was ashore, his mind remained at sea, for
around this time he obtained an eighty-four-year-old copy of Paul
Hoste's naval tactics book *L'Art des armées navales* in its original French,
a language with which Robert was conversant.[7] In the wake of the
Battle of Ushant, there was a growing awareness, not only among
naval officers, that the traditional line-of-battle tactic seemed only to
produce inconclusive results. Literature on naval strategy was scanty,
and while the Scotsman John Clerk of Eldin was working on producing some volumes in English, eventually to appear in the next decade,
the best works available in the 1770s were those by the two Frenchmen
Hoste (originally published in 1697) and Bigot de Morogues (*Tactique
navale*, 1763).[8] Both of them discussed the tactic of breaking through
the enemy's line. Opinion on this dangerous manoeuvre was divided,
for it exposed the ships' vulnerable ends and required firing on both
sides; but it could be decisive. Robert may well have been one of those
who dreamed of such audacious exploits that would bring glory –
without being hanged for the attempt.

★

On 16 June, 'Wednesday P.M: 5 o'clock', Lord Rockingham sent a
note to Arlington Street, asking Charles to call in on him at home
in Grosvenor Square later that evening. As if guessing that the elu-
sive new young duke would not oblige, Rockingham urged that 'your
Grace ought to take your seat in the House [of Lords] tomorrow (if
you have not already) – you certainly should be present on so solemn a
business'. Rockingham's anxiety stemmed from news that the Spanish
ambassador had delivered, as he now told Charles, what amounted to
'a manifesto' that was 'full tantamount to a declaration of War', his
emphatic underscoring pressing his dilatory young friend to act. Obedient for once, on the following day the new Duke of Rutland assumed
his hereditary seat in the House. He was sworn in alongside his friend
John Pitt, the 2nd Earl of Chatham. The earl was not entering politics
with the same fervour as the distinguished 1st Earl, for his priority
was to be a soldier; but, like Charles, he sat with the opposition and

must have sensed his late father's direst predictions being fulfilled as he listened in the House. It transpired that on 12 April, France, having allied with the rebel Americans fourteen months earlier, had signed a secret treaty with Spain. The Spanish, fearful of the consequences for their own American possessions, did not openly support the colonists' rebellion, but were eager to take advantage of Britain's distractions to try and regain lost territory. The Franco-Spanish alliance placed Britain in a dreadful position, for while the country's war effort was principally directed against the American colonies, now Britain's own coasts and its overseas possessions were potentially exposed to Franco-Spanish expeditionary forces. So, too, were Britain's vast fleets of merchant-men, importing supplies for the war effort as well as taxable luxuries.

On 21 June 1779 Spain officially declared war on Britain. By the end of that month, the Spanish had besieged Gibraltar – instituting a naval blockade, constructing forts and batteries, and assembling a large army in readiness for an attack. And all this was taking place just at the moment when Parliament was prorogued, not to sit again until the end of November 1779. During that time, a predicament would unfold more acute even than the threat of invasion by the Spanish Armada in 1588.

It seemed that Lord Sandwich, who had long tried to persuade other ministers that the bulk of the naval fleet should be retained in European waters to defend British coasts, might actually be proved right. While the Spanish were besieging Gibraltar, their ministers had also been planning with the French to take advantage of the weakness of the British Channel Fleet. The arrival of intelligence in June that Admiral d'Orvilliers had left Brest with a large fleet, sailing south to rendez-vous with the Spanish under Don Luis de Córdova y Córdova, was met with alarm. The combined fleets of the House of Bourbon were said to amount to an estimated seventy sails of the line, while some 40,000 French troops were being mustered at Le Havre and St Malo, along with the necessary transports. Was a full-scale invasion about to take place? Sandwich urged his fellow Admiralty Board members to reinforce the Channel Fleet by all means possible, while Sir Charles Hardy hoisted his flag in the *Victory* and took command of thirty-seven ships of the line with attendant frigates. He was ordered to cruise off the Scilly Islands to cover the Channel and protect incoming merchant fleets from the East and West Indies, while guarding against an invasion of Britain's Achilles' heel – Ireland.

Just one month after war was declared, on 28 July 1779, Lord Rockingham – after chivalrously relating that Lady Rockingham had a 'severe attack of head ache and fever on Sunday' – gloomily told Charles he 'understood that the combined fleets of France and Spain are about 51 of the line looking out for Sir Charles Hardy – who has 34 or perhaps 35 or 36. These circumstances in other times would be deemed horrid and alarming – but at present it seems nothing extraordinary. How or how soon – it is all to end – I know not.'

His words, for once, did not fall on deaf ears, for Charles was now attending to his public responsibilities with more gusto than usual. The great fear of a Franco-Spanish invasion shouldered aside domestic issues, such as bickering over adultery, in favour of more pressing matters: such as raising the extra naval manpower needed for the county militias. The tax-paying gentry were already supporting an enlarged army, including the costs of mercenaries, but most of the soldiers were abroad; there were not many eligible people still available to augment the militias which were needed to defend Britain's coast in the event of an invasion.

Some nobles were prepared to contribute from their own pockets by offering to undertake the traditional expedients of raising regiments. Charles himself already had considerable military responsibility, having been appointed by the king in July 1779 to be his Lord Lieutenant of Leicestershire, a position making him the monarch's representative in the shire and the chief officer of its militia. But this did not satisfy the young duke. He was conscious of his family's tradition of being ready to raise a regiment, and before him were the examples of his grandfather during the 1745 rebellion and his father during the Seven Years' War. Charles now wanted to raise his own regiment of light cavalry – as he told Joseph Hill, the 'same plan as the Royal Forresters were last war', referring to the 21st Granby's Light Dragoons raised by the old marquis in the spring of 1760, while he was on leave in England and mourning for his wife. Granby's cavalrymen, commonly known as the Royal Forresters, patrolled England's east coast using horses from the Belvoir Hunt, until the regiment was disbanded in March 1763. But to do such a thing now, it was calculated, would cost at least £12,000.

Charles decided to go ahead anyway, and instructed Joseph Hill that the regiment was to be raised 'at no expense to the government'. Therefore, he had to find the funds from his own resources, but this sent him into little short of panic over how to do it. To his great frustration, the death of his grandfather had not brought an end to his financial problems. Old Rutland had left a number of legacies in his will which had to be fulfilled, and, as Charles confided in Hill, 'The largeness of my bills together with the legacies have entirely exhausted the sum I found in the Bankers hands.' Hill was trying unsuccessfully during the exigencies of war to raise loans on favourable terms, but he was now told by Charles to 'take a large sum on any terms... in God's name apply anywhere you know that money may be procured'.

It had crossed Charles's mind to ask Lord Mansfield for a loan; but he then thought better of it, for he would 'not like to be personally refused'. Mansfield had been giving him some stern advice:

> I think the Trust Deed as far as it relates to your father's debts requires attention... I approve your generosity, but it should be so managed as not to put too much in the power of others. There is one thing I would earnestly recommend to you of your setting out, to look a little yourself into your own affairs; be assured that the best Trustees are nothing but paper and packthread. If you attend a little to your own business you may do great and noble things and live in magnificence and affluence... A little resolution would effect it and a habit of business acquired now would certainly be the greatest service to your Grace through life... If you totally neglect it... you will be a prey and very soon undone.

He had signed off with a judicial flourish, *Dii meliora*, 'may Heaven send us better times'. But Charles's ears were largely deaf to his uncle's pleas to be more self-reliant and business-minded, though in the event his offer to raise cavalry was turned down by the government.

Lord Rockingham seized the chance to score some points for the opposition, telling the House of Lords how generous Charles had been to offer to raise a regiment of cavalry, 'the expense of which the noble Duke had been given to believe would cost him £12,000'. He continued: 'Surely if ministers threw cold water on such an offer they ought to do more themselves. He had not heard of any offer

coming from them. Last war, the noble Earl at the head of the Admiralty [Sandwich] had raised a regiment, had he offered to raise one
now? If he had he [Rockingham] had not heard of it. Had the first
Lord of the Treasury [North] offered to raise one? He believed not.'
Rockingham told them they were 'the most incompetent ministers
this kingdom was ever cursed with. They had themselves occasioned
the cloud which now blackened the British horizon; let them beware
it did not burst upon their own heads!'

That cloud now blackening the horizon – the vast Franco-Spanish
fleet threatening to invade British shores – needed the Royal Navy to be
the first bulwark of defence. But the fleets were already overstretched,
facing multiple problems, including the refusal of many competent
senior officers to serve after the Keppel–Palliser affair, the poor condition of the ships (and their paucity in numbers), and the difficulties
of manning them. Attempting to station ships around the world to
provide support to the army and protect trade routes placed almost
impossible demands upon the Admiralty – and on the subsidiary Navy
Board, the Royal Dockyards and the contracted shipbuilders too. The
entire effort, in turn, placed pressure on Lord North's Treasury.

★

While the navy as a whole was coming under such a massive weight of
expectation, Lord Robert was beside himself with frustration. On the
face of it, he was moving on – Lord Sandwich had taken his request
into consideration and found a vacancy for him on the 74-gun *Alcide*.
Yet, Sandwich had not brought himself to oblige the young Whig
officer completely, for Robert's commission was no higher than 3rd
lieutenant; and his ship was brand new, still on the builder's slipway at
Deptford and in no way near ready to join the Channel Fleet.

As an officer, Robert could at least have on board his own 'servant',
to provide assistance with daily tasks. He had chosen for this role
one Charles Ekins, probably a relative of the Eton tutor John Ekins.[9]
Robert joined his new ship on 15 July 1779. The *Alcide* was one of Sir
Thomas Slade's Albion-class third-rate 74-gun ships. These were the
two-deckers that formed the backbone of the battle fleet's divisions.
And such was the speed with which ships were being brought forward
to join Hardy's flag, there was no time to complete the *Alcide*'s copper

sheathing before she slid down the greasy slipway and into the filthy waters of the Thames on 31 July 1779.

On 5 August 1779, Robert, like many others at this pressing time, made his will, which he did in the presence of Joseph Hill. He left £1,000 to John Ekins, and a further £1,000 to family friend Mun Stevens. The residue of his estate he left to Charles. He left nothing to his sister. This last act was a deliberate and discriminatory decision, for if he died intestate, Frances would be entitled to half of his assets.

Yet more disappointment for Robert came with the difficulties in manning the *Alcide* and the vast amount of work still required to commission her with an initial draft of only 200 men, many of them pressed. The consequence was that, though needed, the *Alcide* could not be part of Sir Charles Hardy's Channel Fleet, which sailed from Portsmouth without her. Thus, Robert found himself still stuck in Deptford with his ship moored alongside an old hulk when, on 14 August, an enormous enemy fleet came within sight of the English coast and appeared to hover off Plymouth, causing a wave of alarm to spread throughout the country. England was ill-prepared to fend off an invasion. Robert's old Newfoundland governor, Molyneux Shuld-ham, now the port-admiral at Plymouth, hurriedly put the place into a posture of defence. Civic authorities began to remove coastal communities inland, and livestock was killed or dispersed and food destroyed so as not to be available to any invading forces. The militias were mustered, horsemen rode along the coast to watch for the enemy, beacons were piled up ready for lighting, and watchmen were stationed on every church tower overlooking the Channel.

Then, to the horror of every witness, and to all who heard of it soon afterwards, the impossible occurred. The combined fleets of France and Spain entered Plymouth Sound and anchored in Cawsand Bay. Plymouth descended into chaos; many of the town's inhabitants fled and the 'Commissioner of the Dockyard', Captain Paul Ourry, had a nervous breakdown. Preparing to take desperate measures, he ranted to Lord Sandwich that 'for some days past I put the question to myself, shall I, Paul Ourry or you Jack Dorvilliers [sic] set fire to the dockyard?'[10]

The news of the enemy fleet spread rapidly, reaching the *Alcide* on 19 August, from whence Robert dashed to the Admiralty in Whitehall to see if he could find out more. There, he scribbled a few lines to Charles, who had gone to Belvoir to gather his Leicestershire Militia:

My Dear Brother, an account is just arrived at the Admiralty from Ld Shuldham that the French fleet consisting of 86 sail 57 or 58 of which are of the line are now at an anchor at Cawsand Bay by Plymouth, & that another fleet has made its appearance but at too great a distance to ascertain whether they are S^r C Hardy's fleet or the enemy's transports. The consternation now is pretty general & the ministers a good deal dejected … I came here this moment from Deptford to hear the news & shall return immediately.

Beneath his signature, Robert added: 'An express is arrived this moment at the Admiralty & no one can guess what it contains.'

What Sandwich and his Board of Commissioners learned when the despatch was unsealed was that on the previous day, 18 August, the enemy fleet had in fact *left* Cawsand Bay. But for where? And where was Hardy with the wooden walls of Old England? Fogs and strong winds meant that reports of sightings could not be relied upon; there was talk of Hardy and his ships off the Isles of Scilly, and of the enemy having been driven far westwards by the onset of an unseasonal easterly gale. The national mood was expectant and greedy for news, and vacillating between fear of invasion and hope that Hardy and his men had already settled matters with the enemy.

Meanwhile, Charles had left Belvoir, and, with his Leicestershire Militia, had reached Plymouth by the end of August. In the camp, morale was low and the strain of anticipation was reflected in the drinking and debauchery that went on after dark. Even Charles felt the pressure. The Duchess of Devonshire remarked, after receiving reports from observers, that: 'In case of the enemy's landing they must all either perish by the invader or be drown'd in making their escape… the Duke of Rutland says he should think himself lucky to escape with the loss of an arm or a leg.'[11] The Whigs were attempting to turn the dramas to their advantage. Robert received a letter from a friend in Charles's regiment, who evidently did not care if it was opened by censors: 'My Dear Lord… You can't think how exasperated everyone is with the ministry… Now whosoever you are who has opened this letter… do carry this intelligence to the First Lord of the Admiralty that the people at Plymouth are so incensed and enraged with him that if he dare shew his head in town he would be torn limb from limb.'

As August rolled into September, there was still no substantiated news of the whereabouts of either fleet. Then Charles received a letter from Admiral Keppel, written on 4 September. The *Victory* and the Channel Fleet had arrived in Portsmouth on the 3rd, undamaged and not having fired a single shot.

Gradually, details of what had happened emerged. Córdova's Spanish squadrons had missed the rendezvous with d'Orvilliers off La Coruña and had been late in joining the French fleet. Within a few weeks of their leaving port, scurvy, typhus and smallpox had broken out among the ships' companies, and spread rapidly to threaten the whole enterprise. D'Orvilliers had lost his only son in an epidemic which so weakened the crews that the handling of the ships was jeopardized. Amid his personal grief, the French admiral had disagreed with orders arriving from Paris to alter the landing place to Cornwall, and any respite at anchor off Plymouth was ended by the onset of strong winds which, combined with poor holding ground, forced their abrupt departure on 18 August. Attempts to engage Hardy failed, for he had succeeded in slipping past them, hoping to draw the enemy's combined fleet east and destroy it close to the cover of Portsmouth.

Their plans bedevilled by the widespread sickness and the prospect of extending the fighting into the winter, the French and Spanish admirals abandoned their campaign and set sail for Brest – where d'Orvilliers resigned in disgust. For the British, the calamity was receding; but it was followed by the usual round of recriminations. Keppel wrote again to Charles criticizing Hardy, railing that the Channel Fleet's failure to bring the Franco-Spanish ships to battle was 'a sorry state of affairs', and the old Lord Chatham would have 'had something to say about it'. In fact, Sir Charles Hardy, old and tired though he might have been, had proved judiciously wily in the face of overwhelming force. Had he fought and lost, the nation's sea power would have been forsaken and Britain's poor and hurriedly extemporized defences would not have been able to stop an invasion.

Eventually, though, it was discovered that a full-scale invasion had not necessarily been the overriding intention of the French and Spanish ministries; rather, they had hoped to take advantage of a weak British fleet – as they perceived it to be at the Battle of Ushant – and at least seize the Isle of Wight to use as a bargaining-counter for Gibraltar. Yet, the invasion attempt still had a sting in its tail, for just three weeks later a homeward-bound Baltic convoy was attacked off Flamborough Head by two men-of-war commanded by that scourge of the British coast, John Paul Jones, whose cruise had been planned as a deliberate diversion from the Franco-Spanish expedition. On 23 September 1779, the convoy's escort, consisting of the frigate *Serapis* and a sloop-of-war, were captured, though not before battering Jones's *Bonhomme Richard*, which shortly afterwards foundered. Having the French and Spanish in the English Channel and the upstart Yankees in the North Sea was an almost unendurable humiliation for Britain. Three days later, Charles received a letter from an eyewitness to the engagement, Samuel Beilby, whom he knew through his electoral interests at Scarborough. 'I thought the above account might amuse you,' Beilby wrote, 'and have therefore sent it. How inexcusable is [the] Ministry in leaving all this coast without a single ship of force! All the [merchant] ships in Hull, Burlington, Scarborough and Whitby might easily be destroyed by any determined adventurer.'

★

While chaos reigned around the coast, Robert was simply bored. 'I have had the Ennui to an excessive degree from the state of Inactivity I have been in, added to my disappointment,' he told Charles. Although he had been made 2nd lieutenant on 2 September 1779, this was still not the 'station of honour' he had hoped for. His envy of Charles's situation was ill-concealed: 'I hear you are in a very active post at Plymouth which if you keep your health, is far preferable to mine.' For Robert was trapped in an unglamorous position, which he described as 'very little employment'. By this he did not mean he had nothing to do, but that it was dull. In hot and sultry weather, he had overseen the crew hauling aboard almost 300 tons of shingle ballast and some 158 tons of guns, including seventy-four cannon and their carriages. Then there was the requisite powder and more than 6,000 round cannon balls, along with musket balls, grapeshot, langridge, bar- and chainshot, cutlasses, boarding pikes and much else besides.[12] Being still short of men, the *Alcide* made use of eighty 'Greenwich pensioners' from the Royal Hospital for Seamen, who knotted and spliced the rigging and cordage that, if put end to end, would stretch to some 25 miles. More than a hundred riggers and labourers from Woolwich and Deptford also assisted.

Then there were the many tons of food and gallons of beer and water to be brought aboard, all by hand or with pulleys, from the ordnance and victualling yards at Chatham and Deptford, and the laying of all the barrels in their tiers. Despite myths to the contrary, the Georgian navy fed its men well enough for them to give 'of their utmost' both in handling their ships and in battle; and the way it achieved this was to issue each man with a standard daily ration. The *Alcide* was loaded for 'Channel Service' – which meant she would have sufficient supplies to feed a complement of around six hundred men for three months. The purser could then calculate how much food was on board at any one time and send weekly 'State and Condition' reports ashore, enabling stock levels to be managed aboard the ships and at the victualling yards. All this effort required fearsome amounts of bureaucracy. Every comestible coming aboard was checked, each stage of the production process having been countersigned – and if breaches

Two days in the life of the Alcide, as recorded in the master's log, 1779.

in standards, weight or condition of victuals were uncovered, those responsible could be made to pay from their own pockets and the suppliers' precious contracts could be terminated. True, the system was not entirely free of corruption, nor did it prevent inedible products arriving on board – such as a cheese so hard that one ship used it in place of wood – but by and large it worked well.

The grand effort to prepare the *Alcide* for sea was overseen by Captain John Douglas Brisbane. He had with him his ten-year-old son, Midshipman Charles Brisbane, along with 1st Lieutenant John Dilkes, Lord Robert as 2nd lieutenant, four other commissioned officers and all the warrant officers. The rest of the complement consisted of an extraordinary melting-pot of men and, unofficially, a number of women too, who – crammed together on this 168-foot vessel – slept at night in their rows of hammocks just 14 inches apart, slung on the gundecks among the cannon. Some of the crew were volunteers, already with sea experience, from places like Whitehaven and Brighton, or had joined via the Marine Society. Others were from inland counties looking for employment and hoping for prize-money. Some were even drafted from other naval vessels or taken from merchant ships and a great many were pressed 'landsmen'. The musters listing their places of birth show they came from all over England, Scotland, Wales and Ireland, and as far as the Shetlands; there were even some from Sweden, and some born in America – in Philadelphia and Rhode Island. Most of them were in their twenties and thirties, but there were a few teenagers and others in their forties. The ship's chaplain, the Reverend Patrick Touch, may have provided spiritual assistance to settle in the new company, while the quota of armed Marines taken on from the barracks at Chatham might have offered a different sort of encouragement.

Many of the new recruits would have been stripped and their clothes destroyed, before being resupplied from the purser's 'slop chest'. One of the real killers in the navy was typhus, carried by lice in dirty clothes. While the true pathology of the disease was not understood, a variety of suspected causes like 'corrupted air', reinforced the officers' attention to the cleanliness of ships and men, undoubtedly helping to limit its effect. By Robert's time, a divisional system was increasingly in use, whereby every man on the ship was known to at least one officer who could keep an eye on his discipline and cleanliness.

But none of this routine was what Robert wanted at that moment. It was little consolation that Hardy's fleet had failed to fire a shot in anger, and he was doubly aggrieved by the feeling he had been deceived, posted to the 'very last ship that was to join Sir C Hardy so diametrically opposite to what [he] ask'd [for] & [Sandwich] promised', as he vented to Charles. He feared he would remain a 2nd lieutenant, being 'in one of the worst mann'd ships in the service & in the beginning of Winter which will', he said sarcastically, 'add to the many pleasant circumstances I have lately met with'. Profoundly frustrated, he made time during October to dine with his uncle Lord Mansfield at Kenwood House, where he solicited the judge's influence as a government supporter to request a promotion to post-captain. Robert also courted the support of Mansfield's nephew, Captain Sir John Lindsay, while the latter's daughter, the mulatto Dido Elizabeth Belle, and Mansfield's niece, Lady Elizabeth Murray, added to the attractions of Kenwood. Robert's hopes of promotion were raised by his visits; he told Charles that Mansfield 'desired me not to be uneasy at its not having been done before as he was certain it would be done in a handsome manner & soon; & assured me he would mention it again to Ld Sandwich'.

By early November 1779, the *Alcide* had at last left the Thames. The Greenwich pensioners and Woolwich and Deptford labourers had been left behind, but so had thirteen of the crew, who had deserted, 'run' from the ship. The weather had turned nasty, so Robert and the other officers had to work the new recruits straight out into 'strong gales and very dirty weather', one man requiring seventy-five lashes to 'persuade' him to his duty as they made their way round to Portsmouth. On 14 November, as they reached St Helens, the wind died to nothing, so the *Alcide*'s boats towed her to an anchor 'between the buoys of Nomans Land and [Portsmouth] Church', as the log noted. The next day, the wind was howling again, so they moved closer to the shelter of Spithead, though the ship dragged her anchor, not finally coming to rest until midnight on 15 November.

The following day, Robert, tired and dispirited, penned a letter to Charles from his mahogany desk – to the sounds of the *Alcide*'s creaking timbers, the thuds and shouts of men as they tidied the ship, and the wind shrieking in the rigging. '*Alcide* Spithead Nov 16th,' wrote Robert, stabbing at the page. 'My Dearest Brother... You might perceive by my last letter I was not perfectly pleased, I have still less reason to be so now, for I discover plainly, my promotion was never intended & that I have been all along amused with specious words & promises which were never meant to be fulfill'd.'

He was sure, he told Charles, that amid the hopefuls showering Sandwich daily with applications for advancement, there were some, such as Lord Charles FitzGerald, who were rumoured to be unfairly close to a promotion. Probably referring to Charles's investment in raising a regiment, he added tartly: 'Thus you see of how little avail are large & liberal donations to a government whose ministers esteem nothing but Parliamentary votes to establish them in their places & carry them through their destructive measures.' Robert then continued his tirade against Sandwich, whose 'character is too well known for any man of higher understanding than an Idiot to put confidence in his promises; I only wonder how Lord Mansfield could pay so much attention to what he said as to relate the conversation to me.'

On paper stained with blotted ink and savage deletions of angry words, Robert ranted: 'Since I saw you there have been numerous opportunities of doing it soon & in a handsome manner, which opportunities have not been lost on other people as I verily believe twenty Captains have been made. I have never yet been so seriously irritated during the course of my service or felt on professional occasion so much as on this.' His sense of entitlement was palpable: 'It is trifling too much with one of the first families in the Kingdom. I hope to God some time or other to have it in my power to shew my displeasure. It is a thing I cannot readily forgive.' And there was yet more to his distress: 'My situation in the *Alcide* (excepting the Captain & officers whom I like exceedingly) is very unpleasant. Conceive a ship by no means a capital one of her class newly mann'd with raw undisciplin'd men & few of them seamen going out in a wintry season to cruize in a boisterous climate & then conclude what our situation must be, at least for a good while, acting against an Enemy prepar'd and fit for service.' Still, even such discomfort he considered 'a thing of too trifling a nature to be regarded, when so important an object as my promotion (if I can get it) is in view'. Then, sensing his impotence in the face of circumstance, he acknowledged: 'However let it be. I must resign myself but it is an extreme hard case.'

Robert's fury was not only the cry of an expectant aristocrat determined to pursue what he considered his natural right. All around
him was intense competition, for places were in short supply even
though the country was at war. In truth, Robert was one of many
hopefuls, some of whom would be successful while others would not;
and he was by no means unique in attempting to call upon whatever
advantages he thought he might possess. It was, however, a deeper
frustration to him than most to find that even with both grandfathers
being dukes, and a duke as a brother, he could not circumvent the
system. He considered, as did others of his ilk, that Lord Sandwich's
insistence on ability as a pre-requisite for career advancement and on
the order of the 'queue' being respected was a form of corruption in
its own right.

Having vented his spleen, Robert's thoughts turned to his brother,
whose love and support he cherished far beyond the role of accomplice to ambition: 'I wish very much to see you, but fear it will be
impracticable at least for some time. In the meanwhile I beg to hear
from you, as you can have no idea what alternate anger & depression
of spirits I have felt. However you must not forget me to the Duchess
who I hope finds no inconvenience from the frequent alarms from
time to time off Plymouth. God bless you my Dearest Brother I am
yours most affectionately Robt: Manners.'

Some days later, Robert suffered the irritation of seeing Sir Charles
Hardy in the *Victory* arriving from a cruise, while in the *Alcide* they
had to attend to varieties of 'dull' business – of submitting Weekly
Accounts, taking on more ammunition from Gosport, washing the
ship with vinegar, fumigating the lower deck, scrubbing the hammocks, while the 'ventilator' – a kind of mechanical windmill in the
bowels of the ship – extracted the damp and foul air during what the
log called 'very dirty weather with Rain and Thunder'. Meanwhile, a
cutter was sent off in search of some deserters, some marines were
punished for fighting, and an officer was sent to witness the execution
of a marine on another ship. No one yet knew where they might be
sailing to. 'The reports are as you may suppose various, West Indies,
America, St Helena, Gibraltar have all been equally talked of,' Robert
told Charles on 30 November.[13] The first of these possibilities was a
worry to him. 'I hope we are not to be sent to the West Indies,' he

wrote, 'indeed we cannot go for some time as we are not sheathed [with copper].'

His fears were then confirmed when scuttlebutt was replaced by firm orders: the *Alcide* and the fleet assembling around her were destined for the West Indies under the command of Sir George Brydges Rodney. This was news indeed, for this highly experienced admiral, whose rise in the navy had been meteoric during the 1740s and 1750s, had not so far served in the war. Although born of poor parents, Rodney had earned a fortune from prize-money, enabling him to buy a country seat and obtain a seat in Parliament; but he had also become unpopular in the service, with a reputation for gambling, misappropriating money and abusing his powers of patronage. In the early 1770s, he was bankrupted and fled to France for four years to escape his creditors; but when Britain and France declared war again, Rodney was given a loan by the Maréchal de Biron, a premier French nobleman, who considered it dishonourable for a British admiral not to serve his country. Sir George returned home in 1778 to find he had attained the rank of Admiral of the White, and that his accrued arrears of pay had cleared his debt.

It was with some reluctance that Lord Sandwich had turned in late 1779 to this now very senior admiral to take command of the Leeward Islands station in the West Indies. For although Rodney was a government supporter, he was still disliked in the navy. But Sandwich was faced with a lack of flag-officers willing to serve the ministry, and he needed an experienced commander who could also undertake a dangerous secret mission, before heading west across the Atlantic. Robert thus informed Charles in early December that the *Alcide* was 'preparing with all expedition for sea though our destination is not known. Certain it is she goes out with Sr G. Rodney, & that pretty soon.'

Still, this did not resolve Robert's anguish, for he could not know whether his new station would be 'desirable for me or not'. He had mixed feelings with good reason. On the one hand, the West Indies were notorious for tropical diseases and ship-worm. On the other, they could provide rich prize-winnings. Yet, more important for Robert was that his situation relieved Sandwich of the pressure to advance him at home, since it was possible for flag-officers on foreign stations to make promotions, away from the glare of public scrutiny. He warned

Charles, with perhaps a little peevishness, that 'there is one thing I beg leave to caution you against, should Ld Mansfield or any person talk to you of a recommendation to Sr Geo: Rodney in the West Indies reprobate the idea, as I know the end of all those vague promises perfectly well. They are the constant recommendations which Ld Sandwich is so liberal of when he wishes to send the person out of his way… I fancy that the Admiralty are determined to proscribe me.' In Robert's eyes, to be overlooked now would be 'so serious a matter to my future expectations in my profession and indeed life'. He urged his 'dear brother' to 'consider these points maturely and deliberately and should your opinion coincide with mine lay them both before Lord Mansfield'.

Lord Mansfield did rally to support his orphaned nephew, reassuring Sandwich on 2 December 1779 that Robert was genuinely keen on the navy, but that 'the same ambition makes him impatient of being humbled, mortified & kept back'. Failure to promote a duke's brother would be felt by 'the whole family… as a personal injury', he went on, pointing out that there would be those 'who will rejoice to exasperate, & ascribe his being neglected to false motives & call it by false names… I conjure your Lordship to consider how prejudicial so bitter an alienation of so considerable a family may be.' A week later, Mansfield again pressured the First Lord. With Charles and his circle already 'very sore & much mortified… [Lord Robert] wishes to continue in the Profession from Ambition and not for Bread', Sandwich was told. 'If he is to rise by the same slow Degrees by which every Cabin Boy may be advanced, there is no Prospect worthy of Ambition, & the same spirit which makes him desire to pursue the Profession, must make him quit from Despair of being early enough in a Rank, which will enable him to make a figure.'

Lord Sandwich was thus placed in an unenviable position. Robert was still just a lieutenant of only eighteen months' seniority. By naval standards, he needed much more experience to have a claim on a command, which given in to now would cause rancour elsewhere. But, such was the ambiguity of his situation that, in social terms, he had every right to a rank that would 'enable him to make a figure', and now he even had the Tory Lord Mansfield fighting his corner. If Sandwich could not speedily find a way to gratify the expectations of Robert and his family, both the First Lord and the ministry could expect to lose another otherwise dedicated sea-officer. Sandwich responded by sending a note to Robert, attempting to placate the young man lest he quit.

But Robert's own correspondence reveals he was not driven by *simply* raw ambition; he had more depth to him. On 5 December, he again took up his pen to confide in Charles: 'My Dearest Brother... I must confess honestly that however decidedly I profess'd to quit in my last [letter,] I find myself, upon tryal incapable of doing [so] & must defer that as my last resource.' It was not Sandwich's note that had placated him, which was 'so vague & unpromising, that so far from my being pleas'd & putting confidence in it, was it in my power by any means other than quitting, I should certainly endeavour to shew my disapprobation', but his own conscience and logic:

> ... when I deliberate on the consequences that must naturally attend such a decision, when I consider the time I have already spent in pursuit of an object which indeed has not answered in the full extent of my wishes yet would be entirely thrown away was I now to quit this line & follow another not to mention the real attachment I always had & still have to the profession. With these reasons however unpleasant & galling it may be to see contemporaries & juniors both in life & service preferred before me (for what Ld Sandwich has averted to the contrary & I avert it to be the fact) I conclude it is preferable to suffer the unpleasing moment of waiting for the present than those constant disagreeable reflections, I certainly should have [if I left now].

Yet even his conscience had limits. Robert then added in a defiant response to Sandwich's note: 'I will by no means be imposed upon for if I find in this instance I am trifled with I shall immediately throw up and suffer any inconvenience whatever rather than to remain much longer in the service.'

With various destinations mooted for the secret mission *en route* to the West Indies, Robert told Charles that the 'report at present is that we are going either to New York or Gibraltar'. He resolved to undertake his next voyage as a 'cruize of service', after which, 'should matters remain in the same state, I can then leave the service without any person venturing to impeach my conduct & with the pleasure of

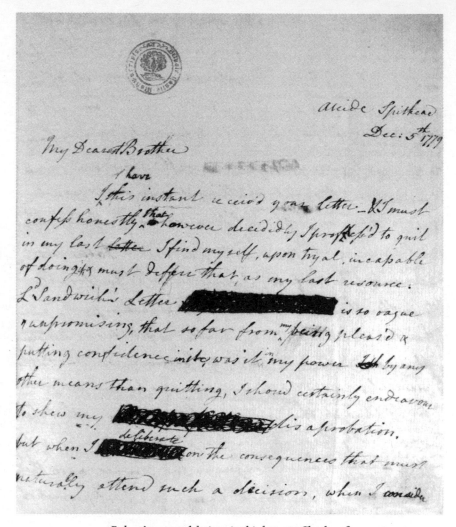

*Robert's savage deletions in this letter to Charles of
5 December 1779 reveal his frustration and irritation.*

being every way satisfied with myself'. He could not, he wrote, 'sufficiently express my thanks to Sr John Lindsay for the trouble he has taken & the kindness he had shown now and indeed on every occasion since my first acquaintance with him'. After sending his 'remembrance & love to the Duchess… as I hear she is at Belvoir', he picked at his wound again: 'Perhaps you may have soon some more satisfactory relation of the method of my obtaining promotion for I confess I cannot call the present one such.'

*

Lindsay's uncle, Lord Mansfield, may well have reflected upon what his sister-in-law Charlotte Somerset would have made of the two grandsons she had cared for so tenderly. She had predicted that Robert would 'be considerable at sea', and so would hardly have been surprised by his ambition. She would not have been surprised, either, that Charles's handling of money was proving no better than it had been during her guardianship. Throughout the momentous months of 1779, he was distracted by his interests, corresponding with Alleyne FitzHerbert over such niceties as the purchase of, *inter alia*, a Rubens and a shipment of some Hungarian Tokay. Even the diplomat felt moved in a letter of 7 September to swipe at Charles's financial chaos, commenting that duties on German wines were not exorbitant and therefore 'will cause no derangement in the rigid system of domestic demony for which you have ever been so remarkable'.

Although Charles's grandmother might have been gratified by his streak of determination to be dutiful to his country's defence, she would have been horrified at the financial risk of his decision, in the summer of 1779, to fund a regiment of infantry. Although his offer of cavalry had been turned down, Charles instead set about raising the 86th Regiment of Foot, which would be known as the 'Rutland Regiment'. He needed at least £6,000 to fund it, a sum that rapidly soared to over £9,000. Eventually Lord Mansfield came to the rescue. 'My dear Lord,' wrote the judge:

> ... I hear you are greatly distressed for the money you necessarily want for raising your regiment [and] that you have offered promising[,] which I greatly disapprove [of] because it blows your credit at the very time of succeeding to your Estate. I can get together about £6000 which I destined for another purpose but it cannot be better employed than to accommodate you. The security proposed by a mortgage on a sufficient part of your Cambridgeshire estate will take up time, [but] I am told you are exceedingly pressed. Therefore I will take your bond and trust to your promise that if the money is not paid at the day and the condition of the bond you will give me a mortgage to my satisfaction.

Charles seemed unable to stop himself from throwing money at whatever he wanted to. Yet ironically he urged economies on others, even his wife. As the invasion threat receded, he left Plymouth and proceeded to London in late November 1779, suffering himself to attend Parliament as it reconvened after the summer break. Meanwhile, Mary Isabella took the children to spend their first Christmas at Belvoir now it was their own country seat. On 8 December Charles wrote to 'rejoice at the receipt of that most desirable letter which informs me that her on whom my soul is [bestowed], is recovered from the sickness which had alarmed me yesterday beyond measure'. He had some serious business to report from London: 'The principal argument which ran through the [Parliamentary] debate was economy,' he told Mary Isabella, which, while admitting economizing was necessary, 'nobody seems to have begun'. Compounding the pressures was the threat of something near 'a universal bankruptcy among the tenants if rents are not lowered', hinting at the strong possibility of disaffection and possibly even revolt if matters did not improve. Charles thought there was little room for optimism, for 'everything bad is to be dreaded. If some alteration does not take place, I fear some dreadful convulsion in this country will arise. Things appear ripe, & people enraged. God Almighty avert the storm & leave the beautiful constitution of the kingdom uninjured & unimpaired.'

Then he turned, for a moment, on his wife. 'It is impossible we can continue our present mode of living long,' he told her. 'Indeed I must press economy to you. You must not purchase everything your eye is attached to – no superfluous cloaths beyond that is requisite for you to appear clean and decent… You must likewise be attentive to the expenses of the children, whose bills, you know, I objected to as extravagant last year.' As if to soften his reprimand, he assured her he would put his own 'affairs under regulation, for I have enormous private debts suspended over my head, besides the appearance of general calamity', before signing off affectionately: 'Embrace all our children from their fond father, and love in the same proportions as I do you which cannot be exceeded…'

*

On the same day that Charles was urging his wife to frugality – probably to no avail – Lord Sandwich was urging Admiral Rodney to get on with his secret mission. 'For God's sake go to sea without delay, you cannot conceive of what importance it is to yourself, to me, and to the public that you should not lose this fair wind. If you do, I shall not only hear of it in Parliament, but in places to which I pay more attention.' Besides his concerns for strategy, Sandwich needed help with removing some thorns in his side. Drawing on the flag-officers' prerogative to make promotions at sea, he asked Rodney to find a way of taking the young aristocrat Lord Charles FitzGerald 'off my hands'.[14] And FitzGerald was not the only such officer the First Lord wished to be free of, telling Rodney: 'There is another young man of fashion now in your squadron concerning whom I am tormented to death; I cannot do anything for him at home, therefore if you could contrive while he remains with you by some means or other to give him rank you will infinitely oblige me. The person I mean is Lord Robert Manners who is now a lieutenant on board the *Alcide*.'[15] Sandwich wrote again to Rodney, on 12 December, enclosing a private missive from an unknown hand (possibly Sir John Lindsay's): 'Sir, I send you in confidence a private letter (which you will be so good as to return) to show you how pressing Ld. R: M:s friends are and what a difficulty you will get me out of if... you can get him off my hands; if he comes back a lieutenant his quitting the service must follow, as it will be impossible for me to promote him at home.'[16]

Robert knew nothing of this, and instead had cause to be further infuriated. A rumour was circulating that he was to join the *Sandwich*, Rodney's flagship, but only as a 9th lieutenant, which would have represented a backwards step. Stung by this seeming ill-treatment, he raged that to remain in the *Alcide* as 2nd lieutenant would be preferable, despite the ship's complement of raw recruits. Luckily, the rumour proved false and by Christmas 1779, when Robert again confided in Charles, his spirits seemed to have lifted: 'I have been turning over in my mind just now Lord Sandwich's letter which he wrote in consequence of Lord Mansfield's application & I think upon reflection that there is a possibility of his speaking the truth <u>for once</u>.'

Towards the end of December 1779, a large fleet and convoy of store-ships gathered at Spithead. The *Alcide* had been ordered to take on victuals for 'Foreign Service' – enough to last her crew for six months – and had received a further batch of marines from the barracks at Portsmouth, though by that time another twenty-four of the pressed men had 'run' from the ship. Meanwhile, the wet and windy autumn had given over to 'pleasant' but cold days, and the officers recorded a crisp frost in their logs. Robert had, by now, formed a close friendship with the *Alcide*'s chaplain, the Reverend Touch, in line with his own 'propensity to divinity'.[17] Perhaps this amity, the clearer skies and a sense of impending adventure all brightened his mood, for on Christmas Day he told Charles that 'the wind is fair & we are preparing to take the advantage of it while it is favourable the signal being made to unmoor; the wind however, not being strong enough for us to push out till the tide turns to our assistance, gives me this opportunity of bidding you for some time adieu'. He added, with a touch of fatalism, 'I am sure that nothing can be done now till I return on your side. It must be left now to their decision whether I am to remain in this service, at least whether this service is to remain an object to me. God bless you, the wind will not permit me to say more...' Expressing his affection for his brother, he signed off.

In the following days, as Rodney's fleet stood out to sea, Lord Robert, in the manner of ambitious young men, made himself a promise. If made a captain, he would resolve never to surrender to the enemy while he remained alive on board.

9

'Now move heaven and earth'

JANUARY TO MARCH 1780

'Now move heaven and earth'

Admiral George Brydges Rodney, the man tasked with the defence of the profoundly significant sugar islands, was an intelligent and aggressive officer, and a stern disciplinarian with high professional standards. He was also, by now, sixty-one years old, with an emaciated look, suffering from gout, and enduring pain from a 'urinary stricture' – probably an enlarged or cancerous prostate. However, the navy remained his passion and he talked of little else, fighting battles with nutshells over dinner tables after the cloth had been drawn. His enthusiasm for the service included a hearty obsession with prize-money and he was a snob, favouring aristocratic connections, although he was invariably courteous to all.

On taking command of the 90-gun *Sandwich* in 1779, for such a critical role in maintaining Britain's empire, he was horrified to find that: 'The unhappy difference between Mr Keppel and Sir Hugh Palliser has almost ruined the navy.' In his eyes, 'Discipline in a very great measure is lost… and officers presume to find fault *and think*, when their duty is implicit obedience. Faction and Party is so predominant.'[1] He would make it his intention to try to rectify this. But first, he had his secret mission to undertake.

Aboard the *Alcide*, Robert, like most others in Rodney's fleet, had no idea of their destination as they set off at Christmas 1779, from Spithead. To avoid any leaks reaching the enemy, usually by way of smugglers, Rodney would not impart their orders until they had cleared the land and the weather was clement enough for him to hoist the signal for 'all captains to repair on board the flag-ship'. In the meantime, they headed south-westwards out of the English Channel.

Some other ships joined them after departure, including Captain Sir Chaloner Ogle in the 74-gun *Resolution* and Captain Philemon Pownoll in the 32-gun frigate *Apollo*, with a midshipman aboard the latter named William Brown – from a family Robert knew, near Belvoir. Rodney's fleet became twenty-two ships of the line plus several frigates covering a convoy of smaller store-ships, victuallers and troopships. With Rodney were two fellow flag-officers to lead the other divisions in battle: Rear Admiral Digby in the second-rate *Prince George* and Rear Admiral Ross in the first-rate *Royal George*.

The new year of 1780 brought fresh and breezy weather, with a confused sea after the gales. At ten o'clock on the morning of 2 January, Rodney signalled his fleet to heave-to and for each ship to send a boat with an officer. Once they were assembled in the great cabin aboard the *Sandwich*, Rodney revealed the Admiralty's secret orders: they were to sail to the relief of Gibraltar. The garrison there was desperately short of supplies of all descriptions, and the governor, General George Eliott, had appealed to London for help. Assuming this mission

Admiral Sir George Brydges Rodney, 1st Baron Rodney (1718–92).

proved successful, Rodney was then to detach some ships to relieve Minorca before heading west for the Leeward Islands station. One of the frigates, the *Triton*, was carrying £25,000 for Minorca along with Sir William Draper – the man who had inadvertently brought criticism on the old Lord Granby – who was to be the new governor there.

Rodney's task was no simple matter, for he had also to protect his valuable convoy. Gibraltar was known to be threatened by the Spaniards on land and blockaded by them at sea, and the Spanish port of Algeciras lay just across the bay from the Rock. At Cadiz, Admiral de Córdova y Córdova had a fleet of twenty Spanish and four French ships of the line, which might well emerge and frustrate Rodney's attempt to reach the beleaguered Eliott. Of even more concern was Admiral Juan de Langára who was thought to be at sea, cruising off Cape St Vincent and on the lookout for a relieving British force having heard that a convoy was likely to be on its way to Gibraltar. To add to the British commander-in-chief's obstacles, there remained a powerful French fleet at Brest.

Once Rodney's captains returned to their ships, word of the mission would have spread like fire through dry grass, passed by senior officers to juniors, picked up by the wardroom servants and carried to the darkest recesses of the vessels. All hands would have wondered what lay ahead, wracked by the mixed emotions of fear and expectation; but the incentives of prize-money were ever powerful, and for the officers, especially, there was the lure of honour and glory. Robert, nursing his frustrated ambition, must have thought that the captaincy he craved – if it was ever to happen – would only come from some lucky happenstance.

After a few days, four sails of the line detached with the supplies for the West Indies, reducing Rodney's main battle force to eighteen. Meanwhile, aboard the *Alcide* Captain Brisbane and his officers exercised their novice sailors at the great guns, hurriedly attempting to bring them up to par with a seasoned crew. From what they knew, it was almost inconceivable that they would not have to fight their way into Gibraltar Bay, sweeping aside the blockading Spaniards.

In an attempt to further deceive the enemy, Rodney had led his fleet far to the west of Ushant and Finisterre, to avoid sightings by fishermen from Brittany and Galicia. However, on the morning of 8 January

1780, when the fleet was about 300 miles west of Cape Finisterre, with the daylight leaching into the eastern sky and the horizon emerging from the darkness, strange sails could be seen to the north-east. Rodney's fleet was proceeding under reduced canvas to ensure all the ships kept together, but now the admiral made the signal to 'set all sail' and give chase, leaving one line-of-battle ship and one frigate to cover the convoy. The *Alcide* was among the chasers, the atmosphere on board quickening with every mile they drew nearer to the unidentified ships, who had passed the British fleet in the dark of night.

As sail after sail lifted over the horizon it was apparent that this was no enemy battle-squadron, but rather a convoy, its ships attempting to escape once the British men-of-war came into view from the still crepuscular west. Soon they were found to be Spanish merchantmen, escorted by seven men-of-war. Robert could see among them one ship whose sides were 'pierced for 64 guns'. Caught out and unable to escape, the Spaniards gave in, Captain Pownoll of the *Apollo* noting in his journal that: 'They hauled down their colours as fast as our ships came up to them.'[2] All were taken, save for one transport that got away.

The prizes had been under the command of Commodore Don Juan Agustín de Yardi, whose broad pennant flew in the 64-gun *Guazpacoano*. De Yardi was escorting twenty-two merchant vessels carrying cargoes freighted by the Real Compañia Guipuzcoana de Caracas (the Royal Company Guipuzcoan of Caracas), in Venezuela. Twelve of the convoy bore naval stores and provisions for Córdova's fleet at Cadiz, while the rest were loaded with a commercial lading of 'Bale Goods' – at this time cloth or domestic utensils shipped in crude burlap bales.

After prize-crews were put aboard, most of the captured vessels were sent home under the protection of the *Pearl* and the *America*; but the *Guazpacoano* was taken into Rodney's fleet. Only six months old, the prize was renamed *Prince William* in honour of Prince William Henry, Duke of Clarence, the younger son of George III who was then serving in the fleet as a midshipman – and who would eventually accede to the throne as William IV. Larger than the *Bienfaisant*, to whom she had struck her colours, the *Prince William* was manned by officers and men from the other ships. It just might have offered the vacancy after which Robert hankered; but her command was given to another officer.

As the ships lay hove-to, and boats plied between them to put the prize-crews aboard, the *Alcide* received fifty Spanish prisoners to be fed on two-thirds rations. If Robert was disappointed at not being given command of the *Prince William*, he could at least anticipate a portion of the prize-money. He just had time to dash off a 'note rather than a letter' to Charles on 9 January, adding in a postscript that: 'The Damage to Spain by this capture is computed by themselves at [£]400,000.' Robert did not relate the whole story since he knew it would be 'more perfectly recited in the *Gazette*, than I shall here attempt' after Rodney's despatches had arrived home.

Robert gave his note to John Dilkes, the *Alcide*'s 1st lieutenant, who was sent to command one of the prizes home. Robert must have had trouble suppressing his glee as he saw Dilkes over the side into his boat, for with him gone Robert now stepped into his shoes as acting 1st lieutenant. Then, somehow, perhaps by being sent to convey Captain Brisbane's report, Robert contrived to get himself onto the quarterdeck of the *Sandwich*, where he came face-to-face with the commander-in-chief. Making his bow, the confident young lieutenant requested that Rodney consider him for the next available vacancy as captain – to which Rodney responded by giving Robert hope that it might be possible at Gibraltar. Fobbed-off or not, Robert would have to bide his time.

As the yards were squared and the two groups of ships drew apart, the *Alcide* settled down with her new acting 1st lieutenant, while the ship wallowed about in no wind before surging forward in weather 'squally with thunder and lightning'. Robert was no longer leading a watch, but as acting 1st lieutenant would have to undertake much of the day-to-day management of the ship, a function that brought him closer to Captain Brisbane and made him the wardroom president. One of his first tasks was to oversee the throwing overboard of 1,499 gallons of beer that were discovered to be 'stinking and not fit for men to drink'.

By the morning of 16 January, the reunited British fleet, with its convoy, was labouring south in heavy swells and poor visibility. These were tiring conditions for all hands. Closing in towards Cape St Vincent, passing Portuguese vessels informed them that a Spanish squadron had been seen cruising off the cape with the intention of

preventing the British from relieving Gibraltar. Rodney, prostrated in
his cabin with gout in his hands and feet, signalled all captains to prepare for battle. By noon, the fleet and convoy had rounded the cape
in a fresh westerly wind and could lay a direct course to the Strait of
Gibraltar. Then, at around one o'clock, the lookouts in the headmost
ships sighted strange sails through the haze. On the quarterdeck of
the *Alcide*, Robert saw the *Bedford* and *Resolution* hoist the 'signal for
a fleet'. From his sickbed, Rodney ordered his men-of-war to form a
line abreast, covering the convoy which followed behind the extending
battle line. The marine drummers beat the men to quarters, the ships
were cleared for action, and the *Alcide* and her sisters bore down on
their quarry.

More sails rose over the horizon ahead, and soon hearts were racing in the British fleet as a Spanish fleet of warships came into view,
in a line of battle heading towards Cadiz, which was 100 miles to the
south-east. From the *Sandwich*, Rodney, fearful that too rigid a control
of his fleet would allow the enemy to escape, threw out the signal for
a 'general chase', releasing his individual captains from the constraints
of the line. Rodney's decision was extemporized, and he relied upon
individual captains 'doing their utmost' as they were bound to do 'at
their peradventure' in accordance with their commissions. He allowed
them to depart from convention, hoping they would run through the
enemy fleet from the leeward position, and cut them off from their
base at Cadiz. Rodney even made provision for a night engagement:
the ships were to 'hoist three lights in a triangle at the mizen peek and
two at the boltsprit end one over the other... the better to know our
own ships and prevent their firing into each other'.[3]

If a battle took place, Robert, as acting 1st lieutenant, would be stationed on the quarterdeck with the captain and the master, a marine
officer and several midshipmen, with 'doggies' to run messages to
the lieutenants supervising the gun-decks. It would be his first action
where he could see the enemy rather than being cooped up in the
deafening world below decks. He would not now supervise any guns
unless they engaged on both sides.

The copper-bottomed British men-of-war drew ahead, gaining
slowly on the hindmost Spanish vessels, while the uncoppered *Alcide*
lagged to the rear of the fleet. The pursuing British observed three of

the enemy ships break away, leaving the main body greatly outnumbered at only eight sails of the line in contrast to Rodney's eighteen. After chasing for two hours, the leading coppered British ships – *Edgar*, *Marlborough*, *Ajax* and *Bienfaisant* – caught up with the trailing Spanish ship *Santo Domingo*. From the decks of the *Alcide*, some half a mile behind, it was hard to distinguish friend from enemy, as Mr Humphreys, the sailing master, noted in his log. Then suddenly, at twilight, the roar of an explosion rent the air and Robert witnessed 'the most tremendous sight I have ever beheld' as a ship blew up. 'The stream of fire clouded by a column of smoke terminated the whole as nothing was left of the ship when the smoke dissappated.' It was the *Santo Domingo* that had exploded, having been fired into by the *Bienfaisant* and the *Edgar*, and it seemed that all on board had been lost. The *Bienfaisant* had been so close that she was swept by the blast, a wave of searing heat threatening to send her to kingdom come. Robert observed later that: 'A very extraordinary thing happen'd which is a man was pick'd up four hours after the *St Domingo* blew up belonging to her & is now alive. The only man that is saved.' As darkness fell and the British men-of-war rushed downwind in a welter of wind and spume, Robert watched as the Spanish *Princessa* surrendered to the *Resolution* after forty minutes of fighting.

Although aware that the wind was pressing them towards the shore, Rodney consulted his flag-captain, Walter Young, and decided to press the pursuit of the Spanish as hard as possible. By about ten o'clock that wild evening, Robert could just see from the *Alcide*'s quarterdeck that most of the British ships ahead of his own were engaged, firing into the dark and squally night. It was obvious, too, that the Spanish ships were overwhelmed, striking their flags in surrender to the British. The weather was 'very tempestuous, with a great sea'; the wind had risen to a gale, and the moon, shining from between the racing clouds, cast a fitful light over the baleful scene.

By the time the *Alcide* caught up, most of the Spanish ships had already given up. Running alongside one of the enemy's ships, which in the dark and confusion Robert thought was the 84-gun *Fénix*, Captain Brisbane ordered his gun-crews to fire into her, though they could not open the lower gun-ports. The Spanish ship returned the fire and shot through the *Alcide*'s main topmast, which crashed down

onto the engaged side and 'disabled us so effectually that we were glad
to haul our wind clear of the action', as Robert later told Charles. As
the mast fell, it cut a pinnace in two and stove it to pieces. Fortunately,
the frigate *Apollo* then took up the attack on the Spanish ship, which
proved not to be the *Fénix* but the 74-gun *Monarca*. Captain Pownoll
gallantly maintained the unequal conflict until the larger ship surrendered to the smaller British frigate. At two o'clock in the morning,
Rodney's flagship, the *Sandwich*, loomed out of the darkness to fire
a thunderous broadside into the *Monarca*, unaware in the confusion
of wind and sea that the Spanish ship had already struck her colours.

The heavy seas hindered the British in putting prize-crews onto their
captures until dawn next morning. The waves ran so high that Lieutenant Nowell, sent by Chaloner Ogle, commander of the *Resolution*,
to take charge of the *Princessa*, was knocked down several times by
broken rigging before he could get on board. The Spanish ship was in
a perilous situation, with 200 men dead and trails of gunpowder running through the lower gun-deck, and it was fortunate that she had not
exploded like the *Santo Domingo*. The *Fénix*, flagship of Admiral Juan
de Langára, had struck her colours to the *Bienfaisant* during the action;
but not only did the *Bienfaisant* find it impossible to lower boats into
the sea, the British ship also had smallpox on board. Captain MacBride
did not wish to spread the infection – not 'even among my enemies',
as he afterwards told Rodney.[4] Instead, he hailed Langára and, securing
his word-of-honour, escorted the *Fénix* all the way to Gibraltar without putting a prize-crew on board. Rodney's fleet had also taken the
Diligente, the *Santo Julien* and *Santo Eugenio*. Six of Langára's vessels
had escaped: four of the line and two frigates.

'The Action lasted til near 4 in the morning,' Robert recalled later
for Charles, 'when we found ourselves so near Cadiz that the *Invincible*
counted all the ships in the Bay. The Spaniards, considering the great
disparity between us, having only 8 to 18 behav'd with the utmost
bravery & did not strike till they had either lost their masts or were so
disabled as not to have in their power to return our fire. Thus ended
the action in their having lost 7 ships out of 8. Our loss is trifling.' He
was right to admire the courage of Langára's squadron, for Córdova's
larger fleet at Cadiz had remained in port, deterred by the onshore
gale. The French *had* known the size of Rodney's force, but did not

pass on the information to their allies. Langára had not known what he was facing until it was too late.

The British fleet was now in trouble too, for by now they had run so far to leeward that they were in danger from the shoals of San Lucar and the guns of Cadiz. The weather was still atrocious and the ships were in danger of being forced aground. With tremendous effort they clawed their way back against the wind into deeper water, though losing two of the prizes, the *Santo Julien* and *Santo Eugenio*, which were driven ashore. The main body of the fleet did not work clear of the shallows until the following morning, after which it bore away for Gibraltar, sweeping all before it.

Having spent most of the action directing the battle from his cot, Admiral Rodney arrived at Gibraltar to a hero's welcome, while the rest of his fleet straggled in as the sudden dying of the wind hindered their entry into the Bay of Gibraltar. The *Alcide* and the *Terrible* had to be towed in with boats, a strong indraught of current driving them so close to the Spanish gun batteries ashore that the *Alcide*'s 5th lieutenant, Sam Higginson, noted in his log: 'The Enemy fired more than two hundred shot at us.' Meanwhile, the *Terrible* received seven holes in her hull, but no one was killed.[5] Both ships eventually anchored on 22 January, near the Rock, where Robert was no doubt interested to see his old ship the *Panther*, now flagship of the Mediterranean station's present commander-in-chief, Vice Admiral Duff.

While General Eliott and his hungry garrison devoured the food brought by the convoy, Rodney sent three ships of the line – *Marlborough*, *Defence* and *Invincible* – to cover the store-ships bound for Minorca. Then, he settled the administration of his fleet, a complex matter of the transfer of officers, since there were 'dead men's shoes to fill', and with so many prizes taken, several lieutenants, besides John Dilkes, had moved to different ships.

On 23 January, Duff, in a boat from the *Panther*, came alongside the *Alcide* with a message for Robert. It was from Admiral Rodney. Whether it was delivered verbally, or in the form of a note, we do not know; but one can only imagine the young man's handsome face breaking out in a broad smile and his expressive eyes filling with delight. The admiral had found a way to remove the thorn in Lord Sandwich's side – by making Ogle a commodore and telling Robert he was now Captain Lord Robert Manners. The commission was to be dated from 17 January 1780, the day after the battle. Rodney had once sought favours for relatives from the old Lord Granby, and perhaps this memory, too, was in his mind as he obliged the young nobleman.

Rodney was able to act in this way because there was some flexibility at the time to make arrangements on foreign stations to suit changing circumstances. It was, in any case, standard practice for flag-officers to have a post-captain to take care of the day-to-day running of the ship and they were often young protégés, able to benefit from the experience of the older man. It was more unusual for a commodore, a temporary rank, to have a post-captain aboard. But Rodney probably knew that Ogle was close to the top of the list to become a rear admiral, so this was not a completely untoward manoeuvre. Also fortuitous was the apparent absence of available smaller naval vessels in which Rodney might otherwise have placed Robert as a master and commander.

The newly made commodore, born in 1726, was the same generation as Robert's father, and a veteran of the Seven Years' War, during which time he had taken a number of valuable prizes. In fact, Robert was very distantly related to the older man, for, like the Manners, the Ogles were also from Northumberland and the families had intermarried. Sir Chaloner had commanded the *Resolution* from 1774, and he had with him a large retinue of 'servants' (captains being allowed one per every hundred men aboard), several of them also 'Ogles'. Some provided domestic assistance, while others might have been young boys hoping to become midshipmen, or more elderly experienced seamen to help with technical duties.

The delighted Robert took leave of his friend on the *Alcide*, the Reverend Touch, and, bringing his own servant Charles Ekins with him, transferred to his new ship on 24 January 1780. The *Resolution*'s master, Charles Young, recorded the moment: 'Got all clear for unmooring. Lord Robert Manners came on board and took command as Captain under Commodore Ogle. Read his commission to the Ships Company & saluted with three cheers.'

Launched on 12 April 1770, the *Resolution* was another Slade-designed vessel, of the Elizabeth class, and like other '74's, she had two gun-decks, the upper one measuring 168 feet 6 inches in length and

46 feet wide. Each gun-deck carried twenty-eight cannon: 32-pounders on the lower deck and 18-pounders on the upper. A further fourteen 9-pounders were on the quarterdeck and four 9-pounders on the forecastle. Some classicist worthy of Robert's brother had fitted the ship with a figurehead depicting Cleopatra clasping the asp, signifying Shakespeare's words: 'My resolution's placed...' Robert would later make a small watercolour study of his ship's 'head' showing this detail. The *Resolution* was also distinguishable from a distance by a red ochre stripe covering the upper gun-ports. Other ships might be painted differently, for this was before the days of Nelson's distinctive black and yellow colour scheme.

Although under the watchful eye of a commodore, Robert would be in command of his ship in all respects other than when an intervention was needed (if he seemed about to act incorrectly) or when going into battle (in which case Ogle would assume tactical direction). To find himself, a few days short of his twenty-second birthday, on the quarterdeck of a 74-gun ship instead of a sloop or frigate was remarkable, even in a case like this where the senior sea-officer could oversee the junior. Being 'made post' so young was an unusual and significant achievement, however it was done. In addition, being distinguished as the commander of a rated vessel, in theory his career was henceforth secure. Further promotion was strictly by seniority, so if he could avoid death or disgrace he would eventually become an admiral.

Nevertheless, in the factious navy Robert's commission could still cause jealousy, and he would have to prove himself. Rodney had a reputation for being obsequious and corrupt in his promotions, and, after all, Sandwich had been 'tormented to death' by Robert. Such considerations made him aware of a further hurdle, in that a promotion made on a foreign station had to be confirmed by the Admiralty – and he did not know what had been said behind his back. On 24 January, once alone in his new cabin, Robert found a moment to write to Charles with his joyous news, albeit tinged with anxiety and remaining sensitive enough to express relief that there were no smaller vessels available that would have made it appear he had been put over the heads of others. Four days later, he read the *Articles of War* to the ship's company for the first time. And three weeks after that, on 17 February 1780, Rodney, catching up with his paperwork, made his order official:

To Captain Sir Chaloner Ogle[6]

Sir,

By the virtue of the power and authority to me given I do hereby constitute an appoint you commodore of His Majesty's squadron under my command with a captain under you, willing and requiring you forthwith to repair on board His Majesty's ship Resolution to the command of which I have appointed the Rt. Honourable Lord Robert Manners; and there to hoist a distinguishing broad pendent as such, and to take the charge of commodore in the said squadron accordingly; hereby strictly charging and commanding the officers and companies of the said squadron, inferior to you, to behave themselves jointly and severally, in their respective employments, with all due respect and obedience unto you their said commodore, and you likewise to observe and execute the general printed instructions, as what orders and directions you shall receive from me or any other [of] your superior officers, for His Majesty's service. Hereof nor you nor any of you may fail as you will answer the country at your peril. And for so doing this shall be your warrant.

⋆

In England, having done all he could for his younger brother prior to Robert's departure at the close of 1779, Charles had swiftly turned his attention to other things. He was keen to get his hands on a painting by Gerard Dow, which Alleyne FitzHerbert had found for him, and also to get hold of some more Tokay. Besides these indulgences, Charles was also occupied with his new 'Rutland Regiment', having been authorized 'by beat of drums or otherwise to raise so many men in any county or part of our Kingdom of Great Britain'. Assisting him with this project was his friend the 2nd Earl of Chatham, a lieutenant in the 39th Regiment of Foot, who unsurprisingly had been forbidden by his father to fight the Americans. Charles and Chatham's friendship had grown increasingly strong, both of them sharing a somewhat indolent and politically unambitious nature contrasting with their highly ambitious younger brothers in the navy.

Chatham set up a headquarters in Grantham and began recruiting for Charles, dispersing a poster calling upon all patriotic young men to join-up and 'chastise the insolence of France and Spain'. On the back of the copy that Charles kept among his papers, someone had written the criteria to be applied by the recruiting sergeants: men of '5 feet 4 inches, not under 17 years of age nor above 40. Growing lads of 5 feet 3 inches and a half each examined by a surgeon', for which sergeants could: 'Beat up at five pounds a man and may go as far as ten pounds a man. But to raise them as cheap as possible.' Meanwhile, Charles footed the bills for such items as '224 white knapsacks' and 'shirts with frills', though a discount was fortuitously negotiated from the suppliers Louch & Straubenzee.

The regiment would be commanded by Colonel Anthony St Leger, a horse-racing friend who had established with Lord Rockingham, in 1776, the 2-mile race at Doncaster later known as the St Leger Stakes. He was also a distant relative of Charles through ancestors George Manners and Anne St Leger, whose effigies lay in the Rutland Chantry at Windsor, and brother to Barry St Leger who had commanded a force in the Saratoga campaign. It was noted in the papers how a number of men of rank had joined the regiment and the fact that 'very few of them, it was well known, would not have lifted a musket against America'. Perhaps with a sense of satisfaction, the columnist continued that 'against good sense and military knowledge [the 86th Foot] are now selected for the service the most disagreeable and dangerous in point of climate'.[7] Indeed, the regiment was to be sent to the West Indies, where the chance of dying of disease was high.

With the administration of his regiment neatly delegated to St Leger, Chatham and others, Charles had also taken on something else to occupy him as Robert had sailed off. A general election was called for September 1780, and Charles had declared his brother as a candidate for the county of Cambridgeshire. On the face of it, there was nothing unusual in this, for it was quite normal at that time for serving naval officers to have seats in Parliament in order to use the connections to help secure advantageous commissions. Their absence did not seem to matter, as they were not expected to represent their constituents in the manner of modern politicians.

However, on this occasion more lay behind Robert's candidacy than just his own or the 'Rutland' interest: his having a seat in Parliament could be useful to those who were calling for electoral reform. Some

To chaſtiſe the

France *and*

Inſolence of

Spain.

ALL GENTLEMEN

VOLUNTEERS,

That have a Mind to ſerve their *King* and *Country*,
Have an advantageous Opportunity of diſtinguiſhing their Valour, by
offering themſelves to the

REGIMENT,

RAISED BY HIS GRACE THE NOBLE AND BRAVE

DUKE OF RUTLAND,

SON TO THE LATE

Illuſtrious and Brave Marquis of *Granby*,

Who, upon a like Occaſion, raiſed a REGIMENT for the DEFENCE
of the *LIBERTY* and *PROPERTY* of OLD ENGLAND, againſt
the Perfidious Attempts of *Frenchmen*.
ALL PERSONS diſpoſed to preſerve every Thing that is *dear to Engliſhmen*, by
TAKING UP ARMS, are deſired to apply immediately

Where a Commiſſioned Officer attends, From whom each Volunteer
will receive

HIS MAJESTY'S ROYAL BOUNTY,

And be Inliſted in the above Regiment.

GOD SAVE THE KING.

*Charles had this poster printed and distributed to recruit for
the 86th Regiment of Foot in 1779–80.*

blamed the dragging-on of the American war on the pro-government voting of MPs from rural and depopulated constituencies, who no longer reflected the shape of the nation – notably Members from the so-called 'rotten boroughs' that still accounted for two seats each. By contrast, growing industry in rising cities such as Manchester had created large populations with little or no Parliamentary representation. One of the strongest voices for reform came from Yorkshire, the largest constituency in Britain and a vital source of textiles and coal; but its sheer size made it inadequately represented. A group of independent MPs had formed the 'Yorkshire Association': frustrated by the soaring costs of the war, they called for 'economical reform', cuts in public spending, a curb on patronage, the shortening of the life of a Parliament, and an increase in the number of seats for larger counties.

The Yorkshire Association's cause was taken up by the Rockingham Whigs, for it suited their underlying aim of reducing the influence of the king and his ministers. Unsurprisingly, Charles's Cambridge tutor, Richard Watson, was foremost among its supporters. It was he who suggested to Charles that, knowing the freemen of Cambridgeshire were sympathetic to electoral reform, Robert should be put forward as a candidate. He stood a good chance too, as 'Granby's son'; after all, his celebrated father had once been a Member for that county. If successful, Robert would make a useful addition in the Commons to support the Rutland and the Yorkshire interest.

Sensing himself caught up in great events, and in a reference to the Whigs' anti-monarchical bent, Charles wrote wittily to Chatham on 30 January 1780, the anniversary of Charles I's execution, that it was: 'The day on which every King in Europe feels a Pain in His neck.'[8] The theme was picked up by the Whigs, and Charles was persuaded to leave Belvoir on 4 February and return to London to hear a motion in the House of Lords.

Lord North had been compelled to confront the Commons with the 'evil of the day' – the proposed taxes needed to help finance the war. They included, following the previous summer's scare, funds for shoring up England's defences against invasion and for improving south-coast fortifications at Plymouth, Portsmouth and Gosport. These taxes were, he said, 'the most arduous, most unpleasant and the most irksome' of any undertaken since he had been First Lord of the Treasury.

The opposition seized the moment. On 8 February, Charles was present to hear the Earl of Shelburne propose that a committee consisting of Members of both Houses should be appointed to examine public expenses, to see what savings could be made in order to lessen the present 'ruinous expenditure and to enable us to carry on the present war against the House of Bourbon'. He said he spoke against the appalling waste of public money. Peace was unlikely, he asserted, at which Sandwich 'gave an affirmative nod', and that the national debt amounted to the 'amazingly enormous sum of two hundred millions', adding that he did not exaggerate the sum. He listed all the dangers facing the country, upholding that if Britain lost the West Indies (for example), then that loss coupled with the load of debt and increasing taxes would make it 'impossible to subsist as an independent nation'.

As ever, the opposition's rhetoric to some extent masked the reality. Although the national debt did indeed swell to £232 million during the war and Britain was undoubtedly very stretched, its economy, agriculture, and banking and insurance system were set up in such a way that they were able to generate surplus capital to largely finance the war. These were advantages that France did not enjoy. The majority of government supporters knew that North was adept at raising finance and that the war was funded not just through general taxes but also through Britain's capacity to trade, which, taxed through Customs and Excise, gave the government solid credit and the ability to borrow. London had the best credit machinery of any country, and redeemable navy bonds enabled the Navy Board to purchase quality timber and hemp from the Baltic, and to finance Sandwich's shipbuilding programme and the laying down of timber for seasoning. Robert himself invested a considerable amount of his own income in navy bonds.

With his inimitable ability to deflect wrath, Lord North defended his position, saying that the task of discussing the budget was disagreeable; but he 'reminded the house that it was not the budget that was to blame or caused the war, but that the war caused the budget and the demands of war were unavoidable and were devouring the resources of the country'. He finished with rhetorical flourish: '[Last summer] we were forced to fit out our fleet and send it against a combined fleet so formidable that [it seemed] the [Spanish] Armada and all the fleets that we read of in history that had ever been sent to sea against Great Britain at former times, were in comparison but mere trifles.'

As the debate swirled noisily in both Houses, the gloom was suddenly perforated by the publication in the *Gazette*, on 12 February 1780, of a letter from Alleyne FitzHerbert in Brussels. Through his diplomatic contacts he had picked up news of Admiral Rodney's defeat of de Langára on 16 January, although the details remained sparse. Soon afterwards, Rodney's despatches arrived describing the victory – and the country was jubilant. Lord Sandwich was especially relieved, having come under so much criticism for the apparent deficiencies of the navy. He later wrote gratefully to Rodney that 'you have taken more line-of-battle ships than had been captured in any one action in either of the last preceding wars'.[9] What came to be known as the 'Moonlight Battle' at last suggested that the First Lord's long tenure of office at the Admiralty might be vindicated, especially as the virtues of coppering the fleet were now more widely appreciated.

The victory, which had been snatched from the potentially insuperable odds of a combined enemy fleet (had Córdova joined Langára), provided a rare moment of national unity. Rodney was publicly thanked in Parliament by Lord North, and even Lord Howe was moved to make the only speech he ever gave in support of one of North's motions, saying how Rodney's conduct had been 'brilliant' and had exhibited an 'uncommon degree of resolution and judgement'. Admiral Keppel arrived late, but said he was sorry to have missed hearing the motion, as he wanted to support it.

However, the opposition did not miss a chance, Mr James Luttrell saying that 'Thanks were not enough' for Rodney and that he must be given support for his next mission to fight the French in the West Indies. 'Let the house send him ships equal to those of the enemy in that quarter of the globe,' Luttrell demanded. And, over the succeeding days, the opposition weighed in heavily against Sandwich again. The British fleet was in bad repair, they said, and greatly outnumbered by the enemy, its ships of the line standing 'at about eighty-two or three with an enemy standing at 120'. The *Parliamentary Register* recorded how: 'Mr Luttrell showed that from the bad quality of the timber particularly the German oak and the mistaken method of preparing it, the men of war in the royal dockyards have... decayed with more rapidity than ever was known in former times. Among others the *Victory* in five years; *Magnificent* in five years; *London* five years; and the *Resolution* built in 1770, was repaired in 1773.'

★

That last-mentioned ship, of which Robert was now captain, was now on her way home, again in need of repair. With Gibraltar and Minorca successfully relieved, on 16 February 1780 Rodney had struck out westwards across the Atlantic to the West Indies, detaching from Rear Admiral Digby's division, which was to return home to convoy prizes and store-ships – a total of twenty-nine sails – and rejoin the Channel Fleet. The *Resolution* was among them, her new young captain unknowingly now a pawn in the bitter politics of the war, both because his ship had been mentioned in Parliament and because of his candidacy for Cambridgeshire to assist the cause of the Yorkshire Association.

Charles might have been troubled that two ships Robert had served on were leaky enough to be mentioned by name in Parliament; but he was probably more interested that his brother's election success might now be more assured – not just because he was 'Granby's son', but because he seemed at last to be making his own reputation. Receipt of Robert's letter of 24 January confirmed what Charles had no doubt already heard on the grapevine. 'I can tell you something about myself which will not displease you,' Robert had written, after recounting the details of the Moonlight Battle. But there was a fragility in his position, and his tone was urgent, imperative:

> Now move heaven and earth, My Dearest Brother make every exertion in your Power to get me confirm'd as I am now Post Captain in the Resolution, being appointed Sr Chaloner Ogle's Captain who is an established Commodore. Sr Geo: Rodney has behav'd exceedingly handsome in it as I am appointed Post at once... I have transmitted home a copy of my Commission to the Admiralty for confirmation. You must use your whole influence to effect it write to Keppel, to Sr John L[indsay], Ld Mansfield immediately... It is so great a point that every endeavour should be used to accomplish it.

Robert's commission as post-captain of the Resolution, *17 March 1780,*
'confirming one given by Adml Sir George Brydges Rodney Bart. Comm: in chief of
His Majesty's Ships and Vessels at the Leeward Islands, 17 January 1780'.

He remarked that he had seen 'Sir William Draper who desired to be particularly remember'd to you', before making his point once again: 'Pray don't delay a moment in applying to Keppel & Co.'

Robert told Charles that if he should meet with 'no difficulty' he should get the commission dated as near as possible to the actual date at sea of 17 January, for Rodney had said this was the day he made the commission. He added: 'There were no sloops or masters and commanders when he made me which will obviate the objection of my having put over anyone's head… There are numerous precedents for it when no sloops are in company. All these things consider'd the Officers in the squadron with whom I have consulted make no doubt of my being confirm'd.' He continued: 'We are going this moment to sea with two copper'd ships under our command. Which makes me in such a hurry that I actually have not read this letter over. Remember most affectionately to the Duchess & Elizabeth & Roos. God bless you my Drst Brother.' Robert's anxiety to have his position confirmed was plain. When the letter caught up with his brother, to Charles's credit he immediately despatched John Glover to the Admiralty to help get Robert confirmed.

Then, in early March 1780, the outstanding news arrived that Robert had taken as a prize the first French ship of the line to be captured since war with France had been declared. Digby's homeward course had brought his ships, on 24 February, across the path of fifteen French supply vessels convoyed by two 64-gun ships. They had been bound for the Île de France in the Indian Ocean, as Mauritius was then known. Setting full sail, the British ships had chased them through the afternoon and on into the night. At two o'clock the next morning, the *Resolution* had caught up with one of the warships, hailed her twice, then fired a gun to make her heave-to, receiving a broadside in response. The *Resolution*'s guns then thundered into her for about half an hour, until the French ship gave up and struck her colours. By this time, three store-ships had already fallen to the British.

Robert's 64-gun prize was named the *Protée*, and was commanded by a Count Dechillou. She had 700 men aboard, 97 of whom were killed or wounded in the action. The *Resolution* had not been unscathed either, sustaining damage to her main topmast, rigging and sails, and 'one shot through the coppers'. But the *Protée* was also found to be carrying about £60,000 worth of silver and base coin. Although Ogle was aboard and, like Digby, would take a large slice of any prize-money, the credit was considered to be Robert's. In due course, seven of the *Protée*'s upper-deck guns would grace the terrace of Belvoir Castle.

The news soon spread, and congratulations to Charles were forthcoming. On 7 March, Bennet Storer, Granby's old army chaplain, offered his 'most sincere, most heartfelt congratulations first on Lord Robert's appointment to so noble a ship as a 74 and next on his glorious success in taking the first ship of force that has been taken from the French during this war. As I well know your affection for Lord Robert I think I see your Grace's transports on the occasion.' This was followed, two days later, by a letter from Mary Isabella's brother, the Duke of Beaufort, who – after complaining that 'we want rain very badly for hunting' – took 'the first opportunity to congratulate Your

A letter from Charles to Robert of 10 March 1780, in which he congratulated his brother
on his promotion to post-captain and capture of a French warship.

Grace on Lord Robert Manners promotion and also on the success
he met with in his return home in taking a French 64 gun ship, &
sincerely wish that his good luck as a captain may continue thro' life'.

Such was the stir caused by the news that even Charles, that most
dilatory of correspondents, was moved to dip his pen into his ink at
Arlington Street and – one imagines with a sigh at the effort required –
address a letter to Sir George Brydges Rodney in the West Indies.
He acknowledged 'the very great obligation you have laid upon my
brother... an event of such essential advantage to him, so long wished
for, so unexpected, and at the same time done in so liberal and particular a manner'. Rodney also received a stream of laudatory letters
for the brilliance of his running fight with Langára. One from Keppel
remarked that: 'You have the Duke of Rutland your warm friend.'[10]
This, no doubt, would have pleased the ingratiating Rodney.

But Charles had other things on his mind that he needed to tell
Robert. On 10 March, with a studied economy of phrase which is to be
admired for its brevity, he wrote: 'My dearest Brother I most sincerely
Congratulate you on all the points on which you are to be Congrat-
ulated.' Charles's real interest was Robert's obligations beyond the
Resolution's bulwarks:

> You are to know... that you are the Declared Candidate (& will
> be the chosen one) for the County of Cambridge. I am advised to
> declare it formally at the Assizes which are next Tuesday & it will
> be necessary (if your absence from your ship can be dispensed
> with) for you to be present. After that there will be a meeting of
> all the freeholders to consider of a Petition on the plan of all the
> other Petitions, when (as you have not an inch of property in that
> county) it will be indispensably necessary that you should attend,
> & make a most violent speech.

Charles's quirky letter ended with his characteristic warmth and
affection. 'Adieu my dearest Boy I will not tell you how my family are
because you must come & see. I am your most attached Friend Rutland.' But before he had time to send the letter, Robert arrived on the
doorstep at Arlington Street.

10

'Whatever expedition we may make'

MARCH TO DECEMBER 1780

'Whatever expedition we may make'

The *Resolution* had arrived on 6 March 1780 at Spithead, where her crew 'Moored ship a whole cable each way [from] Haslar Hospital & South Sea Castle', as her master recorded in his log. Robert did not have the satisfaction of seeing his prize, the *Protée* – whose name was soon to be anglicized to *Prothee* – into Portsmouth, for she had made landfall at Plymouth. After ensuring that the sick went off to Haslar, the Spanish and French prisoners to Forton at Gosport and the Weekly Accounts to Rear Admiral Digby, the new post-captain hurried up to London to see his brother.

He did not have much time there, but stayed long enough to share a glass or two with Charles and Mary Isabella in celebration of his promotion, and to see his nieces and nephew; and possibly to sit again for Richard Cosway, who around this time produced a miniature of him in captain's uniform. Robert also found time to write a speech that could be read out at the Assizes, establishing him as a candidate for election. His words were respectful and humble, and they drew on the memory of his father – though it was not the dramatic entrance into the world of politics that Charles perhaps had envisaged.

Robert was soon back on his ship where his men had begun making substantial repairs, for he had urgent orders to join a detachment under the command of Rear Admiral Sir Thomas Graves. In another strand connecting the brothers' lives, it was Alleyne FitzHerbert at his Brussels listening post who had indirectly brought this about. The diplomat was busy securing for Charles the Gerard Dow at the 'bargain' price of £300. As for the delayed Tokay, the seller was insisting upon FitzHerbert 'tasting and liking it before he suffers it to go out of his cellar', and in order to speed delivery FitzHerbert would 'declare it to be nectar were it no better than bad vinegar'. But FitzHerbert was also picking up naval intelligence. He had heard that the French Brest fleet under the Comte de Guichen was preparing to head for the West Indies, but that it might be suffering an epidemic of sickness. He added hopefully that perhaps it would be 'unfit for service on arrival'. The diplomat warned Charles to keep this to himself: 'I am sure I need not caution you not to follow the example of the *London Gazette* of the other day in making use of my name.' FitzHerbert did not add to the letter some other intelligence that he was simultaneously transmitting back to the government: that a small French squadron with some 3,000–4,000 troops under the command of the Chevalier de Ternay was thought also to be preparing to set out across the Atlantic. De Ternay's destination was given out as being New York, but FitzHerbert was sceptical, since New York was so well defended by the British. He thought it more likely that the French were heading for Quebec.

On 16 March 1780, the Admiralty placed eight ships of the line, including the *Resolution*, under Graves's command, directing him to

A bust of Alleyne FitzHerbert from Tissington Hall, Derbyshire,
ancestral home of the FitzHerbert family.

use the 'utmost despatch' in getting the squadron ready for sea. He was ordered to intercept de Ternay, or at least reinforce Vice Admiral Mariot Arbuthnot, the commander-in-chief of the North American station. But Robert was not happy about being included in this mission. Despite having achieved one objective in his coveted post-captaincy, he craved yet another, revealing a very human capacity always to be striving for something more. Now, he wanted Charles to help him find another ship. He may have suspected that his being sent off with Graves was a way of getting him out of sight of the politically divided Channel Fleet, and he was concerned that his promotion had not yet been officially confirmed by the Admiralty. A further impediment to Robert's ambition was Commodore Ogle's continuing presence, which, although Ogle was aloof from the quotidian concerns of running the *Resolution*, meant that the post-captain was not *quite* master of all he surveyed. Robert's petulance now returned, even contempt for his fellows. On 29 March from Spithead he complained to Charles that:

> I write again to acquaint you of the state of incertitude I am in respecting the change, which we have so anxiously desired. Indeed I wish it the more, as I neither admire the station I am going upon, nor the People I am going to be employed with. I will give you a specimen of them & then judge if I wish to serve with them. The squadron consists of Ad: Graves who is a seaman & a sensible man, but very much disliked in the navy, the rest are Taylor Penny, Mark Robinson, Digby Dent, Samuel Thomson, Sam Burnet, Geo: Falconer. In short not one man of character or ability as a sea officer.

Such was his frustration that Robert told Charles he would even accept command of a 20-gun sloop if she was 'well mann'd & ready'. However, Sir Chaloner had made it clear that his captain should stay with him in the *Resolution*, and so, mindful that it would be inappropriate to go over the heads of others, Robert asked his brother not to mention his desire to anyone unless he could be sure 'it can be done without any great favour or inconvenience'.

Charles, perhaps with a touch of exasperation, suggested his brother write to solicit the support of his old Newfoundland commander, Molyneux Shuldham. Robert did so, and while awaiting the response turned his energy to preparing the *Resolution*. It was one thing for the government to order the dispatch of naval reinforcements to America and quite another for the ships to make a timely departure. Along with the number of vessels requiring victualling and preparing, the dockyard also had to accommodate warships like the *Resolution* just back from Gibraltar, in need of extensive attention and under orders to 'complete' provisioning for 'foreign service' – that is, to take on stores and victuals sufficient for each man for six months.

'We are fitting out as fast as possible, & I hope we shall be the first ship ready, tho we have a very indifferent & sickly ship's company but whatever expedition we may make I don't think the squadron can be ready these eight or ten days,' Robert told Charles on 29 March 1780. In the haste to get Graves's ships to sea, it was said that 'the cordage was taken off the hooks as it was made'.[1] This suggests that parties of seamen under a warrant officer were stationed at the dockyard rope-house to remove rope the moment the laying-engines had finished twisting the hemp strands together, in their lengths of 120 fathoms – one-tenth of a nautical mile. Elsewhere, 'the other ships in the harbour [were] stripped of rigging and boats'.[2]

Robert also had to find time to assemble any further belongings he would need as a captain on foreign service. He had a 'hanger' (type of small sword), a watch – which may have been one of his father's silver pocket watches – a personal seal, 'small clothes' (underwear), a telescope, drawing and writing implements, his own set of signal flags, a new captain's uniform (both full and undress), and possibly some gold coins and Spanish silver dollars for the West Indies. Being diligent and well-heeled, he sent for a copy of the *West Indian Atlas* by Thomas Jefferys, Geographer to the King, which had been published in 1775, and his copy of Paul Hoste's naval tactics book. To furnish his cabin, which was situated in the stern below Ogle's Great Cabin, he had a mahogany writing desk and bureau, and most likely some small decorations; a miniature or two, curtains, crockery and cutlery. Then he would have selected his own cook and a number of 'servants' in addition to Charles Ekins to help him with daily tasks. The Victualling Board minutes recorded supplying him with the quota of oxen tongues he was entitled to as captain, and he would have had other 'luxury' foodstuffs too, including live chickens and possibly even goats. He also received a nice reminder of home in the form of a supply of wine and port from his brother's cellar, for the bottles had the Duke of Rutland's coat of arms glazed on the side.

Regardless of the irritation expressed in letters to Charles, Robert, as a captain, needed good humour and patience to deal with the detail contained in the Admiralty's *Regulations and Instructions Relating to His Majesty's Service at Sea*. Already used to keeping logs as a lieutenant, now he would have to issue his own regulations for the ship, and he would not get paid until his accounts and the officers' logs were submitted, read and passed. Although he would have held money on board for the purser to use to buy fresh food, any additional expenditure would have had to be funded out of his own pocket until it was approved by the Victualling Board. For that reason, naval officers had agents to find credit for them. He would also have to ensure that monthly musters were completed and signed, recording when men embarked or were discharged. The *Resolution*, if fully complemented, would have more than 600 men on her books. At this time, Robert could muster 184 seamen and landsmen and 124 marines, while at least 26 men were recorded as too sick to work.

One of his main priorities during these fraught days of preparation was to get to know his officers, for his relationship with them had to be good, or at least sufficiently cordial, for the ship to operate effectively. Though under the watchful eye of the experienced Commodore Ogle, the twenty-two-year-old post-captain could now dispense patronage and cultivate a 'following'. To this end, he could invite people to dine at his table, a practice that was extended, as Robert had learned aboard the *Panther*, all the way down to the lowliest midshipman. His 'inherited' lieutenants were somewhat ageing: the 1st, 2nd and 3rd were Thomas Arthur Ley, William Reynolds and Richard Shorediche respectively, all aged over forty, though the 4th and 5th lieutenants, William Nowell and William Leggatt, were probably in their mid-twenties. All had been aboard for at least a year under Ogle's command, and now Robert would have to establish his own style of leadership over them.

His warrant officers had also been on the ship for some time. It was one of the Navy Board's wide-ranging responsibilities to appoint the men on whose technical skills the service depended: the sailing masters, boatswains, carpenters, gunners, and surgeons and their mates,[3] but Robert would have had some say in choosing any new ones. The most senior warrant officer was the sailing master, and there was a worrisome moment when the one appointed to the *Resolution*, Charles Young, mysteriously disappeared for a few days in late April – though, fortunately, he returned. Managing the food stocks on board was the purser, Charles Howard, who was also Ogle's secretary, and who had known Robert's father. Taking care of health, and maybe even saving lives during battle, was the Scottish surgeon Robert Blair, a man in his early thirties who had trained at the prestigious University of Edinburgh's medical school.[4] The navy offered career advancement to those who had served an apprenticeship in surgery but lacked the connections or funds to establish a private practice. Blair's enlightened mind would lead him and Robert to develop a close bond. Not all naval surgeons were as able and educated as Blair, but on the whole they were respected, and could influence the officers in matters of diet and hygiene, which was more their daily task than dealing with the frightful wounds inflicted by battle – which happened relatively rarely.

Equally essential as cultivating his officers was Robert's attitude to his crew. As ever, they were a disparate group and included some recently pressed men from Cambridge; but most had been on board for some time under Ogle's command. To some extent, Robert's aristocratic lineage and the influence of his generous father naturally inclined him to extend consideration all those subordinate to him, though it would also have been in his interests to do so. His duty was to develop good working practices between a captain and his officers – both commissioned and warrant – and between them and the crew. Even the most ordinary acts of seamanship could not be carried out efficiently unless the required drills and evolutions went smoothly – and it was so much the more so when a ship had to engage an enemy. To this end, a post-captain, intent on his own goals, whether they were gold or glory, had to study his raw material. If he attained the respect and liking of his men, he would obtain their loyalty and produce an effective fighting force.

Yet, Robert was also to receive a rude reminder of a fundamental aspect of managing his men: prompt payment. The *Resolution*'s company was known to have mutinied the previous year over the constant

William Brown (1764–1814), portrayed as a midshipman in 1780.
He would serve Robert loyally, and would rise to the rank of Admiral.

gripe of back-pay. Under the provisions of what was called Grenville's Act, a ship's company was entitled to receive two months' pay before proceeding to sea, in order for the men to settle their affairs and provide for their families, and many seamen volunteered for the navy precisely to avail themselves of this rather tenuous security. In the case of Graves's squadron, a large number of men had been drafted from ship to ship faster than the paperwork could follow. Robert began to address this issue. On 30 March 1780, he wrote to the Navy Board on behalf of seaman Peter McCormack, requesting he be paid for service aboard his previous ship, the *Richmond*.

As preparations to depart approached completion, Robert and his officers were joined, on 5 April, by some last-minute newcomers. Wearing 'Dead Mens Cloathes' – the clothes of a deceased sailor auctioned off to raise money for his dependents – was sixteen-year old William Brown, from Leesthorpe Hall near Belvoir. His father, John Suffield Brown, served in the Leicestershire Militia under Charles. Probably through this connection, Robert accepted William as a midshipman, which he was entitled to do as a post-captain. The boy had already seen some action – he was in the frigate *Apollo* when she came to the rescue of the *Alcide* during the Moonlight Battle. Another newcomer was William Dawes, an eighteen-year-old 2nd lieutenant of marines, whose father, a clerk in the Ordnance Office at Portsmouth, had helped his son with the 'expense of fitting out' with great parental affection. Both Williams would be among Robert's best friends.

Even as newcomers were stowing their traps below, Admiral Graves was reporting to the Admiralty Board that, with the exception of one ship, his squadron was ready to put to sea, save for loading beer and water. The Board ordered Graves to depart immediately, and to collect beer and water at Plymouth, thereby relieving the burden on Portsmouth. Much to Robert's chagrin, it was the *Resolution* that was not yet ready – and worse was to come. Upon Graves hoisting the signal to get under way on 8 April, the crews of the *Invincible*, *America* and *Shrewsbury* refused to man their capstans to weigh anchor. Aboard the *Invincible*, the seamen assembled between decks, closing the lower gun-deck ports. When ordered on deck they refused to obey, chanting: 'Money! Money!'[5]

Then to Robert's horror, the *Resolution*'s crew came on deck up one hatchway to man the capstan – and then simply went straight back down another. Lieutenants Nowell and Shorediche followed them below to find the men being stirred up to mutiny by one of the carpenter's mates. Nowell stepped forward and punched the ringleader so hard he was knocked off his feet, and the lieutenant said he would fight any man who should attempt a rescue. The moment passed, although the *Resolution* remained at her anchor when Graves set off for Plymouth with six ships of the line. The next day her men did the same again, but this time it took the officers and marines threatening them with arms to persuade them to their duty, though they still declared that they would surrender to the first French man-of-war they came alongside. To this Robert was said to have replied: 'I will take care you shall be placed close enough.'[6] Nevertheless, the *Resolution* was able to 'weigh and proceed' on 9 April, her captain dashing off a note to Charles at Arlington Street. 'My Dearest B[r]... We are under way now, you most likely have heard what prevented us before but it [the mutiny] is now removed.' Now that the moment of departure had arrived, with the promise of adventure ahead, and now that Robert had drawn about him a congenial set of fellows (including family friend Edmund Affleck in the *Bedford*), his morale perked up. He was even contrite

4. Charles Manners as Marquis of Granby in the 1770s, by Joshua Reynolds. Charles was a personal friend of the artist, and commissioned many paintings from him.

5. Frances Manners, older sister to Charles and Robert, by Hugh Douglas Hamilton, shortly before her marriage to the Earl of Tyrconnel.

6. Mary Isabella Somerset, future wife of Charles Manners, with her niece Elizabeth Compton, by Catherine Read.

1. Charles Manners aged eighteen, as Marquis of Granby. Charles himself commissioned this pastel, by Hugh Douglas Hamilton, in 1771.

2. Lord Robert Manners aged fourteen, in midshipman's uniform, by Hugh Douglas Hamilton. The portrait was completed in 1772, after Robert had decided to join the Royal Navy.

3. Frances Manners, Countess of Tyrconnel (1753–93), by Joshua Reynolds. Frances was married to the 2nd Earl of Tyrconnel for four years before causing a scandal by eloping with Charles Loraine Smith, a keen horseman. Tyrconnel and Frances were eventually divorced by Act of Parliament.

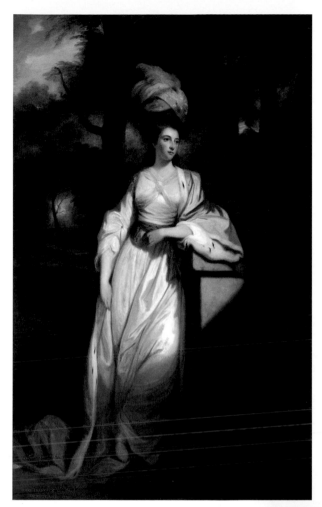

7. Mary Isabella, 4th Duchess of Rutland (1756–1831). This portrait, by Robert Smirke, is a copy of an original by Joshua Reynolds that was burned in the fire at Belvoir Castle in 1816.

8. Charles Manners' lifelong friend Alleyne FitzHerbert (1753–1839), later 1st Baron St Helens, in a portrait attributed to Franciszek Smuglevitz. A diplomat living abroad, FitzHerbert obliged Charles by seeking out works of art for purchase.

9. William Murray, 1st Earl of Mansfield (1705–93), by the portraitist David Martin. Charles's and Robert's great-uncle by marriage, Lord Mansfield was a life-long friend and adviser to Charles.

10. Charlotte, Dowager Duchess of Somerset, Charles and Robert Manners' maternal grandmother, in a copy by Henry Spicer of a pastel by Hugh Douglas Hamilton (1772). Charlotte is in her seventies, and insisted on wearing a hood while sitting because she did not want to 'catch cold', nor let the artist 'see too much of a phiz so near fourscore'.

11. Charles Watson-Wentworth, 2nd Marquis of Rockingham (1730–82) in a pastel copy by Francis Cotes of a portrait by Joshua Reynolds. The son of Charles and Robert Manners' great-aunt, Mary Finch, Rockingham was a leader of the opposition during the American war, and served two brief terms as prime minister (1765–6 and 1782).

12. Charles Cornwallis, 1st Marquess Cornwallis (1738–1805), by Thomas Gainsborough (1783). Cornwallis, who commenced his army career under the patronage of the Marquis of Granby during the Seven Years' War, later endured the humiliation of surrendering to George Washington at Yorktown in 1781.

13. The Battle of Cape St Vincent, or 'Moonlight Battle', 16 January 1780. Richard Paton's painting depicts the Spanish ship *Santo Domingo* exploding, which Lord Robert described as 'the most tremendous sight I have ever beheld'.

14. The bow of the *Resolution*, commanded by Lord Robert Manners. Lord Robert's drawing shows the ship's figurehead, Shakespeare's Cleopatra, holding the asp by whose fatal bite she killed herself, saying: 'My resolution's placed…'

15. John Montagu, 4th Earl of Sandwich (1718–92), by Johann Zoffany. Sandwich served three spells as First Lord of the Admiralty (1748–51, 1763 and 1771–82). After years of resistance, he finally agreed to Robert Manners' promotion to captain in January 1780.

16. Sir Chaloner Ogle, 1st Baronet (1726–1816), by a follower of Joshua Reynolds. He was Commodore in the *Resolution* and Lord Robert's mentor.

17. Lord Robert Manners (1758–82), by Benjamin Wilson. This portrait is believed to have been presented to Sir Samuel Hood in 1784, and came back into the Manners family's ownership when some of Hood's possessions were auctioned off in the twentieth century.

18. A watercolour by Thomas Hearne depicting a scene on board His Majesty's ship *Deal Castle*, during a voyage from the West Indies in 1775. Clearly visible are the wooden compass binnacle forward of the wheel; the officers' chicken coops for eggs and fresh meat; a free-ranging goat (on board for its milk); and an awning providing shade against tropical sun.

about his earlier peevishness, for he had received a reply from his old Newfoundland patron, who advised and encouraged Robert to accept his fate. 'I had not time to answer Ld Shuldham's letter,' he scribbled to Charles, 'but pray inform him that I receiv'd it with the utmost satisfaction, & I see it in exactly the same light with his Lordships & even when I wrote, I thought [a transfer] could not be done with that propriety I could have wish'd it.' At last reconciled to his hand of cards, Robert asked Charles to assure Shuldham 'that I go out perfectly content'. He signed off, sending his 'love to the Dutchess & kiss Elizabeth, Roos etc, Believe me ever your affectionate Brother Robt Manners' – though technically he should have called his nephew 'Granby' rather than Roos, following Charles's inheritance of the dukedom. Then, he turned his attention to such matters as reading out the *Articles of War* and ordering the 'exercising of the great guns and small arms'.

Late in the afternoon of 12 April 1780, Graves in the 90-gun *London* anchored in Cawsand Bay, along with the 74-gun ships *Shrewsbury*, *Bedford*, *Royal Oak*, *America*, *Prudent* and the frigate *Amphitrite*. The *Resolution* soon caught up, arriving on the night of 13 April, to find also anchored there a small squadron under Commodore Walsingham – an escort for a convoy, bound for the West Indies. Among the forces heading for the sugar islands was a substantial proportion of Robert's and Charles's circle. Already on their way out were friends Anthony St Leger and Lord Chatham, on behalf of the Rutland Regiment, while with them, or with Walsingham's convoy, were around 700 of Charles's rank and file, including cousins Francis Sutton and Robert Manners, and Eton friend Henry Fitzroy Stanhope. Even a gardener from Belvoir, one Joe Hutchinson, was among them, and a Sergeant Hall accompanied by his wife Hannah. On the naval side, already out there were Lieutenant James Charles Pitt, Captain George Ann Pulteney (brother to Daniel) and cousin William Clement Finch. Two other cousins, Seymour Finch, now captain of a fire-ship, and Evelyn Sutton, remained in the Channel Fleet. Charles's Eton friend the bookish Thomas Grenville had already dropped out of the Rutland Regiment, perhaps because he did not wish to serve in such a disease-ridden part of the world as the West Indies.

Although speed was of the essence in trying to intercept de Ternay, Graves and Walsingham now found themselves trapped off Plymouth

by a series of westerly gales that caused anchor cables to part, damaged several of the convoy's transports, and occasioned a good deal
of misery and anxiety for those on board, not to mention extreme
frustration for the British government. It was an entire month before
the weather moderated and the wind shifted, finally allowing them
to break their anchors out of the mud, on 17 May. Walsingham's convoy duly headed for the West Indies, while Graves's ships now laid a
course for New York, where they were to join with Arbuthnot and go
on to Quebec.

*

Mercifully, the squadron enjoyed a largely uneventful two-month
passage, though Robert was forced to order the doling out of lashes for
'theft', 'insolence' and 'striking [a] superior officer'; but Graves's ships
approached Sandy Hook, the convenient anchorage for New York at
the western end of Long Island, on 13 July, only to discover that Alleyne
FitzHerbert had been partially wrong: the French had never intended
a descent upon Quebec. Instead, de Ternay had headed straight for
Rhode Island, where he had arrived just two days earlier. The Colony
of Rhode Island had long been a hotbed of opposition to British rule,
but troops had been withdrawn from the coastal town of Newport in
1779 in order to concentrate on New York. Now, as Robert observed to
Charles, 'The report is that the Americans have ceded Rhode Island to
the French & I believe with some truth or else the French have taken
possession of it as the white colours are flying in different parts of the
Island.' He was right – and de Ternay was able to land not 4,000 but
6,000 French troops, under the command of General Le Comte de
Rochambeau. Newport would be the main American base for French
forces for the rest of the war, even though the British continued to
blockade the surrounding waters of Narragansett Bay.

The arrival of French reinforcements was not, however, thought
to be especially alarming, for Loyalist hopes were still buoyed (if over
optimistically) by news of success further south. With a British garrison holding New York, the focus of British military operations had
moved to the southern colonies, and by 12 May 1780, Charleston in
South Carolina had been captured by Sir Henry Clinton and Charles
Cornwallis, backed up from the sea by Mariot Arbuthnot. As the new

arrivals in Graves's ships picked up the news, Robert passed his own wry verdict to Charles on 19 July: 'The taking of Charlestown has infused the greatest spirits into everybody; the affairs in America are now considered as entirely decided.' Then he described, with an equal larding of sarcasm, how many thought the Americans would now have to lay down their arms on any terms 'we may please so graciously to give ... As you see by the above plan there is nothing upon earth so easy.' The reported changing of sides of the population of the Carolinas he saw as pure opportunism, like a 'revolution in an opera'.

Soon after the *Resolution*'s arrival in America, her supplies were topped up with 'ham, beef, flour, raisins, peas and butter' from a transport, though the master's log noted that 'cask of pork no. 4998' was 'short 136 pieces' (someone, somewhere would have been held liable for that). Her coppering had to be repaired, too. Meanwhile, Graves put himself under the command of Arbuthnot, and by the end of July 1780 the *Resolution* and her sisters lay off Rhode Island, observing de Ternay's ships riding at their anchors in Narragansett Bay. For two weeks, the British squadron cruised the stretch of water from Gardiners Bay, at the eastern end of Long Island, to the small offshore Block Island, watching the French and waiting for General Clinton to arrive with 8,000 men from New York to launch an attack on the colony. In the end, the vacillating Clinton decided against it, and Arbuthnot sent the ships into Gardiners Bay to – as Robert recounted to Charles – 'wood & water... and to refresh the people as they begin to grow sickly[,] especially our squadron which came from Europe[,] some ships having 150 and 200 men sick'.

As a captain, Robert now had more sway over the health of his men especially in such matters as scurvy. He could bring to bear what he had learned from a young age: the tables at Belvoir had always been graced with fresh fruit partly for its health benefits, and his father had taken with him to Germany in 1758 '12 pints of orange and lemon juice', for scurvy attacked soldiers as well as sailors. In naval circles it had been known at least since the early seventeenth-century voyages that fresh food, especially fruit and vegetables, revived men suffering from scurvy. By the time Robert joined the navy, when ships were in port salt meat was replaced by fresh meat and served with vegetables whenever possible. Though the concept of Vitamin C did not exist, and certainly there was no formal idea of a preventative, on long ocean passages some varieties of preserved food that appeared to 'cure' scurvy were issued, such as sauerkraut, 'wort' (an essence of malt made from barley) and bottled syrups made of orange or lemon juice; but there was seldom enough of these on board to prevent sickness. Such items were meant to be supplied by the Victualling Board – responsible for the navy's procurement of foodstuffs and drink, and for the control of supply ships and storehouses in ports – and by the Commissioners for Sick and Wounded Seamen (commonly known as the Sick and Hurt Board). But these essentially administrative bodies tended to dismiss the opinions of naval officers in favour of the latest theories from physicians with little or no acquaintance with medicine at sea. In an era when some people even thought scurvy was a kind of venereal disease, the boards avoided the expense of providing sufficient quantities of the preserved foodstuffs for general daily issue.

Robert, his surgeon Robert Blair and purser Charles Howard had done what they could within these constraints, pressing where possible fresh food, sauerkraut and wort on those who had been 'sickly and indifferent' before leaving Portsmouth. Now Robert was able to tell Charles: 'I am I believe in the most healthy ship having only 17 men ill. How long they shall remain so I will not pretend to say as some begin to have symptoms of the scurvy & we have had as yet no fresh provisions or vegetables to correct it. I hear we shall not get any great plenty where we are going.'

By 14 August 1780, they had filled up their water barrels at the eastern end of Long Island and put to sea, though no one knew whither they were bound. A rumour was active that de Guichen was now coming up from the West Indies with fifteen sail of the line. 'If this intelligence should prove true, we shall be soon in a very unpleasant situation. We depend on Sr Geo: Rodney's giving [de Guichen] employment enough on [the Leewards Islands] station or else we shall be blockt up in New York or be obliged to leave the coast' – so Robert informed Charles in a long letter he began on 19 July but did not finish until 14 August, there being no prospect of sending it. 'We remain in the greatest uncertainty in respect to our destination being constantly in readiness for action & not a moment beforehand knowing where we are going.'

He progressed to family matters, revealing his fondness for his nieces and nephew, and despite a certain formality in his expressions he took 'this opportunity of making my most sincere and affectionate love and compliments to the Duchess and to dear little Elizabeth, Roos and Catherine, pray tell Elizabeth I have a great deal to say to her I believe I shall write to her very soon and in return expect a letter with all the news from her.' Charles, Mary Isabella and their children were, after all, the only close family he had.

*

Charles, after Robert's departure, for once had not been idle. In fact, he had been really rather busy, staying at Cheveley Park to canvass on behalf of his brother's electoral prospects, so much so that he was even forgetting to keep Alleyne FitzHerbert informed of the arrival of various art acquisitions. 'I see by Lloyds List that the ship your Rubens was on board of arrived safe in the Port of London some weeks ago I am no longer in pain [anxiety] upon that scene,' noted FitzHerbert. Knowing Charles well, and not being aware he was tied up in Cambridgeshire, he thought Charles's silence was owing to 'the inertia of the morning lives and inertia of the evening parliamentary debates that [left him] no time to write to his friends overseas'.

But then Charles was not *entirely* tied up with electioneering either. An exhausted Lord Rockingham, irritated once again that the young duke was not in London to attend the House of Lords, wrote on 5 April – the day Robert was suppressing mutiny among his unpaid men – to remind Charles that he should be 'present when any great business is being discussed'. He added: 'I am told that Your Grace was a dasher at Hazard at the last Newmarket meeting. I have always held, that playing at dice at Newmarket was – an abomination.'

The 'great business' of the moment that should have called Charles away from the gaming tables was whether George III was increasing his authority at the expense of Parliament. The war had become about so much more than whether or not the American colonies should become independent; it was now also a stark struggle over the power and authority of the king in his own kingdom. Once again, notice of a momentous motion had done the rounds. It was to be made by a Mr Dunning in the House of Commons on 6 April, hence Rockingham's call to arms. Every effort was made to 'get all friends down on both sides and all the cripples'. Charles, of course, missed it and instead received a report from the younger Tom Thoroton, who was no longer serving in America: 'I got to Town soon after five, got out of my chaise in Oxford Road & run to this place where I found Mr Dunning on his legs. I had lost great part of his speech, but what I heard was excellent indeed. He stated the corruption of this house and the increasing interest of the crown and ended with a motion that he thought no one cou'd deny, That the Power of the Crown was Increased, Increasing & ought to be diminisht.'

Tom observed that: 'All the arguments against the motion are that it is an abstract question, no proof, only bold assertions.' But when Lord North was upbraided on 'the numbers of lives which had been lost & the numberless miseries brought on individuals by his most notorious mismanagement as Minister', North was 'enraged to such a degree that he lost all temper' and Edmund Burke made 'a most funny laughable speech at the expense of Lord North'. Burke 'said the minister was a curiosity indeed, fitter for the British Museum than that House and then lanced out into such wit and fun that made Lord North and Germain's faces most extremely grave'. Tom then added what might be construed as a dig at Charles: 'Every creature was forced down that could be carried into the House. And it was exceedingly lamented that neither Lord George nor George Sutton were in the House on so remarkable and critical a day.' The two Georges had not attended because Charles was himself absent.

For once, a motion made by the opposition found fertile ground, and it was carried by 233 votes to 215 votes. This was a high moment for the campaign for 'economical reform', but still this majority was not large enough to satisfy Lord Rockingham. More overtly than the young Tom, he admonished Charles that: 'Your Grace's being absent is thought to have occasioned the absence of L. G. Sutton & Mr Sutton. They are said to have been with you at Cheveley, instead of adding two more to our majority.' As the month progressed, Rockingham was not inclined to let the matter drop. On 24 April, he told Charles in a most reprimanding manner that 'personal credit and honour makes it incumbent upon you to be present in the House on weighty matters and in such times as these'. Rockingham pressed his point; he had heard 'that your Grace is to be at Cambridge today, and possibly to stay there tonight – I therefore send this messenger by way of Cambridge. If you get up early you may be in good time for the House of Lords tomorrow – so you may be back even by <u>dinner time</u> – on Wednesday in Cambridgeshire if you are alert for <u>two</u> mornings.'

Lord Shelburne, on the other hand, was rather more forgiving of Charles for staying away: 'I admire your Grace's philosophy, and will endeavour to imitate[,] by going to Bowood [his country home] as soon as I can without any coquettish principle or wish.' It was true that the business of canvassing votes for Robert was no small undertaking. In May 1780, a friend, Richard Croft, wrote to Charles that 'the very flattering unanimous support that your brother has met with at the nomination for candidates, induces me to take the liberty of congratulating you on the occasion as I imagine his success at the election is now no longer doubtful'. But there was still no guarantee that Robert would gain one of the two available seats. Though many of the seats in the Commons were controlled by the peers, not all were in their 'pockets', and were sometimes bitterly contested.

In one respect Charles was lucky to have an excuse not to be making his way to Parliament on Friday, 2 June. For on this day began the most devastating single outbreak of urban violence in British history. As the peers arrived for the day's debates, they were astonished and terrified to find themselves confronted by a huge crowd of people and assaulted as they went in. Even the *Parliamentary Register* saw fit to record the scene:

> [I]t is hardly possible to conceive a more motley and grotesque appearance than the House exhibited... Lord Bolton came in, not much hurt [but] appeared as if he had just finished a contest with his barber who had parted him half dressed... Some of their Lordships with their hair about their shoulders, other smattered with dirt, most of them as pale as the ghost in Hamlet, all of them standing up in their several places, and speaking at the same instant, one lord proposing to send for the Guards, another for the justice or civil magistrates; many crying out adjourn, adjourn; while the very skies resounded with the huzzas, shoutings or hooting and hissing in the palace yard. This scene of unprecedented alarm continued for about half an hour. We have

subjoined this note, merely to distinguish a circumstance hitherto unprecedented, since the establishment of the monarchy, a
period of above one thousand years.

The rioting, by crowds reaching as many as 60,000, was widespread,
and its causes deep rooted, tapping into social inequity and sectarian
prejudice, always potent springs of action for the London mob. Unsan-
itary and overcrowded conditions in the city, high taxes, unjust and
repressive laws, state-profiteering, and impressment into the army and
navy – all had inflamed the growing working classes and bred discontent. The fuse was lit when the eccentric Lord George Gordon called
for the repeal of the Catholic Relief Act (or Papists Act, 1778), whereby
Parliament had relaxed historic anti-Catholic measures instituted in
the aftermath of the Glorious Revolution of 1688. An articulate pro-
pagandist, Gordon inflamed fears of papism and Jacobitism, and of a
return to the absolute monarchical rule thought to have been ended
by the ousting of the Catholic King James II.

For several days, London was given over to mob rule. The reading
of the Riot Act provided for the use of troops, who managed to rescue
a bigwig or two, including the First Lord of the Admiralty. Charles
learned from his friend Lord George Cavendish, who recounted events
in a letter on 'Tuesday night ten o'clock' at Brooks's, that 'Ld Sandwich
was taken out of his carriage & very nigh torn to pieces but [was] saved
by the Light Horse'. Nor had Charles's relative, the Lord Chief Justice,
escaped the mob's attentions. 'They last night burned Lord Mansfield's
[London] house and destroyed everything in it all his papers etc the
guard fired on the mob and killed six of them and a woman, they then
went back to Kenwood but the soldiers went time enough to save it,'
Cavendish told Charles on Wednesday.

Mary Isabella's niece, Elizabeth Compton, was also in London
during the disturbances. With some *sang froid* she wrote to her aunt
at Cheveley: 'I have been in my habit [travelling clothes] these 2 days,
ready to fly off to you directly & I think it very likely we may be with
you tomorrow. I hope your races have gone on quietly & pleasantly
& that your sweet dear children & your dear self are perfectly well,
& that we shall soon meet in happier times more dreadful ones can
hardly be.' Troops eventually dispersed the rioters, but not before

Newgate Prison had been largely burned down, extensive damage had been inflicted upon Catholic 'chapels' and homes, and several embassies had suffered damage, as had the Bank of England and the Fleet Prison. Estimates of the dead were around three hundred.

The Gordon Riots – as they became known – frightened political opinion on all sides. Some believed a revolution was about to take place. Amid the dreadful turmoil, the Lords resettled their wigs to continue business as usual by 3 June, including the opposition's verbal bombardments on Lord Sandwich, fresh from his narrow escape, who now had to rise in the House to defend himself. As the summer progressed, more bad news arrived in the form of enormous losses sustained by the capture of a very sizeable convoy (under Captain John Moutray) by Admiral Córdova and a Spanish fleet, on 9 August. The City of London took a staggering hit, while commodity and insurance markets were badly shaken. Yet, throughout all these events, the king held steadfastly to his belief that there remained 'the fairest prospect of the returning loyalty and affection of my subjects in the Colonies, and of their happy re-union with their parent country'.

★

Parliament was meanwhile dissolved, ready for the planned General Election in September, which was continuing to keep Charles busy – though not so much that he could not enjoy August in the country with his family. Elizabeth Compton, who did not join them, seemed to yearn to see his children, 'dearest Diddle and Taty [Katherine] rolling in the haycocks', though she was sorry that 'Buffety [John Henry] was in his obstinate humour'. She told Mary Isabella that she hoped 'The Duke... behaved well when he honoured you with his company in the phaeton and did not pull the reins'. Following the shock of the riots, Elizabeth Compton's attention had reverted to her usual trifling interests. She had been 'very busy drawing my basket of flowers these two mornings', while rude interruptions from being 'pestered all day with wasps in my room', made her so cross that she 'laid violent hands on several[,] thank God they have not returned me the compliments'.

Even if he was out taking the air during the harvest, Charles was still having to exert himself (by his standards), for he was also canvassing for seats for Scarborough, and for his friend William Pitt and others.

However, his main concern was Robert, and here he enlisted all the help he could get. Even Charles's chaplain, William Preston, had gone around 'electioneering', which involved drinking punch and beer, and eating bread and cheese with the freeholders during the mornings. 'A very pretty character this indeed my Lord Duke, for a divine,' remarked Preston. Canvassing was indeed a demanding process, and Rockingham confided in Charles that he had 'been so hurried and fatigued with writing letters etc on this subject that I feel quite exhausted'. Charles must have felt the same. He had not as yet secured sufficient support for Robert, who was one of three candidates. The other two were Philip Yorke, son of Lord Hardwicke, and the wealthy Jew Sir Sampson Gideon – a former stockbroker to the Manners family, who, in the 1770s, had rented Cheveley from them to help the family out during the financial turbulence left by the death of the old Lord Granby. They were both supported by the government, and though Charles was often assured that voters would do all they could 'in favour of your brother', there were few guarantees, especially if the competition were dispensing bribes. In addition to his own largesse, Charles called in assistance from every imaginable corner, including old friends like Daniel Pulteney, who produced some anti-Semitic doggerel that targeted Gideon and harped on Robert's martial virtues as Granby's son:

> Whilst Manners in arms at his country's command
> Who by sea has been tried, like his father by land
> Who his youth has midst honor and conquest employed
> And ne'er a foe but he took or destroyed
> Next modestly asks your free vote from his cruize
> He'll return soon to thank you with more glorious news
> Than confusion to slaving to York, and the Jew
> Granby's son! We'll all vote for our freedom and you

'My dear Lord,' Pulteney wrote in an accompanying letter, explaining how the muse had come to him during a quiet carriage ride, 'silence in the chaise enabled me to compose the above elegant and ingenious ditty which I hope you will instruct Thoroton to get printed and make Ablehurst ring it at your public dinners.'

Even Charles James Fox spared a thought for Lord Robert, writing to Charles that: 'I wish you all success possible in your Cambridgeshire business and am with great truth and regard my dear Lord Your Graces most obedient humble servant. C. J. Fox.' Georgiana Duchess of Devonshire was also prevailed upon. 'Lord Richard is very anxious for my father to give his interest in Cambridgeshire to Lord Robert Manners, the Duke of Rutland's brother,' she wrote.[7]

The canvassing process included a visit to Belvoir during August. The Dowager Duchess of Beaufort, keeping track of her only surviving daughter Mary Isabella, was 'vastly sorry to find by your letter wrote the day after your journey that you had been so exceedingly shook and fatigued by it[.] I did not apprehend that the roads which I imagine are all turnpike could have been so very rough and bad. God grant neither you nor your precious inconnu may suffer by this violent exercise.' By 'inconnu', she meant an unborn child, for Charles's wife was heavily pregnant again. Elizabeth Compton wrote too, as usual with other priorities: 'Let me know how your Belvoir uniform chip hat [straw hat] is ornamented as Anne shall make mine the same.'

Then, the young Duke and Duchess of Rutland continued to Scarborough to canvass for their interest there and perhaps attend the town's Fair, which traditionally began on 15 August. Writing on 16 August, Elizabeth Compton asked Mary Isabella to buy her some 'very pretty odd chintz' sufficient for a 'Polonaise' [a fashionable kind of dress]; 'you know I adore having anything smuggled & I know you like emplettes [shopping] particularly in such a place as Scarbro'. Smuggling at that time was at its easiest, for the exigencies of the war meant the coastal watch was depleted.

It is unclear whether Mary Isabella had much time or energy to indulge Elizabeth's penchant for smuggled goods, amid her own role in the canvassing, not to mention travelling back to London where she planned to have her baby. By 12 September, she was at Arlington Street. Her letter to Charles on that day shows how obsessed they both were with the election:

My dearest dear love
We arriv'd very safe here at 4 o'clock tho' I was a good deal fatigu'd with my journey & had a thousand doubts about the little child making its appearance before I got here, however here I am child & all, but I think we shall hardly keep together till you

come my angel, tho' I hope most sincerely I may, for you know
the consolation it is to me to have you with me. Mr Gardener will
attend on Thursday at Cambridge & certainly give Lord Robert a
vote but Sr Sampson is to have the other. Mr Bird at Haverhill will
give Lord Robert a single one. For God's sake let me hear from
you if you can – & for heavens sake come as soon as you can to
your longing loving doating] M[ary] R[utland].

The following day she wrote again:

My dearest love
I shall only write two words to you today as I know how busy
you will be when you receive this at least so anxious about the
election that you will hardly be able to think of anything else even
your Mary tho' I flatter myself I shall certainly be second in your
thoughts perhaps at moments first. I need not tell you that you
are always first in [my] mind. I am still as big as when you saw
me indeed I believe bigger… I hope you will be able to come to
me triumphant tomorrow night or the next… Adieu my sweet
creature nothing can equal the love of your doating affectionate
faithful wife. MR Diddle desires her love & duty & all to Papa.
Success tomorrow is my most earnest wish and prayer & do let
me hear the event.

Those who were eligible to vote could do so either for one or for two
candidates. When the day of voting came – 14 September 1780 – Robert
polled 646 of the single votes compared with 182 for Yorke and 204 for
Gideon; and in all, counting the double votes, they polled 1,741, 1,455
and 1,038 respectively. It was not a secret ballot – everyone's vote was
printed in a purchasable booklet – and so Charles knew, for example,
that the Reverend William Cole had not voted for Robert, despite the
young captain's interest in religion. Horace Walpole, writing to Cole
later, said: 'I am a little surprised at [the Duke of Rutland's] brother,
who is a seaman, having a propensity to divinity, and wonder you
object to it; the church navigant would be an extension of its power.'[8]
    Sir Sampson Gideon, having secured the fewest votes, then with-
drew from the contest, then leaving Lord Robert and Philip Yorke as
the two elected MPs. The still-confined Mary Isabella was 'quite out

THE

POLL

FOR THE

ELECTION

OF

TWO REPRESENTATIVES in PARLIAMENT,

FOR THE

COUNTY OF CAMBRIDGE,

On THURSDAY, Sept. 14, 1780.

CANDIDATES,

LORD ROBERT MANNERS HON. PHILIP YORKE	SIR SAMPSON GIDEON, BT.

THOMAS RUMBOLD HALL, Esq; SHERIFF.

CAMBRIDGE,

PRINTED BY FRANCIS HODSON;

Sold by all the Bookfellers in Cambridge; Nicholfon, Wifbech; Allen, St. Ives; Jenkinfon, Huntingdon; Jacob, Peterborough; Beridge, Chatteris; Claridge, St. Neots; Spencer, Royfton; Payn, Walden; Harwood, Ely; Chapman, Downham; Foreman, Newmarket; alfo by S. Crowder, Paternofter-row, and J. Almon, Piccadilly, London.
PRICE ONE SHILLING AND SIX PENCE.

A booklet listing all those who voted for the three Cambridgeshire candidates in the Parliamentary election of September 1780.

of my wits with joy at our triumph in Cambridgeshire', and letters
of congratulation arrived thick and fast. Although the election had
brought Charles the command of a total of six seats in the Commons,
his great pride was Robert, who had proved popular as 'Granby's son'
and as the successful young captain who had taken the first French
warship prize of the war.

Congratulatory messages began to pour in to Charles. He even
received one from the contentious pen of the scurrilous – and blatantly
anti-Semitic – John Wilkes:

> My Lord
> I beg leave to congratulate your Grace on the splendid victory in
> Cambridgeshire... I am delighted that the Jew was entirely van-
> quished in so well fought a field. It was high time to drive the boar
> out of the garden. I desire to assure Your Grace of the sincere
> esteem and gratitude with which I am always, My Lord, your
> obedient, and very humble servant, John Wilkes.

Another arrived from Charles's friend William Pitt. If having a famous
father influenced voters, it was not a universal panacea for, remarkably,
the younger Pitt had again failed to gain a seat for University of Cambridge, despite being a son of the 1st Earl of Chatham. Nevertheless,
the defeated Pitt wrote graciously to Charles, asking him to: 'Accept
my most cordial congratulations on the glorious triumph of yesterday.
I lament that I had not time to offer them in person and share in your
joy at Cheveley. Besides the advantage gain'd by your victory to the
cause of the public believe me no one can be more truly interested
than I must ever be in the success of all your wishes... Yr ever faithful
& obliged W Pitt.'

However, Charles's sense of triumph was soon overshadowed as he
realized that election expenses were plunging him into further financial crisis. On 21 September 1780, Joseph Butcher told Charles:

> My Lord Duke
> The bill at the Sun Inn, which I take the liberty of sending to
> Your Grace, is so exceedingly large, that I could not think myself
> justified in paying, without receiving particular directions for that
> purpose: the White Bear bill amounts only to [£]450, and those

two houses were reserved for single votes. The bill of the Crown Inn opened jointly for Lord Robert and Mr York, and which bill Mr York has, amounts to six hundred and odd pounds – it appeared to me so extravagant that I refused settling it, and I find Mr York will, by no means, pay his moiety, until he has either seen Your Grace or Lord Robert. The bills of the other houses are entirely settled, but greatly exceed my expectations, yet I flatter myself Your Grace will find the whole expense to be under twelve thousand pounds, which, I am well assured, is not half the amount of Mr York's expense.

Although Butcher might flatter himself on the apparent modesty of a £12,000 cost for Robert's seat, Charles was facing other expenses on top of it: for the other five seats, of raising a regiment, of his passion for art – he had recently bought three paintings by the Spanish Baroque artist Bartolomé Esteban Murillo – not to mention the continuing pressure from his late father's creditors. Joseph Hill was called in to consider what might be done. Among other expedients, it was decided to move forward with Charles's idea to sell the Trowbridge estate – the Wiltshire property inherited from the brothers' long-dead mother. But this was hampered by the necessity of securing Robert's signature on the documents, while Charles's incapacity for order also played its curious part. The family papers were held in the Evidence Room at Belvoir, inaccessibly as it turned out. An adviser had to inform Charles on 1 October: 'It seems the key of the Evidence Room is in Y^r Grace's Library & Y^r Grace has the Library key with you.' In the end, Charles wrote to Robert, just a few days after the election, to tell his younger brother that he was now – like the old Marquis of Granby before him – a Member for Cambridgeshire, but also to procure the necessary signature for the Trowbridge deeds.

Meanwhile, the heavily pregnant Mary Isabella hung on for another month before their fourth child, a boy, also named Charles, was born on 24 October 1780.

★

Unaware of the success of Charles's electoral exertions on his behalf, Robert and the *Resolution* spent most of August and September of

1780 in Gardiners Bay, avoiding, as he described it, 'the boisterous gales which generally blow at the autumnal Equinox on this coast'. But there were storms ahead of not merely the literal kind, too. On 20 September, he told Charles of 'an event that has very much surprised us, which is the arrival of Sr George Rodney with ten sail of the line at Sandy Hook'. With the onset of the hurricane season in the West Indies, Admiral Rodney knew that the French would end operations there and he could go elsewhere. He was expected to send his larger ships out of the way of the hurricane's path, but not as far north as New York. However, having received reports of a French fleet off Rhode Island and thinking that de Guichen might be heading there too, he had decided to reinforce Arbuthnot at the North American station. De Guichen had, in fact, returned to France dispirited, after losing a son in an action against Rodney earlier in the year.

Rodney was now the senior of the two British admirals, and he tried to claim command of both the Leeward Islands and North American stations, which seriously irritated Arbuthnot – not least because it would mean sharing prize-money. 'It is natural to suppose my surprise great at your unexpected visit,' Arbuthnot told Rodney, adding: 'Do not then I beseech you sir let us cause any additional trouble to the Kings ministers, who have lately been sufficiently loaded, without an added weight on our parts... your interference... is certainly unaccountable upon principles of reason & precedents of service.'[9]

Rodney was suffering from chronic gout and had to go ashore, while further abusing his power by promoting his son – at the extraordinarily young age of fifteen – to the command of a small vessel, but with the unfortunate result of missing a chance to engage the French in a combined effort with Arbuthnot. On the other hand, Rodney's arrival had offset the enemy's presence at Rhode Island, disappointing George Washington who hoped that the French fleet would finally bring success to the Patriots.

By now, the *Resolution* was cruising off Rhode Island 'to prevent the French from getting out', as Robert related to Charles on 20 September, with 'a little squadron which consists of 9 sail of the line in sight of the French who do not seem to have any desire of hazarding an action where they have (as they say) so great an inferiority'. Despite the society of Ogle and friends like Edmund Affleck, he longed for

contact with home. 'Let me hear from you immediately,' he demanded
of his brother, 'for I am anxious to know about you and the Dutchess,
as for the riots which are so happily quelled, I have been shocked sufficiently at the accounts of them, therefore I don't want to hear more
about them.' Robert wanted some 'necessaries' – perhaps clothing,
razors and other items of that nature – for 'John Glover or some other
intelligent person to provide me'. Half-joking, he suggested they simply be addressed to 'the old Seaman's direction' of 'Windward Islands,
Jamaica, or elsewhere', meaning he had no real idea where he was
heading next, which was so often the case during this war.

He also wanted 'to hear from Tho[mas Thoroton] make him write
to me, remember [me] to him sincerely'. Commenting on the British
victory at Charleston, under Clinton and their old family friend, he
agreed that: 'Lord Cornwallis has gain'd a very compleat victory at
South Carolina, where he display'd the greatest genius & ability. I have
not seen him since I have been in the country, which I have much
lamented.' Robert signed off with his typical warmth, 'God bless you
my Ever Dearest Brother'; but gone were his former expressions of
being 'perfectly content'. His petulance was back with vengeance: 'I
have been out of the ship but twice since I left England & I do not care
how soon I leave this country,' he told Charles, 'I am heartily tired of it.'

Just a few days later, on 4 October, Robert recounted to Charles 'so
extraordinary an event' as the defection of the American general Benedict Arnold to the British at the end of September 1780. He repeated a
rumour that Arnold had intended 'to have seized Washington & that it
was prematurely discovered; others make Washington an accomplice,
& that it is from a dread of the French' and that Arnold was now said
to be in New York, where Clinton had put him in command of a Loyalist force and soon afterwards sent him on service. What Robert could
not know at that moment was that anger at Arnold's treason would
come to play to the advantage of the Patriots, helping to reverse their
declining morale.

Robert was also seeking more reading material: 'Pray send me a
Delphin Horace[,] Morogues sur la Tactique Navale, a Court Calendar, & any other book or new pamphlet you may think worth my
reading,' he scribbled in the corner of a page to Charles. It is possible
Robert's renewed contact with Rodney inspired the request for Bigot

de Morogues's tome on naval tactics. The admiral, on his arrival in the West Indies in the early spring of 1780, had fought the French near Martinique on 17 April. It had been an indecisive action, but he had again eschewed the traditional line of battle and adopted unorthodox tactics, concentrating his fleet on a part of Admiral de Guichen's line in an attempt to mass his force against the enemy's rear. Unfortunately, his intention was misunderstood by his subordinates in the van, who bore down on the enemy van according to the usual parallel-line formation.[10]

In mid-October 1780, Rodney, at Sandy Hook, sent for the *Resolution*. He wanted Sir Chaloner Ogle, recently promoted to rear admiral, to preside over the court martial of Captain Nathaniel Bateman of the *Yarmouth*. Rodney had been fulminating over what he saw as lack of discipline and political factions among the officers ever since the Keppel–Palliser affair, though his own stern conduct had exacerbated these problems. Insisting upon absolute obedience, he wanted an example made of Bateman for the poor support some captains had given in not obeying his signals during the 17 April action, which he believed had robbed him of the chance of obtaining a decisive victory over de Guichen. Ogle had not been with Rodney at that battle, so he was impartial but of sufficient seniority to preside over the court – to which Robert was also appointed.

By 19 October, Robert had brought his ship to Sandy Hook, where he joined company with Rodney in the *Sandwich* and, among others, Edmund Affleck's brother Philip in the *Triumph* and Charles Thompson, a relation of Mary Isabella's, who was now commanding Robert's old ship, the *Alcide*, which had crossed the Atlantic having had her bottom coppered since the Moonlight Battle. The court martial took almost two weeks from 24 October, aboard Robert's ship, while 'drizzling rain and snow' fell on the decks and 'hard gales' battered the rigging. The facts were laid before Ogle and his fellow judges, which included both Philip Affleck as well as the youthful Lord Robert Manners. It was a duty that the young captain found a 'very disagreeable service', about which he could not convey his true sentiments to Charles 'on account of my oath'. In the event, the court found Bateman guilty of misconduct and dismissed him from the service. It was an outcome for all the captains to reflect upon when it came to their own discipline.

Robert had, by now, been told that the *Resolution* would transfer to Rodney's flag and depart for the Leeward Islands when the hurricane season had passed. Despite the station's dangers, he was pleased, telling Charles that: 'I absolutely loath [the North American station which] besides its natural disagreeable service is render'd more so by the total disagreement of the Commanders in cheif [*sic*] they have both written home complaints of each other. Sr Geo: [Rodney] has taken Clintons side & has wrote also against Arbuthnot. Commodore Drake 2ᵈ in command on this station is hardly on speaking terms with any of the three so you may guess how the service is carried on.' He added: 'I am extremely impatient to be gone, & shall be more so if I do not find a letter for me from you when I arrive in the W. Indies.'

To Robert's delight, some longed-for mail from home then arrived, bringing the good news that he was now an elected Member of Parliament. More soberingly, he also learned how his brother was in even worse financial trouble because of the election expenses. Obligingly, he signed the deeds for the Trowbridge estate, though he had no opportunity to send them before departing.

Taking leave of Edmund Affleck, who was to be employed as a Commissioner of the Port of New York the following year, on 16 November 1780 Robert set sail southwards in a squadron of nine ships. By now, the *Resolution*'s complement was deteriorating as men fell sick or were sent to serve in other ships, and was down to 427 ratings and 114 marines. More promisingly, there were some new arrivals, which included a young 6th lieutenant, Nathaniel Hall, and from 19 October a midshipman from the frigate *Roebuck*, the thirteen-year-old Honourable George Grey, from a Whig family whose ancestors, like Manners and Ogle, were also from Northumberland.[11] (Grey's older brother would become prime minister as the 2nd Earl Grey and give his name to the famous tea.)

The passage south was horrendous. The wind was so strong that the ships sustained damage faster than they could repair it, and the visibility so poor that vessels quickly lost sight of most other ships, the *Resolution* managing to remain in company only with the *Alcide* and the frigate *Triton*. Robert's ship had soon split two topmasts and many of her sails were torn to shreds. Only when the weather moderated, a few days later, 200 miles or so from Bermuda, could carpenter's mate

William Goodwin go aloft to effect repairs. But, as the ship heaved over a wave, Goodwin slipped and fell from the foretopmast. He was killed as he crashed through the rigging onto the deck, at the feet of the men on watch. Goodwin's body was sombrely committed 'to the deep', while his clothes were sold to raise money for his family.

Some on board might have seen the seaman's accident as an ill omen, as they made their way southwards to risk their lives for Europe's profitable and growing addiction: sugar.

11

'The time now seems big with events'

'The time now seems big with events'

Robert's first sight of the West Indies in early December 1780 came after one of the most devastating hurricanes ever known in the Lesser Antilles. The view of high peaks in the blue distance and golden beaches fringed with vegetation was transformed, as the *Resolution*, *Alcide* and *Triton* closed towards Barbados, into a devastating scene – of uprooted palm trees, shattered dwellings and other debris. For the young nobleman, this was a rude awakening to another facet of the sugar islands – the islands so coveted by European nations, from the major powers to even the tiny Duchy of Courland. It evoked less the memories of exotic sweet luxuries on the table at Belvoir, and rather more disasters such as the crop failures on family plantations in Barbados and Jamaica that had driven Alleyne FitzHerbert's father to suicide in 1772.

Commodore William Hotham, who was stationed at St Lucia in command of the ships there, had witnessed the whole terrible event. On the night of 10 October 1780, 'there arose a Hurricane', he wrote, which 'increased by the morning to a Degree of Violence that is not to be described'. It blew for thirty hours, at first with 'an irresistible fury', then with 'redoubled violence and nothing was to be seen or expected but ruin, desolation and destruction in every part... as the day broke after the Storm abated, an unusual and Dreadful scene opened to our view... whole forests were demolished by the roots, scarcely a house left standing, and the aspect of summer was in these few hours changed to all the gloom of Winter'. Hotham added sombrely that 'in short no representation can equal the scene of distress that appeared before us'.[1]

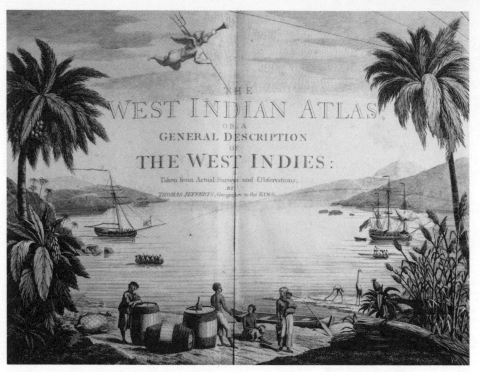

The title page of Robert's atlas that he had with him in the Resolution.

The Great Hurricane killed an estimated 22,000 people through-out the islands, an unprecedented loss of life caused in part by the unusually high military presence in the area. With the entry of France and Spain into the war, and profits from sugar fuelling the British economy more than any other single commodity, Britain had diverted ships and troops away from North America to prevent the loss of the Caribbean colonies. The thousand-mile sprawl of the Leeward Islands station, where Robert now found himself, was the first line of defence for Jamaica, Britain's most vital sugar possession. Barbados, being the most easterly and windward island in the string, was provided with the strongest and largest of the fortifications and garrisons, and the British had even abandoned Philadelphia in order to supply 5,000 troops for the conquest of St Lucia in December 1778. The latter was a highly strategic move, which meant that the island could now be used as a vantage point for monitoring French movements to and from their base at Fort Royal, Martinique, 30 miles away.

Of the British islands, Barbados and St Lucia were the worst hit by the hurricane. The soldiers in their barracks and the sick in the hospitals suffered dreadfully, and ships in the bays were driven from their anchors out to sea or wrecked on the shore. Hotham described the sorry state of his surviving ships at Lucia, such as the *Montagu*, which returned without a single mast standing, 8 feet of water in her hold and all her powder damaged. Several vessels were lost entirely. 'What is truly melancholy,' wrote Hotham, was that 'many of [their] Officers and people perished.'[2] The 32-gun frigate *Amazon*, commanded by Robert's cousin William Clement Finch, made it to Antigua, where she arrived with broken masts and bowsprit, and seventeen of her guns thrown overboard; but her survival was thought to be extraordinary. Two men in particular had worked very hard to save her, one of whom, the *Amazon*'s carpenter, was killed in the process.

If there was a silver lining it was, as Hotham told the Admiralty, that: 'The hurricane by every account has been more fatal to the French Islands than to ours.' He had received a flag of truce from the Governor of Martinique, the Marquis de Bouillé, who wished to return thirty-one men rescued from wreckages close to the island, saying that he could not consider them enemies 'in a time of such universal Calamity and Distress'. Hotham wrote that de Bouillé 'laments only that their numbers were so few and that among them no Officer was saved; in his way of acting he has shewn himself equally humane and generous, and I should be wanting in those sentiments myself, if I omitted to point out to their Lordships his conduct upon this unhappy occasion'.[3]

★

On 6 December, the *Resolution*, *Alcide* and *Triton* came to their anchors in Carlisle Bay, Barbados. There, they found that Rodney and part of the fleet had already arrived, with other ships straggling in. They were greeted by Robert's old friend the Reverend Touch, who had come out from England to rejoin the *Alcide*, but, having escaped from Moutray's captured convoy of August 1780 (and losing all his possessions in the process), he had arrived in time to be caught in the hurricane's devastation. At Barbados, even the cannon in the forts were supposedly flung in the air by the violence of the wind, and some 4,500 people, mostly slaves, and 8,000 head of cattle had been killed. Dead bodies still lay rotting in the pitiless sun. Alleyne FitzHerbert's family estates had been devastated, along with hundreds of other plantation buildings and wind-driven sugar-mills. Slaves had plundered Bridgetown – one of the wealthiest ports in the West Indies – even while troops were patrolling the streets, day and night, to attempt to prevent looting and violence in what was now mostly a heap of ruins.

Robert was called aboard the *Sandwich* and informed that Rodney was about to depart north-westwards for St Lucia, and that he must follow as soon as he was able, so they could station themselves to observe the French at Martinique, which lay immediately north of St Lucia. Four days later, the *Resolution* was sufficiently jury-rigged to set off, and on arrival Robert continued pushing his men to restore the ship to battle-worthy condition, using St Lucia's sheltered west-coast anchorages at Gros Islet (now Rodney Bay) and the Carenage (now Castries) for victuals and repairs, and the river at Cul de Sac Bay for water; but significant refitting was near-impossible to achieve. None of the islands, nor any of Rodney's nine ships of the line – let alone the local ships that had survived the hurricane – had much in the way of spare sails, spars or cordage. It meant that when Rodney tried, unsuccessfully, to recapture the more southerly island of St Vincent in mid-December, having heard it was weakened by hurricane damage, he could not take Robert with him, for the *Resolution* was still not in a position 'to proceed to sea for want of masts sails & rigging'. At least in St Lucia Robert could feel some longed-for connection to Charles and home, for already there was Anthony St Leger, their distant relative now commanding the Rutland Regiment, who was also governor of the island. Charles's regiment, now reduced in numbers through ill-health to 540 men, had 117 rank-and-file stationed on the island, including Joe Hutchinson the gardener from Belvoir and Sergeant Hall and his wife Hannah.

Disease, for which the sugar islands were so notorious, now began to affect Robert's own men too. In the crowded harbours, ships were exposed to the tropical illnesses that killed far more people than any warfare. With the sudden influx of thousands of sailors and soldiers without immunity, the likes of yellow fever and malaria could spread quickly through the ships. Many men would never return home. As the *St James's Chronicle* reported in September 1780, 'near thirty were buried every week' on the islands of St Lucia, Tobago, Barbados,

Antigua and St Kitts. But scurvy also remained a threat, for oranges, lemons, pineapples, bananas and other fresh food-stuffs were in short supply after the hurricane. At least there was plenty of rum available to drown the seamen's sorrows. It was officially issued in the form of 'grog' – a drink that was one part rum to four parts water – in an effort to reduce inebriation; and, if available, brown sugar and lemon juice was added to help prevent scurvy. But occasionally men would risk punishment and temporarily escape to go ashore and get their hands on the neat form of the spirit.

Amid these conditions, the deterioration in manpower was relentless. On 17 December, the new, young 6th Lieutenant Nathaniel Hall died, and the *Resolution* could now muster only 401 ratings and 98 marines. Robert most likely also heard of another local tragedy, one that would be distressingly received in England: the ambitious James Charles Pitt was dead. Aged just nineteen, Pitt had succeeded in gaining a command of the 14-gun sloop *Hornet* in 1780, and, though he had escaped the hurricane by heading to Antigua to refit, he could not escape the region's diseases. As Commodore Hotham was informed by John Laforey, commissioner at Antigua: 'This letter goes by the *Hornet* whose People are mostly recovered, but whose Commander (the Hon'ble Captain Pitt) I am extremely sorry to acquaint you died of a Fever on the 13th [November].'[4] According to rumours, the young Pitt's demise came not before he had sired a child on the island by a slave.[5]

At least the British government did not abandon its men to their fate. It committed a large amount of money to repair the hurricane damage and to treat the sick; and, soon after Christmas, as Admiral Rodney's fleet returned to Barbados, beset by 'fresh gales and squally with rain', there was the cheering sight of reinforcements. On 13 January 1781, Sir Samuel Hood, Rear Admiral of the Blue, arrived with eight ships of the line, including Robert's old ship the *Panther* and the *Prince William*, the ex-Spanish *Guazpacoano* captured in 1780. They brought with them a large convoy of more than a hundred sails carrying food, spare masts, cordage and other stores.

Thus, the beginning of 1781 brought not only the capacity for Rodney to bring his fleet up to twenty-one serviceable line-of-battle ships, but also a moment of joy for Robert: for he now gained what he

had for so long coveted. Amid the turmoil of deaths, new arrivals and
the reorganization of the fleet, the fifty-five-year-old Sir Chaloner Ogle
was to return home. Thus, on 25 January, Robert's immediate superior
transferred to the *Panther* with his large retinue of other Ogles, leaving
only – apart from the training he had imparted and the stories from
old Lord Granby's generation – his table linen and 'other articles',
which Robert, preserving his coins, promised to pay for later. Once
ensconced in the ship's spacious Great Cabin, Robert wrote excitedly
to Charles with the news – but yet again had no opportunity to send
the letter, nor the signed Trowbridge deeds.

Now, just as he was about to turn twenty-three, Robert was going
to be truly in command of his ship – the youngest captain of a '74' in
the Leeward Islands fleet, if not in the whole Royal Navy. The way was
also opening up for him to cultivate his own 'following' more deeply
and further shape daily life aboard the *Resolution*, inspiring the officers and men with his own personality and values. There were many
psychological pressures that might now become more acute: the loneliness of command, the temptations of power, the fear of others' envy,
and the grip of depression could all beset him. Would he adhere to the
era's code of honour – a standard of physical and moral courage that
would enable him to steel himself in the face of death or difficult and
frightening moments? He had already made his private resolution that
he would rather go to the bottom of the ocean than surrender to the
enemy; but what would he do if he had to choose between 'honour'
or chasing a prize?

Ogle's departure was not the only change aboard the *Resolution*. Two
of her ageing lieutenants also now left the ship. Thomas Arthur Ley
departed for England with Rodney's despatches, and William Reynolds
transferred to another ship, leaving Richard Shordiche probably now
as 1st lieutenant.[6] However, perhaps mindful of his own 'thwarted'
attempts to gain advancement, Robert began to dispense favours and
assemble a range of youthful acting lieutenants, supported by Rodney, 3,000 miles away from the watchful glare of Lord Sandwich. The
thirteen-year-old Whig, Honourable George Grey, and the sixteen-
year-old William Brown from near Belvoir were two of them, though
neither had served the requisite six years. Only if they were lucky and
did well would their rank be later confirmed by the Admiralty.

These young men, little more than boys, would be responsible for the ship in a remote part of the world that would severely test their constitutions and seamanship. Although there were not the fierce tides of European waters to contend with, they would face other hazards: intense heat, strong trade winds and relentless ocean currents – along with, as was palpably clear, the hurricane season, lack of supplies and the threat of tropical disease. And although the *Resolution's* mustered ratings continued to fall, to 396 with 98 marines, Robert and his officers still had nearly 500 men whose well-being, discipline and ultimately performance in battle was their responsibility. The future of the American colonies and the sugar islands just might be in their hands, for rumours abounded that the Comte d'Estaing was 'hourly expected in these seas', and even Rear Admiral Hood confirmed the intelligence that the French admiral had sailed from France with twenty-two ships of the line.

Perhaps, with his wardroom dining companions, Robert showed the grave, reserved side of his nature when contemplating the possible appearance of the French or the numerous daily anxieties – concerns over the sick-list, the endless consumption of stores reported by his purser Charles Howard, and the material condition of the ship and her rigging as described to him by the master, Charles Young. But doubtless

A British naval vessel in the West Indies, with an awning to provide shade.

his 'amiable' and convivial side also created lighter moments too. From his childhood at Belvoir, Robert had learned to value the friendship of men from different orders; and now, he seemed to especially appreciate the company of the polymath Surgeon Blair, the intelligent and widely-liked 2nd Lieutenant of Marines William Dawes, and the boy from home, William Brown. With them, he was able to share interests in such matters as the causes of scurvy, and the pros and cons of chronometers versus the complex 'lunar distance' calculations for determining longitude. Both Blair and Dawes came to be influential in these areas – and Brown would one day rise to the eminence of admiral.

Yet, for Lord Robert, the essential reality of the loneliness of command was undeniable, not only because the captain had to maintain a degree of distance from the rest of the crew, but because his high social status also set him somewhat apart. He was inclined, therefore, to look for close associations with those in the wider community of the Leeward Islands fleet, especially some of those on the larger ships with whom he had a family connection. His letters to Charles tended to mention men whom his brother knew, such as Philip Affleck in the *Triumph* and the *Monarch*'s captain, Frances Reynolds-Moreton (later 3rd Baron Ducie), a friend of Mun Stevens.[7]

Whatever their personal situations, this community of men far from home would be expected to unite in their efforts to face bravely what must, at times, have seemed like overwhelming odds. For in addition to the possibility of d'Estaing appearing at any moment, alarming news arrived with Rear Admiral Hood that the British government's relations with Holland had significantly deteriorated.

★

It had already been known for some time that the Dutch had been defying neutrality agreements by supplying arms, munitions and military stores to the rebel Americans and circumventing Britain's blockade of the American coast via Dutch-owned islands in the Caribbean. St Eustatius in particular, lying at the northern end of the Lesser Antilles, was a vital *entrepôt*, operating as a major trading centre in spite of its small size – just 8 square miles. Its harbour was invariably full of the merchant ships of several nations, and it had been the scene of the first formal salute to an American-flagged man-of-war by a foreign power, when the *Andrew Doria* arrived at the island on 16 November 1776 to obtain a cargo of munitions, firing an eleven-gun salute, and receiving one in return. The brig had even brought with it a copy of the Declaration of Independence. More recently, Rodney had been furious that St Eustatius had helped the French, but not the British, with supplies for repairing the ships after his brush with de Guichen off Martinique in April 1780.

Finally, shortly before Christmas 1780, Britain had declared war on the Dutch, on the pretext of discovering of a draft treaty between them and the Americans, which was cited as proof of Dutch non-neutrality. The British government wanted to suppress Dutch trade with France, Spain and America, even at the risk of further isolation without allies in a conflict fought as far afield as the East Indies.

On 27 January 1781, a despatch arrived from England. Admiral Rodney and Major General John Vaughan, the British officer stationed at St Lucia as commander-in-chief of the Leeward Islands land forces, were now ordered to commence an amphibious operation against the Dutch to seize territory. Three days later, Rodney and Vaughan sailed for St Eustatius with 3,000 troops, and Rodney sent for Hood, who had been patrolling the waters between Martinique and Dominica. Lord Robert, sailing with Hood's squadron, was thus also to join the expedition, to comprise fifteen men-of-war.

The morning of 3 February dawned clear and breezy. Four miles from the island, the *Resolution* caught up with Rodney and his fleet in time to observe the admiral, at two o'clock in the afternoon, make the signal to man and arm the boats and prepare to land. There was just one Dutch frigate, the *Mars*, in the bay, and Rodney ordered Robert to anchor within 'pistol shot' of her. From the *Alcide*, it was observed that: 'Between 3 and 4 pm the *Resolution* and a Dutch man of war then lying in the road began to fire upon each other the Dutch friggat soon struck her colours to the *Resolution*.'[8] Not long afterwards, the British colours were hoisted at St Eustatius's Fort Oranje, after Rodney had sent word to the island's governor, Johannes de Graaf, that he should surrender to avoid bloodshed: he agreed. But Rodney then reprimanded Robert for a lack of discipline. The *Mars* had been outnumbered and outgunned, and the *Resolution*'s excited young captain had fired without orders.

Nevertheless, on 6 February Rodney, making use of Robert's enthusiasm, sent him off with the *Barbuda* and the *Alcide* under the overall command of Captain Thompson to capture the island of St Martin. Strong gales caused them to make several tacks to get into the bay, before sending boats ashore with a flag of truce and troops; soon afterwards, the fort there was flying British colours too. The British ships then returned to join Rodney. The admiral had, in the meantime, taken 150 merchant ships, whose cargoes were valued at more than £3 million, and sent 3 men-of-war in hot pursuit of a convoy of 30 Dutch ships protected by a lone 60-gun man-of-war, also called the *Mars*, which had left the island two days earlier. The convoy was brought back, its senior officer, Rear Admiral Willem Krul, having died in its defence. He was buried with full military honours on St Eustatius. Soon afterwards, his vessel was renamed the *Prince Edward* and her command given to George Ann Pulteney, brother of Charles's friend Daniel.

In the days that followed, Rodney did not stop at simply taking the islands; he set about what he considered a 'just punishment upon the insolent and perfidious citizens of Amsterdam'.[9] After ordering the mile-and-a-half of warehouses around the port to be demolished or left roofless, to prevent the island being used again as a trading post, he went far beyond what even his contemporaries considered moral. The impoverished Rodney viewed the immense treasure of St Eustatius as a godsend. He and Vaughan declared it a prize of war, and there began three fateful months of indiscriminate plunder. Rodney reserved his harshest treatment for the Jewish community, ordering that more than a hundred male Jewish merchants be imprisoned and a number of others be deported to other islands, without their wives and children. He even went so far as to order that the lining of the Jews' coats be stripped in an effort to prevent their taking gold coins away with them. Observing matters from the *Resolution*, Robert viewed his commander-in-chief's actions with disapproval; they jarred with his own moral sense and codes of honourable behaviour. Robert owed his being 'made post' to the admiral; but began to find himself drawn instead to the leadership of Sir Samuel Hood.

Hood was a man of greater sensitivity than Rodney, and his letters at that time contained many references to the welfare of individuals.

The eldest son of a vicar, he had not joined the navy until the age of sixteen, in 1740, and had acquired a significant education and a degree of social refinement to become one of a few at the top of the service who combined worldly knowledge, social skills and political aptitude: 'a thinking man'.[10] Robert had several family links with him too, including one of his patrons, the late Captain Thomas Grenville, uncle to Eton friends George and Thomas Grenville.

At the start of the American war, Sir Samuel was already in his fifties and it seemed as though his active career was over, for his battle and fleet-handling experience was limited. Nevertheless, he pressed for a command afloat, and with so many officers either refusing to serve on political grounds or hating the abrasive George Rodney, he had his chance in September 1780, being promoted rear admiral and sent to the West Indies in the 98-gun *Barfleur*. This was not Hood's first experience of subordination to Rodney, for he had first served under the admiral as a midshipman and was confident he could work with him. However, on Hood's arrival in the West Indies, he quickly began to realize why many were now reluctant to serve under the uncommunicative Rodney, a man who ignored the opinions of others.

At the same time as Rodney was exerting his blunt authority in St Eustatius, his third-in-command, Rear Admiral Sir Francis Drake, slightly junior to Hood, had been tasked with scouting for signs of the enemy, but to no avail. Now Rodney ordered Hood in the *Barfleur*, with sixteen other ships of the line, to cruise to the east and windward of Martinique, to be in a position to intercept the French fleet should it appear, without having to then sail upwind to meet them, which was difficult for any sailing vessel, but especially so for the cumbersome, square-rigged ships of the line. However, Rodney himself chose to remain at St Eustatius – on the pretext of ensuring that the island did not change hands again and to prevent illicit trade recommencing, but in fact because naked self-interest had begun to entangle him in a complex web of claims and counter-claims. Large quantities of the sequestered goods had belonged to English merchants, and it would transpire that Rodney and Vaughan were at the cusp of a protracted series of costly lawsuits.

Rather than languish at St Eustatius, Robert requested that the *Resolution* join Hood's squadron, which in any case appeared to have the more exciting prospect of action. Rodney agreed to let him go, and Hood himself was certainly not displeased to be able to take Robert under his wing. Like his superior, Sir Samuel was not unsusceptible to the usefulness of having friends in high places, and he took an interest in the *Resolution*'s aristocratic young captain.

At this point, Robert left behind some more of his inherited officers. His 4th lieutenant, William Nowell, went off to command the sloop *Swallow*, taking with him the master, Charles Young. Robert replaced Nowell with another youngster, Thomas Harrison, and made the assistant master, Charles Martin, the acting master. By 12 February 1781, Robert was on station with Hood patrolling the area to the north and east of Martinique, while Drake was ordered to cruise to the west of Fort Royal, and 'block it up' with a small detachment. The admirals communicated with each other by sending copies of their letters and orders in smaller vessels, via different routes to make sure at least one copy arrived safely.

There followed several weeks spent almost constantly at sea, the British ships expecting all the while a French fleet to appear over the horizon. Rumours abounded. The *Terrible* chased a French lugger and extracted an account that the Comte de La Touche-Tréville, who in 1780 had brought General Lafayette to Boston in the frigate *Hermione* with secret news of reinforcements for Washington, might be now heading for Virginia, where Lafayette was trying to capture the turncoat Benedict Arnold (who had been wreaking havoc there). Meanwhile, other intelligence suggested that de Ternay had slipped away from Rhode Island – but no one knew if he would go to Europe, come to the West Indies or join the operation in Virginia. And Drake picked up four slaves who had escaped from Martinique in a canoe, and were certain 'a large force of men of war 10,000 troops and a large convoy were expected daily commanded either by d'Estaing or Tréville'.[11]

To keep the crews of his seventeen ships fed and watered, Hood rotated them back to St Lucia. While he deferentially commiserated with Rodney over the 'trouble and fatigue' caused by the 'complicated business at St Eustatius', his own experiences were a woeful catalogue of difficulties, in which his inexperience of fleet management had played its part. In a series of letters, he told Rodney the weather had been 'more like that in the English Channel then the West Indies [and] several disasters [had] befallen the squadron'. He wished a 'mast ship' would come from Antigua as they were desperate for a 'supply of sticks for topmasts & yards'. The copper sheets were falling off the bottoms of the ships, which were also leaking, caused by the electrolysis: as Drake said of his vessel, the *Russell*, 'the corroding quality of the remaining copper eating the bolts; and then the working of the ship loosens them; from which they will in a short time fall out; and the ship make much water'. Some ships, including the *Resolution*, were delayed at St Lucia owing to the 'dilatory' attendance of victualling contractors; others came in desperately short of water, with men 'dying so fast' that the sick were put ashore in an effort to save them. The *Prince William* did not even have enough healthy men to work the ship, so Captain Douglas was told to take his crew ashore at Gros Islet and assist with dismantling a church and rebuilding it at the waterside, to be used as a hospital. Hood's own ship appeared to be doing somewhat better. He told Rodney: 'I thank God the *Barfleur* continues pretty healthy, I have got lemons and limes for my poor fellows from every place I could, which has prevented the scurvy, from taking that root [*sic*] I am sorry to say it has in other ships.'[12] To assist in replacing the dead and sick men gone ashore, Hood attempted an exchange of prisoners with Governor de Bouillé on Martinique; but the Frenchman said he could not comply until he had heard from his court, 'though he lamented very much the misfortunes which the chance of war threw upon individuals'.

During this time, Robert stayed with Hood's flag. But on one occasion, as Sir Samuel headed to St Lucia to collect water, the rear admiral noticed that his young protégé had disappeared. On 21 March he told Rodney: 'The *Resolution* is just come in, Lord Robert followed Mr Drake, as I suspected off Fort Royal, from whence his Lordship was sent back to me, upon the admiral's finding he acted without orders.'[13] It seems that Robert had once again, in his enthusiasm, acted on his own initiative, perhaps perceiving there was more excitement to be had with Drake. The tone of Hood's letter suggests it was not a surprise. The admirals probably feared his determination to succeed could lead him into trouble – that he might possess that 'indifference to physical danger that is so often the gift of great wealth or great stupidity'.[14] At

least Robert had so far fared better than the other aristocrat whom
Lord Sandwich had wanted 'off his hands': Lord Charles FitzGerald
had wrecked his ship warping into Carenage Bay the previous year.

By the end of March 1781, all the rumours had proved false, and there
was no sign of d'Estaing, Tréville or de Ternay; so Rodney ordered
Hood to shift his cruising ground to the west – and leeward – side of
Martinique, to impose a close blockade on Fort Royal harbour. The
two British admirals disagreed about this strategy. Hood believed that
Rodney was simply keeping him out of the way so that he could continue to ravage St Eustatius. The junior admiral would have preferred
to collect all their ships together to the eastern side of Martinique to
intercept a 'formidable' French fleet before it could get anywhere near
Fort Royal, for there was now yet another rumour – of 'a big convoy
meaning several men of war, at least twenty', which, as Hood told
Rodney in April, would be 'an object for every ship under your command'. Its commander was unknown but would not be d'Estaing, 'that
officer I understand having retired in disgust'.[15] But Rodney would not
change his mind, and the deferential Hood would not disobey orders:
'My dear Sir George... I most readily submit to your superior knowledge and experience, and shall cheerfully obey your commands upon
all occasions, with the utmost fidelity.'[16]

Hood had to be content, instead, with sending only scouting frigates
out to the east. Then, at last, what was so long expected came to pass.
On 28 April, lookouts in William Clement Finch's *Amazon* spotted the
outline of a multitude of strange sails breaking the horizon. Finch
ventured close enough to make a rough count, then returned to Hood
to tell him of the imminent approach of at least nineteen men-of-war
with a very large convoy. Hood ordered his fleet to start tacking to
windward with all speed to close Fort Royal, while sending word to
Drake and his detachment to join them. At sunset on the 28th, the
enemy fleet could be seen from the masthead beyond Point des Salines
at the southern tip of Martinique; but it was not yet obvious whether
they would pass to the north or to the south of the island to reach Fort
Royal, and Hood was unsure where to position his fleet. At daylight
on 29 April, sightings of the enemy confirmed they had chosen the
southern route, and Hood signalled his fleet to form a close line of
battle and prepare for action. As the French fleet made their way round

the south of the island, they also formed their line, comprising twenty men-of-war, each of seventy-four or more guns. Veterans of the Battle of Ushant, such as Robert, might have recognized the *Ville de Paris*, now with 100 guns, at the centre of the line. At around half past nine, both fleets hoisted their colours.

The British admiral, however, was frustrated, as there was little he could do other than keep his fleet clawing to windward and try to induce the enemy to bear down for close action. Most of his ships, so unwieldy when tacking into the wind, were unable to make substantial ground towards Martinique, while the French refused to take the bait, engaging only in a distant cannonade. 'Never, I believe,' wrote Hood after three hours had been spent in this frustrating situation, 'was more powder and shot thrown away in one day before.'[17] Nevertheless, during the afternoon the two fleets manoeuvred to such a position that a sharp engagement could take place at the rear of the British line. Some ships came under heavy fire, with damage to hulls, rigging and men; and Captain John Nott of the *Centaur* was killed outright, which saddened Robert, who considered him 'a gallant officer'. In the *Resolution*, lying tenth in the line of battle and fourth astern of Hood's *Barfleur*, Seaman James Watson lost a leg, while Robert, standing on the exposed quarterdeck and now directing matters without Ogle's watchful eye upon him, narrowly missed being hit. Right beside Robert, one of his servants, John Kidd, was less lucky, for a ball sheared-off the boy's leg at the thigh. Like Watson, Kidd was hurried below to where Surgeon Blair and his loblolly-boys were plying their grisly trade. Robert observed that the boy 'behaved with the utmost fortitude during the operation down below'; he was moved, too, that Kidd's first words when able to speak again were to enquire after the safety of his beloved captain. Robert would later ask his brother to help Kidd, for whom 'I think you will not blame me if I show some little concern and attention'. Watson, too, was to receive assistance.

The two fleets drew off during the night; but on the following morning, the wind had died away and Hood judged that there was nothing more he could do. With some ships badly damaged and all of them short of men, it was impossible to reach the enemy. He had already failed to prevent about 150 merchantmen passing safely into the harbour at Fort Royal. At eight o'clock in the morning, Hood

François-Joseph Paul de Grasse (1723–88), commander of the French fleet at the critical Battle of the Chesapeake (1781). This statue, in his birthplace of Le Bar-sur-Loup in Provence, describes his 'immortal glory that assured the independence of America'.

withdrew his partially mauled squadron to St Lucia, while sending the badly leaking and now useless 74-gun *Russell* to St Eustatius to break the news to Rodney. Hood also soon learned that the French commander he had faced was none of those from earlier rumours, but was rather the experienced and respected Comte de Grasse, seconded by the Comte de Vaudreuil. The British rear admiral consoled himself in writing a couple of days later that although de Grasse had brought his fleet to close action, the 'zeal' of the British, even with upwards of 1,500 men sick, meant a French victory would not have been easy.

★

Throughout these dramatic events, Robert's thoughts of home and of his brother were never far from his mind. He had received no letters since leaving New York and had only heard about the birth of Charles's new son indirectly; he had even destroyed at least three of his own letters to Charles, for, being constantly at sea, with only a few days at anchor off St Eustatius and brief stops at St Lucia since the end of January, there had been no means of despatching them. But now at last, in early May, though still at sea and heading towards Antigua, to his delight some mail from home caught up with the fleet. Robert began again to write to Charles, on 8 May:

> It is with the greatest joy that I received your letter of the 1st of Dec: The only one I have yet got, I was afraid my letters had miscarried & that you had not heard of the alteration of the *Resolution*'s destination. I had before heard of the birth of your son [Lord Charles Manners] <u>to my further exclusion</u> – & I have had time to vent my greif [*sic*] upon the occasion & to become in a degree reconciled to such mishaps: may you both enjoy many many, many, happy days…

Referring to his own middle name, derived from the early lords of Belvoir, he insisted 'that the next be called after me, Albinine, as you know it is a favourite name of mine, & I, being the only one of the family named so, I take it rather unkind it was not remember'd before'.

Although Robert made light of Charles being too busy with his young family to write regularly, he had something very important to relate: that Ogle had left the ship. With a touch of pride he described how: 'I am now what you so much wisht me to be that is Capt[ain] of a 74 gun ship & what is more, she is allowed in general to be the fastest sailer of any line battle ship or frigate in the West Indies.' It seems, too, that his command of the *Resolution* had improved her performance. 'Without partiality' he could 'assent to that opinion, & what renders it more pleasant is, that before, she never was esteem'd the capital sailing ship she now is.' But he did not labour the point. Gone was his touch of aristocratic arrogance, the obsessive ambition; he was now a more reflective young man with a tremendous responsibility on his shoulders. Neither did he mention the failed Battle of Fort Royal, other than as a 'distant cannonade', but moved on to subjects he knew would be uppermost in Charles's mind. He said he was enclosing the Trowbridge deeds, 'which I have sign'd & executed above 2 months without having had one single opportunity of sending them'. Then, referring to his electoral success of eight months before, he suggested: 'Apropos of opportunity, don't you think it would be amiss for me to make some apology to the worthy freeholders my constituents & others of the county of Cambridge for not having thanked them etc. I will subjoin

a scrap of paper with a hint of something which if you think proper
you will distribute or not if you please.' Feeling justified that service
had kept him from political duty, he added: 'I can do this with some
propriety I think as it is absolutely fact.' Uncertain when he would be
able to send the letter, he trailed off and doodled on the page, remarking with irritation that a vessel had headed home carrying despatches,
but without giving the officers time to write their correspondence. Yet
again, his letter was put to one side. In any case, the greater affairs of
the fleet called.

Sir Samuel Hood's news of his brush with the Comte de Grasse
had reached Rodney. The British admiral at last dragged himself away
from the spoils of St Eustatius to meet up with Hood's fleet on 11 May,
between St Kitts and Antigua, to discuss the reality of a large French
fleet and to argue over the events of the last few days. Rodney blamed
Hood for not making more ground towards Fort Royal during the
night of 28 April, while Hood blamed Rodney for ordering him to
stay to the leeward side of Martinique which had put him at the disadvantage of having to sail upwind. But the squabbling was soon put
to one side, for while their backs had been turned the French had made
a move on St Lucia – albeit unsuccessfully. But worse was to come,
in the discovery that this was in part a diversionary tactic. The true
object of French attention was Tobago, an easier target than St Lucia
and a coveted prize, being a significant exporter of rum, cotton, indigo
and sugar.

Rodney took over command of the fleet. He went with most of
the ships to Barbados's Carlisle Bay to obtain water, while, on 29 May,
despatching Drake with some of Vaughan's troops and six ships of the
line, including the *Resolution*, to the assistance of Tobago. It was some
small comfort for Robert to be going there, for its garrison included
Charles's friend Henry Fitzroy Stanhope and Robert's cousins Francis
Sutton and Robert Manners, along with 297 others of the Rutland
Regiment – although almost half of them were sick. But although
Drake, as Robert recounted in his still unfinished letter, 'was sent to
throw succour in to Tobago... he was prevented from doing by the
arrival of Mons de Grasse with 23 sail of the line'. The French 'chased
us but without effect from some best sailing for 9 hours'. Greatly outnumbered, Drake retreated to Barbados to raise the alarm, prompting

Rodney to join with him on 3 June, where together they made twenty ships of the line, to return to Tobago.

Robert 'expected very severe engagement but to our great surprise found the island taken, the French posted & the [French] Fleet drawn up to defend their conquest'. Unbeknownst to the British, Martinique's governor, the Marquis de Bouillé, had joined forces with the French general Blanchelande; and de Grasse had been able to land their troops unhindered, after chasing off Drake. On a more personal level, Robert had been unable to come to the defence of his cousins. The forces of George Ferguson, its British governor, surrendered on 2 June. They included 207 remaining rank and file of the ailing Rutland Regiment, but Francis Sutton had been killed in action. And Britain had lost another sugar island.

★

Rodney's fleet, arriving in Carlisle Bay, was now in a deplorable state. Although beset by the need to attend to his duties, Robert found time to continue writing to Charles: 'We are just arrived at Barbados', he added on 15 June, 'where I own I hope we may make some stay to recruit our people, who are fairly worn out with keeping the sea & from the want of fresh provisions and vegetables.' He told Charles that the *Resolution*, of which he was immensely proud, 'if compleat in her complement of men and in good repair would be the most desirable ship in the service. But at present is one hundred & twenty five short.'

Such a worrying situation was not caused by a lack of concern from Rodney – who faced bravely the enormous task of maintaining the health of the several-thousand-strong population of sailors and marines. The complexity of managing what amounted to the population of a small and very needy town was compounded by the loss of supply lines from North America as well as by the ferocious hurricane that had robbed the islands of so much of their natural produce. Even though water was fortunately not too difficult to come by, staples such as salt-meat, dried peas, flour, hard-tack and other traditional victuals had to be shipped out by convoyed merchantmen to the islands. Rodney himself made every effort he could to supply the men with fresh provisions and vegetables, being completely aware of their necessity.

Sickly himself, Rodney had appointed his own physician, Dr Gilbert

Blane, as Physician to the Leeward Islands Fleet, to accompany the squadrons and study the health of the seamen. As a result, Blane's correspondence with the Sick and Hurt Board in London reveals tremendous efforts on behalf of the sick men, not just for the purposes of manning the fleet, but also in sympathy with the misery they were enduring. He requisitioned buildings to act as hospitals and asked for a range of items such as 'lavender comp[ound]' and 'tincture of myrrh', as well as sauerkraut and wort, to be sent from England. He was not amused when the Board sent out 'portable soup' that arrived so rancid it 'resemble[d] more an infusion of glue than a pleasant broth'.[18] But his efforts on behalf of the men reduced the death rate from what it would otherwise have been. Indeed, his appointment led to the publication of 'An Address to the Officers serving in HM Ships of War in the West Indies and America', and his studies in the field would go on to make him a major influence on naval medicine, on the use of citrus fruit to prevent scurvy, and on the modern science of epidemiology.

Supplying the fleets came at an enormous cost to the British government, and the Admiralty, so as not to lay itself open to fraud on distant stations, tightly controlled what it was prepared to spend on fresh food, even though scurvy remained a potent threat to the fleet's very battle-worthiness.[19] Blane had told the Admiralty the previous year that Rodney should be given discretionary powers to issue fruit and vegetables at extra expense, which would 'save lives and cost less than having to replace dead men'.[20] Yet still in June 1781, Robert was explaining to Charles that he did 'not see much probability of getting [fresh provisions] even here as it is beyond the price government allows; but unless Sr Geo: Rodney breaks thro' that rule we shall not have men to fight our ships. Some of the ships have lost 70 men & have 200 sick, & should that be our fate, which if we do not get refreshments I think may be the case.'

Robert and his own ship's surgeon, Blair, took an active interest in the diseases prevalent in the West Indies. It was observed by those serving in the *Resolution* that Robert's 'attention to the health of his men had made him so particular in his inquiries concerning [the infections]... which frequently accompanied wounds received in the West Indies'. He would have seen that men ashore collecting wood and water could quickly become infected with the feared 'yellow-jack', though he would not then have known that it was spread by the bite of the female mosquito. He was familiar with tetanus, or 'lock-jaw', which caused fatal muscle spasms, though again it was not then understood that it came from the bacterium *Clostridium tetani*, contained in the manure of horses or mules. When shoes tramped onto the ships from the filthy docksides, and no matter how thorough the cleaning of the decks, *Clostridium* penetrated the wood and could then enter men's bodies through cuts and scrapes, and especially from shards of wood splintered by cannon balls. Similarly it was noticed that long exertion, particularly when men were ashore and denied the cool of the sea breeze, induced heatstroke and that salt was needed as a prophylactic. Yet, despite the ubiquity of salt-preserved meat, often the salt was soaked out as much as possible, because some believed an excess of it caused scurvy. Matters were not helped by the fact that the copious quantities of small-beer imbibed by seamen had the effect of leaching away a good deal of the essential mineral from their bodies, so that a sudden onset of heatstroke could, and often did, prove fatal.

We do not know exactly what Robert suspected was the cause of the fatalities, but if 'obliged on my oath' to venture one, he told Charles that he thought the men 'were starved for though they have the same allowance as in other countries, the salt provision, which by the by is generally very indifferent (& for which are assign'd various reasons) has not nourishment in it sufficient to supply the prodigious diminution of strength caus'd by the extraordinary exudations the body undergoes in this torrid climate, where the thermometer in the coolest place in the ship entirely excluded from the sun or hot air now stands at 86½°'.

While sons and brothers died in Britain's far-flung fleets, the arguments raged in Parliament as how to address the shortage of seamen, the health of those serving and the state-of-repair of the ships. While the Admiralty's failure to authorize the purchase of sufficient fresh food might seem scandalous today, it should be seen in the context of the times. The Admiralty struggled to control expenditure 3,000 miles away, when circumstances inflated prices and when agents and contractors could be corrupt or 'dilatory'. Equally, various attempts to claim financial reward for what turned out to be crank ideas made the authorities suspicious of new-fangled proposals regarding

medicine and nutrition. In the summer of 1781, Parliament debated an
'invention' by a man named Philips, who suggested that many of the
seamen's malaises were due to rats, weevils and cockroaches aboard
their ships. He presented a solution by way of a powder that killed
'caterpillars, flies and other vermin' in his garden, so why should it
not obliterate ship-board pests? But with its failure in trials to control
pests in crops in the West Indies, and with Philips now demanding
£3,600 for his public service, sceptics considered his insecticide more
likely to kill than protect the seamen, for it contained arsenic. 'From
the committee of West India planters and merchants,' Lord Abingdon
told the House of Lords, 'Mr Philips was dismissed with a flea in his
ear, that he might use of his powder on himself and not upon them.
I trust my Lords, that we shall follow the examples of the planters
and merchants, in preference to that of the House of Commons,
and in so doing, give Mr Philips another flea in his ear for the use of
his powder.'[21]

Meanwhile, Robert and the other captains did what they could to
improve matters by carrying out Rodney's and Blane's orders to attend
to hygiene – not an easy business in such high temperatures. With
several thousand men daily relieving themselves into the water at their
ships' heads, some of the resulting foulness could be drawn back into
the ships on the anchor cables, adding to any ship-board noxiousness
created by those men surreptitiously using the shingle ballast for their
toilet. The lieutenants continued to try and enforce personal cleanliness, the ballast was regularly cleaned, and general fumigation – often
by burning loose gun-powder or washing with a vinegar solution – did
at least go some way in improving conditions in the fleet.

★

Sitting at his desk in his baking cabin, Robert himself was fortunate to
be in robust health. He found time to finish his letter to Charles on 15
June, for the consolidation of the fleet meant that a homeward-bound
vessel – the leaky *Triumph* – would be carrying Admiral Rodney's
despatches, and Robert was able to entrust his missive to Philip
Affleck. Back in England, the state of the Leeward Islands fleet – and
all of the navy – was uppermost in the minds of those governing the
country, including Charles, for whom not only was his beloved brother

in danger, but there was the tragedy that had already struck his circle in the death of James Charles Pitt. Of his demise, his sibling William wrote: 'I have to regret the loss of a brother who had every thing that was most amiable and promising, every thing that I could love and admire; and I feel the favourite hope of my mind extinguished by this untimely blow.'[22]

Charles's bond with the Pitt family had continued to strengthen, and though William had failed to obtain a seat for the University of Cambridge at the 1780 election, afterwards Charles persuaded Sir James Lowther, who controlled the pocket borough of Appleby, to let Pitt have an untaken seat there in January 1781. This would later prove to be a profound move for both the future of the nation and the friendship between the two young men. Pitt was grateful: 'Let me rather hope that I shall have the satisfaction of fighting under your banner in the cause to which we are alike attached, and of proving to the world how much I know the value and feel the honour of such a connection.'

William Pitt the Younger (1759–1806):
bust by Joseph Nollekens at Belvoir Castle.

William made his maiden speech in the Commons in February 1781, not long after the news arrived home of his younger brother's death. Over the subsequent months, he entered the fray of debate from the opposition's benches, impressing the House with his eloquence, as he referred to the war with America as 'accursed, wicked, barbarous, cruel, unnatural, unjust and diabolical'.[23]

Time would show that William was a keen observer of the Royal Navy, and would come to oversee significant improvements to the service; but for the moment, he watched and listened to the Members as they debated the welfare of the 91,000 seamen and 20,317 marines – the naval strength voted for in 1781 – as well as the state of the 90 ships of the line said to be in service. Laudatory and patriotic effusions punctuated proceedings: 'With regard to British seamen... if there was one set of men nobler than another, the British seamen were that set. They deserved everything of their country; they were its honour, its support, and its glory!'

Unlike Pitt in the Commons, Charles continued largely to avoid Parliamentary duty in the Lords. During the whole of 1781, he attended just four times out of a possible hundred opportunities.[24] Other matters preyed on his mind. He had not heard from Robert for some time, and his brother's silence had financial implications, quite apart from causing worry over his safety. Joseph Hill expressed relief that Charles had spent much of the spring of 1781 at Belvoir, for 'while your Grace is at Belvoir you are at least not adding to the Debt'. The lawyer was also anxiously awaiting Robert's signature on the Trowbridge estate paperwork. As far as he knew, the documents dispatched the previous September had gone missing:

> I am much grieved that the letters of attorney [were] lost in passage in September. It is attended with infinite inconvenience to your Grace's affairs at Trowbridge and how my letter miscarried I cannot understand; for I gave it to Mr Thoroton who assured me, it went with your Grace's other Dispatches to Lord Robert immediately after the Cambridgeshire election. The sale of Trowbridge, which at present is entirely at a stand, for want of these powers from Lord Robert, would free your Grace from many applications [from creditors], and satisfy many who are at

present much alarmed – these sales and a mortgage are certainly
wanting to make my plan of economy complete.

Then, in late July 1781, Charles received the long letter Robert had
completed on 15 June. Some relief was afforded by the longed-for and
signed Trowbridge deeds, along with Robert's declaration for his constituents; but the letter also spoke of the fall of Tobago, which meant
further damage to Charles's pocket with the surrender of the Rutland
Regiment. At least Robert was in good health. With the fate of James
Charles Pitt in his mind, Charles was no doubt deeply relieved to read
of Robert's seeming imperviousness to the local conditions: 'You will
naturally ask how I like this country and if it agrees with me? I answer
exceedingly well. I do not know that I have ever enjoyed my health better than I have done since I left England... I have never felt the slightest
inconvenience from the climate tho' I have been some considerable
time at St Lucia which is by far the most unhealthy island in the West
Indies.' Charles might also have sensed his conscience being pricked
by Robert's declaration that: 'You need not be at a loss to write to me
as a Pacquet sails every month from Falmouth. Direct to me *Resolution*
Barbadoes or the West Indies.' Mindful of family connections, Robert
had told Charles that '[Philip] Affleck desires most particularly to be
remembered to you and the Dutchess' and that: 'Young Brown is with
me still & a very fine boy he is. I like him extreemly.' Charles could
see that Robert clearly wished Brown to prosper: 'He is rather too
young but however I have got him appointed my acting lieutenant &
if I can by any means overcome the difficulty of his not having serv'd
his [six years], I wou'd get him some time hence a real commission &
if you wish send John Glover to the Navy Office to take out a certifi-
cate of his service, as he once did for me. I may perhaps have it in my
power to serve him.' Then, with perhaps Rodney's fifteen-year-old son
(among others) in mind, Robert added that: 'Indeed there are several
as young actually appointed & I am sure many who are not so able.'
Whether Charles followed up Robert's request for Brown is unknown,
and perhaps unlikely.

Given the delay between the writing and the arrival of the letter,
the duke must have wondered what adventures were now befalling his
younger brother and his friends in the unequal contest that seemed to

be developing. '20 sail of our ships & 24 of the French are in the West
Indies,' Robert had written, and 'there is a report the French have been
join'd by their ships from America which will make their number 34 of
the line but we had no confirmation of this.'

Neither brother knew at that moment that the implications of
Rodney's distraction at St Eustatius would soon become apparent, and
that far to the north-west, a movement had begun that would prove to
be the war's culmination. But, with a certain prescience, Robert had
added: 'The time now seems big with events.'

12

'A slight inconvenience'

JULY TO NOVEMBER 1781

'A slight inconvenience'

Throughout the summer of 1781, Members of the British Parliament fiercely debated the sense in continuing the war for the thirteen North American colonies. Speaking for the opposition, John Wilkes boldly told the House of Commons that whatever was decided would make no difference to the war's outcome: 'It is merely an amusing, curious theme of speculation among a set of idle, listless, loitering, lounging, ill-informed gentlemen at Westminster... It is in this island only that persons are found, who doubt that the present war will end in the acknowledging of American independence.'

Yet still King George III and Lord North's government pressed those in the nation's service to 'do their utmost'. By this time, hope and attention was focusing on General Cornwallis. The man who had begun his army career as an *aide-de-camp* to the old Lord Granby had departed from Charleston after its capture in 1780 to strengthen the British hold on the Carolinas and Georgia, with the help of Colonel Banastre Tarleton – a leader whose name became synonymous with ruthlessness in the American South. On 16 August 1780, at the Battle of Camden, they had beaten Horatio Gates, the victor of Saratoga, and in the long months afterwards turned northwards to attempt to control North Carolina.

The contending British and American forces marched and counter-marched through difficult country, in a cruel partisan war waged upon each other's flanks but settling nothing. Cornwallis had insufficient men to garrison anywhere but his coastal supply-ports, and he was consequently unable to hold territory let alone achieve anything approaching political stability by reoccupation. Everywhere that British arms triumphed, the local population expediently declared loyalty to the king before abandoning it the moment the British moved on, once patchy detachments of Patriot forces turned up. British ambitions in the Carolinas were ebbing away.

Meanwhile, in the early months of 1781, the opposing sides had also gathered in Virginia – a state that had hitherto largely escaped military notice. George Washington had sent General Lafayette there to try to capture Benedict Arnold, supported from the sea by Destouches and Tréville. But Admiral Mariot Arbuthnot had followed Destouches from Rhode Island, and on 16 March 1781, at the Battle of Cape Henry, near the mouth of Chesapeake Bay, Arbuthnot had frustrated the French admirals. This British success enabled Cornwallis to come up from the south with a force of some 7,000 men, to arrive in Virginia in May 1781. Cornwallis, recognizing that most of his enemy's supplies came from Virginia, hoped to cut the supply lines to the Carolinas and make American resistance there impossible. He took over command from Arnold and proceeded to dig himself in at Yorktown, just inside the Chesapeake Capes, with the aim of establishing a naval anchorage close to the Atlantic Ocean. From here, he expected Clinton to resupply and reinforce him from New York, supported by the Royal Navy.

For Admiral Rodney in the West Indies, a difficult decision now presented itself. It was known that the French General Rochambeau had left Rhode Island and marched to join George Washington at Phillipsburg, New York. Rodney did not know whether Washington and Rochambeau would try to attack Clinton in New York or Cornwallis at Yorktown. In either case, the rebel forces would require the assistance of the French ships, and it would be Rodney's task to fend them off.

Rodney's fleet had put into Barbados in June 1781, to ensure the island's protection. But by so doing, he had been unable to prevent the French leaving Martinique. By 9 July, he knew only that the Comte de Grasse's fleet of 28 sails of the line had left with a convoy, but he did not know where they were heading. The rumour that the Comte de Barras, who had replaced Destouches, was sailing south to 'make their number 34 of the line' – as Robert had mentioned to Charles – had so far proved false. De Grasse appeared to be heading north-west,

towards Hispaniola,[1] though Rodney thought they would not attempt
to attack Jamaica so near to the hurricane season. He considered following them; but then again, and confusingly, different intelligence
was emanating from London.

★

While mulling over the options, Rodney took his fleet in mid-July 1781
to Antigua for repairs and provisions. Here, a convoy of supplies and
mail was expected 'with great impatience', as Robert told Charles. The
beautiful island, with its rolling hills covered with palms, its beaches of
golden sand and its turquoise sea, was the centre of British naval power
in the Caribbean. In the south-east of Antigua lay English Harbour,
which had been an official Royal Dockyard since 1725, supporting the
men-of-war assigned to the Leeward Islands station. Here, ships could
obtain more extensive repairs, as well as take on water and victuals.
Yet, though it provided excellent shelter, the harbour was notably noxious: the smells and waste of ships and seamen became trapped in
the hot, airless upper reaches, while mosquitoes bred in the nearby
swamps. So on this occasion, most of Rodney's fleet, the *Resolution*
included, anchored in St John's Road, near the north-western point
of the island, which was a healthier place to lie in the more settled
weather.

At Antigua, John Laforey, Robert's old Ushant captain, was based
as commissioner, and he may have encouraged an unlikely friendship
between Robert and his son-in-law, Captain Anthony Pye Molloy of
the *Intrepid*. Molloy's later attitude to the Manners family suggests that
while he certainly was genuinely fond of Robert, he had also grasped
the chance to befriend a slightly lonely aristocrat who might be of use
to him in the future. The two men were very different, yet they became
close friends. It was also on Antigua that the body of the unfortunate
James Charles Pitt was buried, just outside English Harbour.

To add to Rodney's concerns, the admiral was now much engaged
with efforts to make up the shortfall in his ships' complements. He
continued to support Blane in trying to cure the sick, and he paid some
particular attention to exchanging prisoners of war with the French;
at the same time, any 'English, Scotch, Irish, Italian and Portuguese'

were extracted from American prizes and forced into service,[2] while healthy men were taken off merchantmen and replaced with the sick and wounded to sail the convoys home. A number of former slaves were employed on the ships, too.

Preventing desertion was paramount in the effort to maintain numbers; indeed, it is a wonder that more did not make an attempted getaway, when exposed to so much danger, disease and death. But prize-money provided one incentive to stay aboard, while firm bonds, deriving from mutual dependence in the face of danger combined with the communal nature of ship-board life, provided another. Patriotic pride and notions of duty also played their part in ensuring loyalty, as did acts of solicitude from the captain and knowledge that the wounded – and the widows – would be taken care of.

Of course, as well as carrots there were sticks to instil discipline. In the wake of the Keppel–Palliser affair, Admiral Rodney imposed such overall strictness across his fleet that there were numerous courts-martial and punishments for perceived transgressions, including desertion. Men might have reasonably feared punishment more than the prospect of climbing the rigging in the teeth of a gale or the mighty impact of a French broadside.

Yet, while a level of violence was accepted and tolerated in the service, Rodney had among his captains a growing number of rising stars who, in their general day-to-day management of their ships, largely abandoned old brutalities. Instead, they would scold when others would lash, and lash when others would hang, and they tried to win the hearts and minds of their ships' companies, establishing an understanding that if a man behaved as he was expected to within the pecking-order – essential in a ship of war – he need not fear the cat-o'-nine-tails. There remained the tyrants, the 'flogging-captains' and the outright sadists, but they were increasingly a rarity. As time went on, the effectiveness of the Georgian navy was based upon a reasonable rather than a cruel discipline. If a captain handled his men well, desertion was only likely, for the most part, when men were drafted to different ships and had to re-establish their place within a new company.

As Granby's son, solicitude came naturally to Robert. Although the *Resolution*'s logs are not devoid of punishments, several observers testified to his biographer Richard Watson that Robert only ordered a flogging when absolutely necessary: 'His obligations to use severity were a punishment to himself... he was always unhappy in seeing the necessity of bestowing correction.' In fact, Robert had even come up with an ingenious method of reconciling his men to their duty, by taking advantage of his friend Molloy – one of the remaining tyrants in the navy – who was known to impose a harsh regime to the terror of those who served under him. Robert had told Molloy one day that he had on board the *Resolution* a seaman who was so difficult to manage that the frequency of the punishments invoked was distasteful. Could Molloy break him or reform him? The seaman was accordingly discharged into the *Intrepid*, and 'such was the horror of serving in that ship that Lord Robert made the *Resolution* the smartest of all the fleet by the mere threat to send any other offenders to the *Intrepid*'.[3] So it was that Robert moulded both officers and seamen of the *Resolution* into an effective ship's company by means of a 'strict, steady, temperate discipline' and a 'skilful and intelligent discharge of his [own] duty'.[4] The seamen of the period tended to like the more gentlemanly officers, and they would have known that Robert's father was celebrated for courage and benevolence. In addition, during the capture of St Eustatius and the Battle of Fort Royal, Robert had probably already shown he was the type to lead by inspiring them – boldly facing danger on the exposed quarterdeck, and pushing his ship into action as Lord Granby had led the charge at Warburg, without being afraid to act without orders if he thought circumstances demanded it. Robert was rewarded for his approach by loyalty: at the end of each month the *Resolution*'s musters stated 'No Run Men', while Molloy's *Intrepid* routinely recorded sometimes as many as twenty-four deserters.

On one ship, though, the crew's dissatisfactions had reached breaking point. Earlier in the year, Rear Admiral Hood had been forced to investigate an anonymous letter from the *Santa Monica* alleging that her men had been ill-treated, flogged and confined on the passage from England, even though they had endeavoured to carry out their duties. To the crew's disgust, the letter was judged 'frivolous and without just foundation', coming from new recruits 'unacquainted with the discipline in the Kings Service',[5] and soon after the fleet's arrival at Antigua word of a serious mutiny was circulating. Mutiny, though it contravened the *Articles of War*, played its part in the system of relations

Year	Whither or for what Reason.	Straggling.	Neglect.	Slop Cloaths supplied by Navy.	Venereels.	Trusses.	Cloaths in Sick Quarters.	Dead Mens Cloaths.	Beds.	Tobacco.	Wages remitted from Abroad.	Two Months Advance	Necessaries supplied Marines on Shore.	To whom the Tickets were delivered.	When Mustered. Month May | June Days

No Run Men

These are to Certify that the Articles of War and the Abstract of the late Act of Parliament were publickly Read to the Company of His Majestys Ship Resolution on the 3d May and 7th June 1781

Given under our Hands on Board the said Ship this 30 June 1781

The Resolution's muster for May and June 1781, showing that
no one deserted from the ship during those months.

between officers and men on which mutual respect depended; it was 'the safety valve which blew when complaints were not heeded'.[6] On this occasion, it exploded on 16 July 1781 and involved nearly a hundred of *Santa Monica*'s sailors, many of them Scots.[7] Gradually, the facts emerged: Captain Robert Linzee had been unwilling to quell the mutineers by force, but when he failed with dissuasion, he mustered his marines, hoping to overawe the rebels without bloodshed. He then went below, accompanied by a sergeant and three privates in one final attempt at argument, but the sight of the marines' red coats provoked the seamen who swore violently and hurled whatever they could lay their hands on. Calling up his reserve, Linzee gave the order to fire. A man named Donovan was killed, whereupon the mutiny collapsed.

Robert was now ordered, for the third time in his life, to sit on a significant court-martial, this time of Linzee and the mutineers. He repaired to Hood's flagship, the *Barfleur*, on 20 July. Five days later, Captain Linzee was cleared of any wrongdoing, and his surrendered sword was returned to him. It was otherwise for the mutineers. Some of the accused were acquitted, but, as a matter of course, the death sentence was passed on the rest: sixty-four men.

Rodney, with overall responsibility as commander-in-chief, decided to adopt the most severe form of punishment to discourage others from following suit. He ordered the condemned mutineers to be dispersed among the squadron for execution. To effect such a sentence, the whole of a ship's company would be called on deck, the marines being paraded with loaded muskets. The prisoner, his hands bound and his head hooded, would stand with a noose placed around his neck, the line running up to the fore yard-arm, then back down to the deck, where it was placed in the hands of several seamen. The officers would doff their hats, and the marines would present their muskets to deter the seamen from failing in their duty. Then, a snare drum would roll and the order would be given for the muskets to traverse, as the hanging party ran away with the line, running the culprit up to the yard-arm. Here he would hang, 'dancing the dido of death', struggling for his last breaths. The dead sailor was usually left there until sundown, as a ghastly warning to all. Even in a brutal age, the effect of such a gruesome ritual was powerful, intended to work upon the minds of both officers and crew.

It now fell to Robert and his ship's company to exact this punishment upon thirteen of the mutineers, and the *Resolution*'s company was mustered accordingly. But, on that very morning, the ringleader of the mutiny was discovered – a man named Hirst – and it was decided to pardon the rest of the mutineers. Nevertheless, their reprieve was not made apparent straight away. The different captains were still ordered to make all the preparations for the hangings, then to point out to the mutineers the nature of their offence, before informing them that the sentences had been remitted. On the *Resolution*, witnesses recalled that: 'The suddenness of this order of mercy was too powerful for the mind of Lord Robert. He endeavoured to speak (after many attempts) but could only just get out in short "you are all pardoned" and bursting into tears he was forced to quit the deck and retire to his cabin.'

Rodney, in acquitting the mutineers, used the tactic of threat to enforce discipline, for the fleet would otherwise have suffered from the loss of manpower at such a difficult time. But evidence also suggests that the men were generally of good character and unused to the rigours of the sea. Whatever Rodney's motive, the positive effect of a pardon avoided stoking the sense of resentment that would have simmered had the executions occurred. As for Robert's demeanour on the day, most who witnessed it were moved by the captain's emotional reaction. This was not yet the age of the British stiff upper lip, and it was observed that 'the effect of [Robert's] sensibility was very striking'. The thirteen men from the *Santa Monica* were now mustered in the *Resolution*, and the mutineers, it was said, 'became ever afterwards some of the best seamen in it'. They included a 5th lieutenant, Henry Boyce, who would later appeal to Robert's family for assistance with finding further commissions.

★

Admiral Rodney's attention, momentarily diverted by the *Santa Monica*'s mutineers, had to return to the intractable problem of divining the intentions of the enemy and where to send his fleet. His captains were in the dark, for Rodney changed his mind from day to day or maintained an imperturbable silence. Having initially been told to complete his ship for four months' service, Robert had a reasonable expectation of the *Resolution* soon returning to England, though he thought America more likely, as he informed Charles in June. But when he next picked up his quill in late July he knew he was not to be sent home, writing regretfully: 'I am afraid it is not Europe.'

In his letter, Robert touched on other matters. He alluded only briefly to the mutiny, not wishing to dwell on matters of inhumanity, telling Charles: 'I believe you will not wish me to relate the particulars. I have very little inclination to go over so melancholy and unpleasing a subject.' Nor did he express much appetite for the war, reflecting a growing feeling in the fleet that reflected the views of the jeremiahs in Parliament. 'I don't think things seem to be in the most favourable situation in this country nor indeed anywhere. I wish heartily to hear from home some good news as we are tired & dispirited with hearing of nothing but misfortunes.' Still, duty called and Hood's squadron was under orders. 'Therefore,' he told Charles, 'write to me as I desired in my last to the care of Mr Kemble New York.' Robert's dispirited air was not confined to the strategic situation; he remained as concerned about the condition of his ship as of the state of the war. Like many vessels in Rodney's fleet, the *Resolution* was in a poor repair. The coppered ships were leaking badly, as the effects of electrolysis eroded the iron fastenings that held the hulls together below the waterline. Even Rodney had transferred from the *Sandwich* to the *Gibraltar* for this reason.

By the time Robert wrote, Rodney had at last made up his mind about where the fleet would head. Remarkably, his decision was ultimately based on intelligence from the Admiralty: that fourteen of de Grasse's warships would move station to North America to avoid the hurricane season in the Caribbean, while the rest would return to Europe. This reduction of French sea power offered an opportunity also for Rodney to ease his other concerns, which included his poor state of health, requiring frequent rests, and the necessity of seeing the end-of-season trade convoy safely across the Western Atlantic Ocean. It meant that *he* could return to England, where he was anxious to clear his name of accusations of venality attracted by his plunder of St Eustatius.

So, collecting up some men-of-war (that would otherwise be vulnerable in the West Indies) to accompany the merchantmen, on 1 August 1781 Rodney departed with a large convoy for England before the onset of any hurricanes. He left behind the designated fourteen sails of the line under the command of Rear Admiral Hood, to match the presumed French number. Their job would be to seek out the enemy, and the *Resolution* was among them. Rodney also wrote to Sir Peter Parker, Governor of Jamaica, asking him to prepare to send some additional ships to North America; and on 13 August, a few days into his transatlantic passage, he wrote to Arbuthnot to say that Hood was heading to Chesapeake Bay, 'where I am persuaded the French intend making their grand effort'[8] and where they might be joined by some Spanish ships. He suggested that Arbuthnot should collect all the force he could muster and meet up with Hood, while also indicating that the most 'vigorous campaign' of the French would be in the West Indies in November, after the hurricane months. This message to Arbuthnot never got through, for the ship carrying it foundered.

Hood's fourteen ships, after some more efforts to make repairs, made sail to the north. First, they looked into Virginia's huge Chesapeake Bay area on 25 August to see if the French were there; but Lynnhaven Road, at the entrance, was empty and so they made instead for New York to find out if the fourteen French ships had gone to meet de Barras at Rhode Island. There, on 28 August they found a disconsolate Sir Thomas Graves now in command of the station. It turned out that Arbuthnot had resigned his post in July, on account of his age and infirmity, and had left for England, thereby ending a difficult relationship with General Clinton. Graves, with only a handful of ships in battle-worthy condition, had had no idea Hood was coming; he had also failed to intercept a French convoy said to be bringing much-needed supplies, hard currency and a siege-train for de Barras to deliver to General Rochambeau, who had marched to join forces with Washington. 'All the American accounts are big with expectation,' Graves now told Hood. 'And the Army has lately crossed to the southward of the Hudson and appear in motion in the Jerseys as if to threaten Staten Island.'[9]

However, by contrast with the Admiralty's assertion, Graves had also heard that the French naval commander-in-chief had *not* returned to France. 'We have as yet no certain intelligence of De Grasse,' he wrote, for: 'The account say that he was gone to the Havanah to join the Spaniards and expected together upon this coast[;] a little time will shew us.' Though Graves also thought de Barras was still in Rhode

Island, Hood had picked up from passing vessels intelligence to the contrary. So, Hood refused to bring his ships in over the shallow sand 'bar' at the entrance to the anchorage, persuading Graves – as the senior of the two admirals and now Hood's commander-in-chief – to come out to join him, though Graves had initially refused, saying: 'My squadron is slender and not ready to move.'[10] Robert described the goings on to Charles: 'As soon as we arrived off Sandy Hook from the West Indies, we were order'd to sea without crossing the Bar to look for the Vicomte de Barras with the Rhode Island Squadron, consisting of 7 sail of the line.'

A new order of battle was hurriedly drawn up among the combined ships of Graves and Hood. The *Resolution* was placed in Graves's centre division, with Hood commanding the van and Sir Francis Samuel Drake the rear. On 31 August, nineteen sails of the line and eight frigates headed south, responding to further intelligence that the enemy forces were now moving towards Chesapeake Bay. But Hood had concealed the deplorable condition of his ships from his more timid superior. Graves soon realized the deception when, as the fleet staggered southwards from New York at about 3 knots, the *Terrible* signalled that she was in distress. Her captain was William Clement Finch, who had been transferred from the *Amazon*. Now, to his infuriation, Graves was told that five bilge pumps had been in continuous use on the *Terrible* since she had left the Leeward Islands. Nevertheless, the fleet continued south. Still they failed to locate de Barras and remained anxious as to whether he had combined with the ships of de Grasse.

By 5 September 1781, the British ships reached Cape Charles, the northernmost of the Virginia capes that flank the Chesapeake Bay area, and soon realized that at the entrance to Lynnhaven Bay lay a formidable enemy fleet. Sure enough, among them was the familiar *Ville de Paris*. 'Saw Le Comte de Grasse at an anchor in the Chesapeak,' recounted Robert, 'where he had arrived 2 days before us with 28 sail of the line from the West Indies, 24 of which were actually with him.' It was clear to all that the French admiral had outmanoeuvred the British. The intelligence from England had misinformed Rodney, and neither de Grasse nor the bulk of his fleet had returned to France. The quantity of ships under de Grasse made the British think initially that de Barras had also arrived, bringing the siege-train; the realization that this was not yet the case induced fear that even more French ships could arrive at any moment.

Graves saw the danger these events posed to Cornwallis. He would have to force battle on de Grasse and preferably before he could combine with de Barras. With the wind blowing from the north-east, the British had the advantage of being to windward, and Hood was all for driving in towards Lynnhaven Bay and engaging the French before they had a chance to react. But Graves was beset by anxiety and doubts about his ability to win a battle outnumbered, given that he had a dilapidated fleet two-thirds of which appeared to be already sinking in front of him. Instead, he ordered the ships to clear for action and form a line of battle in the time-honoured way.

As the British closed in towards Cape Charles and the entrance to the bay, a number of French ships began to straggle out to sea. Setting off into the wind, but with an ebb-tide to assist them, twenty-four of de Grasse's vessels now left their anchorage, their aristocratic captains each competing for the posts of honour in the van. With impressive *élan*, they rounded Cape Henry, the southern jawbone of the great inlet. Graves, rather than push into the bay and in effect take up the anchorages being abandoned by the French – a manoeuvre that Hood later suggested would have boldly reversed the strategic situation – held to tradition. In seeing the French willing to accept a conventional battle in line ahead, he ordered his nineteen ships back out to sea by reversing course, just after two o'clock in the afternoon. However, instead of the headmost ship hauling round on a course roughly parallel to that being taken by the jostling French to the south, with each British ship following in the wake of the next ahead, Graves reversed his line in one movement. This meant that Drake's division came to form the van and Hood's the rear. Robert's *Resolution* now lay eleventh in the line, the ship next astern of Graves in his flagship, the *London*.

Around thirty minutes later, Graves signalled to his fleet to turn to starboard so they could manoeuvre into a line parallel to the enemy. However, many of Rodney's Leeward Islands captains, with no time to become accustomed to the signals and instructions that Graves used in the North American station, misunderstood and altered course in succession instead of simultaneously as Graves had intended. The result was that the British van began to approach the French van at an angle.

Although the British were lying to windward, a slight shift in the wind enabled the French to haul up towards them, so that the two forming lines converged. But the enemy remained wary and respectful of British seamanship, suspecting that they might manage to get round behind and cut them off.

From the British perspective, Graves's control of his fleet seemed less assured. At around four o'clock, he told the ships to 'bear down and engage the enemy', intending his entire fleet to turn to starboard towards the French fleet to leeward – and, in a somewhat unorthodox manoeuvre, to try to target his force on the French van. But the British line, being at an angle, was in an awkward position for the leading ships to use their guns, while being simultaneously exposed to enemy fire. Three ships that lay ahead of the *London* opened fire at too great a range, forcing some vessels behind them in the line, including the *Resolution*, to alter course so as not to get caught in the crossfire. Then, according to witnesses later consulted by Richard Watson, 'Lord Robert Manners broke the line of battle, bore his ship into the centre of the enemy and narrowly escaped with his life, the peak of his hat being taken off by grape shot.' In other words, Robert broke out of the British line in responding to Graves's manoeuvre to concentrate on part of the enemy fleet. To say that he had ended up in the middle of the French fleet was a dramatic exaggeration, although in keeping with Robert's growing reputation for 'zeal'. But it was certainly no overstatement that Robert, by a whisker, had once again escaped death or severe wounding.

In the couple of hours that followed, Graves's attempts to manage his fleet caused further confusion. His alternate use of the signals for close action and for the line of battle ahead were misunderstood, especially by Hood in the rear, who was adamant that he had seen both signals flying simultaneously. The result was that the two opposing battle lines did not completely meet, and only the forward and centre sections engaged. The rear division barely took part in the action, Hood claiming that he had not understood what Graves had wanted him to do. By late afternoon, the wind had shifted, causing the fleets to draw too far away to fire effectually. By half past six, in the failing light of sunset, the *London* was flying the signal to disengage, and all firing had ceased. The British fleet had suffered more casualties and greater

*Robert's card from the Battle of the Chesapeake, 1781, showing that if
Graves wished to signal the* Resolution *directly, he would fly a white flag from
the larboard (port) or starboard mizzen topmast yardarm.*

damage than the French; in the *Resolution*, three men had been killed
and sixteen were wounded, one of the latter being Robert's friend the
marine William Dawes.

This two-and-a-half-hour action on 5 September, variously known
as the Battle of the Chesapeake or the Battle of the (Virginia) Capes,
appeared to be yet another tactically indecisive eighteenth-century
naval engagement. But its consequences were infinitely more profound.
Although the two fleets remained in sight of each other for several
days, Graves refused to attempt pressing further into Chesapeake Bay
with his disabled and outnumbered ships; and de Grasse made no move
to encourage him. Robert observed: 'It appear'd extraordinary at the
time that the enemy with 5 sail of the line superiority shou'd avoid an
action, but they had a deeper stake; their object was Lord Cornwallis &
the Chesapeak; where they had disembark'd, as we afterwards found,
3,000 men.'

It is one of the ironies of history that in August Hood and his fourteen ships leaving the Caribbean had only just missed coming upon
de Grasse in Chesapeake Bay, having arrived marginally too early.
In taking a direct course from the West Indies, they had effectively
overtaken de Grasse – the reason why they found the bay empty on

25 August. Yet, hardly had they sailed on over the horizon to the north, than de Grasse was appearing to the south. The French admiral had been advised by General Rochambeau that Cornwallis in Virginia was the better target than Clinton in New York. So, he had sailed from Martinique to Hispaniola, raised a huge sum of money in Havana, embarked his 3,000 French troops, then passed up the coast of Florida, to enter Chesapeake Bay on 26 August and begin disembarking his reinforcements. Meanwhile George Washington and his Continental Army had turned south to Virginia. The result was that the Patriot and French forces had encircled Cornwallis at Yorktown, and Colonel Tarleton at Gloucester on the far side of the York River, also by 26 August. For the British, everything was resting on Clinton's army and Graves's fleet – but, by failing to dislodge the French fleet on 5 September, Graves had also failed to provide relief for the now hard-pressed British land forces in Virginia.

★

By 9 September 1781, the French fleet had disappeared from the British ships' view. On the following day, Graves was forced to make the heart-breaking decision to destroy one of his own ships. The *Terrible*, which should have been in the rear of the fleet, had ended up in the van and therefore taken the brunt of the action. This ship, which Robert had known since his earliest days in the navy and which he described as 'one of the finest 74s we had', was, as he put it, in an 'exceedingly bad state even before she left the West Indies[,] & the firing of her own guns & the enemy's shot in the action, was found in so desperate a state, that she was order'd to be scuttled & set on fire which was done the night after we lost sight of the French fleet, it being thought impracticable to keep her above water, till we got into port.' Referring to his cousin, who had commanded the *Terrible*, Robert described how: 'Poor Finch… has undergone vast fatigue in her both in body & mind[;] his situation has all along been most anxious & distressing & indeed all his friends in the fleet have almost felt as much knowing that her fate wou'd probably be decided either in an action, or the first gale of wind. But fortunately it happen'd, so that we saved all her men.'

Two days later, after what seemed like hours of anguish, Graves had a change of heart as to his strategy. He ordered his fleet to approach

Chesapeake Bay to force a passage. Hood had pressed the matter, for the differences in seniority between them was small: both were rear admirals, as indeed was the third divisional commander, Drake, but Graves was eighteen months the senior flag-officer. Hood, though a man always inclined to obey orders, felt compelled to try and influence his indecisive commander. But, on their second arrival off Cape Henry, they could see that not only was de Grasse's entire fleet snugly back in its old anchorage, but de Barras had by now arrived with his convoy, having slipped past the British unobserved. The combined French fleet now amounted to thirty-six ships of the line, and Washington and Rochambeau had received the heavy artillery of a siege-train with which to pound Cornwallis. With some of his ships barely able to keep afloat, Graves could only abandon Cornwallis for the moment – in the hope that in heading north he might galvanize Clinton to mount a greater relief effort from New York.

Graves arrived at Sandy Hook on 19 September, to find that Rear Admiral Robert Digby had been sent from England with three more ships, to take command of the North American station, even though, technically, Digby was junior to Graves – by just ten days. Graves himself was to head to Jamaica to relieve the commander-in-chief there, Sir Peter Parker. In view of the crisis at Yorktown and the perilous situation of Cornwallis, Digby did not insist on Graves relinquishing command immediately – and it says something for Graves that he did not jump at the chance of relief, but stayed at his post until he had done his utmost to discharge his duties.

Aboard the *Resolution*, Robert recounted the events to Charles in a letter dated 27 September 1781. In a familiar refrain, he admonished his brother for his silence: 'I hope you received all my letters from the West Indies. I have <u>heard</u> you were very well, tho' <u>not from you</u>.' He went on to inform Charles that: 'Admiral Digby has arrived at New York, and there has been a counsel of war held, what the result is I know not, but from the damages & wants of all our ships & the total emptiness of all the store houses, I cannot ever guess when we shall be ready.' The letter revealed the state of the *Resolution* in some detail: 'The ships that wanted but little repair remain at Staten Island, the rest proceeded up to the North [Hudson] River amongst which the *Resolution* is one; having 2 of our lower deck Beams damaged (one of which it is absolutely necessary to shift should there be timber large enough in the yard) & the cathead & rails; main mast and Bowsprit to fish, & a great deal of our rigging to shift.' But knowing that Charles would have little interest in the technical details, Robert passed over 'sev'ral other damages which as you are not seaman enough to understand, & I am not likely to get them repair'd or replaced; I will not trouble you with the catalogue'. He did not mention that his quantity of mustered men had fallen to 389 and that there was a large increase in sickness aboard; though more happily there were still 'No Run Men'. Neither did he relate that John Kidd, his now one-legged servant, had been put ashore in the hospital at Long Island, before being sent to England. A few days later, he wrote a personal note for Kidd to take home with him.

However, Robert did admit gloomily to Charles that although ignorant of the council of war's decisions, he feared 'de Grasse is too good an officer to abandon such a strong post [and] the plight of Cornwallis demanded every effort; & a desperate one it will be if put into execution & if not, Lord Cornwallis & his army I am afraid are in most perilous situation from which they cannot be extricated by any other means; in short it is so melancholy a prospect to look forward on that I wish to drop the subject and wait calmly for the event which one way or another must soon happen'. His conclusion was unequivocal: 'If we do not succeed in our attempt and are repulsed, the fate of America is decided and the West Indies will be left an open prey to the French arms: and should we succeed so as to open a passage to throw in succour, I fear it would be only a temporary relief; as probably in the course of things such superiority must at last carry the point.'

Robert revealed nothing of personal intimacy in his letter, which he rushed to complete, fearing 'keeping this letter open any longer as notice is given that the Pacquet will sail tonight'. But it may have been during this time, while spending a month repairing his ship up the river, that he took an opportunity to sow some wild oats – and possibly give credence to a letter, written centuries later, from an American claiming descent 'from the brother of the 4th Duke of Rutland'. A handful of women were permitted on the ships for one reason or another, and some officers had wives aboard, while others took their pleasures with slave women, as James Charles Pitt was said to have

Resolution News
Oct.r 9th 82

The Bearer John Kidd is the person I mentioned to you in a letter from the West Indies, who was my servant & lost his leg in the action off Martinique if by any accident you should not have recieved that letter. I wish to recommend him to you till I get to England. I had no opportunity to send him home before. I give him this to carry himself to certify he is the person ———

W: ....

Robert Innes

Robert's request to Charles to care for his servant John Kidd,
who lost a leg at the Battle of Fort Royal, 29 April 1781.

done. Undoubtedly, in such entirely or overwhelmingly male environ-
ments, sex between men occurred too, though it had to be carried
out with great circumspection given the official prohibitions – not to
mention the lack of privacy aboard ship for this, or indeed for any
other, form of sexual- or self-gratification when hammocks were a
mere fourteen inches apart. The higher ranks were somewhat luckier.
In the midshipmen's cockpit, there was a tradition that when a senior
midshipman drove a dining fork into an overhead deck-beam, he was
to have some private time – and the juniors made themselves scarce.

★

At last, the British reorganized themselves to make a renewed attempt
to save Cornwallis. In mid-October 1781, 7,000 of Clinton's troops
were gathered and embarked on the British warships and troop-ships
at Sandy Hook. The *Resolution* received a battalion of 125 'Hessian'
Grenadiers and Artillery under the command of Lieutenant Colonel
De Lengereke, who were to be fed 'at 2/3 rations' according to the
ship's muster. From early on in the war, the British had employed a
sizeable quantity of mercenaries, most of whom were German and
from the state of Hesse-Kassel – leading to the generic description
'Hessian' for all the Germans so involved.[11]

On 19 October, the combined squadrons of Graves, Digby, Hood
and Drake departed together as a fleet of twenty-five ships from New
York, expecting to face thirty-six French ships. Unfortunately, they
were already too late. Somewhere off the Virginian coast, they learned
that their efforts were to no avail and that by 19 October Cornwallis – pleading indisposition – had ordered his second-in-command,
General Charles O'Hara, to surrender to Rochambeau. The French
general refused it, insisting it be given to their commander-in-chief,
Washington – who instructed his second-in-command, General Benjamin Lincoln, to accept the surrender. With expressions of disgust for
the troops they had so frequently beaten, 5,000 British infantry threw
down their weapons with ill grace, while their officers ignored the
rebel Americans and saluted only to their French counterparts.

Graves now ordered the fleet to return to the safety of New York
to shelter during the hurricane season. In mid-November, Hood was
dispatched back to the West Indies, to Barbados, with eighteen ships

of the line, including the *Resolution*. During this three-week passage, Robert wrote two (unsent) letters intended for Charles, in which he recited 'the unfortunate capture' of their father's friend Charles Cornwallis and his army.

★

The contrast between the two Manners brothers' lives at this time can scarcely have been greater. While Robert and his fellows, afloat in their wooden worlds, were grappling with their own fears, discomforts and pervading doubts as to whether some other course of action might have prevented Cornwallis's – and Britain's – humiliation, Charles and others of his set continued to enjoy the gaiety of their pursuits. 'I have some thoughts of being in town next week if I can get away,' Lord George Cavendish had written cheerily to Charles on 28 August 1781. 'Charles Fox is here[,] we have had a great deal of turf conversation.' Indeed, Cavendish admitted that, being half-drunk, he had gone so far as to enter the absent Lord Robert into a sweepstake.

Nevertheless, responsibilities lay on them all, should they choose to discharge them. Charles was at this time at Cheveley, occupied sometimes with tasks that in other circumstances should have been his brother's as Member for Cambridgeshire – such as responding to a request from the mayor who wanted assistance to rebuild the town hall, or from the Reverend William Cole for support over issues with the navigation of the River Cam. On the latter, Charles was obliging, even though Cole had not voted for Robert at the general election. 'The Duke of Rutland seems much more liberal [than I], when he is so civil to you, though you voted against his brother,' observed Horace Walpole in a letter to his friend Cole.[12]

Yet, in the foreground of Charles's mind and devouring his energy, were his financial difficulties. He was still struggling to pay off Robert's election bills almost a year after the event, while at the same time pursuing his vision to remodel Belvoir Castle and landscape its grounds, though at least 'Capability' Brown was not yet presenting him large bills. Charles also had to pay off £513 10s 4d demanded by Louch & Straubenzee for the uniform jackets of the now lost Rutland Regiment. This was a bitter pill to swallow in the light of the knowledge that his cousin Francis Sutton had been killed during the loss of

Tobago, while his Eton friend Henry Fitzroy Stanhope and half-cousin Robert Manners were to be court-martialled for their conduct during the affair; and that so many of those connected with Charles and the regiment had been lost through sickness, including Sergeant Hall in St Lucia, leaving his wife Hannah, as she described it, 'at the mercy of Colonel St Leger'.

Charles's money worries even tempted him to consider fleeing abroad. Joseph Hill wrote sternly to the contrary: 'As to your Grace's going aboard, the Remedy would be much worse than the Disease; it would make the creditors more clamorous and would certainly be attended with many great inconveniences (strict oeconomy here would be a much better Plan).' Hill was attending to the sale of various properties as part of his 'Plan'. The receipt of the signed Trowbridge deeds from Robert had gone some way to ameliorate matters, and 'by laying Lord Robert's [£]8400 upon Cheveley', said Hill, 'the Trowbridge Estate will be nearly disencumbered'. However, he was infuriated to find out through a third party that Charles was irresponsibly trying to purchase property in Lincolnshire, instead of paying his debtors. 'I don't myself see at present how otherwise any purchases are to be made, small or great,' Hill wrote, adding pithily: 'so I conclude some great [coal] mine is discovered on your Grace's estate.' He suggested selling Cheveley and acquiring 'any other estate where there was no mansion house', which might present 'a very desirable bargain'.

If Charles was chiefly absorbed in personal concerns, he could not ignore the wider scene, for now even his own extended family was involved in the very global nature of the war. He was at this time receiving a stream of letters from his cousin Evelyn Sutton, who was chasing the French in the Indian Ocean. When incoherent British strategy and overstretched fleets had failed to prevent de Grasse heading out from Brest back in March 1781, at the same time five other French ships, under the command of the Bailli de Suffren, had been able to set off for the Indian coast. However, de Suffren had been hotly pursued and caught up with off the West African coast by Commodore George Johnson, in whose squadron Sutton was serving. The two British officers had had a bitter row after the Battle of Porto Praya on 16 April 1781, and afterwards Sutton flooded Charles with letters to enlist his support.

Then, by mid-October 1781, while Cornwallis was still in the process of surrendering, Graves's despatches arrived in London with the news of the inconclusive Battle of the Capes: even the king was moved to admit that with 'the knowledge of the defeat of our fleet... I nearly think the empire ruined'. Charles heard things first-hand, and not just from Robert's letter describing the battle and the scuttling of the *Terrible*, but from the *Terrible*'s former captain himself, cousin Finch, who had been sent home bearing Graves's despatches. In a decent gesture, Robert commended the bearer to his brother: 'He is a very worthy & honest man.' Finch's mother, Charlotte Countess of Aylesford, also wrote to her nephew on 16 October, telling Charles she had 'the comfort of hearing of my son Williams health and safety after all dangers he encountered in his shatter'd [ship] and beg leave to congratulate your Grace on our dear Lord Robert being safe and well after the engagement.'

In Parliament, however, the woeful news brought renewed acrimony. The Royal Navy had failed to maintain sea power, and no one seemed to escape recrimination. Graves was blamed for incompetence and for not employing better tactics; and Hood was criticized for not supporting his commander-in-chief properly. Some agreed with Hood, while others said that Graves had in fact saved the fleet and that had he followed Hood's aggressive tactics then even more could have been lost. But Rodney, who had by now arrived home with the Leeward Islands convoy, was the greatest target of all. Circumstances were already conspiring against him. A convoy he had sent home earlier in the year from St Eustatius, containing goods worth around £5 million, had been captured by the French; and Rodney was now engaged in a highly public war of words with former Governor Ferguson of Tobago, who said the island had been lost through a failure to relieve it in a timely manner. Rodney was also blamed for the outcome of the Battle of the Capes, because it was said he should have taken command of the fleet himself rather than been distracted by lining his pockets and returning home to defend his interests. Charles James Fox claimed it was 'the most *shuffling shuffle* that ever was attempted in the most *shuffling* times'.

Undoubtedly, whatever the nature of Rodney's distractions, he was outsmarted by de Grasse. While the French admiral had taken twenty-eight ships to North America, Hood had been sent north from the West Indies with only fourteen. 'To this inferiority,' Clinton told Lord Germain, 'and to this alone, is our present fortune to be imputed.' The Earl of Shelburne remarked that such was the British way – of sending too small a force after a large one, and arriving too late anyway – that if the war were continued in the same vein, Britain would have 'another Chesapeake at Jamaica! Another Chesapeake at Barbados! Another Chesapeake at all our West India islands! Nay, he expected to see another Chesapeake at Plymouth, and should not wonder to find a Chesapeake in the River Thames!'

Finally, at midnight on Sunday, 25 November 1781, even worse news arrived in Lord Germain's office: Cornwallis's surrender. Germain immediately set off to inform Lord North who, in the early hours of Monday morning, reputedly flung open his arms and paced up and down the room, exclaiming: 'Oh God! It is all over.'[13] Yet incredibly, when on 27 November 1781 the king opened the second session of the House of Lords of the Fifteenth Parliament of Great Britain, he barely mentioned Cornwallis. He said: 'The war is still unhappily prolonged by that restless ambition which first excited our enemies to commence it… No endeavours have been wanting on my part to extinguish that spirit of rebellion… and to restore to my deluded subjects in America that happy and prosperous condition which they formerly derived from a due obedience to the laws.'[14] While Charles James Fox busily distributed a print of his speech declaring that 'America is now FREE and INDEPENDENT', as far as the king was concerned the war was not lost. After all, Burgoyne had surrendered five years earlier, and the war had gone on. Now Cornwallis had collapsed, but there was still Clinton in New York. Adamant that he would not allow the colonies to break away, George III thought that once Parliament had recovered from the shock, it would rally to his support once again.

Although Charles must have felt acute personal disappointment in, and sympathy for, Cornwallis's predicament, he had his own reasons to hope that the war would now come to an end. So far Robert had been safe, Charles knew, but dangers remained. Robert had been low-key in his 27 September letter, but he was not insensitive to the near miss he had received at Chesapeake. 'I had as nigh an escape in the last affair as I ever wish to have; the peak of my hat was shot off by a ball,' he wrote. He added, with dry understatement, 'I felt a slight inconvenience from it for a few moments but no injury' – though the battle itself would prove rather more than inconvenient for British prospects. Robert had, to date, been luckier than the lad with one leg who arrived on Charles's doorstep in London during the winter, and who bore a note addressed from New York, clearly marked with Robert's red seal:

> *Resolution* New York Oct: 9th The Bearer John Kidd is the person I mentioned to you in a letter from the West Indies, who was my servant & lost his leg in the action off Martinique. If by any accident you should not have received that letter, I wish to recommend him to you till I get to England. I had no opportunity to send him home before. I give him this to carry himself to certify he is the person. Yours very affectionately Robt Manners

'I am not without hopes of seeing you soon,' Robert had told Charles in his September letter, for the state of his ship was so poor that 'another action will render it highly necessary for the *Resolution* to return home, unless they intend she shall share the same fate as the *Terrible*, but my comfort is (if it is any comfort) – there are several ships worse than mine, indeed the *Ajax* is almost as bad as the *Terrible* was, & one or two more not much better'. But Charles must have known it was unlikely that Robert would soon come home. The Marine Royale may have denied the Royal Navy the capacity to sustain British forces in North America, and the British government might now be losing its political will to continue the war: but the future of the sugar islands still hung in the balance.

13

'A very great esteem for the Lady'

DECEMBER 1781 TO MARCH 1782

'A very great esteem for the Lady'

T he battered ships of Rear Admiral Hood's squadron were back in Carlisle Bay, Barbados by early December 1781. They were now very short of food, their crews surviving on salt-beef, hard tack, yams and with dwindling supplies of bread, so Hood sent frigates to other islands to collect what victuals were available. Meanwhile, his captains, Robert among them, did what they could to put their ships back into fighting condition. There were also some personal requirements to attend to. Robert took the opportunity to purchase a 'night spy-glass', an extraordinary quantity of '16 yards of hair ribbon' and 'two small side daggers', all for £12 9s 9d – though his supplier, William Gowdy Joslyne, would not receive payment for almost ten years, having to be content, for the present, with a promissory note.

Now they had returned to the relative safety of Barbados, officers could take advantage of some inter-ship visiting and exchanges of hospitality and Robert still had some bottles of wine and port left which had come from Charles's cellar. Robert mixed with his friends the disciplinarian Captain Molloy, Francis Reynolds and Edmund Affleck, the latter having regained command of the *Bedford* with the rank of commodore. They were joined by a newcomer, William Cornwallis, brother to the unfortunate Charles and commanding the 74-gun *Canada*; he was a man destined for distinction in the years to come. There was at least one departure too: 1st Lieutenant Richard Shordiche had now left the *Resolution*, his position probably taken by William Leggatt, the last remaining of Robert's 'inherited' commissioned officers. Meanwhile Robert had made George Grey an acting 3rd lieutenant,

Robert's promissory note for purchases in Barbados, December 1781.

the teenager having risen steadily upwards from midshipman in less than a year.

As always during this time, Robert's thoughts turned to home as well, as he had heard nothing from Charles for some eight months: 'I hope you receiv'd my letters from America & also from the West Indies, as I sent from thence the deed you sent me to sign,' he wrote on 14 December. He also added to his letter some distressing news: that St Eustatius – that island of so much controversy – had recently been recaptured by de Grasse while he had been returning from Chesapeake Bay to Martinique in November.

By the new year of 1782, the crews' collective efforts at repair had brought the squadron's strength up to twenty-two serviceable ships. Robert even obtained permission from Hood to purchase a new boat for the *Resolution*, a 'six oar cutter with masts and sails compleat 23½ feet in length'. But before he handed over the order, on 14 January 1782 he slipped it temporarily between the pages of his *West Indian Atlas*;

for Hood had passed word for the squadron to put to sea and all was now in a frenzy.

The alarm had been raised on the arrival of a despatch from General Shirley, Governor of St Kitts. Four days earlier, a large fleet had been seen from the heights of the smaller, neighbouring island of Nevis, and, having summoned his captains, Sir Samuel Hood issued his order of battle. The *Resolution* was to be stationed in the rear division, behind Edmund Affleck in the *Bedford*, ahead of which was William Cornwallis in the *Canada*. Captain Molloy's *Intrepid* was to lie in the van, and Francis Reynolds' *Monarch* in the centre. Having passed his captains their orders in writing, Hood dismissed them and told them to weigh anchor, before sitting down to write to the Admiralty. Beset by frustrations since arriving in the West Indies, he was determined now to seize his chance. He assured his masters in distant Whitehall that he would 'seek and give battle to the Count de Grasse, be his numbers as they may'.[1]

As Hood's squadron made its way north, confirmation arrived that the large fleet was indeed de Grasse's, and that moreover on 11 January he had landed 8,000 troops on St Kitts, commanded by the Marquis de Bouillé. The British land forces there had not put up any opposition, having retreated into the fortress of Brimstone Hill, where they remained holed up, leaving de Grasse at anchor in Basseterre Road.

The moderate sea conditions of the Caribbean allowed boats to be hoisted out from the ships, and Hood, unlike most admirals of his day, was thus able to keep his subordinates in the picture, conveying not only his orders but his military doctrine at their daily meetings. On the passage to St Kitts, the squadron anchored off Antigua on 21 January to take advantage of the dockyard there and to effect further repairs, load more victuals and stores, and to embark troops: 2,400 men drawn from the 28th, 13th and 69th regiments of Foot, augmenting the squadron's marines, and all under the command of General Prescott. Hood sent his frigates ahead, to keep a watch on Basseterre Road less than 50 miles away, and with Prescott laid plans with some care.

On 23 January, Hood passed word for his captains to weigh anchor again and proceed towards Nevis. However, that night Captain William Bayne's 74-gun *Alfred* collided with the frigate *Nymphe*, causing a delay for the squadron that turned out to be strangely fortuitous. It gave time for de Grasse to learn of the British approach and prompted him to put to sea, for battle. But the French admiral's move offered Hood something to seize upon, in a daring tactic.

In the first light of dawn, at about half-past-five on the morning of 25 January, Hood hoisted the signal to form the line of battle. This was soon followed by signals to prepare to anchor. It was his intention to head for Frigate Bay, off the little town of Basseterre, taking up the anchorage so lately vacated by de Grasse. This was precisely the manoeuvre that he thought that Graves should have attempted at Chesapeake Bay; but here, Hood had an advantage, for the shallow ledge in the bay that would serve as an anchorage dropped off sharply into deeper water, thus limiting the available space: there was no room for de Grasse's ships to anchor there too. It was a high-risk operation that had the potential to be a brilliant *coup de main* on Hood's part, and would enable him, with an inferior fleet, to form a defensive line in a secure position while concentrating his crews on gunnery. To attack him, de Grasse's ships would need to keep a proportion of their hands to tend the sails, a task made all the more demanding by their proximity to the land.

As de Grasse observed the British head in towards the anchorage, he soon realized he had been outmanoeuvred. Nevertheless, the Frenchman pressed his attack as Hood's ships came to anchor. With Captain Thomas Wells stationed in the 20-gun sixth-rate *Champion*, to repeat signals between Affleck and the rest of the squadron, Hood left the rear division to fend off the approaching enemy, while the van and centre anchored first. De Grasse's flagship, the *Ville de Paris*, was closest to the British, and the French admiral could see that the three rearmost British ships, the *Prudent*, *Montagu* and *America*, had dropped slightly astern, opening a gap in Affleck's rear division as it stood guard over the centre and van. De Grasse pressed forward towards the gap, opening fire at about two o'clock in the afternoon and hoping to cut off the tail of the British line before mauling the rest of the fleet. However, Cornwallis in the *Canada*, just ahead of the gap, hauled his yards and backed his sails, to effectively stop his ship and wait for the slow-sailing *Prudent* to catch up. Ahead of Cornwallis, both Lord Robert and Edmund Affleck saw this initiative; now they distinguished themselves by doing likewise, instantly closing the gap and, with heavy firing, robbed de Grasse of his opportunity. It was a close-run thing. Just for a moment the foresail of the *Ville de Paris* had appeared inside the British line, according to the report of one British officer.

As Hood's van and centre came to their anchors, those men who could be spared set 'springs' to the cables. This entailed running a heavy rope out through an aft gun-port and forward along the ship's side, where it was secured to the anchor cable. Then, by hauling or slackening the spring, it was possible to alter the line of the ship as she lay at anchor under the combined influence of any breeze or current. The gun batteries on one side could then be traversed over a wider arc than was possible when just 'handspiking' them around in their gun-ports. A well-trained crew could set the springs in minutes, and Hood's men did not fail him, enabling the guns of the centre division to cover Affleck's ships, which, although being heavily fired upon by the French, now also came in to Frigate Bay.

These manoeuvres took up the rest of the afternoon, with all the men-of-war within range opening fire on de Grasse as he led his line along the anchored British. Although Hood's fleet conducted itself boldly, individual ships suffered misfortune. The 28-gun frigate *Solebay*, inside the line, ran so close inshore that she was grounded and wrecked. Meanwhile the *Canada*, as she arrived to anchor, found herself lodged on the underwater escarpment and lost two cables before finding the bottom at 150 fathoms.

The *Resolution*, too, had almost been lost. With two cables shot away, she hung only with a third, drifting out of line helplessly towards the nearby French. At that moment, Lord Robert uttered to one of his lieutenants: 'Now you shall see whether I can keep the resolution I have long formed, if my ship should run amongst the enemy, Sir Samuel Hood shall either come down to succour me or I will go to the bottom, for the flag shall never be struck whilst I am alive.' But the enemy was held at bay, and Robert and his ship survived.

As the sun was setting and the French drew off, Hood ordered Affleck's *Bedford* to fill the gap between the end of his line and the shore, so the anchored ships then entirely occupied the shallows across the approach to Basseterre Road. The British were now able to take stock. Robert found that the *Resolution* had been much damaged in her rigging during the engagement; and five of her men had been killed and eleven wounded. The master, Charles Martin, was among the dead. Robert said he would personally provide for his widow, and for the wounded seaman Francis Milladd, who had lost his right arm.

At daybreak the following morning, 26 January, de Grasse renewed his attack. Hood's ships opened a thunderous fire upon the French as they made several fruitless attempts to dislodge the British. The cannonade was furious, the opponents disappearing from view amid clouds of white powder-smoke, and 'whole pieces of plank' were seen flying off the side of one French ship. When the French drew off in the late afternoon, de Grasse had lost 107 men with 207 wounded. Hood 'was left in triumphant possession of the field', but his own casualties of 72 killed and 244 wounded attested to the evenness of the contest.

Over the following few days, de Grasse's fleet hovered nearby, occasionally exchanging shots with the British line, while Hood attempted to put troops ashore to relieve Brimstone Hill. He managed to land some on 27 January, but forty of them were killed or wounded. Like other men-of-war, the *Resolution* was then required to despatch a boat to fetch off the wounded soldiers, an operation with its own attendant dangers. Ten of Robert's men, including his friend William Brown, boarded the *Resolution*'s boat. In quieter moments during these tense land operations, one of Robert's other friends, Marine Lieutenant William Dawes, painted some watercolours of the bay. These too ended up slipped into the pages of Robert's *West Indian Atlas* for safekeeping.

During this hiatus, and although the squadron remained in readiness for renewed close action, Robert was able to put pen to paper again on 8 February, two days after his twenty-fourth birthday. 'My Dearest Brother… I set down to write to you, tho' the signal is now flying to prepare for Battle. The enemy consists of 29 sail of the line & three 50 gun ships standing in for us; therefore you must not expect a long letter or a very correct account, as I am frequently looking out to observe their progress.' He described the scene to Charles:

> The constant sight of the enemy has made them quite familiar to us, tho' at least once a day they form in such a position as to make it appear they are going to attack us, yet when they come near gun shot, they always tack & stand from our fleet. If they mean by this to harass us they are quite mistaken as we have always

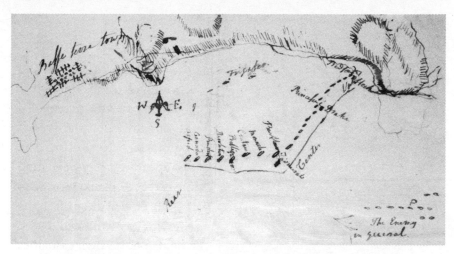

Robert made this sketch of Sir Samuel Hood's squadron at anchor off St Kitts in January 1782. The Resolution *is fourth from the left in the line of vessels.*

time to make our meals in the 24 hours, but it must fatigue them exceedingly, the currents constantly obliging them to carry a great deal of sail to keep their station.

After the earlier failures, it was a 'satisfaction to observe them [damaging] something daily especially those ships which appear to have suffered in the action'. To help Charles grasp the details, Robert made his own drawing, a plan of the bay, in which he marked the three admirals' ships, along with the names of the anchored ships most likely to be attacked by the enemy: he marked 'Resolution' as the fourth ship from the seaward end of the line.

It seemed that the British commanders were not the only ones to be bickering in this war: 'The French commanding officers are all at variance,' wrote Robert, repeating rumours that had reached the British fleet. 'De Grasse is not for risking his squadron, the Marquis de Bouillé declares he will not give the island up tho' de Grasse should leave him, & Bougainville sides with de Bouillé.' Robert also had some disturbing news for his brother:

> With the utmost concern I must inform you of an event which will hurt you much I am sure; which is the loss of poor Brown he went in the long boat in company with other ships boats to bring out a vessel for the reception of our wounded men some days after the action, & has never returned, nor have I had the least

tidings of him or the Boat; another long boat was lost, [probably in the surf] but her people are saved. There were in our boat ten of the best men in the ship which, with him has given me most inexpressible concern. I had a very sincere regard for him. There is but one ray of hope, which is his being taken by some of the enemy's small vessels of which there are a good many cruising under the land, & which might have escap'd us. I have permission & intend to send a flag of truce to the Marquis de Bouillé to enquire if such a capture has been made, but I do not flatter myself much with hopes.

Hurriedly, Robert completed the letter so as to 'send it on board the vessel which is to sail tonight if she can get clear', signing off: 'God bless you my Dearest Brother & be assur'd I shall ever remain yours most sincerely & affectionately Robt Manners.' In the event, it was not possible for a vessel to leave safely with the despatches, and on the following day Robert was able to add with great relief that he had received a polite note from the French: Brown and his other crew were safe but held prisoner on the recaptured St Eustatius, about 20 miles away. 'You cannot conceive what satisfaction I have received by [this news]. The difficulty lyes now in getting them exchanged which I shall use every means to effect. However that is a small consideration to their safety. Poor Brown is at present without a single thing but what he has on him. I do not know how I can convey any things to him but I shall try to send a draft to supply him.' Another captive turned out to be the *Alcide*'s unfortunate Reverend Touch, who, to add to his troubles, had not only been seriously ill since the Great Hurricane, but had also received news of the death of his wife.

★

Despite outwitting de Grasse, Rear Admiral Hood was unable to save St Kitts. The fort at Brimstone Hill had been defended since 11 January by the 15th East Yorkshire Regiment, 'The Snappers', together with the Royal Scots Regiment and 350 of the local militia. But the advance of Prescott's British troops proved a futile gesture in the face of the 8,000 Frenchmen under de Bouillé, and on 12 February the British garrison beat a parley for a ceasefire. With terms agreed, Brimstone Hill surrendered the following day. 'Few situations could have been more unpleasing than ours,' Robert wrote, 'to see an Island surrender in our sight without having it in our power to afford any relief beside that of passively remaining & keeping possession of our ground in sight of it. However we had the satisfaction of reflecting that every exertion which it lay in our power to make had not been neglected. Had the troops we carried from Antigua been sufficient to have thrown themselves into the Hill, in all probability the French wou'd have abandoned their design, in which case I think it would have been one of the most brilliant events this war.' This was, though, but a wishful 'if only' on the young captain's part.

Hood, by contrast, was under no illusions. He re-embarked Prescott's troops to return them to Antigua, which had in the meantime been left virtually defenceless. But his fleet still lay in danger. 'After the surrender of the Island it became highly necessary for us to take some immediate steps for our own safety,' explained Robert. The enemy appeared to have available '34 sail of the line & 13 small vessels, which we imagined to be fireships... on shore they were beginning to raise bomb batteries, & the Marquis de Bouillé, with 3,000 men, was marching to operate against us from that quarter'.

De Grasse, who had neglected to keep his ships adequately provisioned, took advantage of the British surrender to head for Nevis, where his victuallers lay anchored. 'The Admiral [Hood], having some intimation of this, did not, you may imagine, hesitate long what steps he should take,' recounted Robert. On 14 February, Hood called all his captains on board the *Barfleur* and explained his intentions. He told each one that 'he shou'd cut his cables at eleven o'clock that night without making any signal'. And so, his captains set the time aboard their ships by Hood's chronometer. Later that night, 'having regulated our watches accordingly, we each cut our cables at the same precise moment of time, & sail'd out in a line with so little noise or confusion that the Enemy did not miss us for 4 hours after. Nothing could have been more fortunately executed, as not one accident happened from it.'

In their clandestine departure, Hood had worked magic, each ship leaving her cable marked by a buoy, to enable the later recovery of the anchor. On each was left a small lantern too, giving the impression to a distant observer that the British squadron still lay in the roadstead.

De Grasse's blunder had given them the opportunity to escape under cover of darkness, and Robert's description is the first known written record of such a manoeuvre with synchronized watches. To add to the audacity of it, Hood's squadron risked the tricky navigation of a night passage between St Kitts and Nevis before heading for Antigua.

Robert was thrilled to slip out from under the noses of the French under the leadership of Hood, telling Charles that 'taking possession of this Road, was well judged well conducted & well executed... making I think the most masterly manoeuvre I ever saw'. Though they had lost St Kitts, he thought that considering 'the whole in one light, tho' not successful in the point we aimed at, nevertheless it was well conducted, & has given the enemy a pretty severe check, & if you give him half the credit the enemy does, Sr Samuel Hood will stand very high in the public estimation'. He was proud of British superiority in seamanship, in the company of men like Cornwallis and Affleck; and his sense of being close to the heart of decisive events found expression in a greatly increased volume of correspondence to Charles, in which he could boast of the French officers confessing 'they cannot keep the line of Battle with that precision we do, & manoeuvre with so much sail out without the danger of running aboard each other. The [French officers] set no bounds to their praises; they speak in the highest terms of our manoeuvres & contrasting them with their own, draw a comparison not very flattering to the latter.'

Robert, after so much personal frustration, could no longer feel bored by his naval service. Even if Charles so rarely responded, for Robert the act of writing was an outlet – for describing adventures, assuaging anxieties, soothing his isolation aboard the *Resolution*, and for expressing his innermost ambitions and his pride in – at long last – serving under a flag-officer who truly knew his business. Although he realized that they had not achieved all that was wished for, writing that 'de Grasse sent to the M de Bouillé two days before the surrender to say that if the Island did not surrender by that day week he would positively leave it, whether he chose to embark or not. (I wish it had held out long enough for them to have put his resolution in practice).'

By 16 February 1782, Hood's fleet lay at St Johns Road, Antigua, in 'fresh breezes and rain'. On arrival, Robert had gone to the assistance of the packet ship *Grantham*, which had almost foundered while entering the bay, and whose name must have evoked thoughts of home. But it was now that the French plan of campaign became clear – indeed, brazenly laid bare by the French themselves. As Robert described to Charles on 22 February:

> Comte Dillon, who is appointed [the French] governor of St Kitts, told an officer of the navy who was sent with a flag of truce by Sr Samuel Hood that it was not necessary to keep their intentions any longer any secret, that Barbadoes & Antigua were the next objects, then Jamaica, & lastly New York, & then they will consent to make peace; and in my conscience I believe they intend all this, as we have just received accounts of the arrival of the remainder of the Marquis de Vaudreuil's squadron, which together with 4 Spanish men of war also arrived, make their fleet now lying within 12 leagues of us, 44 sail of the line, a most astonishing fleet, & out of those only 5 of 64 guns; ours to consist of 22 of the line.

As for the British response, Robert wrote: 'We are taught to expect Sr Geo: Rodney with a large reinforcement, but have not as yet heard nothing to be depended upon.'

Robert was also still trying to secure the release of William Brown and the other men from the *Resolution*'s boat. 'I have not got Brown yet, but the Comte de Grasse has promised he wou'd send him & all my people, & long boat, & I believe would have done it had we remain'd a day longer in Basseterre Road.' All would be well with the captured seaman, for Robert later recorded how 'Brown is return'd to me with all my people from St Eustatia, from whence they were sent by the Comte de Grasse', emphasizing for Charles's benefit the humanity of the Frenchman 'who very politely lamented the loss of the boat as it prevented him from sending them immediately & in the same state they were taken'. And with perhaps a sigh of homesickness, he signed off: 'Adieu dearest brother for the present, but you shall hear very soon again from your ever sincere & affectionate R Manners. Pray remember me to all with you.'

Shortly afterwards, British naval intentions did become clear. Hood's squadron, having set off from Antigua on 23 February 1782 to return to Barbados, fell in with the returning Admiral Rodney just two days later. Given a shortage of available flag-officers to choose from, Lord North's increasingly desperate government had had little choice but to retain Rodney and to reject the attempts of Edmund Burke in Parliament to make a political issue of the admiral's dealings at St Eustatius. Thus, Rodney had been asked to return to the West Indies to resume his command there, bringing reinforcements with him. He had departed in mid-January 1782 into the teeth of a severe westerly gale. Thrashing through mountainous seas, he cleared Ushant by just two leagues, saying that he had risked the danger for the sake of public service, in order to connect with Hood in mid-February.

Rodney's twelve ships of the line brought the British fleet up to thirty-six, and Sir George had as his flagship the *Formidable* – the 90-gun ship in which Sir Hugh Palliser had served at Ushant in 1778. With his health temporarily improved, the British senior admiral was back in control. Hood had to revert to being second in command. Rodney, catching up with recent events, penned a note to de Grasse that says much about the cordiality between enemies:

> Sir, I am honor'd with both your Excellency's dispatches, and am truly sensible both of your Excellency's politeness and humanity and shall always be happy whenever I can have an Opportunity of shewing my personal Respect and Esteem for you. I beg you will accept my thanks for restoring the Boat & Crew belonging to Lord Robert Manners, as likewise of the men belonging to the King my master's Brigantine called the *Alert*, when under the protection of the French Flag.

In the margin of his letter book, Rodney added: 'NB the French admiral had sent me two Chests of Liquors.'[2]

The combined British fleet put into St Lucia for repairs and victuals where, to Robert's delight, a bundle of letters from Charles finally caught up with him. 'Your correspondence now Dearest Brother makes ample necessity for your former neglect; you cannot conceive the satisfaction the receipt of your letters gives me.' The letters included the news of the birth of another son on 14 December 1781, named Robert William after his uncle – but not 'Albinine', as Robert had requested, which would be reserved for a future child. Referring to gossip in the fleet that Charles was the worse off for gambling, Robert confessed

to being 'much concern'd at what you informed me of in your letter, the loss you met with at Brookes' and hoped it was 'not to the
extent of what I heard'. Charles's letters might have been brought by a
new addition to Robert's crew, William Robinson, a middle-aged and
experienced seaman who, it seems, arrived with Rodney's squadron
and joined the *Resolution* as captain's servant. He hailed from a family
that Robert knew from childhood visits to Scarborough. Another newcomer to the *Resolution* at this time was one William Raven, to take the
place of the deceased master, Charles Martin.

On 10 March, Robert told Charles of Rodney's arrival 'with a force
which gives a new face to the affairs of this country'. Robert did not
think 'the lost Islands will be recovered', but he was of the opinion that
'the few remaining windward Islands are safe & that the designs of the
enemy on Jamaica will be frustrated. The very defenceless state of all
our Islands through the want of troops will always oblige [Rodney] to
act upon the defensive as no Island is safe but the one we are immediately protecting.' Despite such demands on the navy, Robert was still
hopeful that he might get home, and to the bosom of his brother's
newly expanded family:

> Next month [my] ship will have been three years copper'd &
> out of dock, which is the usual time of their service, & from the
> loss of the *Terrible*, & the very bad state of the ships of the same
> standing with her, it is probable they will go home at nearly the
> same time. It is remark'd that copper bottom ships, when they
> once begin to show their defects, drop all at once, which is the
> case of the *Invincible*, who is now in as bad a state as the *Terrible*
> was & several others which they are even afraid to trust home.

His love of his ship was as palpable as if she were, indeed, the only
mistress he had ever really had:

> The *Resolution* is order'd to sea this morning and I fancy will
> proceed tomorrow & not in the most pleasant condition being
> entirely destitute of stores, and all our rigging condemn'd
> as unserviceable & none to be had to replace it: & to say the
> truth, she herself complains a little. I am administering to her
> the most salutary and efficacious remedies that can be apply'd in

this country, & there is soon to be a consultation of carpenters upon her, as it is generally supposed a change of climate will be found the only means of restoring her health, which has been lately very much impair'd; and as her disorder is cheifly [sic] a violent relaxation in all her parts so as to admit of the free ingress & egress of water (the reverse of a diabetes) I opine a northern climate is the most proper to brace her up & restore many of her faculties which she has now (I grieve to say) entirely lost. Her speed is gone & she is no longer the chasing ship but as I have notwithstanding a very great esteem for the Lady, I shall certainly attend her in her Illness and accompany her home, should that be the result of the consultation before attended to which I am apt to think will not be a very distant period.

And while he could write with such sensitivity, and at other times with humour, he could still fall prey to the moroseness and sense of frustration exhibited in earlier days, almost as if serving under Rodney once again had somehow smothered the mood of high hopes: 'You cannot conceive anything so intolerable as the dull uniformity of our situation in this place.' He was sorely conscious of losing the company of his closest friends among the other captains, those who had also experienced the loneliness of command on the quarterdeck. 'The people I usually live with,' he wrote miserably, 'happen to be in ships worse than my own & are going home immediately. One particularly by whom I beleive [sic] I shall send this letter will be a great loss: Capt: Molloy of the *Intrepid* with whom I lived most intimately. If you shou'd meet him pray be acquainted with him as a friend of mine, "et fortem crede Bonumque" ["Believe to be both brave and good"].' In fact, he did not give his letter to Molloy, who was sent to Jamaica instead. It was eventually entrusted to the hand of another.

*

As Robert was writing, those at home were as yet unaware of Hood's naval masterstroke at St Kitts. But a creeping realization that the American colonies were now, *de facto*, independent, had though spread throughout Britain in the aftermath of the Yorktown surrender, and the king's persistent desire to pursue the war was no longer shared by the majority of his ministry. Indeed, Lord George Germain was almost alone in his belligerent desire not to give up America; but this 'cold, arrogant and isolated, distrusted and distrustful' minister,[3] the 'Coward of Minden', was forced from office in January 1782 following irreconcilable differences with Lord Sandwich, who, despite the vitriolic attacks on him by the opposition, clung to his post.

Various Members of Parliament called for motions to discontinue the war, and an enquiry into the mismanagement of naval affairs was proposed. The potential disaster of Britain's insufficient naval power was expressed in a few simple words: 'If the sea is lost, all is lost.' Thus, a detailed document was produced, laying before the politicians all the relevant papers, including intelligence reports and analyses of the states of various naval squadrons during the previous year. Charles, on reading his copy of the *Parliamentary Register*, would have seen his brother's name printed in the order of battle for the action of 29 April 1781, off Martinique. But such deliberations were merely tinkering at the margins.

By February 1782, although a House of Commons vote had effectively conceded American independence, confusion still reigned as to what fate might befall the sugar islands. On 10 March in Brooks's, Mr Aston bet Mr Crewe 6 guineas to 4 that St Kitts was still in English possession. Just five days later, Mr Crewe found himself the winner,[4] for on 15 March the *Gazette* published the news of its loss. Some compensation came in the reports of Hood's triumph over de Grasse, which, against the background of the surrender at Brimstone Hill, was seized upon, not least by Lord Sandwich as a proof that his efforts to build up the naval fleet were bearing fruit. Hood was, accordingly, the hero of the moment; but Charles was delighted to find that Robert did not escape notice, for Sir Samuel had drawn attention to him in his despatches, when describing the anchoring manoeuvre at St Kitts: 'The enemy gave the preference to Commodore Affleck, but he kept up so noble a fire, and was so well supported by his seconds, Captain Cornwallis and Lord Robert Manners, that the loss and damage sustained in those ships were very trifling, and they very much preserved the other ships in the rear.'[5]

Charles proudly sent copies of the *Gazette* to his friends. Thomas Thoroton responded immediately: 'Ten thousand thanks to your

Grace for your most kind letter and the *Gazette*. It has raised all our spirits to a high degree. We all join in most sincere congratulations on these fresh honours Lord Robert has so fairly won, and on his safety. And our heartiest wishes are for more and more honors to him till we see him at the head of his profession.' Richard Watson was not tardy in his compliments either. 'I heartily congratulate you on the honour which your brother has gained; his reputation, which is a great matter is now established, and you can push his interest, when opportunity offers with credit.' A day later, John Ekins, the brothers' old Eton tutor, added his voice: 'I beg your grace to accept my most hearty congratulations and hope it will please God long to spare a life which promises to be so useful to his country, and so honourable to himself and his family.' Charles was doubtless warmed immoderately by this reflected glory. Richard Watson said it was 'a circumstance which strongly marked the character of Lord Robert', though wisely left it 'to military men to fix the precise limits beyond which true courage ought not to advance, being satisfied that they will applaud rather than condemn in a young man at least, that intrepidity of spirit which in the pursuit of glory forgot the care of life'.

As the congratulations over Hood's action rippled out, like circles made by a stone cast into a pond, they naturally also dissipated over time. The actual loss of St Kitts enabled the opposition, soon afterwards, to revive its hostility to the government. A bravura display of sea power could not ultimately offset the impact of the island's loss, and indeed this moment marked the lowest point of North's ministry. Ekins, in concluding his letter of 18 March, expressed his wish for change to improve the chance this 'poor country once more has of recovering from the calamities and disgrace which have so long depressed her'. He hoped Charles would be a part of a new government, adding with a flourish that managed to be both obsequious and admonitory, 'few from their abilities if they were properly exerted... are better able to assist her in this time of distress'.

On 20 March 1782, there was an unusually large attendance in the House of Commons, where some 400 Members were preparing for a vote of no confidence in the ministry. They anticipated a long and rancorous debate, and as Lord North entered the chamber in full court dress, his blue Garter ribbon over his coat, he was greeted with howls of 'Order' and 'Places'. But moments later the House was silenced. North announced his resignation and thus that of the ministry. Although his political skill had kept him in office for the few months following Yorktown, he had decided irreversibly that he could not 'with prudence, oppose the deliberate resolution of the House of Commons'. After the announcement, Parliament adjourned. Even at the end, North managed to wrongfoot his opponents. Expecting a long session, most of the opposition had sent their carriages away, and were now forced to stand in the rain; but North had his ready and waiting. The departing prime minister turned to them and remarked: 'Good night, gentlemen. You see what it is to be in on the secret.'[6]

In truth, Lord North had never felt himself up to the burden imposed upon him by his loyalty to the king. His reservations about the use of military force in North America were not conducive to his being an effective war leader, though he had other attributes that had kept him in office and enabled the war to continue. Nevertheless, until the day of his death he maintained that the long struggle had been 'unfortunate but not unjust', emphasizing his belief, honestly held, that it had been fought not for tyranny but to uphold the right of Parliament to govern the people under its jurisdiction.

For some time afterwards, the loss of those colonies damned the reputation of North's ministry. Certainly, British strategy had been hampered by the political tensions between North, Sandwich and Germain, and by the contentiousness between commanders of the army and navy. However, many of the strategic blunders and failures in co-ordination were attributable not so much to incompetence as to the sheer practical difficulties presented by vast distances, slow communications by sail, and the terrain and resources in North America – all of which bore little resemblance to the European theatre with which the British military hierarchy was familiar. British ministers performed better than history has given them credit for, and the British military effort in America was remarkably well supplied considering the logistical difficulties involved. But what was undeniable was the seeping away of political will, and the facts of military defeat.

★

Having been deluged with praise at his brother's part in Hood's victory, Charles now received a stream of letters of congratulations on the change of government. Great things were hoped of him, though not all came as carrots without sticks. The Marquis of Lothian wrote: 'I sincerely hope you will now exert yourself and prove that you can be of great use to your country... that I may wish you joy of having some employment yourself that is suited to you, and that may bring your talents forth and rescue you from that inactivity which is your greatest fault.' But despite encouragements, Charles was not destined to join the new ministry that was formed by the Marquis of Rockingham, on 27 March 1782, and reluctantly accepted by King George. Charles simply headed instead to Belvoir, in torrential rain and on slippery roads, arriving on 31 March, there to be followed by a succession of guests, including his friend the 2nd Earl of Chatham.

Although peace negotiations now began, and the war with the Americans had run to a temporary stalemate – with Clinton still holding on in New York – the war with France, Spain and the Dutch raged undiminished. Gibraltar remained under siege by the Spanish, the East Indies were still being fought over, and of course the West Indian islands remained under threat from de Grasse, their fate resting with admirals Rodney and Hood. In London, the ousted Earl of Sandwich was replaced as First Lord of the Admiralty by Augustus Keppel, raised to the peerage as a viscount. Sandwich would also not be treated kindly by historians; but more recently his unequalled experience, first-class mind, determined energy and remarkable record of even-handedness in promotions have come to the fore. It had been his political misfortune to have been relatively poor and appointed on merit, and thus never really able to cultivate an ample enough 'interest' to support him.

Keppel had no time to waste in getting his feet under the desk. Intelligence had been unearthed that a Spanish military doctor-turned-government-agent, named Saavedra de Sangronis, had passed himself off as a merchant when captured by the British in 1780, and then travelled throughout Jamaica; and that in 1781 he was colluding with de Grasse. The resulting de Grasse–Saavedra Accord thereafter underpinned Franco-Spanish operations in the Caribbean, from July 1781 to the end of the war. The strategic intention was, of course, to seize all of Britain's West Indian possessions. The most important of these was Jamaica, and it had been Lord Germain's last task in office to ensure the island stayed safe.

What was understood in London of de Grasse's movements was sketchy, and out at St Kitts Rodney's fleet had heard a Frenchman's version of it, but in early April 1782 Charles James Fox received further intelligence from Alleyne FitzHerbert in Brussels, dated 29 March. It suggested that de Grasse intended to set sail to Hispaniola, there to join up with Spanish naval forces, bringing the combined fleet to fifty-two ships of the line. These, with 12,000 French and 8,000 Spanish troops were intended to comprise the forces for the de Grasse–Saavedra Accord, in particular for the conquest of Jamaica.

Charles's visitors at Belvoir, Chatham especially, brought the news of this Franco-Spanish threat hotfoot, and the duke must have feared for his brother, 3,000 miles away in his leaky *Resolution*. In early April, in his study at Belvoir Castle, Charles drew his brother's letter of 8 February towards him to refresh his memory of its contents. Robert's anxious words were sprawled across the page: 'I want much to hear from England, how you take the loss of St Kitts... & also what is going on.' Robert had concluded with his invariably thoughtful solicitations: 'I have nothing more to add at present than my most fervent wishes for your health & of your family's, which be assured is ever the most sincere hope and prayer of your ever affectionate Brother...'

Charles picked up his quill, spread a sheet of paper before him, dipped his nib and began to write. There was a good deal to tell Robert. But the usually reluctant correspondent was too late. Robert had already written the last lines he would ever send, and Charles was now scribbling words his younger brother would never read.

14

'My dear little Lord'

March to May 1782

'My dear little Lord'

F ar away from Charles, on the hot, disease-ridden island of St Lucia, Robert had at long last succumbed to the effects of poor food and stagnant water. For the first time since he had been in the West Indies, he was, in March 1782, in imperfect health, complaining to his ship's surgeon of a 'bilious disorder' and causing Robert Blair some anxiety. But the young captain still had to attend to his duties.

The combined squadrons of Rodney and Hood were hurriedly repairing any battle damage and taking on what supplies could be had. At least their ships' crews were now in good shape, Gilbert Blane's efforts having made a considerable difference. This did not stop some men from deserting – the frigate *Andromache* lost nine on 28 March. The *Resolution*, however, now mustering 399 men and none recorded as sick – apart from her captain – could still boast 'No Run Men'.

As yet, the commanders had no idea that Lord North's government had fallen; nor were they aware of the size of the huge Franco-Spanish fleet that Alleyne FitzHerbert had heard was gathering. However, they did know they had to watch like hawks for the departure of Admiral de Grasse, for he had returned to Martinique's Fort Royal after the St Kitts battle, and that they had to try and stop him from heading towards Jamaica and joining up with the Spanish.

The British had established a signal station on Pigeon Island, which lay at the entrance to Rodney's St Lucia anchorage of Gros Islet Bay. In combination with the frigates cruising between St Lucia and Martinique, the station would enable news of enemy movements to be communicated rapidly in the 30-mile stretch of sea between the two islands. De Grasse now commanded thirty-six ships of the line, though some were of only fifty guns, and his intention was, in reality, to meet up with twelve Spanish ships and fifteen thousand troops at Hispaniola for the attack on Jamaica. However, the French commander-in-chief had a problem: there was a large convoy of around 150 merchantmen waiting to sail to France. He therefore had to devise a plan for seeing the convoy clear of the islands before taking his battle-fleet, with the Marquis de Bouillé's siege train. Thus, de Grasse intended to use his warships first to accompany the merchantmen along the western (and leeward) side of the long arc of the Lesser Antilles, with its safe havens, until he was sufficiently confident to send them on their way. Then he would sweep round to the north-west and fall upon the largest of the British sugar islands.

The British could not, of course, know all the details of de Grasse's intentions, and were anxious to be alerted to any sign of his departure from Fort Royal. On the evening of 5 April the ships in Gros Islet Bay hosted the arrival of a small vessel with some deserters from Martinique. They reported that de Grasse had embarked 9,000 troops in transports, intending to sail on 8 April to join the Spanish fleet for the Jamaican attack. What value could be put on intelligence from such a source was questionable. As for Robert, he was still feeling ill enough for his friend Blair to record, two days later, that 'his Lordship... took an emetic'. The surgeon advised his captain to take an additional 'opening medicine' the next day, but in the event a better treatment was at hand.

★

At daylight on 8 April, the watch aboard the *Resolution* saw the station on Pigeon Island make the signal for 'six sail in different quarters'. Captain Byron of the *Andromache*, cruising between St Lucia and Fort Royal, sent the news via the *Alert* to inform Rodney that a large fleet and an enormous convoy had come out of the French harbour and were heading north-west. A frisson ran through the British ships – and, as Blair noted, Lord Robert felt instantly better. His laxative was 'delayed on account of the appearance of the French fleet early in the morning, a circumstance which as it prevented his lordship from taking his medicine seemed also to render it unnecessary as he immediately appeared in high spirits and his disorder was forgotten'.

At quarter past nine in the morning, Rodney made the signal for all officers to return to their respective ships, soon followed by a signal to prepare for action. Robert put his watch in his pocket, left his cabin and gave his own orders for the *Resolution* to make ready for sea. From his quarterdeck, he would have seen his French prize the *Prothee* – recently come out from England with Rodney and under the command of Captain Charles Buckner – head out to sea as Rodney sent her to trail the French. Shortly afterwards, the *Resolution* received a draft of twenty men from the *Shrewsbury*, which was to be left behind for repairs. The new men were sent to haul up the anchor as, overhead, the agile topmen worked out along the yards, casting loose the sails.

By noon, the thirty-six British ships of the line were under way and in hot pursuit of their enemy. The vast mass of shipping under de Grasse moved ponderously, enabling their pursuers to begin gradually to catch up. Two-and-a-half hours after leaving Pigeon Island behind, Rodney's advance frigates were in sight of the enemy; and by sunset, the French were visible from the mastheads of the British fleet's main body.

Rodney's ships, their signal books updated, lay in three divisions, a formation loosely kept until they closed the enemy. Hood led, with the van. The *Resolution* lay in the centre division, two ships behind Rodney in the *Formidable*. The admiral might have been moved by self-interest in placing a promising, gallant and well-connected young aristocrat under his wing; but he may have wanted to keep his eye on the captains who had acted with such decisive initiative at St Kitts too, for he also deployed Edmund Affleck's *Bedford* and William Cornwallis's *Canada* in the centre.

Besides the *Prothee*, also in the centre, Rodney's fleet comprised other ships familiar to Robert. The *Prince William* was in the van, while the 70-gun *Princessa*, taken in the Moonlight Battle of 1780, was the flag-ship of the rear division, flying Sir Francis Samuel Drake's flag. John Nicholson Inglefield, nephew of Sir Thomas Slade who had designed four of the ships Robert had served in, commanded the *Centaur*, while Charles Thompson, Mary Isabella's relation, was in Robert's former vessel the *Alcide*. (Even an old adversary was there: Taylor Penny, captain of the *Marlborough*, whom Robert had once accused of being a poor seaman.) There were numerous other men of distinction in the fleet, too. Rodney's Captain-of-the-Fleet with him in the *Formidable* was Sir Charles Douglas. Known as a mechanical genius, Douglas was experimenting with improving guns' arc of fire, and making them safer and quicker to reload, with goose quills for priming and flintlock ignition replacing matches. Within the fleet, the *Duke* and the *Formidable* were already making use of his ideas to good effect.

On 9 April, the tropical calm of dawn brought word that the French were still in sight. By this time, both fleets, heading northwards in order to stay close to the string of islands, had become extended, with de Grasse's huge armada spread out between 4 and 12 miles from the British. Rodney's 'lookout' frigates reported some of the French ships to be becalmed in Prince Rupert's Bay, off the north-west corner of Dominica; but the calm would not last long, and Rodney signalled for his fleet to form a line ahead and prepare for action.

All hands were wakened and sent to breakfast; but at around six-thirty in the morning, Rodney's signal was hauled down, for the admiral anticipated a long day ahead and did not wish to wear the men out by being precipitate. His fleet was still behind de Grasse's, although the leading British ships were beginning to overlap some of the rearmost French ships. The enemy van, however, had now cleared the shelter of Dominica and, picking up the trade-wind, was beginning to draw ahead. But the breeze then also reached the leading ships of Hood's van, and at about seven o'clock they too began to creep forward faster – so much so that they threatened to cut off two French vessels that, in the night, had become detached from the rest. The 80-gun *Auguste* and the 74-gun *Zélé* strove to rejoin de Grasse, sailing boldly across the head of Hood's rough column and indeed approaching so closely that the *Alfred*, Hood's headmost ship, was obliged to alter course to avoid colliding with the *Zélé*. As the two passed each other, their crews glared while the officers doffed their hats. Hood, in perfect obedience to the ever punctilious Rodney, disdained to open fire in the absence of an order to do so, allowing the *Zélé* and her consort to rejoin their admiral unharmed.

By that time, it was about half past eight; and it was now that de Grasse's fleet hoisted its battle-ensigns. The French van, under the Marquis de Vaudreuil, lay in the strait between the north of Dominica and Guadeloupe; it tacked, and headed towards Hood, who had also reached the strait. Meanwhile the French centre and rear divisions were still shuffling northwards along the Dominican shore, but de Grasse hoped that as soon as they picked up the breeze, their superior speed would throw off his pursuers and he could continue with his plan to head for Jamaica. The French ships were better sailers, and the copper bottoms of the British ships might not make up for the difference.

It was well nigh impossible to determine from the quarterdeck of the *Resolution* what was happening ahead, but by late morning the *Formidable* had again hoisted the signal to prepare for action and the marine drummers sounded their imperative rat-a-tat-tat as they beat to quarters. The *Resolution* was cleared for action and sand was scattered on the decks, while gun-captains selected the roundest shots, and their crews opened the gun-ports and readied the tools of their grim trade. Robert, who, like the other officers, would have donned clean underwear to avoid infection if wounded, now stood on the quarterdeck with his senior officers, eager for news of what was going on far ahead.

As the morning progressed, the ships' companies in the British centre and rear worked their yards and sails to catch every small waft of air that troubled the blue surface of the sea, desperate to catch up with de Grasse's main body of ships as it began to clear Dominica. In the distance to the north, the British van appeared to have caught the trade-wind, but to those in the *Resolution* the sound of gunfire and a haze of smoke breaking on the horizon suggested that Hood was engaging with some French men-of-war.

It was only later, as the British fleet lay-to overnight and repaired battle-damage, and as ships' boats plied about the fleet, carrying news and orders, that events concerning Hood's van became clear. The fluky wind that had speeded Hood onwards had not held, preventing Rodney's and Drake's divisions from catching up with him. His isolation from Rodney's main body had tempted de Grasse to send the Marquis de Vaudreuil's division to fall upon Hood, and, while under cover of this manoeuvre, had sent the merchant convoy into the shelter of Guadeloupe, escorted by two 50-gun warships. Despite the advantage of numbers, because more of their ships had reached the strait, throughout the action the French kept their distance, robbing them of decisive effect – although the distance also cheated the British out of effective use of their new short-range carronades, known as 'smashers'. It was

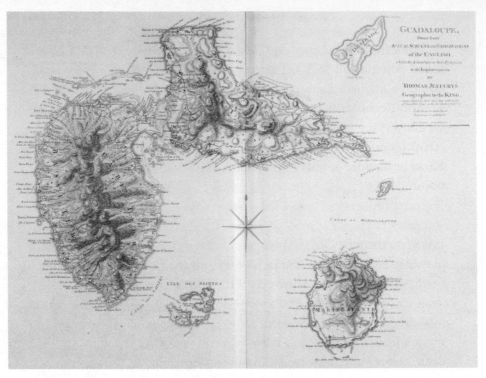

*A chart showing the location of the 'Isle des Saintes' (the archipelago of the Saintes),
from the atlas Robert had with him on the* Resolution.

not the French admiral's intention to submit to the risks of close action
if he could avoid it, for he had a more important objective in Jamaica.
But it was a fatal error, for although de Vaudreuil attacked repeatedly,
Hood stood his ground. Had de Grasse thrown the *whole* of his battle-fleet down upon Hood – for which wind conditions had eventually
been favourable – he might have annihilated the British division. At the
very least, he would have so damaged Hood's ships that Rodney would
have been compelled to withdraw, allowing the French an unopposed
passage to Jamaica. As it was, although mauled, the British ships had
mainly suffered damage to their rigging – and nothing was beyond the
competence of their crews to repair. Rodney nevertheless went on to
alter his order of battle, placing Drake's division in the van and leaving
the rear to Hood while he made repairs.

For Robert and the company of the *Resolution*, the day had seen
no action and had proved frustrating. How the young captain must
have rued not being in Hood's division; but there was nothing to be
done about it. News reached the *Resolution* that things had been quite

different for those aboard the *Alfred*, whose captain, Bayne, had been killed when a ball took off his leg. He had died before a tourniquet could be applied. By way of reciprocal gossip, Robert sent word to Francis Reynolds in the *Monarch* that he had seen a badly damaged 64-gun French ship, noticeable because of a painted black-and-white streak along her topsides, making for Guadeloupe. Robert thought he knew her name, but his ship-recognition skills were not his strongest point.

★

It was on the next day, 10 April, that the vagaries in the wind strength played in favour of the British, for although Rodney's fleet had paused to effect repairs, at the same time de Grasse was unable to gain much distance, as he tried to throw off his pursuers by heading eastwards into the prevailing wind, to the south of Guadeloupe. At daylight, the French fleet were about 14 miles to windward, 'just in sight from the deck'. They were drawing away, but the British hung on doggedly; in the *Resolution*, the sailing master, William Raven, ran up every yard of canvas he could stretch. Dominica was now behind them and to the north, in the distance, lay the twin peaks of Guadeloupe and to the east loomed the island of Marie-Galante. The closest land, ahead to the north, was a cluster of small islands, islets and reefs called the Saintes.

The hours dragged by, and the watches rotated. Men stuck to their posts, eating there by day (and dozing there at night). When the wind was ahead, captains fumed and officers fretted as the ships crept too slowly through the water, their yards braced sharp-up on the catharpings, and the hands sent to the braces from time to time as the ships tacked in order to claw their way to windward. This produced successive manoeuvres that disrupted the formations, but with greater consequences for the French – who were doing the same – than for the British. What the British lacked in the sophistication of their ship-design, they partially compensated for with their technical skill, the little tricks that their hard-bitten sailing masters and masters'-mates had learned in their harsh lives.

That evening, Rodney ordered a 'general chase' to free his captains from the constraint of what had become, anyway, a mere pretence at maintaining station in battle order. Now they would be able to make the best use of their individual sailing qualities. However, the result was no pell-mell action as the Moonlight Battle of 1780 had been; as each side sought to gain its objective – contact for the British, escape for the French – it was a slow business of patient manoeuvre, where advantage would have to be seized if it offered itself. Drake, in the *Princessa*, led the fleet as the new van of the now reversed line. With him were Charles Thompson in the *Alcide*, James Saumarez in the *Russell* and Lieutenant Thomas Foley in the *Prince George*, all three men destined for distinguished careers. But Drake was in some disarray, confused as to his instructions and driven to despatch Captain Byron of the *Andromache* with a note to his commander: 'Dear Sir George. There is not anything that I have so much pleasure in, as obeying the orders of my commanding officer; nor do I ever experience so much uneasiness of mind; as when I am at a loss to know what I am to do; as I am in this present instance.' Rodney's signals appeared to him to be contradictory, including ordering one ship in Drake's division with almost no sail set to reduce sail. Drake wished to be afforded the 'great satisfaction' of knowing 'what I am to do'.[1]

Night closed on them once again. Still to windward, the enemy ships betrayed their positions in the darkness by 'making signal by rockets and guns'. Despite all the British efforts to catch up, the distance between the two fleets had increased when day broke on Thursday 11 April. The fact that the French could maintain superior speed even though their ships were cluttered by the troops intended for Jamaica said much about the differences between the two navies' vessels. By noon, the bulk of the French fleet had worked to the windward side of the little archipelago of the Saintes – and it looked as if de Grasse would escape his pursuers.

During the day, Drake, from his vantage point in the van, wrote again to Rodney: 'Dear Sir George. I am sorry to see so many ships split their sails; and make known to you by signal; that they are disabled in their mast.' Drake had also sailed close enough to Guadeloupe to observe the worrisome sight of additional French ships: 'I saw [in the bay] one sixty four; one fifty; and three frigates today. The enemy's fleet are so nearly equal to yours; that I apprehend; you will not be able to do any thing with them; unless you cou'd bring up your whole force; well connected; and that appears unpredictable to be done; from the disabled state many of your ships appear to be in.' He was still perplexed by Rodney:

> You will do me a great favor if when; you think proper to send me any orders; by a frigate; that you would let me know whether I am, or not to regard any signals that may be made; after your orders or message was sent away; for I am at a loss to know how to act when signals are made that contradict the orders brought... I have the Honor to be, Dear Sir George, with great respect, your faithful, and obedient humble servant. Fra: S: Drake.[2]

Yet, unbeknownst to the British, the light winds had also been causing confusion in the French fleet. One of their ships, the *Zélé*, had sustained damage in a collision with the *Jason* and had been unable to keep up with the main body. Another French '74', the *Magnanime*, was also lagging behind, detached. Should they fall to the British, de Grasse's fleet would be further reduced, a circumstance that the French admiral could not contemplate. Judging Rodney's fleet to be sufficiently distant to effect a rescue before the pursuers caught up, de Grasse turned back to close with the damaged *Zélé* and the laggardly *Magnanime*. Having gathered in his stragglers, he turned eastwards again, relying upon the greater speed of his ships to make up the ground he had just lost between him and Rodney.

But in rescuing the *Zélé* he had unwittingly drawn a viper into his bosom. At two o'clock on the morning of Friday, 12 April, the wounded *Zélé*, passing de Grasse's *Ville de Paris* on the opposite tack, collided with her. It was said afterwards that the officer-of-the-watch aboard the *Zélé* was a mere *enseigne* – a midshipman – instead of an experienced lieutenant. Whatever the truth, the *Zélé* was badly damaged, especially her bowsprit, rendering her unmanoeuvrable. De Grasse had no option: he was obliged to dispose of the *Zélé*, which was now a liability, and the frigate *Astrée* was ordered to tow her into the shelter of Guadeloupe. As first light broke on 12 April, the rear of the British fleet, still to the south-west, caught sight of the *Zélé* and *Astrée* breaking the eastern horizon, only 6 miles from Hood's *Barfleur*. As the light grew brighter, it revealed that although the bulk of the French fleet was about 10–15 miles away, the *Ville de Paris*, delayed by her collision, was no more than 8 miles distant. Shortly before six o'clock that morning, Rodney ordered Hood to attack and take the *Zélé* and the *Astrée*, and Sir Samuel promptly detached the nearest vessels – his four rear-most ships – to chase the two French men-of-war.

On seeing four British ships set off in pursuit of two of his own, de Grasse, instead of abandoning them, signalled his entire fleet to turn back, and he himself in the *Ville de Paris* went to the assistance of the *Zélé* and the *Astrée*. So once again de Grasse attempted a rescue, but, whether the decision was chivalrous or foolhardy, at a stroke he threw away his precious advantage of distance to windward. With the wind now blowing from behind him, the French three-decker sought to intimidate Hood's four ships of the line. Watching from the *Formidable*, Rodney sensed matters swinging in his favour. He threw out the signal to tack in succession and form the (still-reversed) line of battle – with Drake's division in the van and the rest of Hood's ships in the rear – so as to close with the enemy. Now the wind, blowing from the south-east, favoured the British, Robert's *Resolution* among them, as they took up their stations.

At daybreak of 12 April 1782, Robert sent a manservant, John Benson, to fetch his telescope before climbing to the main-top to observe what was going on. It was plain to see that events were coming to a head. Once back on deck, he buckled on his hanger – and bid his officers make ready. At seven o'clock, as the British line began to coalesce, Rodney recalled the four ships chasing the *Zélé* and the *Astrée* before making another signal, the one they had all been waiting for. It was to close the line of battle until each ship was no more than four ship-lengths' distance apart. Having passed his instructions, Rodney left the deck to the Captain-of-the-Fleet Sir Charles Douglas, and retired to his cabin to await events.

The British fleet, still numbering thirty-six ships of the line, fell into their stations, with Drake's division leading. The wind, though still light, was now steady enough to permit the rigid formation of the line. In the centre, the *Resolution* lay three ships ahead of the *Formidable*, the two between them being the *Agamemnon* and the *Duke*, the latter bearing a figurehead of the Duke of Cumberland in his red coat. Perhaps it reminded Robert of his father, who had fought with the 'Butcher' against the Jacobites in the '45 rebellion. His old prize, the *Prothee*, lay immediately ahead of him.

The enemy's formation was, by contrast with the British, loose and reduced in number to thirty-two ships of the line after the damaged ships were sent in to Guadeloupe. De Grasse's captains had run down-wind to follow their commander as he attempted to protect the *Zélé* and were now in some disorder. Their line was, like the British, reversed, heading southwards towards Dominica and extending to windward of the British line, which was moving northwards. The nearest land was the little archipelago, the Saintes. There was a chance that the two fleets would pass each other. If the French could inflict sufficient disabling damage, they might yet be able to retreat for the greater prize of Jamaica; but it would require a steady wind, which was unlikely as the day heated up, for hot air rising from the islands would cause local wind shifts. In the French rear, de Vaudreuil's flag-captain, du Pavillon – a noted tactician – was heard wondering 'what evil genius' had inspired their commander-in-chief to have turned round.[3] Aboard the *Formidable*, spirits were rising. Sir Charles Douglas sent word below to rouse his flag-officer – 'I give you joy, Sir George!'[4] – as Rodney came on deck to observe the opposing lines closing in on each other. Thereafter, the British admiral took his place on the quarterdeck, sitting in a chair.

Then, in the next few moments, the light breeze shifted to the east, allowing the French to alter course and carry their leading ships across the British line of advance and out of range. But the wind shift was no disadvantage to the British either, and at around eight o'clock the leading ship of the van – Taylor Penny's *Marlborough* – finally came close enough to fire at the ninth ship in the enemy line, the 74-gun *Brave*. Penny thus led Rodney's line along the line of de Grasse's ships. The two fleets were on a divergent course, bringing each successive French ship in range for sufficient time to receive punishment from every British vessel it passed – and without being able to make a reciprocal onslaught. In such conditions, British gunnery – fast and aimed low, its hard-hitting upper-deck carronades wreaking horrible carnage – inflicted the maximum damage possible upon the French. Meanwhile, Rodney had hoisted the signal for close action, followed by an order to turn further to starboard and close the range, for he was dissatisfied with the line Penny had adopted.

Fifteenth in the line behind Penny, the *Resolution* opened fire at quarter past eight – just a few minutes before the *Agamemnon*, *Duke* and *Formidable* did likewise. In the aftermath of her first broadside, her quarterdeck was wreathed in thick gun-smoke. There was little that anyone could see beyond the next ship, ahead and behind, as each French line-of-battle ship appeared out of the dense fog, passing slowly in the opposite direction. Robert's officers bellowed their orders and the cannon belched fire, smoke and iron, leaving the decks trembling as the recoiling gun-carriages rolled back. Amid the cacophony, Robert knew of Rodney's signal for close action, for it had been seen through the smoke, repeated by the *Agamemnon*, and in the ensuing half hour the *Resolution* steadily and 'very desperately [engaged] nine or ten of the French ships'.

It was not, though, one-sided, for the *Resolution* was under severe fire herself. At a quarter to nine, an iron ball flew across the quarter-deck and struck Robert across the legs, before also taking off the arm of seaman Thomas Noon nearby. In that same instant, a splinter of wood struck Robert's breast and tore into his right arm. He crumpled to the deck, but for several moments continued to give orders: it was said that 'in this miserable situation the fortitude and firmness of his mind did not forsake him for a moment'. Yet, with blood pouring from him, his strength soon began to fail.

Robert tried to drag himself below, from where he intended to continue to 'give orders for the fighting of his ship'; but a group of officers and sailors near Robert, probably including William Dawes and William Brown, seeing his distress took him in their arms and carried him straight to the orlop deck. There, Robert Blair was horrified to see that his friend and captain was the first man brought below for surgery. The surgeon saw that Robert's right arm was fractured and that both legs were shattered. His left leg was beyond saving, but the young captain at first refused to permit amputation, pleading that he would not be able to continue serving in the navy with a leg lost above the knee. Blair soothed his anxiety, claiming that others similarly maimed had continued to serve, until Robert became reconciled to his fate – so much so that bravely he accepted the loss of his leg as 'immaterial' to him and granted permission for it to be taken off.

The captain was then stripped by the surgeon's assistants and prepared for surgery. His watch was taken from his pocket and put aside for safekeeping. Blair applied a screw tourniquet, pulled up the skin of the thigh, then picked up his knife. He drew it swiftly around the firm flesh above the wound, first to divide skin and fat, and a second time around muscle. He sawed through the bone and tied off the blood vessels with silk or linen ligatures. The surgeon observed that: 'During the most painful moments of the amputation, [Robert] was so far from betraying any symptoms of imbecility of mind or depression of spirit that he made jocular remarks on the operation with a smiling countenance, seriously declaring that he would not leave his ship but at all events continue in the command of her during the remainder of the campaign and circumstances of victory.'

Once Blair had applied linen roller bandages, Robert was made as comfortable as possible. He lay in the gloom of the orlop deck, where the air reeked of blood and was punctuated by the groans of the wounded as Blair and his mates plied their gruesome but essential craft. The 1st lieutenant – probably William Leggatt – had in the meantime taken command of the *Resolution* and was periodically sending below news of what was happening; but *Resolution*'s fire slackened at about nine-forty, by which time she had passed the rear of the enemy line. Soon thereafter, her guns fell silent until, shortly before sunset, there was a brief but furious discharge.

Later on, as the demands of attending the other wounded diminished, Blair conscientiously placed the remains of Robert's left leg in a barrel of spirits to preserve it: he wanted to ensure it could be inspected by 'the most able anatomists' to prevent any suspicion that it had been removed unnecessarily. Robert trusted his friend to have done the right thing, and said he did not care one way or another.

★

Gradually, as the day drew to its close, accounts of the battle reached Robert. He learned, for instance, that a few moments before his own injury, Captain William Blair of the *Anson* had been killed. As the boats of the fleet conveyed news, Robert also learned that while his leg was being amputated, the two fleets had continued to pass each other, and that the wind had shifted back to the south-east, throwing the French line into *echelon* and forcing their bows towards the British, while Rodney's ships were freed to alter course towards the French. Although what happened next is unclear, it is likely that Sir Charles Douglas, swiftly noting the wind shift, advised Rodney to turn to starboard, break the enemy's line and thereby cut off and corner de Grasse's van, which had already passed the *Formidable*. The admiral refused to follow the advice – but Douglas ordered the course alteration anyway. Rising from his chair, Rodney furiously castigated Douglas for his presumption, but then, realizing the chance now presented to an admiral willing to break with hallowed tradition, he icily acknowledged to the equally angry Douglas: 'Very well, Sir Charles, you may do as you please.'

The *Formidable* broke through the French line under the stern of the *Glorieux*, which was the nineteenth enemy ship, and ahead of the *Diadème*. Rodney's flagship was followed by the ships immediately behind him, and Edmund Affleck in the *Bedford*, lying six ships further down the line behind the *Formidable*, also broke through. Alan Gardner in the *Duke*, ahead of the *Formidable* and wondering to himself about the propriety of such a manoeuvre, did likewise, but the *Resolution* did not, as she had already passed by the tail of the French line. As the British vessels barged through, they were able to rake their enemies, pouring shot the length of their ships and causing immense damage. The *Glorieux*, holed six times, was helpless and shattered, while other French ships lay in a similar sorry state. By about half past eleven that morning, all of Rodney's fleet was to windward of the now disorderly and scattered French ships.

Meanwhile, de Grasse had attempted to reform his fleet but had lost effective control. The *Glorieux*, *César* and *Hector* lay dismasted, and a fourth ship, the *Ardent*, surrendered when overwhelmed by the British. She had on board de Bouillé's siege artillery, intended for Jamaica. Other French vessels were severely damaged, the morale of their crews as shattered as their ships. The French practice of shooting high had availed them little – in one case doing nothing more than shooting the trucks off the three mastheads of the *Princessa* – while the effect of the low British gunfire had been devastating. British losses in what became know as the Battle of the Saintes amounted to 243 killed and 816 wounded. French losses are unknown, but were certainly in the thousands; the number killed in the *Ville de Paris* alone was thought to have exceeded three hundred.

The French were fortunate in that the breaking of their line at least allowed the bulk of their ships, hitherto trapped between the British and the land, to escape to the westwards. Admiral Rodney, however, surprised his men by not ordering them to pursue the fleeing enemy and instead hauled down the signal for close action, frustrating Hood, who was expecting the command for a general chase. Unable to order a chase himself, Hood instead sought to lead by example, getting his boats out to tow the *Barfleur*'s head around – for such was the lack of wind – so he could make after the French ships. The apparent slackness on Rodney's part probably owed much to his debilitating illness and a desire to preserve his fleet as the evening drew on, as well as not to risk a night action. But, although the British pursuit was 'languid', it managed to take five French ships – including de Grasse's flagship, 'the finest ship of war' afloat. So shattered was the *Ville de Paris*, with scarcely a man left to stand on her upper deck, it was said that de Grasse had lowered the colours himself. Captain Lord Cranstoun boarded the great ship, 'over his shoes in blood', to accept the sword from the tall and robust figure of the French admiral.

The chief architects of this notable capture were Hood in the *Barfleur* and James Saumarez in the *Russell*, which had caught up with the *Ville de Paris* just before twilight; but they were not the only participants. Lieutenant Leggatt in the *Resolution* had pressed after the *Russell*, and that final burst of the *Resolution*'s guns had been the noisy evidence of his ship's gallant part in the action, as his men 'tried some of our shot at the *Ville de Paris*', as Lieutenant George Grey recorded in his log. When Robert was told of the capitulation, it was with the greatest difficulty 'that he restrained his emotions', for he 'felt his blood flow with such violence to give him apprehensions that his wounds would burst'. So shattered was the *Ville de Paris* that she would not survive a hurricane during her homeward Atlantic passage; but the prestige attached to her capture was such that the British later built a namesake, to retain the memory of their moment of triumph.

*

Despite the day's victories, the mood aboard the *Resolution* after the action was sombre. In addition to her maimed captain, she had suffered four dead and thirty-three wounded, three of them fatally, although Thomas Noon, who had been hit by the same shot that struck Robert, survived. Amid the criticisms of Rodney's failure to order a vigorous pursuit of the fleeing French – the disapproval chiefly voiced by Hood, supported by Douglas – was another suggesting that the *Resolution* had not done her utmost. With Robert known for his 'Zeal and desire to distinguish Himself upon such occasions, [many] had expressed a wonder that His ship had not been in a conspicuous situation during the day'.⁵ But such pejorative comments were short-lived once it was known that within thirty minutes of carrying his ship into action Lord Robert had been gravely wounded, and that Rodney had subsequently ordered the ship to stay out of the action.

As night drew on, the British fleet hove-to, and the remaining French ships slipped away. At nearly midnight, the darkness was pierced by a sudden flame followed by an explosion, as someone in search of liquor on the captured *César* upset his candle with catastrophic consequences. More than 400 Frenchmen aboard perished, along with the British prize-crew of Lieutenant Hayes and 58 seamen.

Daylight found the ships refitting – 'knotting and splicing' as the logs had it – while around them in ghastly attendance cruised hungry sharks. Gradually, news spread around the fleet that Robert had lost a leg. Cornwallis, as soon as he heard, 'immediately went on board the *Resolution*' where he found Robert, as he recorded, 'in very good spirits I thought with every prospect of doing well, but he Lamented the Idea of not being able to serve with one Leg'.⁶ Cornwallis almost certainly repeated the scuttlebutt that Hood was criticizing Rodney. But, as Cornwallis later observed regarding Rodney's failure to chase: 'The trials of Keppel & Palliser, which had taken place at the beginning of the War, had taught those most apt to talk upon such occasions to be silent.'⁷

Robert 'conversed with great ease and cheerfulness' with the flag-officers and other friends who came to visit him while he lay in his cot. Perhaps one of them relayed the anecdote regarding the poultry coup smashed by enemy fire on the *Formidable*. A surviving bantam cock had flown aft and perched nearby Rodney from where, at every broadside, it flapped its wings and crowed. Given the derisory association of cockerels with the French, Rodney decided to keep the bird until it died a natural death.

Such frivolities could not distract the wounded young man for long. His future troubled him, and although he bravely displayed 'great composure and serenity of mind', encouraging Surgeon Blair to think his 'symptomatic fever was slight and soon over', he fretted over the ship that had been his responsibility for so long. At one time, as Blair recounted afterwards, 'he talked seriously of remaining in the command of her as before'. The patient managed to pen a short, querulous note to Francis Reynolds, who had brought him a gift:

Dear Reynolds

I am as well as a man can be with one leg off one wounded & right arm broke. The doctor who is sitting by me at present says there are every hope of recovery. I thank you much for your present. Whenever it should suit you I shall be happy to see you.

Believe me dear Reynolds most humbly R Manners

On the same day, Sir Samuel Hood was also putting pen to paper, to Philip Stephens, Secretary to the Board of Admiralty: 'I am grieved most exceedingly for that truly gallant and amiable young nobleman, Lord Robert Manners. One leg gone and the other wounded, and his right arm broke; but I think his habit of body is good, and therefore hope and trust he will do well.'

On the next morning, Sunday, 14 April, the *Resolution* received fifty-six French prisoners. By now the ship was lying about 15 miles south-west of Guadeloupe, and her crew were busy repairing damaged sails. And now Robert learned that he was not to remain in command of his beloved ship, for on the same day Captain John Symons – Rodney's captain from the *Formidable* – came aboard to take over. Later still, Captain Byron of the frigate *Andromache*, having been scouting for any lingering French vessels, learned from Rodney that he was to be tasked with taking home Captain the Honourable James Cranstoun with the admiral's despatches – and giving passage to the wounded Lord Robert. It was thought that the young aristocrat's best chance of recovery was to return to England, away from the heat of the West Indies. When told of his fate, Robert 'ordered every man who had behaved well during his command to come into his cabin, thanked him for his attention to his duty, and gave him a present of money with his own hand'.

Monday, 15 April dawned clear with light airs. As Robert and his belongings were being transferred to the *Andromache* on a stretcher, he suddenly asked whether the colours of ships that had struck to the

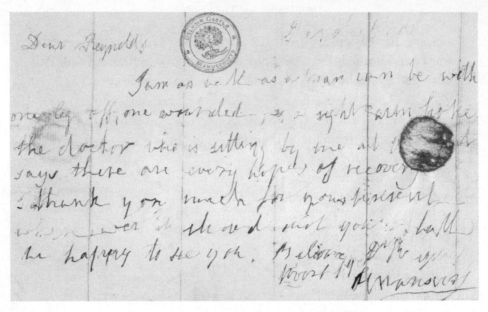

The note Robert wrote to his friend Francis Reynolds,
after being wounded at the Battle of the Saintes.

Resolution during his command were in his baggage. But recollecting himself, he apologized. 'I beg pardon it is mere folly and vanity, I am sorry such a weak idea has escaped me. Give yourselves no trouble about them.' As Watson, ever the hagiographer, later observed, 'It was natural for a young hero to make the inquiry, but the reflection on having made it would have done honour to the oldest.'

The *Andromache*'s sailing master noted in his log: 'Came on board Lord Robert Manners and his attendants.' With the wounded man were his servant Charles Ekins, Acting Lieutenant William Brown, Surgeon Robert Blair, and others of Robert's retinue – James Hughes, Richard Redman and James Russell. The frigate was also to give passage to a French officer and his servants, probably from the *Ville de Paris*, and Lord Cranstoun, bearing Rodney's despatches. Sometime during the day, Hood visited too, pressing his own letters into Cranstoun's hands – letters to influential individuals containing his vigorous views on Rodney's failure to pursue de Vaudreuil. He then went straight to the *Formidable* to try to persuade Rodney to chase and defeat the rest of the French fleet, for Jamaica remained threatened. But Rodney thought enough had been done to secure British sea power.

As the admirals argued, the *Andromache* set sail. In light and variable airs, she 'parted company with the fleet, the latter keeping to the west-ward', and headed north-east. She was taking Lord Robert Manners from that which he loved, and from that by which he lived.

★

At the Battle of the Saintes, the navy's *Fighting Instructions* had been disobeyed, and the fleet had performed an unconventional manoeu-vre in breaking the enemy's line. It remains the greatest sea battle ever fought in the Caribbean, and it marked a change in the fortunes of the Royal Navy. However, of itself the battle did not save Jamaica, though it was indeed the catalyst for what followed. The island was secured instead by subsequent actions, including that of Sir Samuel Hood, who persuaded Rodney to let him detach with a few ships to pursue the French. He was successful in taking some stragglers, the *Caton* and the *Jason*, together with a frigate and a corvette. Eventually, the French abandoned the venture, their motivation sapped by dis-ease-ridden troops and worn-out ships. In the meantime, Hood had remained deeply frustrated with Rodney. He wrote Robert a letter in the hope that his words might find an ear in Parliament via the young captain's influential brother, the Duke of Rutland:

> Barfleur off Alcavala St Domingo April 22nd 1782
>
> My dear Lord
> I most sincerely hope and pray this may find your Lordship as well as your unhappy misfortune will possibly allow, and that you may be restored to perfect health, and long enjoy it, with every blessing and comfort of life your own wishes can suggest. From the Andromache where I had the honor of paying my respects to your Lordship, I went to the Formidable… Now where my Lord was Sir George Rodney's judgment to subject me with only ten sail of the line to fall in with at least twenty of the French and at the same time to keep twenty two sail of the line with him to take care of the Ville de Paris without the shadow of a prospect of meeting a single ship of the enemy's… If divine providence was not to assist us, as it has most kindly done, in many instances since we left St Lucia, what would become of our poor distressed country?… I have the honor to be with the purest sentiments

of regard and esteem My Lord Your Lordships most faithful and
most humble servant Sam: Hood

Francis Reynolds wrote too, from the *Monarch*, in a more informal vein
of real friendship:

Monarch May 2nd

My dear little Lord
I hope this will find you perfectly recovered, but to hear of this
from yourself I despair of, knowing by experience how apt you
all are to forget your friends in these parts, after stepping upon
British ground... The Caton the ship with the black and white
streak is ours her commander the Cont le Framond was my guest
for some time and the very agreeable person I found him and
sorry I was when he left me. By him I was confirmed in what I
so often told you that you did not know one of their ships from
another and that you had misled me very much... I have taken
up a good deal of your time and I find my letter longer than
intended, which impute my dear Lord to the very sincere regard
with which I am, your very sincere friend
        Fra[ncis] Reynolds

The news of Robert's misfortune spread through the Caribbean. On
4 May, Anthony St Leger of the Rutland Regiment, now a brigadier
general, wrote from St Lucia to Charles. At the time of his writing,
Charles had no idea what had happened to Robert; but St Leger must
have calculated that his letter would reach Charles after the news had
reached England. St Leger wished to enquire whether the gift of some
earrings for Mary Isabella and some pineapple plants had been well
received, and to let Charles know that those men of the Rutland Regiment still with him at St Lucia (including Joe Hutchinson, the gardener
from Belvoir) were 'a well behaved lot'. But the main thrust of his
letter was clear:

Before this your Grace have heard of the terrible wound poor
Lord Robert received in the action with the French fleet by letters
I received he was in as fair a way as could be [expected] and trust
in God he will recover he is an honour to his king and country, the

whole fleet lament the accident but the whole world must admire
his conduct on that memorable day. I entreat your grace to give
me a single line as my anxiety about him is not to be expressed...

As it turned out, St Leger's anxiety was not unjustified. Some days
before that letter was written, the *Andromache* was working to windward in light north-easterly zephyrs, as Robert lay in his cot. By 18
April, she was passing the Bahamas, heading towards Bermuda but
beset by calm spells and hazy visibility. The familiar routines went
on – exercising 'the great guns and small arms', bracing the yards and
altering the sails, and washing and cleaning between the decks. On
20 April, Seaman William Chilton was punished for drunkenness. A
couple of days later, Marine Nicholas Alexander died on board of an
unrecorded cause. Occasionally a strange sail was to be seen in the
distance.

Throughout these days, Robert remained cheerful and the attentive
Blair was struck by his 'serenity of mind'. The patient spent the time
reading, conversing with friends such as William Brown, and asking
for music to be played, 'which he generally accompanied with hum-
ming or whistling'. His appetite was good, and his wounds appeared
to be healing. 'In short being perfectly freed from the cares of a command his mind seemed perfectly at ease and he declared he never was
easier or better in his life,' Blair observed.

On Sunday, 21 April, there 'sprung up a breeze from the southward',
and the *Andromache* began to reel off the knots as the wind increased
to squalls from the south-west. But the progress of the frigate was not
to be matched by that of her august passenger. It was now that Robert
began to feel the symptoms of tetanus. '[H]e was perfectly acquainted
with the symptoms of lockjaw which generally accompanies those
[wounds] received in the West Indies,' not least because 'his attention
to the healths of his men had made him so particular in his inquiries'.
He mentioned it to Blair 'but in so composed and unconcerned a manner' that the surgeon 'thought his Lordship was bantering him'.

It was not so. Robert told Blair 'that it was now over with him, that
it was needless to take any more medicines and that his mind was
resigned and made up to every event which can possibly happen'. However, the persuasive Blair made him take some kind of medicine, on

the basis that even if it failed as a cure, it would at least 'have the advantage of alleviating pain'. Robert 'seemed at first to receive considerable benefit, but the symptoms soon recurred with redoubled violence, and swallowing which had been very difficult, became impracticable'. During the night of Monday, 22 April, Blair's patient grew delirious, his speech becoming 'wild and incoherent'. He continuously called out 'the enemy is approaching! – get the ship ready! – bear down close!', 'giving orders as if in real action'.

On Tuesday, 23 April, St George's Day, the *Andromache* reached latitude 35° North. As the day dawned, the skies were dark and the rain heavy, while the squally wind veered to the north-west as a weather front passed through with 'much thunder and lightning'. On that morning, Robert lay calm again, 'thoughtful, composed and alert for some time'. On seeing Blair, he asked the surgeon through clenched jaws 'to repeat the Lord's Prayer', to which Robert 'attended with the utmost reverence, bowing his head and making a sign of his faith'. Less than an hour later, 'as the sun passed the meridian', Robert expired, 'without a groan, or struggle, or the smallest sign of uneasiness'. Thus eleven days after the Battle of the Saintes, the *Andromache*'s master recorded in his log that: 'Departed this life Lord Robert Manners late captain of His Majesty's ship *Resolution*.' He was aged just twenty-four years, two months and seventeen days.

It is not possible to know from Blair's description whether Robert really had contracted full-blown tetanus or an attenuated *'forme fruste'* kind, a septicaemia, from the surgery. In the case of the former, the symptoms would typically have been prolonged and severe muscular spasms involving the whole body, the clenched jaw leading to exhaustion and starvation, sometimes for as long as three weeks. But Blair had reason to spare the feelings of those reading his description, and so perhaps he held back on some of the more unpleasant detail.

There began a protracted discussion as to what to do with the young man's body. Captain Byron initiated it by asking Blair how long they should wait before 'committing Robert's body to the deep'; but others pointed out that Robert's friends in England would expect him to be brought home, though there were doubts as to whether it would be possible to preserve a corpse for that long. Robert Blair was especially concerned about what Charles would want. 'And it was also mentioned that his losing his life in a manner so gallant, and on an occasion so glorious and so beneficial to his country, might well entitle him to every mark of respect that could be showed by his country,' recorded Blair. By contrast, Cranstoun and Byron, 'endeavouring to judge how themselves would be influenced on a similar occasion', felt that 'the Funeral ought to take place immediately; and with respect to the other consideration that a monument might equally be erected notwithstanding'. Blair agreed: 'Considered abstractedly, it certainly appears of little moment and I ventured to give it as my opinion that Lord Robert, had it been possible to consult him, would have co-incided with theirs.' Eventually, they concurred that if carried home, Robert's body would be 'beat[en] to pieces in the cask', and, fittingly for someone who was a naval man to his core, that '[t]here seems to be some degree of propriety in committing the body of a sea officer to the element on which he has passed the most active part of his life, and where he had so gloriously distinguished himself'.

Robert's remains were thus prepared in the traditional way. A lock of his hair was cut off. Surgeon Blair placed the preserved leg in its rightful place, remarking that he 'thought it proper that it should accompany the body'. With two iron shot at his feet to ensure sinking, Robert was shrouded in canvas, sewn from the feet upwards, the last stitch being passed through his nose to verify death. When all was made ready, the entire ship's company was mustered on deck. At five o'clock on the afternoon of 24 April 1782, the *Andromache*'s main-yards were hauled aback and the frigate lay hove-to. The marines were

Lord Robert's hanger he had with him in the Resolution.

paraded and Robert's faithful followers took their places. The dead captain was brought from below, as the *Andromache*'s 1st lieutenant ordered 'hats off! Robert was placed on an eight-man mess-table, then covered with an ensign and positioned at an entry-port in the ship's bulwarks. Captain Byron stepped forward with the *Book of Common Prayer* and intoned the words of the committal: 'We therefore commit his body to the deep, to be turned into corruption, looking for the res-urrection of the body, (when the Sea shall give up her dead,) and the life of the world to come, through our Lord Jesus Christ...'

A volley of shots from the marines rang out, the mess-table was upended, and the body slipped from beneath the ensign into the sea. 'Granby's son' sank beneath the waves. Byron ended with the Grace: 'In the sure and certain hope of the resurrection to eternal life through our Lord Jesus Christ, we commend to Almighty God Captain Lord Robert Manners and we commit his body to the deep... The grace of our Lord Jesus Christ, and the love of God and the fellowship of the Holy Ghost, be with us all evermore. Amen.' Then, as the hands were dismissed, the yards were squared to the wind and the *Andromache* gathered speed once more. The ceremony had, as Blair recorded, been attended by 'all the honours of war', involving 'a company of marines, a band of musick and all the usual military honours and solemnities'.

The frigate was, at the time of Robert's burial at sea, 700 miles south-west of Cape Race and 300 miles north-east of Bermuda, with almost a month of sailing ahead of her before she would reach England. As darkness fell the weather grew squally, with 'much lightning', and shortly after the main topsail was torn from its yard. Thereafter, the *Andromache*'s track towards home took them close to Newfoundland and the 'isles of ice' that Robert had witnessed in his earliest naval days. As the vessel approached England in early May, the wind drove them off course, so Captain Byron considered he could get Lord Cran-stoun to London with Rodney's despatches more quickly by making for the Bristol Channel. Nine miles north of Lundy, Byron and Cran-stoun were put ashore on 17 May 1782 at Ilfracombe, on the North Devon coast, while the *Andromache* continued on to Portishead, near Bristol. Here, Robert's personal effects were wrapped up in 'canvas to be placed on a wagon at the first opportunity and thirty guineas were distributed among his three attendants'.

Robert Blair had proposed that 'all his Lordships papers and effects should immediately be sealed up and delivered untouched'. Their recipient would be Charles, who as yet had no inkling that he had lost his beloved brother. The effect on him was to prove catastrophic.

15

'The darling of your soul'

MAY 1782 TO FEBRUARY 1784

'The darling of your soul'

'J amaica Saved!' ran the headlines. News of the Battle of the Saintes broke across London early on the morning of 18 May 1782, after Byron and Cranstoun had travelled post-haste through the night. The rejoicing was widespread – illuminations and the firing of cannon – as word of the victory spread throughout the country. It was the one bright spot in Britain's dark hour, evidence that the lion could still bite. And, in contrast to the whirl of controversies surrounding Admiral Rodney's behaviour just months before, he was now the hero of the hour. The ageing, gout-ridden admiral, with his troublesome prostate and his grim visage, was raised to the peerage by a grateful King George.

But the victory had come at a price. Heading the list of the fallen were the three post-captains William Bayne, William Blair and Lord Robert Manners. For a while, the papers seized on any details they could get, with little regard to accuracy, one even reporting the return of Robert's body to Belvoir for burial. Of the three men, it was Robert who most caught the public imagination, perhaps because of his aristocratic allure but his resolute, fair-minded and gallant nature had also played its part and the king, when he heard, told the Duke of Portland that he 'would rather have lost three of the best ships in his service'.[1] Almost immediately, a proposal was made in Parliament for a monument to him in Westminster Abbey; but, as he had not been killed in a moment of heroic endeavour that affected the course of the battle, this singular distinction was denied him. Heated discussion about the virtues of dying in action rather than afterwards of wounds led to the decision to acknowledge the triple deaths together, thus avoiding an appearance of partiality. Such was the strength of feeling regarding the victory, though, that the 'Three Captains' monument was to be paid for by public subscription. The sculptor Joseph Nollekens was commissioned to execute the work, and to this day it remains one of the very few in the abbey to be funded in this way.

The battle, coming after so much bad news, bolstered the national mood and gave Britain's new government a better bargaining position for peace negotiations. Something of the sense of relief found expression in panegyric and eulogy. Verses commemorating the battle appeared, as did some written in Robert's honour, including lines that one anonymous woman sent to Charles:

> A feeling heart, humanity was thine
> That gives true lustre to a noble line
> In the high bloom of youth he meets a grave
> His injured country much he wished to save
> Britannia's many wounds he died to heal
> His own alas he would not timely feel
> A limb torn off could not abate his zeal,
> Still, still, he fought, and fell for England's weal
> A nation sighs shall consecrate thy bier
> Each Briton sure will pay the feeling fear
> Their own, and noble Rutlands loss deplore,
> Their hero falls, His Brother is no more;
> With wonder struck thy prowess we admire,
> Amazement strikes us at thy martial fire
> Till memory tells us Granby was thy sire.

Inevitably, comparisons were made with Robert's father. 'Would that such should be the death of a son of Lord Granby can be matter of no surprise to no-one, how much so ever we may regret it,' wrote another scribbler. Dr Knox, old Granby's doctor during the Seven Years' War, wondered: 'Might not [Robert's] friends… shed a tear to the memory and recollection of such a father! Such a son!?' Others emphasized the loss to his calling: 'He appeared from his amiable temper and extraordinary talents joined to the advantages of his birth and connections to be a person from whom the public had reason to promise themselves the most valuable and important services.' Although Robert was, by

1. A sketch of the island of St Kitts, by William Dawes, 2nd lieutenant of marines in the *Resolution*. Drawn in January 1782, soon after the battle in Frigate Bay, Dawes's sketch was slipped between the pages of Lord Robert's *West Indian Atlas* for safekeeping.

2. The Battle of the Saintes, 12 April 1782, by Lieutenant William Elliott RN. Elliott's painting was executed in 1784–7 and exhibited at the Royal Academy in 1787.

3. Thomas Stothard's painting, *The Death of Lord Robert Manners*, in fact depicts the moments after he was wounded during the Battle of the Saintes on 12 April 1782. It is believed that the man at Lord Robert's head is Lieutenant of Marines William Dawes, and the young man kneeling at his feet is Acting Lieutenant William Brown. The latter was later involved in advising the artist over details of the scene.

4. The surgical set, by Evans and Co. London surgical instrument makers from 1676 to 1874, used to amputate Robert Manners' left leg following his wounding at the Battle of the Saintes.

5. Lord Robert Manners by Joshua Reynolds, who was paid £210 for the full-length portrait. Lord Robert is wearing a captain's full-dress uniform with white cuffs; his lapels should be white also, but for an unknown reason the artist painted them blue.

6. Charles, 4th Duke of Rutland, wearing the robes of Viceroy
of Ireland (1784–7). Joshua Reynolds's portrait was presented to
the 5th Duke of Rutland by the Prince Regent in 1816.

7. The Three Captains memorial in the north transept of Westminster Abbey, by the sculptor Joseph Nollekens. The monument, completed in 1793 at a cost of £4,000, commemorates Royal Navy captains William Bayne, William Blair and Lord Robert Manners, all of whom died in 1782. On a column are relief portraits of the three with their names and ages (50, 41 and 24 respectively), Lord Robert is the topmost of the three reliefs. A figure of Fame surmounts the column and below is Neptune on a sea-horse and Britannia with a lion.

8. John Henry and Elizabeth (Diddle), the two eldest children of Charles, 4th Duke of Rutland, with their favourite dogs Turk and Crab. The painting, by Joshua Reynolds, dates from around 1783.

9. Mary Isabella, Duchess of Rutland and Vicereine of Ireland, driving her phaeton in Dublin, Ireland, as depicted by the Irish artist John James Barralet. Unusually for a noblewoman, she liked to hold the reins of her horses herself.

10. Wine bottles showing the coat of arms of the Duke of Rutland. Lord Robert Manners took them to the West Indies in the *Resolution*. They were returned to Belvoir Castle after his death, whereupon Charles, 4th Duke of Rutland, left instructions for them not to be touched. Two of them were drunk in 1909. The label is in the hand of the 9th Duke of Rutland, and dates from the early twentieth century.

11. Three out of four new wings of the fourth Belvoir Castle had been completed by 1816. On 26 October of that year two wings, one new, and the one remaining old wing, were totally destroyed by fire. Staff and local villagers rescued many precious objects, but some treasured items were lost. This painting was based on an illustration from a local newspaper.

12. A clutchbag embroidered by Mary Isabella, 4th Duchess of Rutland, containing locks of hair of her husband Charles and his brother Robert.

13. The fourth Belvoir Castle. Its footprint is the same as the second castle, and one wall still retains some of the original stone. Building of this fourth castle began in 1801, was interrupted by the fire of 1816, and was not completed until c.1830

14. Cannon from the *Prothee*, the French prize Lord Robert Manners captured in 1780, being fired by Robert Osborn, a Scots Guardsman. Osborn lost his left leg after being injured during the battle for Mount Tumbledown in the Falklands War, 1982, exactly 200 years after Lord Robert lost his in the Battle of the Saintes.

all accounts a well-liked, competent and brave sea-officer, the praise
was somewhat overdone because the circumstances of his death, combined with his aristocratic status, exemplified the contemporary ideal
of a glorious death in battle, embracing both victory and tragedy. Robert's lineage and youthfulness spoke of heroism and patriotism, but
also of self-sacrifice.

In the wake of the Battle of the Saintes, Britain clawed back some of
her lost prestige. The navy, too, regained its self-respect following the
destructive divisions of the Keppel–Palliser affair, and the accusations
that it was blundering into unpredictable encounters around the world
while failing to protect home waters or blockade the French in their
ports. And whether it was Rodney, Captain Douglas or a fortunate
wind shift that was responsible for the Saintes' unorthodox but effective manoeuvres – it would be debated for years to come – the way
had been paved for greater role of *initiative*. In all these efforts, Captain
Lord Robert Manners had played his full part, to the end.

*

Lord Rockingham told Charles that: "The general joy in this great
and important victory gained over the enemies of this country is even
checked and damped by the general sense of affliction which is felt for
his loss.' As Robert began to fade from public acclaim and attention
moved to the winding down of war with America, a different and more
lingering sort of profound personal tragedy was developing. After all,
as Sir Thomas Gascoigne told Charles: 'Alas one of the proudest victories this country had to boast of robs you of the darling of your soul.'

Somewhere within Belvoir Castle, in a spot he would not forget,
Charles had received the terrible news of his brother's death. He was
inconsolable. Friends tried to rally round, as they had done for his
grandfather on the death of the old Lord Granby. An anxious Henry
Fitzroy Stanhope urged him: 'For God's sake my dear dear friend arm
yourself with all the fortitude you are master of and if possible bear
up against this horrid calamity.' Trying again, Stanhope wrote: 'It is a
consolation to reflect… the death itself is to be envied… For Gods sake
my dearest duke reflect upon the applause of a whole nation, and the
immortal honors which crowned him in his last moments reflect on
these Triumphs and admit them as consolation to your afflicted breast.'

A succession of carriages and horses arrived at Belvoir bringing
friends who tried to comfort Charles, but who mourned with him.
Mun Stevens, now a colonel, wrote: 'What I feel... for the loss of one
of the most valuable friends of men that ever existed... I really have
neither power or word to express... Time and reflexion, I fear, can only
relieve you.' Lord Rockingham tried a different tack: 'Lord Cranston
& Captain Byron were with me yesterday. The accounts they gave me
of the fortitude with which your dear brother bore the misfortunes &
pains of his wounds while the expectation of the possibility of his life
existed & the calmness & resignation of his mind when the fatal turn
appeared are circumstances I trust will afford great consolation to
your grace in your most serious thought on this most heavy calamity.'

Charles seemed particularly affected by the absence of a body. 'I
firmly believe there never was a more awful melancholy burial,' Byron
afterwards admitted. 'If I had known the Duke of Rutland would have
wished his brother to be brought home at all events I would have
endeavoured to have done it.' Robert Blair, having written an account
of Robert's last days, waited upon Charles in person. 'Nothing was left
undone which could contribute to his relief,' he informed the griev-
ing duke. Charles pressed a large sum of money on the surgeon, but
Blair would not accept a present. Instead, he left at Belvoir the set of
instruments with which he had removed Robert's left leg, as a kind of
memorial. They could never be used again on anyone else.

Even the Comte de Grasse – who became a prisoner of war in
England for a time – in the gentlemanly spirit of warfare that obtained
at the time, troubled himself to write to Charles, on 10 August 1782:

> Monsieur le Duc, J'ai été d'autant plus sensible a la perte de
> Lord Manners, que j'avois déjà eu l'honneur de le connoitre. Son
> courage et sa bravoure lui avoient acquis mon estime et mon
> admiration, et sa mort m'a fait beaucoup de peine. Elle m'en
> cause encore aujourd'huy [sic], puisqu'elle me prive du plaisir de
> vous voir fair ma cour. Recevez, Monsieur le Duc, les temoignages
> de toute ma reconnaissance pour ce que vous aves la bonte de me
> dire de flatteur... Votre obéisant serviteur Le Comte de Grasse[2]

Such sentiments have the ring of authenticity rather than opportunistic sympathy to gain favour, though from the perspective of centuries

later it is not always easy to tell. But some of Charles's friends took pains to relay Robert's qualities as an officer as expressed by his naval peers, men who had no reason to be obsequious.

William Pitt's mother, the Dowager Countess of Chatham, understood the nature of Charles's grief, having lost not only her son, James Charles Pitt, to fever, but also her brother, Thomas Grenville, to enemy action in an earlier war, in a similar way to Robert. She now wrote to a friend: 'Nobody knows better than myself, by early, sad experience, what the Duke's sufferings must be.' But Charles's distress was something beyond ordinary mourning: he had broken down and gone to pieces. Although the brothers had not seen each other for two years, the bond they had formed from the circumstances of their childhood had been maintained by Robert's correspondence, even if Charles had been parsimonious in his replies. This may have added to his grief a poignant regret, perhaps even guilt. He was not of the kind of robust character that had experienced the discipline Robert had voluntarily submitted himself to when choosing to go to sea; and now his inconsolable sadness, his distraught countenance and his self-imposed isolation at Belvoir not only affected his close friends but became a subject for social gossip. Stanhope was so concerned that on 3 June he pleaded with Charles to abandon Belvoir, where:

> Everything I know reminds you of your poor brother... you reflect upon the different situations in which you have seen him there. You remember him there when a boy in all his puerile amusements, and there too you remember him whilst age had brought his talents and his virtues to maturity. You think of all the intermediate passages of his life and alas you reflect with sorrow on that spot you received the fatal account of his heroic death. For God's sake therefore my dearest Duke, leave that melancholy scene where all your misfortunes present themselves to you and where I am sure it will be impossible for you to recover your spirit. I conjure you to act like a man and to rouse up all your courage and all your good sense.

But then Stanhope followed sympathy with moral exhortation, a call for Charles to recollect his manhood and to take a lesson from Robert's stoicism: 'You have paid the most ample tribute to the memory of your poor Brother and your present conduct is diametrically opposite to what he would wish it to be if he could dictate to you. The eyes of all your friends and all those who look up to your character are fixed upon you, they revere pious lamentations but they require you not to forget the duties you owe as a Husband, as a Father, and as a good citizen.' Charles's misery was later prodded, on 19 June, by the arrival of Sir Samuel Hood's letter to Robert as well as the one from Francis Reynolds addressed to 'My dear little Lord'. Both men had assumed that their young friend would live. On the back of each letter Charles wrote: 'My dearest Bob died of His wounds April 23d 1782.'

Already arrived at Belvoir were Robert's possessions, tangible connections with his late brother: a mahogany desk and table; papers concerning his personal estate; letters from home – from Charles, Mary Isabella, Thoroton, Ekins and Mun Stevens. All were placed in Charles's dressing room in the north-west corner of the castle. There was also Robert's sea-chest containing his two seals, his drawings and doodles, his copy of the Jefferys *West Indian Atlas*, his Paul Hoste and Bigot de Morogues texts, a set of signalling flags, the 'night spy glass' bought at Barbados, the watch taken from his pocket at the time of his wounding, and not least the symbol of an officer's very *ésprit* – his hanger. Other remnants included some rum and some bottles of wine and port, bearing the Duke of Rutland's coat of arms, which he had perhaps been saving as a reminder of home; the table linen Robert

Charles annotated letters from Samuel Hood and Francis Reynolds with the words: 'My dearest Bob died of His wounds April 23d 1782.'

had bought from Chaloner Ogle; and the remainder of his clothes and uniforms. Most poignant of all was a *memento mori*, the lock of chestnut hair Blair had cut from Robert's head shortly after he gave up the ghost.

Charles took the hair and the most personal items into his care, and had the bottles placed in his cellar, with strict instructions that they were not to be touched. The flags he had draped through the archway that joined Belvoir's south wing with the external Picture Gallery his grandfather had built. With these relatively few physical artefacts from Robert's life, Belvoir became a mausoleum to the dead hero. Somebody – probably William Brown – told Charles that William Dawes had executed drawings of the fleet at St Kitts, and Charles, after asking Dawes for one, was directed to look inside the pages of the *West Indian Atlas*. And there they still were, for in all the haste of transferring Robert to the *Andromache* Dawes had forgotten to remove them. Still tucked in the book, too, was Robert's order for the *Resolution*'s cutter.

On 14 June 1782, responsibilities elbowed their way into Charles's hermetic world, for he was obliged to prove Robert's will. There was almost £2,000 in his bank account with Snow & Denne, besides a quantity of South Sea Company annuities inherited from their mother. Among Robert's other investments were those accruing to Navy Bonds funded by his annuity of £2,100 from Charles, while his prize-agents Ommaney & Page were still collecting what was owed to Robert. Charles asked for the accounts to remain open in Robert's name and for Joseph Hill to keep a watchful eye. Robert had requested that £1,000 be given to his old Eton tutor Ekins, and another £1,000 to Mun Stevens, amounts that were paid out quickly.

There was also other sad administration to attend to. Captain Symonds had to be reimbursed for deductions in the *Resolution*'s pay for errors in the ship's books – it seemed that an impatience with book-keeping was something of a family trait – and wounded seamen such as Francis Milladd, who had lost his arm at St Kitts, asked for the assistance they would have received had his captain lived. The sale of Robert's uniforms to Captain John Nicholson Inglefield, nephew of naval architect Sir Thomas Slade, must have been a wrench. On his return from the West Indies, Inglefield had been caught in the hurricane

Account Current with Ommanney & Page, — Cr.

1780			£ s d	£ s d
Mar. 1	By ½ pay – to 30 June 1779	13.6.6		13 0 0
	Comm.ⁿ 0.6.6		
May 16	By Ocean Prize Money of Geo. Agar	9.15.6		
	By Victory D.º of D.º	56.1.6		
		65.17.0		64 4 0
	Comm.ⁿ 1.13.0		
30	By ½ Pay – 1.st & 14 July 1779	2.1.6		2 0 6
	Comm.ⁿ 0.1.0		
July 4	By Resolution Pr. Money Prothee 3526 Dollars	764.2.3		745 0 3
	Comm.ᵈ 19.2.0		
17	By Victory wages 2.d Aug.t 1778 & 14 April 1779	53.12.0		
	Servant 6.15.0		
		60.7.0		58 17 6
	Comm.ⁿ 1.10.0		
		£ 883 2 3		
Sept. 1	By Balance from above			880 14 3
Nov. 14	By Alcide – Prize Money – Sundrys	82.4.0		80 3 0
	Comm.ⁿ 2.1.0		
Dec. 12	By Ocean – Wages 20 May & 25 Aug.t 1778	24.2.0		
	Servant 3.1.0		
		27.3.0		26 9 6
	Comm.ⁿ 0.13.6		
1781				
May 4	By Resolution – Prize Money – Prothee	380.2.0		370 8 0
	Comm.ⁿ 9.14.0		
Aug. 4	By Alcide – D.º – Sundrys 2.d Payment	60.5.6		58 15 6
	Comm.ⁿ 1.10.0		
				£ 1425 10 3

An account of the prize-money Robert won while serving on various ships, including his capture of the Protée (later Prothee).

of 1782 in which, besides the *Ville de Paris*, Inglefield's own ship the *Centaur* had foundered. He had survived but lost all his possessions.

Unable to throw off his grief, Charles rallied sufficiently to set about memorializing his brother. His chaplain George Crabbe was to write a long eulogy, likewise Lorenzo Pignotti, Mary Isabella's tutor from her days in Italy. Richard Watson, who that year became Bishop of Llandaff through Charles's patronage, consulted William Brown and others for details for 'Anecdotes of the Life of Lord Robert Manners'. Hill was drawn into the morbid enterprise and asked to organize the commissioning of Dominic Serres the Elder to paint battle-scenes of St Kitts and the Saintes. The artist consulted an eyewitness from the Saintes to help make the scene authentic, but William Brown was called in to help instead, to 'give some account of the particulars of the action, the seaman not being able in the least to make Mr Serres comprehend anything about it'. Meanwhile Sir Joshua Reynolds was paid £210 for a full-length portrait of Robert, the likeness taken from Richard Cosway's miniature executed when Robert was last in England – except the hanger, which, now in Charles's possessions, could be copied direct. Sir Joshua was to paint a second, three-quarter-length version for Francis Reynolds. The artist wrote:

> I shall certainly execute the commission which His Grace has ordered with the greatest care possible... I knew very little of Lord Robert but was very well acquainted for his Grace's great affection to him, I therefore felt and sympathised with him. I really think in losing him we have paid the full value of what we got, it is the general opinion that we have lost the most promising youth in the whole navy, and I am sure from what I saw of him and the letters I have seen from him, I am most perfectly inclined to confirm their opinion.

Thomas Stothard was commissioned to depict the scene of Robert's fatal wounding, and he too most likely consulted with William Brown. The resulting painting is thought to portray William Dawes at Robert's head and Brown at his feet.

Nearly a year after Robert's death, Charles still felt the loss keenly. During this doleful period his prolonged grief exacerbated his habitual unreliability – 'Your attendance at any time or any place is never a

certainty,' as a friend commented; and it did nothing to improve what
the army chaplain Bennet Storer described as 'your grace's aversion
to writing'. Others tried to persuade him to take up a role, something
that might take his mind off the memory of Robert. Trying to convince him that having nothing much to do would lead to no good, an
old friend wrote moralistically:

> A laudable or true ambition is certainly an object for every young
> man and relieves the mind from little objects which impercepti-
> bly involve us in expensive trifles of which we soon weary. This
> I take to be one reason of so many of young nobility falling into
> the deceit of gaming and ruining their fortunes almost before
> they can recollect themselves. This is a proof the mind must be
> employed and that idleness is the mother of vice.

Some tried to draw the Duke of Rutland into government. After
all, there was still plenty to do – the war in America was not quite

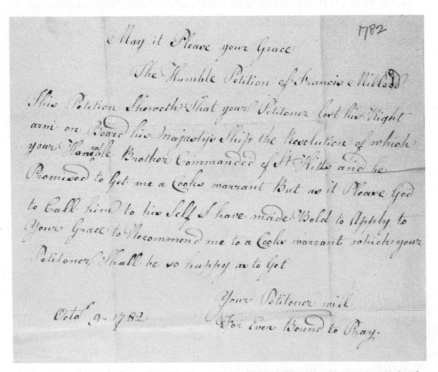

After Robert's death, Francis Milladd, a seaman who had lost an arm in the Battle of
St Kitts, wrote to Charles to request assistance with obtaining a cook's warrant.

over, and there was as yet no peace with France (while the Spanish still besieged Gibraltar). Charles resisted these overtures, although, as a kind of morbid memorial to his brother, he remained engaged with the affairs of the navy. Friends kept him informed – of the loss of the *Ville de Paris* in 1782's hurricane; and of the tragic fate of the 100-gun first-rate *Royal George*. This ship, once Hawke's flagship at the celebrated 1759 victory of Quiberon Bay, was lying at anchor at Spithead, where she was heeled for some repairs to the coppering below her waterline. Then, in the words of William Cowper: 'A land breeze shook the shrouds / And she was overset.' Water flooded into her open lower gun-ports causing a disastrous capsize that drowned more than 800 souls, including her commander Rear Admiral Sir Richard Kempenfelt. Of this great ship – whose exploit in having 'twirled a French ship round till it sunk' had inspired the five-year-old Charles to want to join the Royal Navy – only the masts remained above the grey waters.

Charles's friend Stanhope, now cleared by court-martial of wrongdoing at the fall of Tobago, when with the Rutland Regiment, was waiting at Portsmouth to board the *Courageux* with troops; he described the shocking spectacle of 'dead bodies... floating round her, and fresh ones rising as they are taken up'. To this general evocation of death, Stanhope could not help but maladroitly add a more personal one for Charles. Remarking upon the 'party of young men' with whom he was sharing quarters, which included some Finch cousins, thought them 'all perfectly good humoured and very hospitable but not very polished in their manners. I cannot help reflecting however painful the recollection may be to you upon the difference of your poor brother's behaviour. With the most consummate bravery he united all the good breeding of a fine gentleman, a character totally unknown here. Forgive me my dear Duke for this digression.'

★

For all sides in this war that had begun from American rejections of Parliamentary sovereignty and escalated into a global conflict, weariness had set in. It was as true for the colonists themselves, who had few resources left with which to fight, as it certainly was for the British, who, again, this time under Admiral Howe in the *Victory*, had to relieve Gibraltar from its Spanish siege in October 1782. But it would

not be Lord Rockingham as prime minister who oversaw peace negotiations, for this tenacious politician and inveterate goader of Charles
to apply himself to his duty died from influenza in July 1782, soon
after taking office. Instead, it was Lord Shelburne who now headed the
ministry. Although initially reluctant to accept the total independence
of the thirteen colonies, instead proposing a form of dominion status,
he bowed to the inevitable. Alleyne FitzHerbert was sent to Paris as
plenipotentiary. His task was to negotiate peace with a France that had
been virtually bankrupted by the strains of war – in contrast to a Great
Britain which, though fatigued, was still economically resilient owing
to its ability to finance war not just through taxation but through borrowing – the concept of the national debt elaborated from the end of
the previous century. FitzHerbert, a prudent man with quiet, polished
manners, played a significant role in obtaining favourable terms and
also in laying the foundation of the final peace treaty with the American colonists, thanks largely to his excellent relations with Benjamin
Franklin, one of the American peace commissioners.

And finally, Charles agreed to participate in affairs of state. King
George made him a Knight of the Garter in October 1782, and then
in February 1783 he joined the government as Lord Steward of the
Household. This was not by then a Cabinet post, but involved, among
other things, presiding at the 'Board of Green Cloth', which audited
the accounts of the king's household and made arrangements for
royal travel – which might have raised a few eyebrows given Charles's
own shortcomings in managing his own household. He was willing
to serve under Shelburne, for the new prime minister was a protégé
of the old Lord Granby *and* a disciple of the 1st Earl of Chatham.
Charles Howard, the purser of the *Resolution*, wrote on 20 February
1783 to congratulate Charles on the appointment, bluntly hoping
that 'however trivial to you, yet [is] to be wished by your friends as
it will in some degree prevent your indulging in that retirement and
pensiveness you have so much given way to since the loss of your
most excellent Brother and will oblige you to take part in the business of your country which at this time is much wanted in men of
your Grace's integrity and virtues'. But by April, Shelburne was out of
office, to be replaced by the uncomfortable coalition of Charles James

Fox and – again – Lord North. Although that unlikely alliance lasted only eight months, it was during its term that the war saw its formal end in September 1783, with the final incarnation of the British–American Treaty of Paris and the two treaties of Versailles with France and Spain. The former was momentous, bringing independence for the thirteen former American colonies and designating the boundaries of the new nation with Canada. Despite the years of hostilities, within months trade between Great Britain and the new United States had been revived by the common interests between the two economies with a shared language, negating the long fought-over argument that losing the colonies would destroy Britain. France held on to some minor territorial gains including Tobago, which could not outweigh the costs of the war; and Spain was still denied Gibraltar.

In Britain, some political stability at the top arrived under the leadership of Charles's great friend William Pitt, who, at twenty-four years of age, became Britain's youngest ever prime minister on 19 December 1783. He described himself as an 'independent Whig', though others called him a 'new Tory'; whatever he was, he was able to command the support of both the king and the Commons. Charles loyally aligned himself with his friend, which suited a disposition that was always uncomfortable with being forced to take sides, and Pitt was able to lure him into government as Lord Privy Seal. Mary Isabella also now came into her own as a political rival to Georgiana, Duchess of Devonshire, who stayed loyal to the ever more outspoken Charles James Fox. Georgiana related that, during one evening at the opera, where women sometimes had political fights in public, the 'Duchess of Rutland jumped to her feet and shouted, "Damn Fox!" at the boisterous crowd below; Lady Maria Waldegrave retaliated from the opposite box, "Damn Pitt!"'[3]

It was now twelve years since Charlotte Somerset had told her eldest grandson in no uncertain terms that: 'You must turn out either Surprisingly Good or remarkably the Contrary for your Composition allows of no medium.' In those intervening years, Charles had lived up to, what, to her, would have been mostly the 'Contrary'. But his friend and now prime minister, William Pitt, with perhaps a greater sense of Charles's capacity for 'Good', had in mind a grander position than

Lord Privy Seal for his friend. He was prepared to give the nobleman a substantial chance. On 11 February 1784, Pitt appointed Charles to be 'Lord Lieutenant', or Viceroy, of Ireland, with an annual salary of £20,000.

Perhaps the dilettante Duke of Rutland finally had his role.

16

'Claret is a bad medicine'

FEBRUARY 1784 TO OCTOBER 1787

'Claret is a bad medicine'

When Charles's carriage drew away from Belvoir towards the end of the hunting season in 1784, he could not know then that he would never return to his beloved castle, for Ireland was to consume him, and eventually, his life. He had gathered up some possessions and, more importantly, his wife and children, for he did not wish to leave his sons behind to the vagaries of Eton schoolmasters, and set off to Dublin in late February. There, they were to take up residence in Dublin Castle and the Viceregal Lodge in the city's Phoenix Park. Charles cannot have had much time for reflection on arrival, for his duties began immediately, finding Dublin, as he observed to Pitt, 'under the dominion and tyranny of the mob [and] persons are daily marked out for the operation of tarring and feathering'.

In 1784, the Viceroy of Ireland needed to be a man of some sensibility. Britain was, quite simply, afraid that her oldest and nearest colony might try to copy the Americans. Two years earlier, the Irish Parliament in Dublin had achieved a measure of independence, after so many Irishmen had fought on Britain's behalf, and 'patriot' sentiment was on the increase. In accepting the viceroyalty, Charles was stepping into the precarious position of managing an Anglo-Irish ruling elite – the Protestant Ascendancy – in a country where the vast majority of the population were Catholics with neither the vote nor political office.

Possessing greater powers than a colonial governor elsewhere, the viceroy – more officially, Lord Lieutenant – was usually a peer. Although not sitting in Cabinet, Charles would be expected to act in

concert with Downing Street and Westminster. A previous viceroy
and old Eton friend George Grenville, now Earl Temple, confirmed
that the 'government of that kingdom is indeed most delicate', and
that the task was 'difficult'. Temple then gave Charles a grave warning: that the expense of living in Ireland would 'much exceed your
ideas'. For the annual £20,000 salary would soon be used up, and he
would need to find, from his own pocket, a further £15,000 each year
to spend on patronage and entertaining, which were unofficial, inde-
finable but necessary ingredients of the role. Charles was in a weak
position financially to take on the viceroyalty, not least because he was
still paying off old Granby's debts – and still running up his own. But
Temple told him, perhaps with veiled irony, that with 'your principles,
firmness and moderation I have no doubt but that you may govern
with advantage to the empire and credit to yourself'. So Charles had
accepted Pitt's offer, and took office on 24 February 1784.

Now everyone wanted something from Charles, and his duties
proved varied and complex. Soon after his arrival, he was baffled by
a dispute that had arisen between the Archbishop of Canterbury and
the Archbishop of Dublin. It concerned the order of precedence in
the ceremonies of the Order of St Patrick, recently founded by Earl
Temple as a means of patronage. 'My dear Lord,' wrote Charles to
Temple with dry humour:

> Being very incompetent to decide in matters of form and finding
> no one here more helpful than myself… I apply to your Lordship
> for your opinion… Trifling as this difference seems I assure your
> Lordship that it is conducted with great heat likely to be produc-
> tive of much ill blood between the parties. The matter in question
> is simply whether the Primate as Prelate and representative of
> St Patrick should walk by himself, or whether the Archbishop of
> Dublin should walk with him on the left hand.

From the very start of his tenure, Charles's relationship with Pitt
remained extremely close, providing the prime minister with valuable
insights in what, compared with his previous reluctance to put pen
to paper, might be considered a remarkably energetic volume of correspondence. Charles was soon warning Pitt of political rumblings:
'I cannot consistently with my zeal for the King's service, and my

affectionate attachment to you, omit transmitting to you as speedily
as possible a very flagitious publication which has just been put into
my hands.' He elaborated:

> I have some time entertained suspicions that the lower classes of
> the people may have been wrought upon by French or American
> emissaries, from a general endeavour to mix the Roman Catholics
> with questions of parliamentary reform, and I have therefore on
> my part endeavoured to detach them as much as possible from
> mingling with those pursuits... The question, therefore, is, what
> is now most prudent to be done, for I shall most cheerfully exe-
> cute whatever shall be thought wisest and best [but] I ask myself,
> whether the present, like former seditious publications, may not
> die away.

To Charles the situation in Ireland was hardly a surprise, given his
opposition to the previous ministry, for a 'government whose schemes
extend no further than the exigencies of the day cannot expect any decisive good effects from its measures. Ireland has already been reduced to
its present state of faction and confusion by the not daring to meet and
oppose difficult questions in a manly and undaunted manner.'

However, Charles's real strength in the role was less as a political
mover and shaker and more as an enabler, a host. Indeed, reflecting
Lord North's view of him as an intermediary, he took the task of
entertaining Irish high society to new heights of brilliance, displaying an adroitness in balancing competing interests. While expensive
obligations came with such an elevated position, Charles *exceeded*
expectations with his lavish hospitality. As a result, he was received as
'witty, gallant and convivial', while the beauty and temperate conduct
of his wife won all hearts. It was said his court 'outrivaled that of
Comus himself'.[1] Sir Jonah Barrington recalled that Charles's establishment was 'more brilliant and hospitable than that of the monarch:
the utmost magnificence signalized the entertainments of the Duke
and Duchess of Rutland, and their luxury gave a powerful impulse
to industry... The Duke was singularly popular... His Grace and the
Duchess were reckoned the handsomest couple in Ireland.'[2]

★

Charles had not, though, undergone a Damascene conversion and become an entirely reformed character. From the stupefaction of his intense grief following Robert's death, when Charles was finally sprung from the confines of Belvoir and London and released into a new environment, he emerged confirmed in his tendency to libertinism. The viceroyalty gave him spectacular licence to throw off the 'blue devils' of his depression – or at least to sublimate them through indulgence.

One winter evening in 1784, the courtesan Margaret Leeson – who was more commonly known as the whore Peg Plunkett – was drinking tea with friends at her business premises in Dublin's Pitt Street (later named Leeson Street in her honour). Suddenly, they 'were surprised with the trampling of horses at the door and a monstrous tantarara when behold to our amazement who should be announced but his Grace himself attended by two of his aid-de-camps and a troop of horse'. Charles and his staff 'stomped in', the two aides 'soon decamped with an *impure* each', but, as Peg herself described, 'as for honest Charley, he and I, *tete-a-tete* drank and spilled three or four flasks of sparkling champaigne, after which we retired together, for his Grace would take no partner but myself'. By his own admission, the viceroy was already heartily drunk, and he completely forgot he had left his military escort outside. In the morning, Charles showered Peg with compliments, saying he would give 'ten thousand pounds' for 'his beautiful, his divining Dutchess' to be as much a 'mistress of the art of pleasing' as Peg was. On the spot, he promised to put the courtesan on the government pension list under an assumed name for the annual sum of £300. 'Oh how pleasing 'tis to please,' thought Peg.[3]

While Charles had been satiating his lust, his cavalry escort had 'remained on horseback armed cap-a-pee with swords in hands from one o'clock in the morning 'till five in the afternoon the next day, sixteen hours!!' recorded a delighted Peg. This spectacle drew crowds from 'the entire city who all flocked to behold the state', to the vexation of the viceroy when he emerged. Peg had, at least, spared a thought for the hapless cavalrymen, having taken 'care of the poor fellows and had them properly plied all night with the *pure-native* [whiskey] and a large portion of Maddock's Irish porter'.[4]

Dublin loved the scurrilous and salacious gossip. The broadsheets teemed with anecdotes of 'Peg and Charley'. At the theatre a few nights later, some of the audience spotted Peg entering and roared out 'Peg who lay you with last?'; to which she, harking back to Peg Woffington's old riposte concerning Charles's grandfather, nonchalantly replied 'MANNERS you black-guards'. The cheers that greeted the repartee were 'astonishingly great'. An unabashed Charles himself was in the royal box, *and* with Mary Isabella, who was 'observed to laugh immoderately at the whimsical occurrence'. Peg wrote in her memoirs that 'tis a known fact that this most beautiful of woman-kind that ever I beheld never troubled herself about her husband's intrigues'.[5] In public at least, and for now, Mary Isabella did display the imperturbable indifference expected of her; and Charles returned several times to Peg's bed, though never with quite so much panache as on that initial visit.

Unfortunately, sexual frolics, with their attendant dangers of syphilis and the clap, and over-spending were not the only excesses Charles found hard to resist. His breakfast alone was said to consist of six or seven turkey eggs washed down with port. Late in 1784, he was seized by a dangerous fever such that those close to him feared for his life. Lord Mansfield, whose beloved wife had now died and who maintained a deep friendship with his nephew-by-marriage, was perhaps the only man bold enough to tell the viceroy that he was drinking too much and staying up too late. There was one other person who felt able to speak her mind, and that was Charles's half-sister Anne, daughter of old Granby and Mrs Mompesson. Married to Charles's legitimate cousin John Manners Sutton, she had not seen her half-brother since the 3rd Duke's funeral in 1779. She now wrote to Charles during his illness:

> I have long been uneasy on your account, as it is universally thought that the life your Grace leads is far too irregular for it to be possible for you to live long, much less is the chance of continuing in health, suffer me to look back some years when you used to tell me that the faculty were of opinion that your constitution was far from strong and that it had been represented to you your necessity of being abstemious both in eating as well

as drinking, would to heaven that I could say anything to influence you to take care of yourself, health takes a sudden flight and
death happens as unexpectedly…

The fever did not, however, kill Charles, and he was able to return to
his public duties, where, to counterbalance his private behaviour, he
was showing some talent. While the age generally drew a line between
the expectations of public and private life, Charles's dissolute habits
did attract criticism, which in some cases grew vitriolic (and which
his supporters classed as 'libel') and threatened to undermine his
achievements. At the end of the viceroy's first year, his friend Charles
Greville pointed out that 'the generosity you showed to the distressed
did not immediately gain you the praise you deserved and your desire
to gain popularity by the conviviality of your table, by your enemies
was misinterpreted'. As Greville remarked, there was promise, for:
'The alteration which you have made shows the world that you are
not a slave to indolence or dissipation, and your steady adherence to
the measures of decision will I hope save the country and establish
your name and reputation as a firm and able statesman.' Greville was
not merely being obsequious. In fulfilling his official duties, Charles
had revealed a greater capacity for responsibility that might have been
expected, as well as a desire for modest reform, gaining, on the whole,
popular support.

★

Throughout such a complete change in his circumstances, Charles
continued to maintain his personal interests, as he had habitually done
from an early age no matter what else occupied him. The most central of these remained the acquisition of paintings for his collection.
During his time in Ireland, to his delight he was able at last to purchase the set of the *Seven Sacraments* by Nicolas Poussin, which he had
unsuccessfully tasked Robert with viewing all those years ago. The
pope's embargo on their export from Rome had been circumvented
by subterfuge, the agent James Byres having had copies made and
covertly substituted for the originals, which were then smuggled out
in the summer of 1786. There was some talk that the paintings might
be exhibited in London as a national treasure; but Charles forbade

it, saying that the Poussins were to stay at Belvoir Castle as long as 'the name of Manners and its splendours endures'. In an aside, Byres enclosed with his bill for the Poussins the news that: 'Our friend Sir William [Hamilton] is well. He has lately got a piece of modernity from England, which I am afraid will fatigue and exhaust him more than all the volcanoes and antiquities in the kingdom of Naples.' He was referring to Charles Greville's lover, Emma Lyon/Hart, who when married as Emma Hamilton would go on to achieve a starry notoriety as Horatio Nelson's mistress in a rather public *ménage à trois*.

At the same time, Sir Joshua Reynolds was trying to find an artist to paint for Charles. He recommended two possible candidates, John Webber and William Hodges, both of whom had sailed around the world with Captain James Cook on his voyages of discovery. Eventually, Charles took on the Irishman Solomon Delane, who produced four splendid scenes of Dublin and the surrounding area, which were to remain thereafter in the Manners family. Here, there was a connection with Robert's life, for Delane's daughter was married to Robert Home, the artist who had run away from home and sailed with Robert in Newfoundland in 1772.

For underlying the gaudy glamour of being the most powerful man in Ireland, was Charles's touching and loyal devotion to the memory of his younger brother, whose life still discharged its unfinished business. Odd bills run up by Robert caught up with Charles, among them those for the expensive and possibly aphrodisiacal strawberries that Robert had enjoyed in London in 1779. As memorials, Joshua Reynolds' full-length portrait and Thomas Stothard's painting of Robert's mortal wounding were copied as engravings, made into prints and distributed among friends. A print was also made of one of Lord Robert's own drawings, with copies sent to acquaintances, including to the Scarborough family of William Robinson, the former manservant in the *Resolution*. In 1784 Charles presented Benjamin Wilson's portrait of Robert to Sir Samuel Hood, who was extravagantly thankful:

> I am unable to express what I feel for the very great honour your Grace has done me by the commands you so obligingly left with Mr Hill for sending me the portrait of your late most dearly and justly beloved brother. Your Grace could not have made me a

more acceptable present or one I could prize with such enthusiastic warmth of veneration and esteem, for I not only loved and respected Lord Robert Manners but much lament his loss and a very publick one, and honor and revere his memory as long as I live.

The painting was later reacquired by the Manners family, when some of Hood's possessions were auctioned off. Around this time, too, Charles wrote the words for a memorial tablet for Robert to be placed in Bottesford Church alongside the Manners ancestors, including the words: 'He expired with all the philosophy and content of death which would have distinguished a Roman.' We can never know if Robert was truly resigned in his last moments, but it comforted Charles to believe it so.

In emerging from his depressed state, Charles assumed some responsibility for those who had served in the *Resolution* and who would, had their captain not died, have looked to Robert for relief. These men were now fortunate in having a duke to turn to in their hour of need, and Charles responded warmly to the one-armed, one-legged and one-handed petitioners, helping with recommendations to the Navy Board for warrants as ships' cooks or other suitable positions. There were other beneficiaries too. Reverend Touch wrote a most grovelling letter describing his 'weighty and inevitable misfortunes' and averring that he would 'rather rush again among all the thunder of battle and the horrors of that horrendous hurricane' than ask for help; but he was sure that 'were that Noble young hero… who when lieutenant of the *Alcide* honoured me with his particular notice' still alive he would help him.

Charles, as well as presenting Hood with the painting, also assisted him in gaining a Parliamentary seat as a Member for Westminster. And most notably among his efforts, in 1785 Charles persuaded William Pitt to establish a Professorship of Practical Astronomy at the University of Edinburgh, and to confer the office upon Robert Blair. Sir Henry Dundas wrote that 'it gives us all great pleasure that at the same time we are gratifying a wish of your Grace, we are serving a very meritorious man'. Charles also tried to obtain an award for Blair from the Commissioners of Longitude – who were still encouraging improvements in navigation and related sciences. Robert Blair proved a true child of the Scottish Enlightenment and is today best remembered for his work on improving the performance of achromatic prisms and lenses, though he also made a significant contribution in the 1790s towards banishing scurvy from the navy.

William Dawes, late of Robert's naval 'family', wrote asking for support for a position whereby he could relieve his impoverished father – the father who had once funded his son's appointment to the *Resolution*. Dawes became a respected, scholarly, scientific and conscientious 'gentleman', who, in 1788, would accompany hundreds of convicts in the 'First Fleet' to Australia. There, he joined the few free men supporting Governor Phillips to establish the new penal colony. He built an observatory at Dawes Point,[6] from where his contributions enriched the fields of astronomy, meteorology and surveying, and he worked also on unique and enduring documentation of the local language. An observer of human misery, Dawes would be involved, too, in the fight for the abolition of slavery.

William Brown was another beneficiary of Charles's interest. He almost joined the *Bounty* for Captain Bligh's doomed expedition of 1787 in search of bread-fruit, but was posted elsewhere at the last minute. He would go on to play a 'useful supporting role'[7] in command of the frigate *Venus* during Admiral Lord Richard Howe's 1794 victory of 'The Glorious First of June' against republican France. But in 1805, he became embroiled in giving evidence at a court-martial and so narrowly missed fighting alongside Nelson at Trafalgar. Notwithstanding this, Brown died an admiral in 1814 while serving – perhaps fittingly – as commander-in-chief of Jamaica, and was described by First Sea Lord Lord St Vincent as 'my inestimable Friend'.[8] A print of Thomas Stothard's depiction of Robert's wounding, with William kneeling at Robert's feet, found its way into Brown's family at the time and today still hangs on a descendant's wall in Australia.

While these former associates of Robert found ways to improve their positions, helped by Charles, others foundered, among them the 'flogger' Captain Anthony Molloy. Always short of money, he badgered the Manners family for years. He claimed dramatically that: 'Death would be infinitely more welcome to me than to be thought unworthy of the House of Manners, a name that has ever been from my first knowledge of it, dearer to me than any other.' But his own career would fall apart after his court-martial for disobedience during the Glorious First of June battle, and he was dismissed from the naval service. If a contemporary poem is anything to go by, his marriage to the daughter of the *Ocean*'s Captain Laforey was also in trouble:

> I, Anthony James Pye Molloy
> Can burn, take, sink and destroy;
> There's only one thing I can't do, upon my life!
> And that is, to stop the d-d tongue of my wife.[9]

★

Communications with these men from Robert's past naturally also brought painful reminders of his younger brother, as did the thought of returning to Belvoir, which Charles considered doing but never managed to achieve for the duration of his Irish posting: the numerous duties of his office prevented it. Nevertheless, the castle was often in his thoughts and he corresponded regularly with Hill and Thoroton, whom he had left to oversee the management and finances of the place.

Belvoir Castle was, by now, in a very poor state of repair. Since inheriting the estate, Charles had been up to his neck in war-related expenses, debt and collecting art; he had commissioned Capability Brown's redesigns, but events – not least Robert's death – had caused him to lose interest in the architectural and landscaping projects. Brown had prompted him in 1782 to leave a legacy for future generations, lamenting on 1 October: 'Brown grows very old and nothing done to ornament the castle.' Some works were then set in motion. Thoroton informed Charles later that month that: 'I have minutely lookt for Places to Plant the Lucomb Oaks which Your Grace intends sending to Belvoir... I mean it to be exactly what Brown has drawn in his Plan which I have consulted.' But Brown was indeed growing old; in 1783 he died, with the consequence that the plans to alter Belvoir were largely shelved. With Charles now away in Ireland, Hill, intent on saving money, advised that nothing more should be done other than to 'fasten and secure' the structure, funded by selling timber from the local Barkestone Wood.

Charles in Dublin was kept informed of what modest works did take place. In 1785, Thoroton let him know that the 'Duke's Dressing Room… where Lord Robert's bureau and table stand' had been freshly painted. And, showing sensitivity to Charles's sentiments about his brother, Thoroton added that 'poor John Hodgkins death has left us somewhat in the dark as [to] old wines which are in your cellar. As to your brother's wines and rum, they are all safe, clearly understood, and not a single bottle either has or will be touched.' Belvoir was, Thoroton wrote reassuringly, 'in high beauty as the late rains have given a verdure which is very uncommon at any time of the year'. Perhaps tempted by such evocative reminders of the place, not long afterwards Charles was back to his grandiose schemes. He became friendly with a Dublin architect called Frederick Trench, to whom he showed Brown's plans. In a bid to outdo Capability himself, Trench thought he could 'improve' on them and drew up some new ideas of his own for the castle. Joseph Hill was much against it, arguing the foundations would not support the proposed designs and would cost too much, but Charles in 1786 pressed ahead, insisting that some alterations be initiated in the grounds at least.

Wildly inconsistent, Charles's conduct is open to interpretation. While he loved Belvoir and was mindful of passing on his legacy there, he was incapable of executing any restraint or handling his affairs with maturity. True, he did not lose his family estate on a fall of the dice, as did some of his peers. But he was not far from bankruptcy. The valiant Hill managed to prevent Charles from spending on Belvoir; but from afar he could not control Charles's indulgence in paintings, patronage and much else. Charles needed money from England to pay his expenses in Ireland, as Earl Temple had predicted. Yet, while trying himself to bring in funds through buying lottery tickets, at the same time he was despatching a member of his military staff, George Kendall, to France to secure only the best wines for Dublin Castle, and asking his Eton friend Daniel Pulteney to send over French truffles. An increasingly troubled Hill thought the consumption of food in Ireland 'incredible', the quantity of meat alone 'very sufficient for a Battalion of Foot', before adding deprecatingly: 'But perhaps your Graces Establishment may be equal to one.'

Hill attempted to rein in costs, suggesting, for example, that the Belvoir foxhounds be lent out to 'make a great saving'. He also did what he could to divert estate income to pay off Charles's immense debts. In this manner, one liability of £19,000 was reduced to £10,000. But hitherto unknown debts were emerging too. In 1785, an advertisement was placed in the newspapers asking any unsatisfied creditors of the late Marquis of Granby to come forward. One of these was the old marquis's apothecary, who presented an account for over £1,000, dating from 1769. Desperate for new sources of funds, Hill thought the continuing wrangling over the spoils from St Eustatius would turn up something – for Robert was still owed some prize-money and, he felt, 'Lord Robert's money… it would double in about 15 years – or sooner (in value) if Stocks rise considerably some years hence,' by which time, Hill added wryly, 'Your Grace must be very fond of your Irish Friends if you stay with them until this happens.' Indeed, Hill realized that Robert's legacy could become 'a considerable fund', for he had been doing as Charles had requested and investing the interest on the account. By contrast, the rest of Charles's accounts were 'at present in all other respects very low'. Hill suggested investing Robert's money in a 'Family House in Town' – a good 'Destination for that Fund when it is grown to a proper size'.

Irresponsible though Charles may have been with money, he fared better in oiling the political wheels as viceroy. He succeeded in establishing in law that a Protestant militia could be called upon in case of Catholic rebellion. In 1785, William Pitt proposed removing tariffs thereby creating a British–Irish free-trade area – in effect, a partial union on a commercial basis, bartering Irish freedom of trade for a larger financial contribution to British defence. But the so-called 'Commercial Propositions' raised a storm on both sides of the Irish Sea. Attempts to compromise pleased nobody and the propositions were withdrawn from the Irish Parliament in August 1785. Helpfully, Charles was able to mediate with those around him to calm the situation, and there is no doubt he had a degree of talent for the diplomatic side of his job – even if he was to confide privately to a friend that he was 'getting the potatoes out of the Irishmen's heads'.

Charles did retain his dislike of public speaking, though of course it was unavoidable on occasion. Rather, his skills lay in charming people around him, in listening to them and in his capacity to influence Pitt. While never a statesman of Pitt's calibre, Charles was capable of being a 'shrewd politician',[10] and he was undoubtedly a successful choice of viceroy for that delicate time so soon after the war with America. He was generously open-handed of course, which commended him to the Irish as he ran up debts with tradesmen to build a hospital, and with Frederick Trench for the creation of Dublin's Rutland Square, with its drinking fountain for horses. 'His courage, the affability of his manners, the hospitalities of his table, and the generosity of his disposition, justly acquired him universal popularity,' Sir Nathaniel Wraxall remembered. 'Never was a viceroy more formed to conciliate affection throughout that convivial kingdom.'[11] A contemporary reference to Charles in the *Belfast News Letter*, while opining that he 'possessed no degree of political abilities and was by no means remarkable for attention to business', yet affirmed that:

> ... he possessed all those social qualities which constitute an agreeable companion. And either as a visitor or when presiding at his own board, he was equally pleasing. In company he was somewhat reserved, but always anticipated the wishes of his guests. If the bottle circulated His Grace was never deficient but when alone was remarkably temperate. After dinner if no one was present save the gentlemen in waiting it was customary with him to doze for an hour or two in his chair.[12]

Perhaps Lord Mansfield's and his half-sister Anne's warnings about drinking were having some effect after all.

Charles' friends in England jested he was like a 'king' and would never be allowed home, and indeed Pitt kept him on as viceroy beyond the customary term, even though Charles did express, from time to time, the desire to return to Belvoir. During the remainder of his time in office, Charles refrained from embarking on controversial policies following the failure of Pitt's Commercial Propositions; instead, his time was taken up with the formal business of government and with a task that irked him – the dispensing of patronage to keep the local nobility tame. He told William Pitt's older brother John, the 2nd Earl of Chatham that he preferred hunting and drinking: 'I would rather be at Belvoir breaking my neck all morning, & Bottles & Glasses all the

Evening than Disposing of Bishoprics Peerages, &c, However Pleasant Power & Patronage most certainly is.'[13]

Perhaps the most notable of the patronage requests came from Richard Wellesley, Earl of Mornington, whose younger brother Arthur was in need of employment. Mornington asked Charles in 1786 to consider 'the case of my brother to whom you were so good as to promise a commission in the army'. Early the following year, Charles found Arthur a place in the artillery, but Mornington regarded it as unsuitable; instead, Arthur accepted an offer from Sir George Yonge of an ensigncy in an infantry regiment serving in India, the 73rd Foot, a Highland unit. But Mornington had no intention that Arthur should serve 'under all the disadvantages of that station' and so obtained for him a leave of absence while waiting for Charles to find him something better to give him a 'next step'. In the event, Arthur Wellesley would indeed one day serve in India; but he would go on to distinguish himself as the nemesis of Napoleon and as a future prime minister: the Duke of Wellington.

Chatham was a most loyal friend to Charles all through this time. He also managed some of Charles's political influence in England. The affection between them, embracing a common loss of a much-loved younger brother, was evident in Charles's declaration that:

> ... the Little Ambition I have in my Composition & the great attachment which I bear to yourself & your family bind me to my present Situation as long as I can render Service to our Country & Strengthen your Brother's able and Honourable Government I shall never desert you, & by the strict union which Subsists between us we shall ever mutually assist each other... God Bless you my dear Friend and Love you as much as I do.[14]

In contrast, Daniel Pulteney, who had spent a great deal of time at Belvoir and Cheveley with Charles over the years, became an increasing nuisance, complaining that it would cost Charles 'less than the price of a picture' to help him to stand on his own feet. Although Charles had been fond of him, he now 'found him a very troublesome friend afterwards, and a person who having encouraged it was impossible to get rid of'. Charles still took advantage of the man though, by putting him in the Commons as Member for Bramber, and relying on him

for Westminster gossip and reports of Parliamentary debates over the
still-unresolved St Eustatius prize-money claims.

There were many other old friends and associates to whom Charles
remained loyal. John Ekins, the Eton tutor and a beneficiary of Robert's will, wrote in June 1786: 'You have made me the happiest of men
by the appointment to the Deanery of Salisbury.' After compliment-
ing Charles on hearing the government of Ireland was going well, he
added: 'I have had the addition of a son to my family, whom in remembrance of your dear brother, I have named Robert.' Others Charles
helped included Hannah Hall, who had returned to England after her
husband had died serving in the Rutland Regiment; and the younger
brother of Robert's lieutenant, George Grey, whom Charles took on
as an *aide-de-camp*, as he did the brother of Lord Mulgrave, captain of
the *Courageux* at the Battle of Ushant.

★

If in his treatment of long-standing friends (and friends of Robert)
Charles revealed a nature that was generous and steadfast, his greatest
love and devotion were reserved for his family. He went so far as to
keep his and Mary Isabella's children with them in Ireland, thereby
breaking with the family tradition of sending sons to Eton. Perhaps he
was inspired by his old preceptor John Locke, who thought children
should be raised and treated as children and not as 'little adults' –
though his own memories of a childhood largely separated from his
parents might well have exerted a strong influence too. Their youngest
surviving child was Lord William Robert Albanac Manners, who had
been born in 1783 and was known as 'Billy'. With him, Charles had
finally acceded to his late brother's request to name a son with something reflecting his middle 'Albinine' name.

As for Charles's wife, it is true that he may have found her less
adept in bed than Peg Plunkett; and of Mary Isabella's thick layers of
make-up, the duke once declared: 'I detest it [applied] without mercy',
and pointedly mentioned a lady who wore less, 'which believe me,
'increases her beauty wonderfully'. It was said the duchess wore so
much rouge that she dare not sit too close to the fire in case it melted.
Undeniably too, Peg Plunkett was a symptom of the fact that Mary
Isabella could not fulfil all his needs, as Charles sought, not untypically

of his class, intellectual and physical satisfaction elsewhere. 'Charley' is also reputed to have had an affair with – and possibly a child by – the opera singer Elizabeth Billington during her appearance in Dublin.

Nevertheless, Mary Isabella herself was both the mother of his children and Charles's greatest companion, earning her own form of devotion. She endured his philandering and even became pregnant again, though she miscarried in 1786. And Mary Isabella had many of her own admirers, including Anthony St Leger's nephew, John 'Handsome Jack' Hayes St Leger, who was also living in Ireland. He paid her extravagant compliments, going so far at one dinner party 'to drink the water with which she had just cleaned her teeth'.[15] But in 1787, it appears that Mary Isabella could not remain as tolerant of her husband's affairs as Peg had thought. Professing that she no longer enjoyed being in Ireland, in April she returned to England amid a swirl of speculation as to why. Some said her health had suffered through the continuous entertaining and that she was seeking medical help; others thought that she and Charles had fallen out because he was jealous of the attentions paid to her beauty and irritated that she tried to stop his gambling.

On her return journey to England, she was accompanied by John Glover, who met her from the packet at Holyhead. She took children Diddle, Taty and Billy with her, but left Buffety (John Henry) and his younger brothers Lord Charles and Bob (Lord Robert) behind in Ireland. The trip, which encompassed a visit to Blenheim Palace before arriving in London in early May, where she fell ill, produced an eye-watering bill. Indeed, she might well also have borne some responsibility for the parlous state of the Rutlands' finances. When Joseph Hill learned that he was now to scrape together the means to support two separate Rutland family establishments, he sent a cautionary note to the viceroy: 'Claret is a bad medicine for disorders of the Breast.'

Mary Isabella's absence triggered in Charles a stream of emotional effusions towards his wife. Undoubtedly genuine, perhaps they were also fuelled by guilt. He instructed her to send for Dr Knox – his father's old physician – and wrote often, calling her 'My dearest life', or 'the sweetest girl in the world' and declaring: 'I love you as much or more than I did on our wedding day.' He obsessed about a gumboil she had, in case it should damage her looks, for 'that beautiful mouth deserves every care'. And he felt lonely. 'Alas my dear it is very melancholy to go to bed night after night without you. I lie on your side, but I long to be turned out and sent to the other side of your bed.' Of the young charges left in his care, he informed their mother that: 'The boys are all very well and riotous.' In another letter, he worried in a most fond and tolerant manner that the boys were not attending school and were becoming backward in their reading, for the five-year-old Lord Charles 'should have started Latin and he cannot even read his name'.

On her recovery from her 'indisposition', however, Mary Isabella showed no signs of wishing to return to Ireland. Instead, she busied herself with supporting Charles's political interests in England. On hearing of a proposed visit to Scarborough, Charles wrote poignantly that he hoped 'you will stop for a day or two at Belvoir on your way down to see a place where we have been so happy and where I hope we may be so again'. From England, Charles's friends commented upon the duchess's beauty in their letters to him, and Thomas Gascoigne described her routine as 'swimming before nine, horseriding, at dinner gets regularly drunk then sleeps it off while her hair is being done for the evening's entertainment'. In Gascoigne's eyes, Charles's separation from Mary Isabella was a 'state of widowhood' in which, he surmised, Charles 'must be quite the man *a bonnes fortunes* and I doubt not your sprinkling your seed in many a hotbed'.

In fact, Charles now wanted to go home to see his wife. But he was told he could not, for his absence would leave 'the kingdom... open to cabal and faction', as he explained to Mary Isabella. Perhaps as an antidote to the pain of this physical separation, Charles embarked on a whirlwind tour of his domain, encompassing the north of Ireland. Leaving his sons in Dublin, he rode for up to 70 miles a day between destinations. In three months, he travelled more than 2,000 miles; but it was not only his riding that was intensive. His programme was so gruelling and the social obligations so laced with heavy drinking that a young *aide-de-camp*, Captain Sloper, died of exhaustion, while a string of the horses they rode were simply described as having 'foundered'. Ironically, Sloper had been given the position at the request of his father, who had wanted his son to get the 'same protection that he felt when serving under Granby in Germany'.

This frenetic expedition ended when news arrived of events in the Dutch states, as Prussia intervened to restore Prince William V and his 'Orangists' to power over the rebellious republican 'Patriots', prompting a mass exodus of the latter and a bigger European crisis. Charles was back at his residence in Phoenix Park by the end of September 1787, offering to raise an army from Ireland to fight on behalf of England if required.

Captain Sloper proved not to be the only victim of the Irish tour. Charles himself felt unwell on his return, and a few days later was complaining of a 'bilious fever' and calling for his physicians. Led by a Dr Quin, their opinion was that, after all the hard drinking and hard riding of his three-month excursion, his blood 'was extremely heated'. Over-eating was added to the causes of his distemper, as Charles tossed uncomfortably on his bed. Then, he took a turn for the worse, finding himself unable to get out of bed or even to raise himself. With a sense of foreboding, on 17 October Charles wrote to Mary Isabella to inform her of his illness, signing the letter: 'Adieu my life very your affectionate husband Rutland.'

His doctors now advised a change of air and said he should be sent to Scarborough; but by that time travel was impossible. Charles asked Dr Knox to come over to Ireland and attend him; and he expressed a wish to see Mary Isabella too. Word was sent to England, and she set off on Sunday morning, 21 October, from her mother's house at Stoke, intending to travel day and night to reach him.

Charles knew she would be too late. As he remarked to Quin, 'In point of time it will be impossible. I must therefore be content to die with her image before my mind's eye.' He summoned his sons 'in the most affectionate manner, who were accordingly brought in to take a last leave of their illustrious parent'. Perhaps, in the Manners' tradition, he instructed them to be ready to raise regiments and not to seek political posts for profit rather than duty. Soon after seeing his boys, he became delirious. Neither Mary Isabella nor Knox arrived in time. Charles Manners, 4th Duke of Rutland, died just after nine o'clock on the evening of Wednesday, 24 October 1787. By a strange coincidence, it was also the seventh birthday of his second son, who carried his name.

*

The 4th Duke of Rutland had been just thirty-three years old at his death. Although many thought he had died from exhaustion after his travels, the next morning his body was opened up and his liver was found to have been irreversibly decayed. His remains were placed in a double lead-lined coffin and soldered up.

Three couriers set out on the road to carry the news to Mary Isabella – who was intercepted before reaching Ireland – and to London, where William Pitt and the Home Secretary, Lord Sydney, were the first to receive it that Sunday. For Pitt, this meant more than having to find a new Viceroy of Ireland. As well as being Charles's long-standing friend, he was also an executor of his will and guardian to John Henry, who now became 5th Duke of Rutland at the age of nine.

Charles had always had his critics, but Ireland – and individual Irish men and women – regretted his loss. Unsurprisingly, he was Peg Plunkett's favourite nobleman, both because of his genial personality and his egregious inclusion of her on the pension list. She mourned the 'excellent, generous, noble Rutland, whose like we shall never behold again'.[16] Others were kind too: 'The Duke of Rutland's incessant conviviality deprived... the British peerage of an honourable, generous and high-minded nobleman.'[17]

Three weeks later, at six o'clock in the morning on 17 November 1787, the 'minute guns' in Phoenix Park began to fire and the church bells to ring 'dead peals' – which they kept up for the entire day. Ireland was in mourning. The body of the popular young viceroy left Dublin in a grand procession on its way back to Belvoir Castle. A contemporary account noted that 'funeral honours so magnificent and yet so grave were never paid in any quarter of the globe to the Representative of Majesty. A decent sorrow was visible in every countenance.' No expense had been spared. It was said that 800 pieces of linen were purchased, enough to make 6,000 scarves. The hearse, drawn by eight horses covered with velvet, was followed by a long procession of nobility and dignitaries, with the chief mourners in coaches. They in turn were followed by a detachment of artillery and several battalions of infantry with drums and fifes. Huge crowds of spectators turned out to watch.

The coffin, placed upon His Majesty's yacht *Dorset* and escorted by the frigate *Perseus*, crossed the Irish Sea to Parkgate, near Liverpool, arriving on Sunday evening. And Charles's three boys John Henry, Lord Charles and Lord Robert reached Holyhead on a packet named – appropriately enough – the *Duchess of Rutland*. On the next morning, another grand funeral procession escorted the coffin, this time through Chester and on to Nottingham, arriving on Friday evening. On Saturday, the hearse was finally taken to Belvoir Castle, drawn by six horses with 'the largest and grandest Plumes of black Feathers ever seen on such an Occasion', followed by five mourning coaches and troops of Light Horse. The old Lord Granby's former batman, John Notzell, was present, carrying Charles's coronet on a crimson velvet cushion, his horse led by two pages and supported by soldiers on each side.

During Saturday night, Charles's remains lay in the private chapel at Belvoir Castle. Lit by candles, the chapel had been 'suitably decorated for this mournful occasion'. On Sunday, 'all people of genteel appearance' were allowed to see his corpse lying in state and 'pay their last tribute of respect to so exalted a character' – a man whose clutch of non-hereditary titles alone encompassed Lord Lieutenant and Custos Rotulorum of the County of Leicester, Knight of the Most Noble Order of the Garter, one of His Majesty's Most Honourable Privy Council, Grand Master of the Most Illustrious Order of St Patrick, and, of course, Lord Lieutenant General and General Governor of the Kingdom of Ireland.

On the Sunday evening, the procession reformed as before but with the addition of Charles's favourite horse, Tolbay, at the head. The hunter was draped in black and led by a page on foot; behind it came nearly a hundred of Belvoir's tenants on horseback, wearing white gloves and black hatbands. Charles's body was taken to Bottesford Church where the altar, monuments and pulpit were hung with black cloth. Here, the Reverend Dr Ekins, now Dean of Salisbury, performed the obsequies for the man whom he had spent so much time nurturing, almost as a surrogate parent, and who in return had received his patronage. The number of spectators that jostled outside the church to watch the proceedings was said to be so great 'that many persons lost their hats and several coats and cloaks were torn in the crowd'. The funeral had been organized by John Glover, who had witnessed so many tragedies within the family.

In traditional eighteenth-century deference to 'noble Rutland', verses were written to commemorate Charles's life, one being a 'solil-oquy... wrote in the Chancel of the Church at Bottesford soon after the interment':

> Within a solemn gloomy vault behold I see,
> CHARLES Duke of RUTLAND, aged thirty-three;
> Cropp'd like a flower he wither'd in his bloom,
> Tho' flatt'ring life had promis'd years to come.

A thirteen-verse 'elegy' of rambling flattery stressed traits inherited from his father:

> Friend to affliction and distress,
> Rutland was always known to be;
> Poor widows and the fatherless,
> Now miss his well tim'd charity.

Mary Isabella was said to have been so afflicted by the 'violent shock' of Charles's death that she fell ill, her own life despaired of for a short time. She appeared to forget all Charles's vices and was perhaps consumed with guilt for having left him in Ireland. She went to stay at the seat of Lord George Cavendish, now married to her niece Elizabeth Compton. The *Belfast News* reported that Mary Isabella had 'ordered an urn to be made of pure gold with an elegant device in which the heart of her beloved Duke, whose last sighs breathed conjugal and parental fondness, [was] to be deposited'. Whether his heart actually was extracted from the corpse in the double lead-lined coffin is doubtful; but a lock of his glossy brown hair had been cut off and given to her. She carefully labelled it and placed it in a purse she had embroidered, where it nestled alongside the lock of Robert's hair.

★

On 27 November 1787, a new session of the London Parliament opened. Charles was not mentioned in the king's opening speech, and it was left to Richard Watson, now Bishop of Llandaff, to stand up in the House of Lords and say some words to mark his friend's death:

> The world, My Lords, was not aware of his ability, was not conscious of half his worth; I had long and just experience of

them both. In the conduct of public affairs, his judgement was
equalled, I verily believe, by few men of his years; his probity and
disinterestedness were, I am confident, exceeded by none. [He
had] a liberal spirit [and] noble tendency – not that of aggrandiz-
ing Great Britain by the ruin of Ireland, not that of building up
Ireland at the expense of Great Britain – but that of promoting
the united interests of both countries, as essential parts of one
common empire.

He went on to say that: 'In private life, My Lords, [he imitated] his
illustrious father in the practice of one [his] most characteristic principles – in being alive to every impulse of compassion. His family, his
friends, his dependants, all his connections can witness for me the
warmth and sincerity of his personal attachments… His memory I
trust, will be long, long revered by the people of this country [and]
long held dear by the people of Ireland.'

The speech was well received by the House, and Richard Watson
was later thanked by the Prince of Wales for expressing such fulsome
sentiments. Kind, generous, loyal, vulnerable to sycophants, hopeless
with money, but in his heart always well-meaning, Charles had perhaps managed to turn out 'Surprisingly Good', as his grandmother
would have had it. At a fragile time in Ireland's history, he had risen to
the occasion in the last three years of his life, proving to have the diplomatic skills required. Within a little more than a decade after his death,
Ireland would experience something quite different: violent rebellion
and French invasion, before Irish MPs voted their own Parliament out
of existence – and ushered in years of decline. But Charles had always
lived in his father's shadow. Even when given the Freedom of the City
of Carrickfergus in 1786, he was told that 'the lustre of the patriotic
heroism of the Marquis of Granby your late father, which remains
bright in the recollection of every member of the British Empire…
gives your Grace a just claim to the gratitude and attachment of the
nation'.

Charles also never seemed to recover fully from the death of his
younger brother. It disturbed what his contemporaries would have
called 'the tranquillity of his mind' and fuelled the self-indulgent
pleasures to which his position in society provided such easy access.

Perhaps Charles, always conscious of Robert's naval achievements, felt keenly Samuel Johnson's opinion that 'every man thinks meanly of himself for not having been a soldier, or not having been to sea'. His own efforts at serving with the militia cannot have redressed the balance, for the scales were too much weighted in the other direction. Charlotte Somerset had been right when she predicted that 'according to my notion of Bob he will be considerable at sea'. And, at the other end of Robert's life, Rockingham had told Charles with all the hyperbole of the age: 'No young man ever rose faster to a high pitch of honour, repute and glory in his profession than your beloved brother.' Such a legacy left brother 'Charley', with his distractions, his amiability, his easy propensity for a jolly whore, his wit and his avoidance of exertion to enter history with little more than his ducal coronet.

Just days after his death, on 13 November 1787, the *Belfast News Letter* reminded its readers:

> The late Duke of Rutland's only brother, Lord Robert Manners, was in the Navy and continued in that service until April 12 1782 when his Grace received at Belvoir the melancholy news of his brother's death. He was for some time stupefied with grief, was long inconsolable and never perfectly recovered the loss he and his family had sustained...[18]

Even in death, Charley was overshadowed by Bob.

17

Epilogue:
'The dear old chateau'

1787 TO 1816 TO TODAY

'The dear old chateau'

I n December 1795, the seventeen-year-old John Henry Manners, 5th Duke of Rutland, rode up the steep hill to Belvoir Castle. He had not been back there since his father Charles's funeral, almost half his life-time ago; now he wanted to make the castle his principal home and to revive the plans for repair and alterations he knew his father had abandoned.

The old place was by now in a 'miserable plight', virtually unoccupied for a decade, its interiors uncared for, the furniture covered in dusty cotton, the paintings hanging mournfully, their gilt frames dulled, the corridors dark and forbidding, and the servants' quarters crusty with flaking paint. Even the private Chapel was described as 'shabby'. Various odd items had been randomly left as if in want of somewhere proper to put them: 'three bed-horses' stood in the Picture Gallery, while outside Diddle's room, in the Long Passage, eight cases of books lay unpacked. The harpsichord once played by Charles and Robert's mother had been shoved into a closet at one end of the Music Room; the cues and balls in the Billiard Room lay idle, untouched. No rustle of silk gowns, no gaiety, no laughter, no surge of welcoming conversation had graced the castle's halls since Charles had departed, 'stupefied by grief', eleven years earlier, and the housekeeper in the meanwhile had been of 'a very drunken, dawdling appearance'. A visitor had noted in 1789 that: 'Out of doors there [were] no Improvements, no Pleasure Grounds... not a Rose Bush to be seen; as if for the last 100 years all had been left to Ruin.'[1]

For John Henry, the castle was a stark memorial to his father and uncle. Its gloomy interior was redolent of their lives; even Charles's

childhood model ship from Scarborough sat there, dust-covered, in
an alcove up the Best Stairs. Some of Lord Robert's brightly coloured
signal flags were still draped along the passageway and up the staircase
leading to the Picture Gallery; the rest of them lay in a bundle in the
Armoury closet. His mahogany writing desk containing his personal
papers was in the duke's Dressing Room. His bottles of wine, rum and
brandy lay untouched in the cellar.

The Long Gallery contained sculptures – the busts by Nollekens,
Wilton's bust of the 1st Lord Chatham and Ceracchi's of Admiral Keppel, all standing on their columns as ossified reminders of Charles's
interest in these prominent figures of his day. One – perhaps that of
Robert – stood alone in a passage leading to the Nursery Rooms,
where John Henry had lain in his cradle before the family had gone
to Ireland. The Armoury contained 28 pistols and 116 Brown Bess
muskets from the 1730s; 3 swivel guns and 292 iron 'mortuary pattern'
swords from the Civil War, 192 brass-hilted swords and 7 stands of
military colours (of which 4 of the dirty silk standards were from the
Rutland Regiment). In an underground chamber nicknamed 'Hell',
eight militia drums had been piled, and on the ground floor were three
Mudge fumigators.

The number of paintings in the house, many of them the result
of Charles's ferocious collecting, was immense. There were seventy-
three in the Picture Gallery, forty-one (along with fifty miniatures) in
the Drawing Room, six 'old paintings' in the Musick Room, eleven
in Charles's and Mary Isabella's old bedroom, thirteen in the Marble
Hall, twenty-eight stored in a closet and forty-eight lining the Best
Stairs. As a visitor observed, 'with judgement, for finer pictures are
not to be seen; but they are all tost about in confusion'. In the Long
Gallery were twenty-two pictures, 'a wonderful collection of ancient
and modern skill', though 'not yet hung up', while 'a large room like
an auctioneer's room, leading from this is filled by fine paintings, piled
about at all corners'.[2]

The Poussins were in the Great Yellow Room; the Rubens, Murillos and Henry VIII hung in the Best Dining Room, and the eyes of
Van der Eyden's nine Earls of Rutland gazed down upon John Henry
as he made his slow inspection of his ancestral pile, just as they had
stared down upon young Charles and Robert before him. In time, John

Henry would come across the 'two evidence rooms which are very curious and one whose contents have entertained us much being full of old letters from all our great grandfathers and grandmothers for many generations back of Dukes and Earls of Rutland and of their wives etc'; but for the time being, he formed his resolve to implement the shelved plans of his father, quietly vowing to create a new vision for the castle and grounds.

*

After Charles's funeral in November 1787, Mary Isabella had settled in London, sending her boys to school in Ealing. She did not remarry, though she appears to have maintained an intimacy with John Hayes St Leger. John Henry's maternal grandmother, the Dowager Duchess of Beaufort, told the young duke that as he was 'deprived of a father [he] must act a good one to his brothers' – though these were fewer in number after the youngest, 'Billy', died aged ten in 1793. Holidays were spent at Ramsgate and Southampton, where the young John Henry, inspired by his 'heroic' Uncle Robert, developed a love of the sea. Picking up a pebble from the beach one day he pocketed it, took it home and made it his personal seal.

By the 1790s, the sea was once again uppermost in the national consciousness as France felt the brisk wind of change from across the Atlantic. Bankrupt from the American war – and suffering poor harvests and a rising tide of discontent among the 'third estate', resentful of burdensome taxation – France dissolved into revolution and another new republic was born, destabilizing the whole of Europe. In 1793, following the revolutionaries' guillotining of King Louis XVI and his Austrian wife, Britain was drawn back into war with its neighbour across the Channel. In that year, too, the 'Three Captains' monument was at last completed after remaining covered for eleven years while William Pitt had dragged his feet on deciding the final wording for its inscription. It was eventually unveiled just in time to inspire naval officers – both contemporaries of Robert and those newly commissioned – as they jostled for command in this new conflict.

John Henry, having already inherited, had no need of a career, naval or otherwise. He went up to Cambridge but left in 1794, unsurprisingly more interested in taking on his family seat at Belvoir and involving himself in the family's political interests. During his minority, the Belvoir estate was managed under the loyal partnership of Joseph Hill and Thomas Thoroton, and after the latter's death in 1794 by Thoroton's son, Sir John. Mary Isabella's brother, the 5th Duke of Beaufort, also held a significant advisory role. These men took care of inherited family obligations too, and both Mrs Mompesson and the old hussar Notzell received annuities until their deaths in 1799 and 1804 respectively.

The son of Charles and Robert's long-estranged sister Frances, 'Poor Little Leslie', was also taken care of. Frances herself died in 1793. Some forty years later, her portrait by Hugh Douglas Hamilton, which Charles had commissioned in 1772, was returned to the family along with a letter from William Jeffs, the son of a couple who were friends with her. Jeffs begged acceptance of the picture, describing Frances as a decent person 'pitied' by his parents, who in the 'unfortunate circumstances of her life' was 'most assuredly far more sinned against than sinning'.

In the wake of John Henry's resolution to reoccupy the castle, Mary Isabella began to stay at Belvoir once again, calling it 'the dear old chateau' and, indeed, staying so long that her brother was 'afraid she will trim the old port'. John Henry's ambitions for Belvoir were, for now, stalled by Hill and guardians Beaufort and Pitt, who reminded him he had no money to spare, since paying off his father's debtors was the first priority. Still only eighteen, John Henry was soon diverted. In 1798 he was obliged to sail for Ireland at the head of the Leicestershire Militia, which was required as a reinforcement in suppressing the French-backed rebellion of the United Irishmen, led by the Protestant republican Wolfe Tone. The news of his departure struck his mother 'like a thunderbolt'. In Ireland, John Henry found himself serving under none other than Charles, Earl Cornwallis, now Viceroy of Ireland – to Mary Isabella's delight, who remarked that Cornwallis 'was an elève and great friend of Lord Granby's and from that a great friend of your father's'. It was one of her rare references to her late husband. But she added a warning – with its own veiled reference to the 4th Duke – that John Henry should not allow the 'kind and hospitable welcome I know you will find in Dublin induce you to drink too much'.

On his return from Ireland, John Henry married Elizabeth Howard, second daughter of the Earl of Carlisle; and then, on 4 January 1799, he finally came of age. The event was celebrated by a huge party at Belvoir, with illuminations in every window and fireworks sparkling and shooting into the sky from the roof. Attaining his majority – not to mention marriage – freed John Henry from constraint, and he could now begin to realize his ambitions for the estate. That November, he employed a relative of the distinguished architect James Wyatt to draw up plans for the refurbishment of Belvoir, plans which caused Mary Isabella to rejoice that they 'will not be very expensive' and 'will not destroy the original and famous old walls which would have quite broke my heart and yet it will by all accounts be very comfortable and handsome'. She was not keen on *all* the ideas for the 'dear old castle', for she did not 'quite like the idea of every room having a balcony'.

The first task was to demolish the 3rd Duke's external Picture Gallery, the work beginning in earnest in 1801; but notions of inexpensive alterations soon evaporated. The new Duchess of Rutland had grown up amid the splendours of her father's great house, Castle Howard in Yorkshire, and she had grander ideas than her husband. The newlyweds soon engaged James Wyatt himself, who was joined by Frederick Trench junior, whom John Henry had met in Ireland and who came over to Belvoir. He remained a life-long friend. An ambitious scheme was conjured up to create a spectacular fairy-tale Regency country home, with turrets and towers. Sir John Thoroton was drawn in, and Capability Brown's plans for the landscaping of adjacent parkland were brought out and pored over, elements of them adopted to realize Elizabeth's vision for the castle's surroundings. James Wyatt's elaborate scheme incorporated some of the old foundations and the castle's former skewed-quadrilateral footprint, in combination with some of the younger Trench's ideas. From 1801, the castle was rebuilt, wing-by-wing, and augmented on the south wing with a large Round Tower, said to have been inspired by the one at Windsor Castle.

Some way had to be found to finance such grandiose plans. But the family finances had improved vastly in the years before John Henry came of age. There had been the business of paying off his father's debts, of which Irish liabilities alone were said to have amounted to

£30,000. Most of this money was owed to tradesmen. But at least the young duke had had his team of executors and guardians at hand to help matters. The executors of the will, including William Pitt (to whom Charles left £3,000), discovered a special instruction inserted by Charles in 1782, directing them to keep open Lord Robert's bank account until John Henry reached maturity. During that time it was to be managed, re-invested and eventually used to buy land in Leicestershire or within 10 miles from Belvoir Castle, specifically for the benefit of John Henry or, in the case of his premature demise, the oldest living son. Prize-money from the *Ocean*, *Victory*, *Alcide*, *Resolution* and from St Eustatius, the Navy Bonds, the South Sea annuities and other stocks had been found to be, at Charles's death, worth a handsome £24,000: they were the most valuable of all Charles's liquid assets, which otherwise ranged from between £1,000 and £8,000. It seemed that, despite his spendthrift tendencies and his desperation, Charles had never touched his dead brother's treasure – a measure perhaps of his deep respect for Robert.

And so, all the time that John Henry was a minor, Hill and the executors had been quietly carrying out Charles's directions, re-investing Robert's funds and securing what they could from the St Eustatius prize-money – though that process would drag on for years yet. They also tied up some loose ends, in 1790 paying Sir Chaloner Ogle for the table linen he had sold Robert, and closing Robert's account with his prize-agents Ommaney & Page by transferring the balance to their executors' account held by Snow & Denne. Due diligence almost cleared up both old Granby's and Charles's debts – though several mortgages were still outstanding, awaiting John Henry's majority. The long hiatus had allowed those men responsible – Hill, Thoroton *et al.* – to avoid excessive and profligate expenditure, removing much of the debt and encumbrance.

Now, however, John Henry's new freedom combined with the imprudent ambitions of his headstrong duchess threatened to undermine all their hard work. His advisers therefore confronted him with reality: despite the achievements on his behalf, a decision was made to sell outlying land in Yorkshire and Nottinghamshire to clear outstanding mortgages and to raise capital to finance the grand reconstruction plans. And, when John Henry had turned twenty-one, Uncle Robert's account had been finally closed down. It is perhaps ironic that Robert's was the largest of the family investment funds available to the young duke. It was, by 1799, worth £81,000. The money was used – in accordance with Charles's will – to acquire the village of Eastwell and some nearby land, all within 10 miles of the castle. The purchase of a corner of the English Midlands with prize-money from the American War of Independence seemed a fitting outcome.

Thus, against a background of what would become the long national struggle with Revolutionary and Napoleonic France, the rebuilding of Belvoir proceeded. Although John Henry benefitted from Robert's financial legacy, he found he could not escape his uncle's moral legacy, too, as Robert's heroic end continued to prompt the appeals from those in distress. In 1811, Captain Sir Michael Seymour tugged at the 5th Duke's heartstrings on behalf of his own brother who 'fell in action... and did not survive the amputation of his left thigh and breathed his last nearly in the same manner that your Grace's noble and heroic uncle did, whose memory the service must ever cherish'. Soliciting money, Seymour was embarrassed about discussing so 'delicate' a subject and offered in return a portrait of Robert as a midshipman, painted by his friend the artist Robert Home when they were together on the *Alborough* in Newfoundland, under Captain James Hawker. (Seymour had married Hawker's daughter, while Home, having been a pupil of the artist Angelika Kauffman, had become a notable portrait-painter.) A year later, John Henry received a petition from Thomas Noon, the man struck by the same ball that hit Robert. Down on his luck, Noon was now a sixty-one-year-old widower with a second family of very young children. John Henry authorized Joseph Hill to give the man 'a chaldron of coals'.

Meanwhile, the duke acquired seven cannon from Robert's 1780 capture, the *Prothee*. In September 1795, the old ship had been 'reduced' and converted into a prison-hulk, moored in Portsmouth Harbour for the detention of French prisoners-of-war. Hearing of this, John Henry was able to purchase at auction several of her guns, made by the French gun-caster J Berenger in Strasbourg in 1758 – by strange coincidence the year Robert was born. They were brought to Belvoir and in due course placed on the newly constructed terrace, their muzzles dominating the steep ascent to the castle's new entrance.

Tho.ˢ Noon aged 61 — a Widower
with three Children vizᵗ

Henry Noon aged 6 years
Thomas Noon aged 4 Years
Ann Noon aged 9 Years

Served under Lord Robᵗ Mannexs
3 Years & had his arm shot away
on the 12ᵗʰ April 1782 supposed
to be with the same Shot that
struck his Lordship —

Daughter by 1.ˢᵗ Wife 29 —
lives with him & looks after
the Children —
Can do nothing else

9 July 1812 On presenting this to the Duke
of Rutland, his Grace authorized me to assist Noon
by advancing him &c. would purchase a Children of
Coals & measures to retail at out as an addᵗ to his Subsistence.

A note in the hand of Charles's lawyer Joseph Hill, July 1812,
responding to a request for help from seaman Thomas Noon, who
was maimed by the same cannon-ball that wounded Robert.

By the time Napoleon was definitively vanquished in June 1815, three of Belvoir's new wings had been completed, and only the north-east wing, in which Charles and Robert had stayed as children, had yet to be started. But the next year, on the night of 24 October 1816, the whole of the new north-west and the old north-east wings were burnt down, in a fire that also consumed the Serres paintings of the battles of the Saintes and St Kitts, Robert's writing desk containing Charles's letters to him, the Dance portraits of Robert, and many other treasures, including several important works by Reynolds. Luckily, Sir Joshua's full-length portrait of Robert was saved, having been in Diddle's room; so too were the Poussins – all but one, which mysteriously disappeared, probably stolen. Also escaping destruction among the paintings were the portraits of the nine earls of Rutland, of King Henry VIII, of King John and Magna Carta, as well as the Murillos, the Gerard Dow and a Rubens, the Delanes, and the Stubbs and Gainsboroughs. Suspicions swirled in the aftermath of the conflagration. At a time of post-war demobilization, unemployment, rising bread prices and economic dislocation, there was widespread hardship and unrest in the country. It was strongly believed by staff, tenants and local villagers that the fire was not accidental. Arson could not be proved, though everyone on the Belvoir estate was interviewed and asked if they had seen strange characters in the vicinity. Someone said that there would be 'a lot more of this before the winter is out – burning of great houses'.

Undaunted, John Henry and Elizabeth turned to the task of rebuilding the two ruined north wings. But for the 5th Duke of Rutland there was further family tragedy, in the devastating death of his wife in 1825, aged forty-five. He never married again, and she had not lived to see the completion of the great Elizabeth saloon that would be named after her, in the Roos Tower, which formed part of the new north-east wing. It was Sir John Thoroton who stepped in to help complete the castle, adding, in his own style, the Ballroom and the Portico inspired by Lincoln Cathedral. A mausoleum was built in the grounds, where Elizabeth's body was placed, along with those of Charles, Lord and Lady Granby, and the nine-year-old John, all of whose remains were removed there from Bottesford Church.

The ageing Mary Isabella – now unkindly referred to by some as Mary 'Was-a-bella' – had her own rooms in the castle until she died in

1831. Also with rooms in the castle was John Henry's great friend the Duke of Wellington. John Henry's two younger brothers, Lord Charles and Lord Robert, had served under him as lieutenant generals during the Peninsular Campaign (1809–14) and at Waterloo in 1815. Another regular visitor was John Pitt, 2nd Earl of Chatham, who became a close friend and possibly something of a father-figure to John Henry. He was lent Cheveley to use as his home for many years. While France and Napoleon had threatened Europe, both Pitt brothers had played their parts in the nation's story – William pre-eminently, who, as prime minister, transformed British politics and rebuilt the navy before his early death in 1806; and to a lesser extent John, who, though somewhat indolent (like Charles), was First Lord of the Admiralty before holding other positions in the ministry. Unfortunately, Chatham's reputation was severely battered by military disaster off the Netherlands in 1809, in which thousands of troops died of sickness. But it was he who said 'few feel as you do on the loss of Nelson', after Trafalgar in 1805, which reminded John Henry so much of his own uncle's heroic end.

At the time of Robert's death, Richard Watson had written that the nature of it 'secured him from the oblivion which waits upon the many millions who in every century take their turns upon this stage of human life and depart undistinguished by the performance of any actions eminently great or good'. Yet, Robert's memory was eclipsed, like that of so many of his generation, by a succession of British naval victories in the Revolutionary and Napoleonic wars made possible by officers who had been blooded in the American war, and none more so than Vice Admiral Horatio, Viscount Nelson of the Nile. Picking up where Rodney had left off, at Cape Trafalgar on 21 October 1805, Nelson broke the enemy's battle line multiple times. Had Lord Robert lived, he too would doubtless have embraced the new naval orthodoxy, and perhaps become a distinguished exponent of it. Following Nelson's death at Trafalgar, the Honourable George Grey – once the boy so speedily promoted by Robert – commanded the vessel *Chatham* bearing his mortal remains up the Thames to Greenwich. There they lay in state until their interment, in St Paul's Cathedral in January 1806, in a ceremony overseen by Charles's and Robert's cousin Charles Manners-Sutton, Archbishop of Canterbury. Nelson's *Victory* survived, as she does to this day in Portsmouth Harbour, defined by her association with the pre-eminent naval man and Trafalgar rather than the American war – though she is the only surviving ship from that earlier struggle.

A love of the sea remained with the 5th Duke of Rutland throughout his life. After the peace of 1815, he commissioned the building of a large and very beautiful yacht, which, in his uncle's honour, he named *Resolution*, fitting her with a figurehead of Cleopatra and her deadly asp. He enjoyed many enchanting voyages in her, accompanied by his friend the marine artist John Christian Schekty. Sailing, as John Henry noted in his diary, was a good way of finding peace and solitude away from the intensity of social and political obligations, and he continued to sail up until his death in 1857.

★

In the twentieth century, the Manners family had to sell much of the land surrounding Belvoir to pay death duties and to finally discharge debts that were still outstanding from the reconstruction – the last stonemason's bill was not paid until 1940. But today, Belvoir Castle remains much as it was when rebuilt under John Henry and stands as one of the finest examples of a grand Regency home, its interior largely unaltered.

Charles in particular, but Robert too, remain bound up in this incarnation of the castle, even though they did not live to see it take shape. Were it not for Charles's obsessive collecting, its walls would not be adorned with so many magnificent artworks or its library so full of interesting books. Even some of his Rutland Regiment colours hang to this day in the castle's Guard Room, almost disintegrated but with '86th' still just visible. A few mementoes of Robert also remain: the tiny model of the *Resolution* and his drawing of her 'head', his sword, his books, and Surgeon Blair's grim tools used to amputate his shattered leg, a stark reminder of what so many naval men endured. Some of Robert's bottles lie, even now, untouched in the cellar. His captured French cannon stand upon the terrace, and the lock of his hair lies with that of Charles in the purse that was, as a note within states, 'embroidered by my dear wife 1781'. In the purse, too, is a newspaper clipping describing Charles as the 'idol of Ireland'.

United in death, the two brothers' ends were as great a contrast as their lives. Charles, remembered, mainly for his amiability exceeded only by his extravagance, had a reputation, summed up by the Duke of Leinster, as a man who 'provided he gets his skin full of claret, he cares little about anything else'.[3] He had an indolent nature, of that there is no doubt. He was also an emotional character, torn between 'virtue and pleasure', a victim to the rise of 'luxury' Georgian society. Today, addictions such as gambling and alcohol are classed as diseases, but to a late-eighteenth-century Georgian they were moral lapses. Yet, his public persona hid his private self. While primogeniture delivered to him the title and the estate, it also wrapped around him a strait-jacket of dynastic responsibility, which could be at odds with other expectations of the role he was expected to play. In Charles's ostensible political apathy, he was governed by the desire to uphold his title and his family legacy. The result was that he could never wholeheartedly support a potentially treasonable political opposition. In some ways, he showed presence of mind in resisting – as his grandmother had demanded – the pull of political faction. And even Horace Walpole, a man so often critical of others, said of Charles: 'I am not acquainted with his grace, but I respect his behaviour; he is above prejudices.'[4] But still, his heart was with those whose strategy, though not coherent enough to prevent bloodshed in America, had a hand in 'liberty' and American independence.

By contrast, aristocratic younger sons had more freedom to be architects of their own lives – though it was often a necessity. It was the more reserved yet ambitious younger brother Robert whose 'resolu-tion' shone through. He created his own wealth by serving and saving, and he achieved a place in the nation's consciousness in a monument positioned in the North Transept of Westminster Abbey, alongside the memorials of the more famous elder and younger Pitt and his relative Lord Mansfield. Robert's part in Admiral Rodney's great victory over de Grasse achieved for him the eighteenth-century 'desire of fame, the applause of men directed to the end of public happiness'. He took risks in naval engagements, to be sure. Yet, though the boundaries between the code of honour and overambition are difficult to determine, he did his duty and that was an honourable alternative to earning a vast fortune through prize-money and he was deemed worthy of the early opportunities he demanded by birth-right. In the words of Richard Watson: 'Green in years, mature in glory… he took care that the short fate which God had allotted him should not be a period of inactivity and oblivion.'

Both Charles and Robert never quite escaped their father's shadow. But both, in their own ways and different legacies, lived up to Capability Brown's words to Charles in late 1782: 'Since it is denied us to live long, let us do something to shew we have lived.'

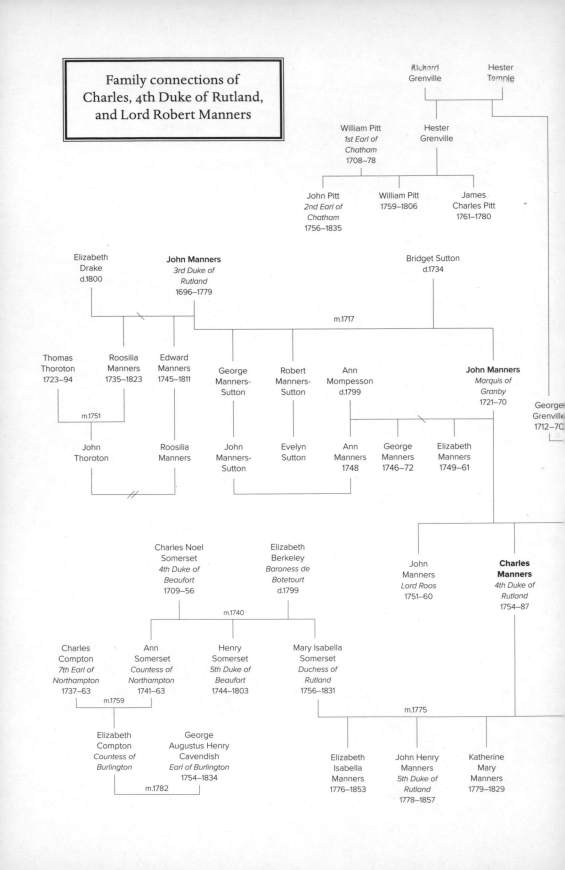

Family connections of
Charles, 4th Duke of Rutland,
and Lord Robert Manners

Richard Grenville — Hester Temple

William Pitt
1st Earl of Chatham
1708–78

Hester Grenville

John Pitt
2nd Earl of Chatham
1756–1835

William Pitt
1759–1806

James Charles Pitt
1761–1780

Elizabeth Drake
d.1800

John Manners
3rd Duke of Rutland
1696–1779

Bridget Sutton
d.1734

m.1717

Thomas Thoroton
1723–94

Roosilia Manners
1735–1823

Edward Manners
1745–1811

George Manners-Sutton

Robert Manners-Sutton

Ann Mompesson
d.1799

John Manners
Marquis of Granby
1721–70

George Grenville
1712–70

m.1751

John Thoroton

Roosilia Manners

John Manners-Sutton

Evelyn Sutton

Ann Manners
1748

George Manners
1746–72

Elizabeth Manners
1749–61

Charles Noel Somerset
4th Duke of Beaufort
1709–56

Elizabeth Berkeley
Baroness de Botetourt
d.1799

John Manners
Lord Roos
1751–60

Charles Manners
4th Duke of Rutland
1754–87

m.1740

Charles Compton
7th Earl of Northampton
1737–63

Ann Somerset
Countess of Northampton
1741–63

Henry Somerset
5th Duke of Beaufort
1744–1803

Mary Isabella Somerset
Duchess of Rutland
1756–1831

m.1759

m.1775

Elizabeth Compton
Countess of Burlington

George Augustus Henry Cavendish
Earl of Burlington
1754–1834

Elizabeth Isabella Manners
1776–1853

John Henry Manners
5th Duke of Rutland
1778–1857

Katherine Mary Manners
1779–1829

m.1782

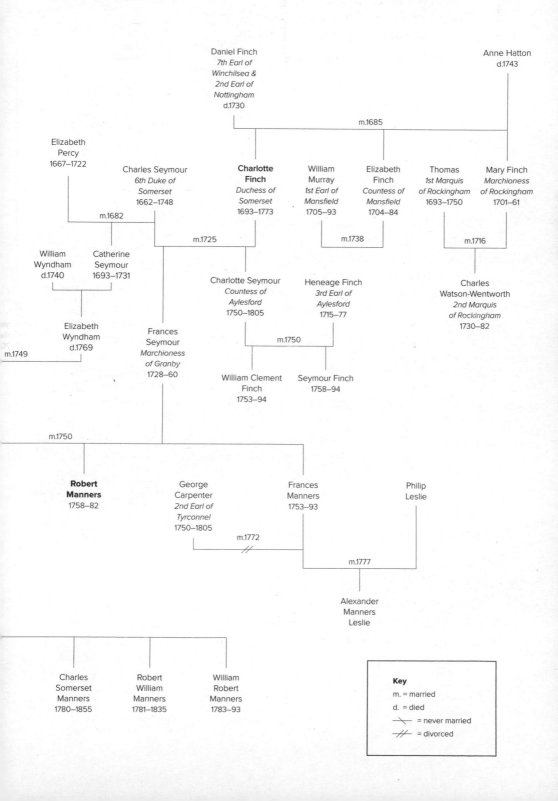

Daniel Finch
*7th Earl of
Winchilsea &
2nd Earl of
Nottingham*
d.1730

Anne Hatton
d.1743

m.1685

Elizabeth
Percy
1667–1722

Charles Seymour
*6th Duke of
Somerset*
1662–1748

**Charlotte
Finch**
*Duchess of
Somerset*
1693–1773

William
Murray
*1st Earl of
Mansfield*
1705–93

Elizabeth
Finch
*Countess of
Mansfield*
1704–84

Thomas
*1st Marquis
of Rockingham*
1693–1750

Mary Finch
*Marchioness
of Rockingham*
1701–61

m.1682

m.1725

m.1738

m.1716

William
Wyndham
d.1740

Catherine
Seymour
1693–1731

Charlotte Seymour
*Countess of
Aylesford*
1750–1805

Heneage Finch
*3rd Earl of
Aylesford*
1715–77

Charles
Watson-Wentworth
*2nd Marquis
of Rockingham*
1730–82

Elizabeth
Wyndham
d.1769

Frances
Seymour
*Marchioness
of Granby*
1728–60

m.1750

m.1749

William Clement
Finch
1753–94

Seymour Finch
1758–94

m.1750

**Robert
Manners**
1758–82

George
Carpenter
*2nd Earl of
Tyrconnel*
1750–1805

Frances
Manners
1753–93

Philip
Leslie

m.1772

m.1777

Alexander
Manners
Leslie

Charles
Somerset
Manners
1780–1855

Robert
William
Manners
1781–1835

William
Robert
Manners
1783–93

Key

m. = married

d. = died

⟋ = never married

⫽ = divorced

Glossary

The use of SMALL CAPITALS below refers to words and phrases with their own definitions in the glossary.

Admiral. A flag-officer, i.e., senior officer in command of a group of ships. He was distinguished by flying a flag appropriate to his rank as either a rear, vice or full admiral. For administrative purposes, the seniority list of admirals went in ascending order from rear admiral of the blue, white, red, to vice admiral of the blue, white, red, then up to admiral of the blue, white, red. The admiral of the red was admiral of the fleet. Admirals flew a square flag of the appropriate colour on their MASTS to distinguish their rank: a rear admiral's from the mizzen mast, a vice admiral's from the foremast, and a full admiral's from the mainmast. All the men-of-war commanded by POST-CAPTAINS under the operational control of an admiral flew an ENSIGN appropriate to the flag-colour of the admiral under whose immediate command they came.

Admiralty, the (Board of). The body that translated the strategic wishes of the Cabinet into reality. It issued regulations, ordered the building of ships and decided at which station each ship would serve.

Aft. The rear of the vessel, and thus the opposite of 'forward'. 'Going aft' implies moving towards the rear.

Anchors. A man-of-war carried several anchors, the heaviest of which was the sheet anchor carried in the middle of the upper deck. The usual working anchors were the 'best bower', kept in readiness on the STARBOARD BOW, and the 'small bower' stowed on the LARBOARD (port) BOW.

Back a sail/yard. To reverse a sail/YARD, so that the wind blows onto the forward surface of the canvas, thus arresting the movement of the ship.

Bar-shot. Two cannonballs with sliding bars between them, which on discharge expanded and whirled through the air to damage the sail, masts and rigging of an enemy vessel.

Batten down. To close and secure hatches and other openings in the deck.

Beat to quarters. To call the crew to action-stations by drum.

Bilges. The inside of the bottom of a ship.

Binnacle. The cabinet in front of the ship's wheel, housing the compass.

Boarding-pike. A short spear ranged at the base of MASTS, which could be seized by seamen in the event of having to defend themselves against an enemy who was boarding.

Bomb-vessel. A ship carrying a heavy mortar.

Bow. The forward part of a ship.

Bowsprit. The SPAR protruding from the bow to support the foremast stays.

Brace. To swivel the YARDS into different angles in order to trim the sails to the wind direction. The term 'braces' also referred to the tackles used to 'brace' the yards round.

Broadside. The simultaneous firing of all the guns on one side of a ship.

Bulwark. The side-rails of the ship, protruding up above the level of the upper deck.

Bum-boat. A small boat used to ferry supplies to ships moored away from the shore.

Cable. The thick rope that attached the ship to its anchor.

Captain. *See* POST-CAPTAIN.

Captain of the Fleet. The officer on a flagship who assisted the ADMIRAL when he had ten or more ships to command. It was a post, not a rank, and the admiral would issue his orders to the rest of the fleet through him.

Carronade. A short-barrelled gun named after the Carron Company of Stirlingshire, Scotland. It was used to cause maximum damage at close range, as it carried a heavier ball than carriage guns of a similar calibre. It was usually mounted on a slide.

Catharpings. Ropes in the upper part of the lower rigging for the purpose of supporting the MASTS to tension them. When the YARDS were braced at a sharp angle to enable the ship to sail towards the wind, they would come up against the catharpings.

Chain-shot. Two cannonballs chained together, which, like BAR-SHOT, spun on discharge to injure the MASTS and rigging of an enemy vessel.

Chronometer. A timepiece capable of keeping accurate time despite the motion of a ship at sea (and thus allowing LONGITUDE to be calculated).

Colours. A ship's national ENSIGN, which she 'wore'; all other flags were 'flown'.

Commodore. The senior captain among a group whose ships were acting in concert. It was a temporary appointment, rather than a rank as it is today.

Courses. The lowest sails on the MASTS (fore course, main course).

Cutlass. A crude form of sword issued to seamen in action.

Cutter. In this context, one of the smaller of a man-of-war's pulling boats.

Ensign. The national flag flown at the STERN (= the COLOURS).

First/1st lieutenant. The commissioned officer next in seniority to the captain, who assumed command in the event of the latter's incapacity.

First-rate ship. A SHIP OF THE LINE with three gun-decks, carrying 100 guns or more.

Flag-captain. The captain actually commanding an ADMIRAL's flagship, and so distinct from the CAPTAIN OF THE FLEET.

Flag-officer/Flag rank. Synonyms signifying an ADMIRAL.

Fleet. Either a large group of ships comprising two or more squadrons under a senior ADMIRAL, or a nation's combined strength of men-of-war.

Frigate. A rated ship of at least twenty-eight guns, used as a scouting vessel and for the repeating of signals in battle, but without a place in the line of battle.

General quarters. An announcement signalling that all HANDS aboard a ship should go to battle-stations as quickly as possible.

Grape-shot. MUSKET balls and small ROUND SHOT fired from a gun in a bag, as anti-personnel ammunition.

Gun-room. A MESS for the WARRANT OFFICERS and MIDSHIPMEN, usually presided over (during this period) by the gunner as one of the senior warrant officers, hence the name.

Halyards. Ropes used to raise or lower the YARDS, or to hoist signalling flags.

Hands. The seamen and landsmen on a vessel who worked a ship; synonymous with 'the people'.

Head. Either (a) the forward section of the ship, or (b) the place where men could go to the lavatory.

Holystone. To scrub or scour the decks with a piece of soft sandstone.

Hove-to and **heave-to.** A combination of drawing and backed sails, which had the effect of holding the ship more or less stationary in the water, so that she might lower or hoist a boat. Also, to ride out strong winds and heavy seas under a minimum of sails. A ship could *hove-to* (active) or lie *hove-to* (passive).

Impressment. *See* PRESS-GANG.

Jury-rig. To make temporary repairs to the rigging and so enable a ship to reach a destination where more permanent repairs could be made.

Knot. Nautical measurement of speed per hour. 1 knot = 1 nautical mile per hour (1.15 statute miles per hour).

Knotting and splicing. In the context of this book, joining the ends of ropes, especially when commissioning a ship or making repairs after battle or storm damage.

Langridge. Scrap iron or a collection of small shot in a loose case, fired from a cannon, used in the same way as GRAPE-SHOT.

Larboard. An eighteenth-century word for the port or left-hand side of a ship, as seen from the STERN and facing forward.

Latitude. Conventionally, a parallel horizontal geographic coordinate that specifies the north–south position of a point on the earth's surface.

Lead-line. A lead weight on the end of a long piece of rope, swung and dropped to the sea-bed to measure the depth of water. Tallow on the bottom of the weight picked up sand and shells, if present, and so this was also used as a way of ascertaining location.

League. A nautical measurement of distance, equivalent to 3 NAUTICAL MILES.

Lee/Leeward. The opposite side of the ship to the one from which the wind is blowing.

Line ahead/abreast. The direction of the line of battle, usually BOW to STERN (line ahead), but sometimes side by side (line abreast).

Linstock. A burning piece of taper, or slow-match, fixed to a wooden handle in order to ignite gunpowder and set off the main charge.

Loblolly-boy. A surgeon's assistant, who, among other duties, gave the soup to patients.

Log. Either (a) the journal kept by the sailing MASTER, lieutenants and captain; or (b) a device for measuring speed through the water.

Long-boat. One of the ship's boats, usually fitted with masts and sails or pulled by oars.

Longitude. Conventionally, a vertical geographic coordinate that converges at the North and South poles and specifies the east–west position of a point on the earth's surface.

Marines. Soldiers serving at sea, and who acted as the ship's policemen.

Master and commander. An officer commanding a vessel of below twenty guns and without the full rank of captain, who also carried out the function of a sailing MASTER.

Master/Sailing Master. The WARRANT OFFICER responsible for navigation, stowage of stores in the hold and for the fabric of the vessel.

Masts. The vertical SPARS holding the yards and sails. The ships and frigates mentioned in this book had three masts: a fore, main and mizzen. The masts were in three joined sections of lower masts, topmasts (hence foretopmast) and topgallant masts (hence foretopgallant).

Mess. The space between the guns where a hanging table allowed the seamen to eat their meals.

Midshipman. A candidate for commissioned officer. The word derives from the area 'amidships' where he was berthed. Midshipmen were not always boys, or 'young gentlemen', and could be older, more experienced seamen.

Mizzen. The rearmost of a ship's three MASTS.

Musket. A smooth-bore, long-barrelled flintlock small arm carried by a ship's MARINES.

Muster. Either (a) to gather the ship's crew, or (b) the name given to the book in which all their names were recorded.

Nautical mile. A distance equivalent to 1.15 statute miles.

Navy Board. A subsidiary Board of Commissioners responsible for the maintenance of the fabric of the British fleet, the laying-up 'in ordinary' and the bringing forward of men-of-war as required.

Observations. Measurements (using specific instruments) of the angle of elevation of a celestial body above the horizon – most commonly the sun at midday – to determine LATITUDE. Later known as 'sights'.

Ordinary. A ship out of commission, with a small complement, tended by 'standing WARRANT OFFICERS'.

Orlop deck. A ship's lowest deck, below the waterline, where the MIDSHIPMEN slept and where, in battle, the surgeon and the LOBLOLLY-BOYS were stationed.

Packet/Pacquet. A small courier vessel.

Pinnace. A ship's boat used to transport junior officers around a harbour or anchorage.

Port. The left-hand side of the ship, when looking forward from the STERN.

Post-captain. An officer holding the full rank of captain, as opposed to a commander with the courtesy title of captain.

Press/Press-gang/Impress. All referring to the act of taking men into naval service by compulsion, with or without notice. Patrolling in or near sea-ports, the press gang would try to find men with merchant-navy, fishing or river-boat experience. In times of war and the 'hot press', they would first ask seafarers to volunteer for naval service, and on refusal would ply them with alcohol or simply seize them. At these times, 'landsmen' were also pressed, for normally they would be exempt. It could be a brutal process, but not to the extent of the inhumanity portrayed in literature and film.

Purser. The WARRANT OFFICER who handled money aboard ship and who was in charge of supplies such as food and drink, clothing, bedding and candles.

Quarterdeck. The 'after' portion of the upper deck, from which a ship was commanded and manoeuvred. It was the preserve of the officers, occupied by the seamen only when they were on a specific duty.

Rake. In battle, to pass the ship at right angles across the BOW or STERN of the enemy in order to fire guns the length of his decks and destroy as many of the enemy's people as possible at one stroke.

Rated ships. *See* FIRST-RATE; SECOND-RATE; THIRD-RATE.

Reefed. The upper parts of the sails drawn up to the YARD, furled and tied; this was a way of reducing sail area in heavy weather.

Riding to the anchor. Another way of saying that a ship was lying securely anchored to the sea-bed (in order to hold a stationary position in a place of shelter).

Round shot. Cannonballs.

Scuttlebutt. Sailors' gossip or rumour, so-called after the scuttlebutt, a cask for serving water, around which they gathered to talk.

Second-rate ship. A SHIP OF THE LINE with three gun-decks, carrying between ninety and ninety-eight guns.

Ship of the line. The major men of-war that formed the line of battle.

Sick and Hurt Board. A common name for the Commissioners for Sick and Wounded Seamen, responsible for the Seamen's Hospital at Greenwich.

Sloop. A warship with a single gun-deck carrying up to twenty guns.

Slops. A supply of clothing on board a ship, which could be sold to the crew (i.e., usually offset against their pay).

Sounding. The depth of water, or the process of ascertaining the depth of water, using a LEAD-LINE.

Spanker. The quadrilateral fore-and-aft sail at the STERN of a ship, hoisted from the lower MIZZEN mast.

Spar. A collective noun referring to the MASTS, YARDS and BOWSPRIT.

Sponging. Using a rod with sheep's wool on the end, dipped in a bucket of water and then sloshed down a gun barrel, to ensure that all burning embers were extinguished.

Squadron. A group of warships acting in concert under a single FLAG-OFFICER; a sub-section of a fleet when several ADMIRALS were present.

Starboard. The right-hand side of the ship, when looking forward from the STERN.

Stern. The extreme AFT (rear) part of a ship's hull.

Strike colours. To haul down one's COLOURS (or ENSIGN), signifying submission and surrender.

Tack. To change direction by putting the BOW of the ship through the wind. Ships cannot sail directly into the wind, hence 'tacking to WIND-WARD' – to make ground to windward by zig-zagging towards the wind.

Third-rate ship. A SHIP OF THE LINE with two gun-decks, carrying between six-ty-four and eighty guns.

Top/Tops. The platform at the lower masthead, primarily intended as part of the support arrangement for the topmast, but also serving as lookout, and for sharp-shooters in battle.

Topgallant. The highest of the three wooden sections joined to make a MAST; hence topgallant mast, topgallant sails, etc.

Topmen. The most able and nimble seamen who worked aloft handling the upper sails.

Topsails. During this period, the middle sails on a MAST, always the last to be furled. Usually, in action, the COURSES (lower sails) were brailed or 'clewed-up' and a ship was manoeuvred under her topsails.

Victualling Board. The body responsible for the navy's procurement of foodstuffs and drink, and for the control of supply-ships and storehouses in ports.

Wardroom. A MESS for the commissioned officers.

Warrant officers. Non-commissioned officers with specific responsibilities, who formed part of the standing (permanent) crew. They handled all technical aspects of the ship's running, such as navigation, ammunition, stores, victualling and encompassed trades such as carpentry and maintenance of the rigging.

Watch. The officers and crew working the ship for a fixed period of duty. There were usually two watches: the STARBOARD watch and LARBOARD watch.

Wear ship. To put the STERN of the ship through the wind to change direction (opposite of TACK).

Weigh the anchor. To raise the ANCHOR.

Windward. The side of the ship upon which the wind is blowing, or the position closest to the direction from which the wind is blowing.

Worming. Pushing a wooden rod with an iron spiral on the end down a cannon, to remove the remains of the burning wadding from the previous shot.

Yards. The horizontal SPARS across the MASTS, from which the sails are suspended.

Notes on the text

Books cited below in short form appear with their full publication details in the Select Bibliography.

I. ISLES OF ICE

1 Frederick Chamier, *The Life of a Sailor*, quoted in Cavell, *Midshipmen and Quarterdeck Boys*, p. 12.

2 Cavell, ibid.

3 J. Raigersfeld, *The Life of a Sea Officer*, quoted in Adkins & Adkins, *Jack Tar*, p. 88.

4 To determine longitude (east–west position) involved knowing the time at the ship's point of departure (not yet replaced by the Greenwich Meridian) and comparing it with local time at sea. It was not yet accepted that the clockmaker John Harrison's innovative chronometers could prove sufficiently accurate in a ship's damp, unstable conditions. So, in this period, and weather permitting, mariners were still depending on the lengthy calculations involved in establishing the time at their departure point by the measuring of angles between the moon and stars.

5 Land granted by William the Conqueror, including the site where Belvoir Castle was built, passed from de Todeni through the female line first to the de Albini family and then to the de Ros family, who brought land in Nottinghamshire and Yorkshire and a considerable fortune to the match. Eleanor stood to inherit the castle and lands because her brother and her sister had no heirs, but she died before they did, leaving her son George to inherit Belvoir.

6 The Duke of Rutland's full set of hereditary titles was (and still is): Duke of Rutland, Marquis of Granby, Earl of Rutland, Baron Roos of Hamlake, Trusbut and Belvoir, Baron Manners of Haddon. The title 'Marquis of Granby' (also used as the courtesy title for the eldest son, and not using the alternative spelling 'Marquess') derives from a village near Belvoir but historically part of the Haddon inheritance. The Haddon title derives from Haddon Hall, a Derbyshire estate that was acquired by marriage to the Vernon family in 1563. The Roos title (used as the courtesy title for the

447

eldest grandson of the duke) derives from Baron de Ros, an early Lord of Belvoir. The royal connection to Edward IV and Richard III enabled the lion of England and the fleur-de-lys of France to feature in the Manners'

blue-and-yellow-striped family shield. The ducal coronet, motto and the peacock were added to the shield to make the ducal family crest.

7 Collingwood to Mrs Moutray, quoted in Cavell, op. cit., p. 3.

2. GOING AT IT BALD-HEADED

1 Horace Walpole, *Letters* (1840 edition), Volume II, quoted in Dale, *The History of the Belvoir Hunt*, p. 46.

2 Ibid., p. 45.

3 Ibid., p. 47.

4 Dale, op. cit., p. 44.

5 Lord Berkeley of Stratton, diary (in the Belvoir Archives).

6 British Library Sloane MS 4045.

7 British Library Add. MS 32729 fol. 4.

8 Horace Walpole, quoted in Manners, *Some Account*, p. 82.

9 J.W. Fortescue, *History of the British Army*, Volume II, Book 10 (1899), p. 512.

10 De Mauvillon, quoted in Manners, op. cit., p. 139.

11 Christopher Rowell, *Petworth: The People and the Place*, National Trust (2012), p. 36.

12 British Library Sloane MS 4045.

13 Granby's younger brother Robert took the name Manners-Sutton as a proviso for inheriting their mother's Kelham estate in Nottinghamshire – her name was Bridget Sutton. She was also known as Lady Lexington, being heiress to the Lexington properties and fortune. Robert Manners-Sutton had one illegitimate son, known as Evelyn Sutton. On Robert's death, Granby's youngest brother George took the Kelham estate and the name Manners-Sutton.

14 Further afield, one town in Canada and four in the United States are named 'Granby' after the marquis.

15 Quoted in Kelly, *Beau Brummell*, p. 81.

16 Eton College Archives: ED 361, Nugae Etonenses, 1765–66.

17 Arthur Richard Austen-Leigh, *The Eton College Register*, p. xxi.

18 Kelly, op. cit., p. 93.

19 Patrick O'Brian, *Joseph Banks*, London: 1997, p. 19.

20 Eton College Archives, op. cit.

21 Kelly, op. cit., p. 77.

22 Both George and his brother Thomas were Charles's friends at Eton, sons of the prime minister, George Grenville, whose government the Marquis of Granby served during the 1760s. Their mother was a distant relative via Charles and Robert's grandfather, the 6th Duke of Somerset, and their aunt was the wife of the 1st Earl of Chatham. George would one day become Nugent-Temple-Grenville, 1st Marquis of Buckingham, while his younger brother Thomas was a future First Lord of the Admiralty, and would bequeath his enormous collection of books to the British Museum (and now in the British Library).

23 Eton College Archives, op. cit.

24 Derbyshire Record Office, F6525–6548 (Letters of William FitzHerbert to his son William).

25 Kelly, op. cit., p. 65.

26 Eton College Archives, op. cit.

27 Christopher Hollis, *Eton*, p. 147.

28 Ibid.

29 Anecdote quoted in Sterry, *Annals of the King's College*, pp. 181–3.

30 Dale, op. cit., pp. 6–7.

31 Daniel Defoe, *A Tour Through the Whole Island of Great Britain* (1724–7), edited by Pat Rogers, London: Penguin, 1971, p. 424.

32 The Manners and the Howes had intermarried over the centuries, and their respective country seats of Belvoir Castle and Langar Hall were close together. Richard and William's elder brother George had been killed in North America, at Ticonderoga, during the Seven Years' War, leaving Richard to inherit the family title.

33 Quoted in the Duchess of Rutland, *Belvoir Castle*, p. 40.

34 Manners, op. cit., pp. 55–8.

35 Janet Camden Lucey, *Lovely Peggy: The Life and Times of Margaret Woffington*, London: Hurst & Blackett, 1952, p. 69.

36 'Junius' Letters (17 February 1769) quoted in Manners, op. cit., p. 356.

37 Ibid.

38 Horace Walpole, *Memoirs of the Reign of George III*, quoted in Manners, op. cit., p. 398.

39 Manners, op. cit., p. 99.

40 'Pocket boroughs' such as Bramber, in Sussex, had very small electorates and could be used by a patron to gain unrepresentative influence within the House of Commons. The Manners family underwent many difficulties in maintaining control of this one.

3. GRANBY'S SONS

1 Richard Watson was a university tutor to Charles who became a mentor and family friend. After Robert's death, he wrote this short biographical piece, more of a hagiography than a biography, but based on interviews with those who personally knew Robert. Watson, though he had reason to exaggerate Robert's qualities, claimed that he had done due diligence in remaining impartial and objective.

2 According to John D. Baird's article on William Cowper in the *Oxford Dictionary of National Biography*, 'Joseph Hill (1733–1811) was the son of an attorney, and something of a protégé of Ashley Cowper's. He qualified as both attorney and solicitor, and developed a highly successful practice among the wealthy and powerful, recommended by a well-deserved reputation for discretion.' Hill was articled with the poet Cowper and Edward Thurlow, lord chancellor from 1778 to 1792. Hill's father Francis had been Secretary to Sir Joseph Jekyll, Master of the Rolls. Hill and his sisters Theodosia and Frances lost their father when they were very young in 1741, which may have given Hill some empathy with the Manners children. Despite his connections to some of the top lawyers in eighteenth-century London, Hill worked his way up as one of the junior clerks in Chancery. Charles and Robert may have been among his first private clients. 'Joe Hill' may have been introduced to the Manners boys at Eton, where his brother-in-law John Tickell was a private tutor. He would become indispensable to the Manners family, providing a quiet but essential service for two generations. He himself had a house at Wargrave in Berkshire as well as offices in the centre of London.

3 Gainsborough produced an original and two studio copies, of which Charles kept one (now at Belvoir Castle). The copy he gave to Dr Barnard, Provost of Eton, still hangs

today in one of the school's boarding houses. The original went to the family of the Earl of Chatham, and it is believed to have been 'wantonly destroyed by a domestic servant' in New York in 1941. Hugh Douglas Hamilton (c.1740–1808) was an Irish portrait-painter, who, often overwhelmed with work, found great success in London for his pastel oval portraits depicting the head and shoulders of the sitters – often royalty, politicians and celebrities of the day.

4   Quoted in N.A.M. Rodger, *The Wooden World*, p. 255.

5   First performed at the home of Frederick Prince of Wales (Cliveden), the masque was intended to link Alfred the Great's victories over the Vikings with the idea of a revival of British sea power following Admiral Vernon's recapture of Portobello, in Central America in 1739: hence many places in Britain called Portobello.

6   The phrase is from Voltaire's *Candide*: 'In this country, it is wise to kill an admiral from time to time to encourage the others.'

7   Another connection may have been through General Lord Robert Manners, Member for Hull and a half-brother of the 3rd Duke of Rutland. The vessel was sold to the navy along with another, the *Marquis of Rockingham*, and they were renamed *Resolution* and *Adventure* respectively for Cook's expedition. There is some evidence that the Manners family may have taken an interest in the voyages of discovery: their account ledgers suggest that the 3rd Duke lent Sir Joseph Banks, the botanist aboard Cook's first voyage, the then vast sum of £15,000 to assist with a 1766 voyage to Newfoundland with Yorkshireman Constantine Phipps. This was

during the time that Granby was Master General of the Ordnance, a department responsible for producing maps. Cook, who had played a key role in the 1759 capture of Quebec using his surveying skills, also surveyed the coast of Newfoundland in the 1760s to make sea-charts.

8   In 1714, Isaac Newton (who was born just 14 miles from Belvoir) was one of those who instigated the Longitude Prize, to be awarded for solving the problem of finding longitude at sea. Although he knew that finding a way of telling accurate time at sea was the answer to the problem, in his view a clock could not be made to withstand the damp and turbulent conditions of a ship, and so like others he considered that the answer lay in celestial navigation. Newton's friend and biographer, William Stukeley, also one of the first to attempt to date Stonehenge, was a friend of the 3rd Duke of Rutland and helped him discover, in the 1720s, the stone coffin of Belvoir's Norman founder, Robert de Todeni. The 3rd Duke was interested in archaeology, and the family certainly had a great interest in clocks and watches, for timepiece repairs feature consistently in the account ledgers of the period.

9   Evelyn Sutton was the illegitimate son of Lord Granby's younger brother, Lord Robert Manners-Sutton, who had died of illness in 1762 at the end of the Seven Years' War.

10 Roland Thorne, 'Manners, Charles, Fourth Duke of Rutland', *ODNB*.

11 The portrait was then probably lost in Belvoir Castle's fire of 1816, and so it has not been possible to reproduce it here.

12 *Somerset v Stewart* (1772) is a famous judgement of the English Court of

King's Bench, which held that chattel slavery was unsupported by the common law in England and Wales, although the position elsewhere in the British Empire was left ambiguous. Mansfield made this ruling on 22 June 1772, the day Robert Manners first dropped anchor in Newfoundland.

13 Cambridge University accounted for two Parliamentary seats until 1950, as did Oxford University.

14 In 1773, Parliament enacted the Tea Act, which, although it imposed no new colonial taxes, helped the East India Company to export its stockpile of tea to North America at a favourable price. Colonial merchants perceived the tea shipments as a threat to their businesses from a corporate giant backed by the British state.

15 Parliamentary speeches were supposedly secret until 1775, when, in the aftermath of the Wilkes Affair and other incidents encouraging free speech, John Almon and John Debrett began to publish verbatim reports. Charles Manners was a subscriber. These were eventually taken over by Thomas Hansard after 1812.

16 Jeremy Black, *Crisis of Empire: Britain and America in the Eighteenth Century*, London and New York: Continuum, 2008, p. 136.

4. A PLACE WITHOUT HONOUR, PROFIT OF PLEASURE

1 The Reverend Doctor James Bennet writing in 1777, and quoted in Leonard White, *The Story of Gosport*, Southampton: Ensign Publications, 1989, p. 45.

2 Janet Macdonald, *Feeding Nelson's Navy*, p. 120.

3 Richard Watson, *Anecdotes of the Life of Richard Watson*, pp. 49 and 54.

4 Another term for these principal divisions of the Ottoman Empire is *eyalets*. They had varying levels of autonomy across the empire.

5 Captain Augustus Hervey, described in N.A.M. Rodger, *The Wooden World*, p. 255.

6 N.A.M. Rodger, *The Insatiable Earl*, p. 31.

5. THESE ARE THE TIMES THAT TRY MEN'S SOULS

1 E.H. Chalus, 'Manners, Mary Isabella, Duchess of Rutland (1756–1831)', *ODNB*.

2 Nathaniel Wraxall, *Historical Memoirs of My Own Time*, p. 370.

3 Chalus, op. cit.

4 Michael Talbot, 'From Giovanni Stefano Carbonelli to John Stephen Carbonell: A Violinist Turned Vintner in Handel's London', Göttinger Händel-Beiträge, Volume 14 (2012), pp. 265–99.

5 The Pennsylvania Assembly described Magna Carta thus in 1765; quoted in Stephen Conway, *The American Revolutionary War*, p. 43.

6 Richard Watson, *Anecdotes of the Life of Richard Watson*, p. 50.

7 Ibid., p. 51.

8 Ian Kelly, *Mr Foote's Other Leg*, London: Picador, 2012, p. 296.

9 The prime minister, whose official Cabinet title was First Lord of the Treasury, was also expected to be the minister best able to command a majority in the House of Commons.

10 Quoted in Charles Sebag-Montefiore *et al.*, *Brooks's*, p. 206.

11 Quoted in Jacqueline Reiter, *The Late Lord*.
12 One of the family's lawyers, Levett Blackborne, wrote these words to Charles.
13 Quoted in N.A.M. Rodger, *The Command of the Ocean*, p. 328.
14 Sebag-Montefiore et al., op. cit., p. 183.
15 Susan C. Law, *Through the Keyhole*, p. 121.
16 Among their number, as Charles may have noted, was *aide-de-camp* Lord Petersham, the former Eton boy who had damned his father on the occasion of the schoolboys' rebellious truancy in 1768.
17 G.H. Guttridge, *English Whiggism*, p. 101.
18 G.R. Barnes and J.H. Owen, *The Private Papers of John, Earl of Sandwich*, p. 292: Sandwich to Gambier, 13 April 1778.

6. THE OAK OF OLD ENGLAND

1 N.A.M. Rodger, *The Command of the Ocean*, p. 336.
2 These, and several other uncredited quotations in this chapter, are taken from the transcript of Keppel's 1779 court-martial, of which Charles's own copy is held in the Belvoir Archives.
3 Horace Walpole, quoted in J.H. Broomfield, 'The Keppel–Palliser Affair', p. 198.
4 J. McDonnell (ed.), *A History of Helmsley, Rievaulx and District*, York: Yorkshire Archaeological Society / Stonegate Press, p. 865. The *Courageux* had been captured from the French and substantially rebuilt using English oak.

7. PRODIGIOUS BICKERINGS

1 Quoted in J.H. Broomfield, 'The Keppel–Palliser Affair', p. 200.
2 Now the Duke of Westminster (created 1874).
3 Fanny Burney, 'Two Celebrated Duchesses Discussed', in *The Diary and Letters of Madame D'Arblay*, London: Vizetelly, 1890.
4 E.H. Chalus, 'Manners, Mary Isabella, Duchess of Rutland (1756–1831)', *ODNB*.
5 Quoted in Gomer Williams, *History of the Liverpool Privateers and Letters of Marque, With an Account of the Liverpool Slave Trade 1744–1812*, Liverpool & Kingston, Ontario: Liverpool University Press / McGill-Queen's University Press, 2004, p. 226.
6 *Liverpool Advertiser*, quoted in ibid., p. 225.
7 Janet Macdonald, *Feeding Nelson's Navy*, p. 80.
8 Quoted in Broomfield, op. cit., p. 202.
9 Quoted in ibid., p. 203.
10 Ibid., pp. 203–4.
11 Piers Mackesy, *The War for America*, p. 242.
12 Ibid., p. 204.
13 Taken from the transcript of Keppel's 1779 court-martial (Charles's own copy held in the Belvoir Archives).
14 Mackesy, op. cit., p. 204.
15 Ibid.
16 Charles Sebag-Montefiore *et al.*, *Brooks's*, p. 184.

17 John C. Miller, The Origins of the American Revolution, London: Faber and Faber, p. 317.

18 National Maritime Museum: NMM/ADM/L/V132.

19 Broomfield, op. cit., p. 205.

20 National Maritime Museum: NMM: SAN/3/6.

21 The House of Commons attendance records were burned in the Parliamentary fire of 1834.

8. AN EXTREME HARD CASE

1 Cyril Bruyn Andrews (ed.), Clouds & Sunshine, p. 44.

2 He later transferred to the North American station in 1775, from whence he sent home 'disagreeable' accounts of the war. British Library MSS Add 69795 Folios 89 and 90.

3 The last descendent of the 3rd Duke and Mrs Drake to live there was Fursan Manners. Eventually, the house was knocked down, but the properties now on the site – near Harrods – are named Rutland Gate

4 Robert may have been aware of the Olney Hymns of 1779, created by William Cowper and his curate friend John Newton. (Joseph Hill was a friend of Cowper.) They included Cowper's lines 'God moves in a mysterious way / His wonders to perform / He plants His footsteps in the sea / And rides upon the storm' and Newton's 'Faith's Review and Expectation', which was to become famous as the song 'Amazing Grace', associated with the anti-slavery movement. Newton had been pressed into the navy, became involved in the Atlantic slave trade, and had experienced a spiritual conversion after pleading with God to save his ship from a storm in 1748.

5 Its evocative title in full was Trials for Adultery, or, The History of Divorces. Being Select Trials at Doctors Commons, for Adultery, Fornication, Cruelty, Impotence, &c. From the Year 1760, to the Present Time. Including the Whole of the Evidence on Each Cause. Together With the Letters, &c. That Have Been Intercepted Between the Amorous Parties. The Whole Forming a Complete History of the Private Life, Intrigues, and Amours of Many Characters in the Most Elevated Sphere: Every Scene and Transaction, However Ridiculous, Whimsical, or Extraordinary, Being Fairly Represented, as Becomes a Faithful Historian, Who is Fully Determined Not to Sacrifice Truth at the Shrine of Guilt and Folly. Taken in Short Hand, by a Civilian.

6 William Wilberforce, quoted in Susan C. Law, Through the Keyhole, p. 19.

7 Robert's copy of Hoste was inscribed as having belonged to a James Hubbard, and it might have been captured from a Spanish ship in 1711.

8 John Clerk of Eldin was not a sailor himself, but he knew the stultifying Fighting Instructions for battle and by 1779 had begun writing an English equivalent of the Morogues and Hoste studies. Clerk's 'An Enquiry Into Naval Tactics' and 'An Essay on Naval Tactics' were not published until 1782 and 1790 respectively, and it is questionable as to whether he influenced any of the sea officers of the era. Nevertheless, his efforts were symptomatic of the growing interest in this subject.

9 It has not been possible to discover exactly who this servant was. He probably was not the later Admiral Charles Ekins, a nephew of Robert's

Eton tutor John Ekins, but most likely another relative of the same family.

10 J.D. Davies, 'Woodcote's Admiral: Sir Charles Hardy and the Franco-Spanish Invasion of 1779', unpublished paper given to the Britannia Naval Research Association, 25 March 2007.

11 Amanda Foreman, *Georgiana, Duchess of Devonshire*, p. 70.

12 As a sample specification, the 74-gun *Bedford* in 1779 carried the following (as quoted in Brian Lavery, *The Ship of the Line*, Volume 1, London: Conway Maritime, 1983):
  'Weapons: 230 muskets, 230 swords, 70 pairs of pistols, 60 poleaxes, 100 Half pikes
  400 barrels of gunpowder
  Shot of 18lbs: round 2800, grape 116, 84 double head, 115 langridge, 173 canister

  Shot of 9lbs: round 1800, grape 99, 54 double head, 74 langridge, 131 canister
  Shot of half lbs: round 720, grape 144
  Musket shot: 24,900
  Pistol shot: 9880'

13 The island of St Helena would be for the purpose of convoying East Indiamen for their homeward passage from India and China.

14 David Syrett, *The Rodney Papers*, p. 270: Sandwich to Rodney, 8 December 1779.

15 Ibid.

16 Ibid., p. 282: Sandwich to Rodney, 12 December 1779.

17 Horace Walpole, *Letters from the Hon. Horace Walpole to the Rev. William Cole*, p. 234.

9. NOW MOVE HEAVEN AND EARTH

1 Quoted in Donald Macintyre, *Admiral Rodney*, p. 106.

2 Quoted in Alastair Rowland Brown, *My Inestimable Friend*, p. 33.

3 David Syrett, *The Rodney Papers*, p. 308: Memorandum by Rodney.

4 Ibid., p. 312: MacBride to Rodney, 20 January 1780.

5 National Maritime Museum: NMM/ADM/L/A/256.

6 David Syrett, *The Rodney Papers*, p. 368: from Rodney's order book.

7 *London Courant and Morning Chronicle*, 24 January 1780.

8 TNA: Hoare MSS PRO 30/70/5 f 356, dated 30 January [1780].

9 David Syrett, *The Rodney Papers*, p. 375: Sandwich to Rodney, 8 March 1780.

10 Ibid., p. 373: Keppel to Rodney, 6 March 1780.

10. WHATEVER EXPEDITION WE MAY MAKE

1 Among the Navy Board's other responsibilities were the building, maintenance and repair of ships, the management of the Royal Dockyards, the supply of stores and the manning and paying-off of ships. In addition, the Board was also responsible for transporting troops, naval stores, military clothing and equipment, playing a crucial role in supplying the fighting forces in North America.

2 Robert Blair (1748–1828) was born in Merchiston near Edinburgh, the son of a minister. He was a product of the Scottish Enlightenment which was in full swing by 1750, with spectacular developments in intellectual life originating in Glasgow and spreading to Edinburgh. Surgeons such as Blair arrived to do their apprenticeship in the navy having been trained in the new medical schools of Aberdeen,

Glasgow and Edinburgh, where they learnt new standards of care and performance. A good naval surgeon enjoyed the confidence of his captain, which would help elevate his social status.

3   David Syrett, 'A Strategy of Detachments', p. 5.
4   Ibid., p. 6.
5   Amanda Foreman, op. cit., p. 83.
6   *Royal naval biography: or Memoirs of the services of all the flag-officers, superannuated rear-admirals, retired-captains, post-captains and commanders, whose names appeared on the Admiralty list of sea officers at the commencement of the year, or who have since been promoted; illustrated by a series of* historical and explanatory notes. With copious addenda, by John Marshall, 1784?–1837, published 1823, Volume 2, p. 589.
7   TNA: PRO 30/20/12.
8   Sam Willis, *Fighting at Sea in the Eighteenth Century*, pp. 130–1.
9   George's father, who became the 1st Earl Grey, had been a successful general in America in the early part of the war, earning the nickname 'No-flint Grey' in 1777 when, to ensure surprise in a night attack on a rebel encampment, he ordered his infantry to remove the flints from their muskets and use only their bayonets.

II. THE TIME NOW SEEMS BIG WITH EVENTS

1   TNA. PRO 30/20/12.
2   TNA: PRO 30/20/12.
3   TNA: PRO 30/20/12.
4   TNA: PRO 30/20/12.
5   Roy and Lesley Adkins, *Jack Tar*, p. 167.
6   Existing records do not reflect all the changes of officers that occurred on foreign stations, and it is unclear who now became Robert's 1st lieutenant.
7   Francis Reynolds-Moreton, 3rd Baron Ducie (1739–1808), first became a naval officer during the Seven Years' War. From 1784 to 1785 he served as Member of Parliament for Lancaster before inheriting his title from his brother Thomas. Ducie Island, in the Pacific Ocean, was named after him by Captain Edward Edwards of the *Pandora*, who had served under Ducie during his time in command of the *Augusta*. 'Reynolds', as he is referred to in correspondence, gave passage to Mun Stevens when the latter was serving in America in the 1770s.
8   TNA: ADM 52/1557.
9   TNA: PRO 30/20/12.
10 Andrew Lambert, *Admirals*, p. 161.
11 TNA: PRO 30/20/12.
12 All quotations from this paragraph are from TNA: PRO 30/20/12, Hood to Rodney.
13 Ibid.
14 Ian Kelly, *Beau Brummell*, p. 179.
15 D'Estaing had indeed returned to France, and he never served again on the western side of the Atlantic.
16 All quotations from this paragraph are from TNA: PRO 30/20/12.
17 Ibid. Shortly after the battle, Hood wrote for the Admiralty a long description of the action, to extricate himself from any blame regarding its inconclusiveness and the failure to prevent the French convoy reaching the safety of Fort Royal.
18 TNA: ADM/99/49.
19 Rodney's purser would collect the weekly State and Condition reports from each ship, then a victualling agent – one John Blackburn, for St Lucia and Barbados – would

resupply the ships from stocks of convoyed stores or produce from negotiated local contracts. Pursers and agents had to work to detailed instructions, and they collected newspapers, invoices and other items to justify when they had to pay above what was considered a 'fair price', otherwise they themselves would not be paid. The British government sent out Spanish silver dollars – the West Indies' currency – to pay local shipwrights, artificers and victualling contractors. If the currency ran out, the British credit system was sufficiently respected that contractors would accept interim payment by way of bills drawn on London.

20 TNA: PRO 30/20/12.
21 TNA: ADM/111/83.
22 William Hague, *William Pitt the Younger*, p. 54.
23 Ibid., p. 52.
24 *Journal of the House of Lords, Volumes XXXV (1776–79), XXXVI (1779–83) and XXXVII (1783–87).*

12. A SLIGHT INCONVENIENCE

1   Today's Haiti and Dominican Republic.
2   TNA: PRO 30/20/12.
3   Sir Richard Vesey Hamilton, *Letters and Papers of Admiral of the Fleet Sir Thos. Byam Martin*, p. 114.
4   Ibid., p. 113.
5   All quotations from this paragraph are from TNA: PRO 30/20/12.
6   N.A.M. Rodger, *The Command of the Ocean*, p. 322.
7   Names such as 'Magnus Ninian' also show that there were a number of Orcadians and Shetlanders among them.
8   TNA: PRO 30/20/12.
9   Ibid.
10 Ibid.
11 About 30,000 German soldiers fought during the war, making up a quarter of the troops the British sent to America.
12 Horace Walpole, *Letters from the Hon. Horace Walpole to the Rev. William Cole*, p. 234.
13 William Hague, *William Pitt the Younger*, p. 76.
14 Piers Mackesy, *The War for America*, p. 435.

13. A VERY GREAT ESTEEM FOR THE LADY

1   Quoted in Andrew Lambert, *Admirals*, p. 166.
2   British Library: MSS Rodney's Correspondence, 1782.
3   N.A.M. Rodger, *The Command of the Ocean*, p. 331.
4   Charles Sebag-Montefiore et al., *Brooks's*, p. 186.
5   John Clerk of Eldin, *An Essay on Naval Tactics*, second edition, Edinburgh & London, 1804, p 231.
6   William Hague, op. cit., p. 82.

14. MY DEAR LITTLE LORD

1   TNA: PRO 30/20/12.
2   TNA: PRO 30/20/12.
3   A.T. Mahan, *The Major Operations of the Navies in the War of American Independence*, p. 215.
4   Quoted in Richard Woodman, *The Liberty War*: Endeavour Press (e-book, forthcoming 2017).
5   G. Cornwallis-West, *The Life and Letters of Admiral Cornwallis*, p. 125.

6   Ibid.   7   Ibid., p. 126.

15. THE DARLING OF YOUR SOUL

1   *Royal naval biography: or Memoirs*
    of the services of all the flag-officers,
    superannuated rear-admirals, retired-
    captains, post-captains and commanders,
    whose names appeared on the Admiralty
    list of sea officers at the commencement
    of the year, or who have since been
    promoted; illustrated by a series of
    historical and explanatory notes. With
    copious addenda, by John Marshall,
    1784?–1837, published 1823, Volume 2,
    p. 620.
2   My lord Duke, I am all the more
    sensitive to the loss of Lord Manners

for having had the honour of
knowing him. His courage and
gallantry brought him my esteem
and admiration and his death has
caused me much sorrow. It causes
me even more sadness today since it
deprives me of the pleasure of seeing
you pay court to me. My lord Duke,
please accept my gratitude for the
compliments that you have been kind
enough to pay me. Your obedient
servant, the Count de Grasse.
3   Amanda Foreman, op. cit., p. 140.

16. CLARET IS A BAD MEDICINE

1   Comus being the Greek god of
    festivity, revels and nocturnal
    dalliances. Quoted in Julie Peakman,
    Peg Plunkett, p. 128.
2   Jonah Barrington, *Historic Memoirs of*
    Ireland, Volume II, London: Colburn,
    1865, p. 216.
3   Peg's words are from Mary Lyons
    (ed.), *The Memoirs of Mrs Leeson,*
    Madam, 1727–97, p. 144.
4   Ibid., pp. 144–5.
5   Ibid.
6   Dawes Point is where the southern
    approach to Sydney Harbour Bridge
    now runs.
7   Alastair Rowland Brown, *My*
    Inestimable Friend, p. 93.
8   Ibid., p. 2.

9   Notes & Queries, Volume 11, London:
    George Bell, 1855, p. 513.
10 James McGuire and James Quinn
    (eds), *Dictionary of Irish Biography:*
    From Earliest Times to The Year 2002,
    9 vols, Cambridge: Cambridge
    University Press, 2002, p. 344.
11 Nathaniel Wraxall, *Posthumous*
    Memoirs of His Own Time, Volume II,
    London: Bentley, 1836, pp. 365–7.
12 *Belfast News Letter,* The Northern
    Ireland Library Authority.
13 TNA: Hoare MSS PRO 30/70/3 f 145.
14 Ibid.
15 Peakman, op. cit., p. 121.
16 Ibid., p. 167.
17 Barrington, op. cit., pp. 224–5.
18 *Belfast News Letter,* The Northern
    Ireland Library Authority.

17. EPILOGUE: DEAR OLD CHATEAU

1   Cyril Bruyn Andrews (ed.), *Clouds &*
    Sunshine, p. 44.
2   Ibid.
3   Arthur Foss, *The Dukes of Britain,*
    p. 82.

4   Horace Walpole, *Letters from the Hon.*
    Horace Walpole to the Rev. William Cole,
    p. 234.

Manuscript sources

The majority of the primary sources used in this book, including most of the unreferenced quotations, are held in the archives at Belvoir Castle, which are known today as the Muniment Rooms. The manuscripts drawn upon include marriage settlements, wills, charters, accounts, correspondence between the characters in this book, and various contemporary printed documents such as Augustus Keppel's court-martial report and Charles Manners' copies of the *Parliamentary Register*. There is even a detailed set of eyewitness accounts taken after the fire of 1816, enabling us to piece together such fine details as the time at which the 5th Duke rode up the hill.

Researching this book was facilitated by the present Duke of Rutland's grandfather, John Henry Montagu Manners, 9th Duke of Rutland, who gathered together the family papers in what had previously been the Estate Office, long before his accession to the dukedom. Ancient charters were already in the adjacent Evidence Room, where the young John had boxes specially made to prevent seals being damaged, and he supplemented the charters with series of royal grants – including Lord Robert's commissions – and family settlements. He began to catalogue and index the archive, beginning with the medieval charters, entails and accounts, but never finished the task. He hired a translator, Isaac Jeays, and a typist, Sister Catherine, and today there is a wall of typescript lists and handwritten card indexes.

The earliest documents had already been published by the Historical Manuscripts Commission, between 1895 and 1905. A precedent had been set of binding up historic correspondence in order, and the 9th Duke continued it; but when he died tragically young in 1940, some eighteenth-century letters were still only roughly sorted into blue file boxes, chronologically arranged, where we found them while researching.

Ledgers line the corridors, but more ephemeral accounts vouchers of the past 300 years were in disarray until we recently began sorting through them. This process brought us many discoveries which individually were minor but collectively have added colour and richness – such as the dish of strawberries that Lord Robert enjoyed in the summer of 1779.

Today, the 11th Duke is embarking on a project to pick up where his grandfather left off.

★

In addition to Belvoir's own resources, we drew on ships' logbooks and musters held by The National Archives (TNA) in Kew. These include:

For the *Panther* (1772–5):
Master's Logs ADM 52/1902 (1771–4), ADM 52/1903 (1774); Captain's Logs ADM 51/671 (1764–83); Musters ADM 36/7661 (1772–3), ADM 36/7662 (1773–4).

For the *Enterprize* (1775–7):
Master's Logs ADM 52/1722 (1775–7), ADM 52/1724 (1777–9); Captain's Logs ADM 51/314 (1775–84); Musters ADM 36/8563 (1773–6), ADM 36/8564 (1776–7).

For the *Ocean* (1778):
Master's Logs ADM 52/1891 (1770–8), ADM 52/1897 (1778–9); Captain's Logs ADM 51/649 (1776–83); Musters ADM 36/7788 (1778), ADM 36/7789 (1778–9).

For the *Victory* (1778–9):
Master's Logs ADM 52/2060 (1778–80), Captain's Logs ADM 51/1036 (1778–83); Musters ADM 36/8479 (1778), ADM 36/8487 (1778–80), ADM 36/8480 (1779), ADM 36/8481 (1779–80).

For the *Alcide* (1779):
Master's Logs ADM 52/1557 (1779–81); Captain's Logs ADM 51/33 (1778–83); Musters ADM 36/8916 (1779–80), ADM 36/8922 (1779–83).

For the *Resolution* (1780–82):
Master's Logs ADM 52/1954 (1779–82); Musters ADM 36/8709 (1780), ADM 36/8710 (1780–1), ADM 36/8711 (1781), ADM 36/8712 (1782).

Other manuscript sources at TNA include:
ADM/111/83, 87,88 (Victualling Board minutes); ADM/99/49 (Sick and Hurt Board minutes); ADM/8/56, 58 (Ship disposition books); PRO 30/20/12 (Admirals' correspondence).

At the National Maritime Museum (NMM) we drew on:
NMM/ADM/L/R/102 (Lieutenants' Logs, *Resolution*); NMM/ADM/L/R/101, NMM/ADM/L/R/100, NMM/ADM/L/A/256 (Lieutenants' Logs, *Alcide*); NMM ADM/L/A/84, NMM/ADM/L/O/10 (Lieutenants' Logs, *Ocean*); NMM/ADM/L/O/11, NMM/ADM/L/V/132 (Lieutenants' Logs, *Victory*); NMM: SAN/3/6 (Sandwich appointment books).

Other manuscript sources include:
Eton College Archives (with thanks to the Provost and Fellows of Eton College); Tissington Hall (with thanks to Sir Richard FitzHerbert, private papers); Derbyshire Record Office (for the papers of Alleyne FitzHerbert); and The British Library (BL).

Select bibliography

The works listed below, as well as additional ones cited in the Notes on the Text, contributed in greater or lesser ways to our research, and we would like to express our gratitude to all these authors and editors.

Adkins, Roy and Lesley, *Jack Tar: The Extraordinary Lives of Ordinary Seamen in Nelson's Navy*, London: Abacus, 2009

Andrewes, William J.H. (ed.), *The Quest for Longitude*, Cambridge, Massachusetts: Collection of Historical Scientific Instruments, Harvard University, 1996

Andrews, Cyril Bruyn (ed.), *Clouds & Sunshine By an English Tourist of the Eighteenth Century: Part I of the Tour of 1789, From the Torrington Diaries By the Hon. John Byng (1743–1813)*, Marlow, Buckinghamshire: Roy Patrick Smith, c.1935

Austen-Leigh, Arthur Richard, *The Eton College Register*, Eton, Berkshire: Spottiswoode, Ballantyne, 1921

Barnes, G.R. and J.H. Owen (eds), *The Private Papers of John, Earl of Sandwich, First Lord of the Admiralty 1771–1782*, 4 vols, London: Navy Records Society, 1933

Baugh, Daniel (ed.), *Aristocratic Government and Society in Eighteenth-Century England*, New York: Franklin Watts, 1975

Boatner, Mark M. (ed.), *Cassell's Biographical Dictionary of the American War of Independence 1763–1783*, London: Cassell, 1973

Broomfield, J.H., 'The Keppel–Palliser Affair, 1778–1779', in *The Mariner's Mirror*, Volume 47, No. 3, 1961

Brown, Alastair Rowland, *My Inestimable Friend: An Account of the Life of Rear Admiral William Brown (1764–1814)*, forthcoming e-book, 2017

Cannadine, David, *The Decline and Fall of the British Aristocracy*, London: Papermac, 1996

Cavell, S.A., *Midshipmen and Quarterdeck Boys in the British Navy, 1771–1831*, Woodbridge, Suffolk: Boydell Press, 2012

Chalus, E.H., 'Manners , Mary Isabella, Duchess of Rutland (1756–1831)', *Oxford Dictionary of National Biography*, Oxford: Oxford University Press, 2004; online, May 2008

Conway, Stephen, *The American Revolutionary War*, London and New York: I.B. Tauris, 2013

Cornwallis-West, G., *The Life and Letters of Admiral Cornwallis*, London: Robert Holden, 1927

Dale, T.F., *The History of the Belvoir Hunt*, Westminster, London: Archibald Constable, 1899

Dickinson, H.T. (ed.), *Britain and the American Revolution*, London and New York: Longman, 1998

Dull, Jonathan R., *The Age of the Ship of the Line: The British and French Navies, 1650–1815*, Barnsley, South Yorkshire: Seaforth Publishing, 2009

Eller, Irvin, *The History of Belvoir Castle: From the Norman Conquest to the Nineteenth Century*, London: British Library, 2011 (reprint of 1841 work)

Foreman, Amanda, *Georgiana, Duchess of Devonshire*, London: HarperCollins, 1999

Foss, Arthur, *The Dukes of Britain*, London: Herbert Press, 1986

Guttridge, G.H., *English Whiggism and the American Revolution*, Berkeley and Los Angeles: University of California Press, 1966

Hague, William, *William Pitt the Younger*, London: HarperCollins, 2004

Hamilton, Sir Richard Vesey, *Letters and Papers of Admiral of the Fleet Sir Thos. Byam Martin GCB*, Volume I, London: Navy Records Society, 1903

Hannay, David, *Naval Courts Martial*, Cambridge: Cambridge University Press, 1914

Hollis, Christopher, *Eton: A History*, London: Hollis and Carter, 1960

Kelly, Ian, *Beau Brummell: The Ultimate Dandy*, London: Hodder and Stoughton, 2005

Knight, Roger, *The Pursuit of Victory: The Life and Achievement of Horatio Nelson*, London: Allen Lane, 2005

Lambert, Andrew, *Admirals*, London: Faber and Faber, 2009

Law, Susan C., *Through the Keyhole: Sex, Scandal and the Secret Life of the Country House*, Stroud, Gloucestershire: History Press, 2015

Lyons, Mary (ed.), *The Memoirs of Mrs Leeson, Madam, 1727–1797*, Dublin: Lilliput Press, 1995

Macdonald, Janet, *Feeding Nelson's Navy: The True Story of Food at Sea in the Georgian Era*, London: Frontline Books, 2014

McGuire, James and James Quinn (general eds), *Dictionary of Irish Biography: From the Earliest Times to 2002*, 9 vols, Cambridge: Royal Irish Academy / Cambridge University Press

Macintyre, Donald, *Admiral Rodney*, London: Peter Davies, 1962

McIntyre, Ian, *Joshua Reynolds: The Life and Times of the First President of the Royal Academy*, London: Penguin, 2004

Mackesy, Piers, *The War for America, 1775–1783*, Lincoln, Nebraska: Bison Books, 1993

Mahan, A.T., *The Major Operations of the Navies in the American War of Independence*, London: Sampson, Low, Marston, 1913

Manners, Walter Evelyn, *Some Account of the Military, Political and Social Life of the Right Hon. John Manners Marquis of Granby*, London: MacMillan, 1899

Mitchell, Leslie, *The Whig World, 1760–1837*, London: Hambledon Continuum, 2007

Norman, Jesse, *Edmund Burke*, London: Collins, 2013

O'Day, Rosemary, *The Family and Family Relationships, 1500–1900*, Basingstoke: Palgrave Macmillan, and New York: St Martin's Press, 1994

O'Shaughnessy, Andrew Jackson, *An Empire Divided: The American Revolution and the British Caribbean*, Philadelphia: University of Pennsylvania Press, 2000

—, *The Men Who Lost America: British Command During the Revolutionary War and the Preservation of the Empire*, London: Oneworld Publications, 2013

Peakman, Julie, *Peg Plunkett, Memoirs of a Whore*, Quercus, London, 2015

Poser, Norman S, *Lord Mansfield, Justice in the Age of Reason*, Montreal and Kingston, Ontario: McGill-Queen's University Press, 2013

Reiter, Jacqueline, *The Late Lord: The Life of the 2nd Earl of Chatham*, Barnsley, South Yorkshire: Pen & Sword, 2017

Rodger, N.A.M., *The Wooden World: An Anatomy of the Georgian Navy*, London: Fontana Press, 1988

—, *The Insatiable Earl: A Life of John Montagu, Fourth Earl of Sandwich, 1718–1792*, New York and London: Norton, 1993

—, *The Command of the Ocean: A Naval History of Britain, 1649–1815*, London: Allen Lane, 2004

Rutland, Duchess of, with Pruden, Jane, *Belvoir Castle: 1000 Years of Family, Art and Architecture*, London: Frances Lincoln Limited, 2009

Sebag-Montefiore, Charles and Crook, Joe Mordaunt, (eds), *Brooks's 1764–2014: The Story of a Whig Club*, London: Brooks's, 2013

Spinney, David, *Rodney*, London: Allen and Unwin, 1969

Sterry, Wasey, *Annals of the King's College of Our Lady of Eton Beside Windsor*, London: Methuen, 1898

Syrett, David, *The Royal Navy in European Waters During the American Revolutionary War*, Columbia: University of South Carolina Press, 1998

—, *The Royal Navy in American Waters, 1775–1783*, Aldershot, Hampshire: Scolar Press, 1989

—, 'A Strategy of Detachments: The Dispatch of Rear-Admiral Thomas Graves to America in 1780', in *The Northern Mariner/Le Marin du Nord*, Volume XIV, No. 4, 2004, pp. 1–9

— (ed.), *The Rodney Papers: Selections From the Correspondence of Admiral Lord Rodney*, Volume II, 1763–1780, Abingdon, Oxfordshire: Routledge/Navy Records Society, 2007

Thorne, Roland, 'Manners, Charles, Fourth Duke of Rutland (1754–1787)', *Oxford Dictionary of National Biography*, Oxford: Oxford University Press, 2004; online, January 2008

Trew, Peter, *Rodney and the Breaking of the Line*, Barnsley, South Yorkshire: Pen & Sword, 2006

Vale, Brian and Edwards, Griffith, *Physician to the Fleet: The Life and Times of Thomas Trotter, 1760–1832*, Woodbridge, Suffolk: Boydell Press, 2011

Walpole, Horace, *Letters from the Hon. Horace Walpole to the Rev. William Cole, and Others: From the Year 1745, to the Year 1782*, London: Rodwell and Martin, 1818

Watson, Richard, *Anecdotes of the Life of Richard Watson, Bishop of Llandaff, Written by Himself at Different Intervals and Revised in 1814*, London: Richard Watson LL.B, T. Cadell and W. Davies, 1817

White-Spunner, Barney, *Horse Guards*, London: Macmillan, 2006

Willis, Sam, *Fighting at Sea in the Eighteenth Century*, Woodbridge, Suffolk: Boydell Press, 2008

—, *The Struggle for Sea Power: A Naval History of American Independence*, London: Atlantic Books, 2015

Acknowledgements

Isaac Newton, who was born just a few miles from Belvoir Castle, famously said that if he had seen further it was by 'standing on the shoulders of giants'. This book would not have been possible without the assistance of many 'giants'.

The authors would especially like to thank Captain Richard Woodman LVO FRHistS FNI and Elder Brother, Trinity House, whose generous sharing of advice as a seafarer and writer have guarded us against foundering on a number of rocky shores. Captain Woodman has been awarded – for various historical works and for advancing the importance of our maritime sector – the Society of Nautical Research's Anderson Medal, the Desmond Wettern Maritime Media Award, the Thomas Gray Medal, the Merchant Navy Medal and the Fellowship of the Maritime Foundation.

We would also particularly like to thank Peter Foden MA (Cantab), MArAd, Archivist at Belvoir Castle and specialist in reading and interpreting historic manuscripts. Peter's skill and patience have enabled us to understand many esoteric documents, including the Marquis of Granby's marriage settlement (on parchment made from 246 sheepskins). Entail and settlement were immensely complex in the eighteenth century, and without Peter this book would have missed some essential understanding.

Our grateful thanks also go to those 'giants' who have written scholarly and insightful works on which we have relied heavily, in particular N.A.M. Rodger, Dr Roger Knight and Dr Andrew Jackson O'Shaughnessy.

Our thanks go to the team without whom the production of this book would not have been possible: Barbara Levy, Anthony Cheetham and the staff at Head of Zeus, and especially Richard Milbank and Mark Hawkins-Dady, both of whose patience and attention to detail have been a particular asset. Also to Nick Hugh McCann, whose skill and professionalism in illustrating this book so beautifully has been so much appreciated.

A number of individuals have been enormously supportive and helpful. They include, in particular, Dr Roger Knight for essential input and for rescuing us from errors; Nicholas Rodger for important encouragement at the start of the project; Dr Carole Taylor, an independent scholar whose work will put the 3rd Duke of

Rutland on the map of British art collectors; Lord and Lady Edward Manners from Haddon Hall; Sir Richard FitzHerbert from Tissington Hall; Michael Crumplin FRCS FRHistS, medical military historian and Hon. Curator, Royal College of Surgeons of England; Peter Symonds from Petworth House; Patrick Villiers from the University of Littoral-Côte d'Opale; Charlotte Manley from St George's Chapel; Dr Sophie Forgan from the Captain Cook Memorial Museum, Whitby; Dr Pieter van der Merwe, MBE, DL; Brenton Simons; Jim Ginn, who patiently transcribed the *Belfast News Letter* for us; Ian Daisley; Sir Ben Slade from Maunsel House; Lord Sandwich from Mapperton House; Lord and Lady Mansfield from Schoon Palace; Robert Osborn, who has done sterling service firing Lord Robert's cannon over the years; and Boo Mellows, Angela Ryland, Robin Hart, Jane Pruden, Ian Kelly, William Thuillier, Alastair Brown, David Hilton, Mark Bowden, Andrew Norman, Julie Peakman, Janet Saunders-Watson, Margaret Scard, Harvey Proctor, Geoff Butterworth, Richard Seymour, Richard Hiscocks and Ben Sinclair.

Thank you to Andrea Burle Schmidt Dubeux Webb for your support and encouragement.

We are indebted to the helpful staff at Eton College, St George's Chapel Windsor, Westminster Abbey, Brooks's, Christie's, Rockingham Castle, The National Archives, the National Maritime Museum and Portsmouth Historic Dockyard

Our appreciation goes to those who took the trouble to read the manuscript and make pertinent suggestions, including Roger Knight, Andrew O'Shaughnessy, David Hancock, Hamish Laird, Alex Laird, Butch Dalrymple-Smith, Carole Taylor, Simon Grantham, Malcolm McKeand, Michael Head, Jacqueline Reiter, Rodney Atwood, J David Davies, and William M. Fowler, Jr. (Distinguished Professor of History, Northeastern University) and Professor Robert J. Allison PhD.

Thanks to all the team at Belvoir Castle who have supported us over the years, especially Debbie Griffiths for helping with many administrative tasks, Fay Lawrence for keeping the finances in order, Chris McCallion in the early days and then Suzanne Charlton for keeping us fed and watered, Stuart Foster for keeping our spirits up, and Wendy, Linda and Paul, Vendo and Blanka, Ricky and April, and Ray and Tony. Also, thanks to all of the Nadfas team including Glenda and Jill for helping us find the books we needed in the Belvoir Library, and with great appreciation to our committed guides and volunteers who do so much to help at Belvoir, including John Daybell and Bill Whittaker who have especially supported this project, among many others too numerous to mention here but all appreciated. Special thanks to Rhi for her continued passion over the years in relating the Lord Robert story to the castle's visitors.

This book would not have been possible without the unswerving belief in the project and support given to us both, throughout, by Emma, Duchess of Rutland, and the children: Violet, Alice, Eliza, Charles (Marquis of Granby) and Hugo. Our very grateful thanks go to them all.

And last, but in no way least, our gratitude goes to Dominic Dobson for introducing the authors.

Image credits

All the rest (for Chapters, 1, 4, 7, 8, 10, 11, 12, 13, 14) have been extracted from illustrations in Robert's own copies of Jefferys' *West Indian Atlas*, Hoste's *L'Art des armées navales* and Morogues's *Tactique navale*.

COLOUR PLATE SECTIONS

Plate Section 1

1. Etal Castle © Historic England Archive
15. An English man-of-war entering Portsmouth Harbour by Dominic Serres © 2009 Christie's Images Limited

The following images are reproduced courtesy of 9th Duke of Rutland's will trust/Nick Hugh McCann © Belvoir Castle:

2. *View of Belvoir Castle from the South West with Belvoir Hunt in Full Cry* by Thomas Badeslade, 1730.
3. John Manners, 3rd Duke of Rutland.
4. Charlotte Finch, 6th Duchess of Somerset by Thomas Hudson.
5. Rutland House.
6. John Manners, Marquis of Granby by Jean-Etienne Liotard, 1740.
7. Frances Seymour, Marchioness of Granby by Sir Joshua Reynolds.
8. A miniature of John Manners, Marquis of Granby by Henry Spicer.
9. Spurs and watch worn by the Marquis of Granby during the Seven Years War.
10. John Manners, Marquis of Granby by Joshua Reynolds.
11. John Manners, Lord Roos.
12. A print of *The Marquis of Granby relieving a Sick Soldier* by Edward Penny, 1765.
13. Cheveley Park by Jan Siberechts, 1671.
14. Newmarket Heath by Peter Tillemans.

Plate Section 2

8. Alleyne FitzHerbert, later 1st Baron St Helens: Courtesy of Sir Richard FitzHerbert Bt / Ian Daisley © Belvoir Castle / Sir Richard FitzHerbert Bt
11. Charles Watson-Wentworth, 2nd Marquis of Rockingham, by Francis Cotes, copy of a portrait by Joshua Reynolds: Courtesy of James Saunders Watson, Rockingham Castle © Andrew Norman
12. Charles Cornwallis, 1st Marquess Cornwallis, by Thomas Gainsborough 1783: © National Portrait Gallery, London
13. The Battle of Cape St. Vincent, or 'Moonlight Battle' by Richard Paton: © National Maritime Museum, Greenwich, London
15. John Montagu, 4th Earl of Sandwich by Johann Zoffany: Courtesy of a private collection © Private Collection

16. Sir Chaloner Ogle, by a follower of Joshua Reynolds: © 2009 Christie's Images Limited

17. Lord Robert Manners by Benjamin Wilson: Ian Daisley © Belvoir Castle / Rutland Hotels Ltd

18. A scene on board His Majesty's ship *Deal Castle* by Thomas Hearne, 1775: © National Maritime Museum, Greenwich, London

The following images are reproduced courtesy of 9th Duke of Rutland's will trust / Nick Hugh McCann © Belvoir Castle:

1. Charles Manners, Marquis of Granby by Hugh Douglas Hamilton, 1771.

2. Lord Robert Manners by Hugh Douglas Hamilton, 1772.

3. Frances Manners by Hugh Douglas Hamilton, 1772.

4. Charles Manners, Marquis of Granby by Joshua Reynolds, 1770s.

5. Frances Manners, Countess of Tyrconnel by Hugh Douglas Hamilton, 1753–93.

6. Mary Isabella and Elizabeth Compton by Catherine Read.

7. Mary Isabella, 4th Duchess of Rutland, by Robert Smirke, copy of an original by Joshua Reynolds.

9. William Murray, 1st Earl of Mansfield by David Martin.

10. Charlotte, Dowager Duchess of Somerset by Henry Spicer.

14. The bow of the Resolution by Lord Robert Manners.

Plate Section 3

2. Battle of the Saintes by Lieutenant William Elliott RN, 1787: Courtesy of the Jamestown-Yorktown Foundation, Williamsburg, Virginia, USA © Jamestown-Yorktown Foundation, Williamsburg, Virginia, USA

6. Westminster Abbey © Dean and Chapter of Westminster

13. The fourth Belvoir Castle © Belvoir Castle

14. Cannon from the Prothee firing: Courtesy of RDC Osborn © RDC Osborn

The following images are reproduced courtesy of 9th Duke of Rutland's will trust / Nick Hugh McCann © Belvoir Castle:

1. A sketch of the island of St Kitts by William Dawes, 1782.

3. *The Death of Lord Robert Manners*, by Thomas Stothard.

4. The surgical set by Evans and Co.

5. Lord Robert Manners, by Joshua Reynolds.

7. Charles, 4th Duke of Rutland, by Joshua Reynolds.

8. John Henry and Elizabeth (Diddle) by Joshua Reynolds, c.1783.

9. Mary Isabella, Duchess of Rutland and Vicereine of Ireland by John James Barralet, 1786: Courtesy of Dowager Duchess of Rutland.

10. Wine bottles showing the coat of arms of the Duke of Rutland.

11. Fire at Belvoir Castle.

12. Clutchbag embroidered by Mary Isabella, 4th Duchess of Rutland.

Index

Italic page numbers refer to illustrations. Charles Manners is CM and Robert Manners is RM throughout. 's.' represents son and 'd.' daughter.